DISTANT SHORES

HISTORIES OF ECONOMIC LIFE

Jeremy Adelman, Sunil Amrith, Emma Rothschild,
and Francesca Trivellato, Series Editors

Distant Shores

COLONIAL ENCOUNTERS ON
CHINA'S MARITIME FRONTIER

MELISSA MACAULEY

PRINCETON UNIVERSITY PRESS

PRINCETON & OXFORD

Copyright © 2021 by Princeton University Press

Princeton University Press is committed to the protection of copyright and the intellectual property our authors entrust to us. Copyright promotes the progress and integrity of knowledge. Thank you for supporting free speech and the global exchange of ideas by purchasing an authorized edition of this book. If you wish to reproduce or distribute any part of it in any form, please obtain permission.

Requests for permission to reproduce material from this work should be sent to permissions@press.princeton.edu

Published by Princeton University Press
41 William Street, Princeton, New Jersey 08540
99 Banbury Road, Oxford OX2 6JX

press.princeton.edu

All Rights Reserved
First paperback printing, 2023
Paperback ISBN 9780691214887
Cloth ISBN 978-0-691-21348-4
ISBN (e-book) 978-0-691-22048-2

British Library Cataloging-in-Publication Data is available

Editorial: Thalia Leaf
Production Editorial: Jenny Wolkowicki
Jacket/Cover design: Layla Mac Rory
Production: Erin Suydam
Publicity: Alyssa Sanford and Amy Stewart
Copyeditor: Anita O'Brien

Jacket/Cover art: A Chinese trading junk flanked by an American full-rigged ship (left) and a British brigantine (right). CPA Media Pte Ltd / Alamy Stock Photo

This book has been composed in Arno

Printed and bound by CPI Group (UK) Ltd, Croydon, CR0 4YY

To the Memory of Clara Brown Macauley

CONTENTS

JIAYINGZHOU

FUJIAN
PROVINCE

Dabu

Fengshun

Raoping

Han River

Haiyang
(Chao'an after 1914)
● Chaozhou

Rong River

Jieyang

Chenghai

Nan'ao
Island

Puning

● Swatow
(Shantou)

Chaoyang

Huilai

Lian River

HUIZHOU
PREFECTURE

| 0 | 10 | 20 | 30 | 40 | 50 km |
| 0 | 10 | | 20 | | 30 miles |

- - - - - District boundaries

⁓⁓⁓ Mountains

Rivers and creeks

MAP 1. Chaozhou Prefecture, Nineteenth Century

MAP 2. Maritime Chaozhou, Nineteenth Century

The Great Convergence

There the pilgrim on the bridge that, bounding
Life's domain, frontiers the wold of death.

—CHRISTOPH AUGUST TIEDGE

CHEN JINHUA WAS BORN in the Chaozhou region of southeastern China in
1911. His parents cultivated a fruit orchard on 15 *mu* (2.47 acres) of land, which
was not a particularly large property—the average farm size in the area was
9.43 *mu*—but local communists reviled his family as "rich." His village comprised about a thousand Chens, but they also had kinfolk overseas who owned
businesses in Siam and the British Straits Settlements. Jinhua decided to leave
his homeland and join them in 1932. His village was located in the once-
thriving commercial district of Puning, which had fallen on hard times after
the fall of the Qing dynasty in 1912 and the eruption of communist insurgencies and Nationalist counterinsurgencies in the 1920s. A communist base had
been established in mountains nearby, and comfortable farm families like the
Chens were constantly harassed. "This is why I went to Siam, because of this
situation," he recalled years later in an interview:

> There was nothing you could do. Because of this, our large household of
> twenty or thirty people all escaped. There was no way we could stay. Our
> family could not live in peace and enjoy our work. We lived in suspense the
> entire day. We were terrified the Nationalist army would come, and we were
> terrified that the communist army would come. If the communists came,
> even if you had no money, they would say "you're rich" and take it, whatever
> the amount. Otherwise they would detain you. . . . And if the Nationalists
> came, they would also detain you arbitrarily, and then beat you, beat you
> just shy of death. So we all fled.[1]

Jinhua sailed to Siam, where his sister's husband owned a three-hundred-acre sugar plantation and refinery. The spread was so enormous, they rented most of the land to local Thais. Jinhua went to work in the refinery, which was staffed by Chaozhou émigrés who spoke his own Puning-inflected Chaozhou dialect. The business suffered during these Depression years, however. Perceiving that opportunities for advancement in his in-laws' rural businesses were limited, he first moved to the nearby city of Bangkok to work for a cousin and then hitched a ride on a Chinese-owned steamer heading south for Singapore, where his older brother peddled fish. Most of the Chinese migrants in his new village also hailed from the Puning district of Chaozhou and specialized in vegetable production. Encouraged by his brother to start at the bottom, Jinhua took the backbreaking job of "night soil" collector, someone who lugged buckets from gate to gate to gather excrement for use as fertilizer. His wages were relatively high, he recalled, laughing, because "no one else wanted to do it." His early sojourn in the British colony was full of such travails, but in time he made a new life for himself. After a decade trudging as a fruit peddler, he managed to establish his own fruit shop and, later, other enterprises. He married a woman his mother, back in China, selected for him. He raised a family, sent remittances home, endured the horrors of the Japanese occupation, and retired a moderately successful businessman who served the Chinese community in a number of philanthropic capacities.[2]

Chen's life story is unique in some ways, but it is emblematic of the larger trends characterizing the social and economic connections between southeast coastal China and Southeast Asia from the seventeenth to the early twentieth century. Sojourning overseas had become fairly normalized by his day, but catastrophes big and small—a feud, a flood, a government campaign—inclined villagers and urbanites alike to embark on foreign journeys for work and sanctuary. Many of these sojourners already had relatives or acquaintances living overseas on whom they could rely initially. Absent that close connection, they turned to other expatriates from their native place in China. A significant number of émigrés who achieved fame and fortune hailed from the trading classes at home or had family overseas who were engaged in commerce, shopkeeping, or other small businesses. Because of that overseas connection, families like the Chens tended to own more property and have more financial resources back home than their neighbors who lacked that lifeline. Although the vast majority of Chinese emigrants were males, female relations played an important role in commercial networking across the South China Sea. Siam was the default destination of the Chaozhou overseas sojourner after the eighteenth century, but the prosperous colonies of the British in Malaya and the French in Indochina also beckoned ambitious or desperate young migrants.

The most significant feature of Chen Jinhua's life for our purposes was his birth in Chaozhou, a commercialized region on the eastern seaboard of the great maritime province of Guangdong on the southeast coast of China. Chaozhou—known as Teochew (or Teochiu) in Southeast Asia—was simultaneously an administrative prefecture and a local culture in which people shared a common dialect and repertoire of ritual, spiritual, and social practices. After the seventeenth century, natives of this region joined the Fujianese and Cantonese in an astronomical migration of Chinese laborers and merchants to Southeast Asia. Ng Chin-keong long ago characterized the emergence of Chaozhou at this time in the larger history of the South China Sea as unprecedented; the Fujianese and Cantonese, in contrast, had long been commercially dominant.[3] This emergence was a uniquely modern phenomenon, reflecting the expansion of the opium trade, the formalization of colonial rule in Southeast Asia, and the political decline of China. The rise of Chaozhou across the watery domain of overseas Chinese was one of the more remarkable social developments in the interconnected history of China and Southeast Asia. This book attempts to tell that story and consider its historical significance. How did natives of this smaller, poorer, and phenomenally ungovernable corner of imperial China emerge among the commercial masters of the South China Sea by the twentieth century?

The history of southeast coastal Chinese at home and abroad cannot be recounted merely within the geographical framework of the colony, nation-state, village, macroregion, or treaty port, or within the social framework of the "Chinese" or "overseas Chinese." Traditionally, the cultural identity of sojourning Chinese was determined by native place of origin, reinforced by common dialect and personal connections. If they did not entirely embrace this identity when they departed their villages, it was strengthened and reinforced simultaneously by the overseas native place institutions that advanced their interests and by colonial authorities, who were intent on classifying the identities of those who arrived on their shores. The history of transnational Chinese capitalism and migration must be grounded in the cultural dynamics of native place affiliation. Millions of Chaozhouese migrated to Southeast Asia from the mid-eighteenth to the mid-twentieth century. Many of those travelers remitted a portion of their earnings to their families back home and stayed in touch in other ways. Chaozhou thus was distinguished by a territorial boundlessness.

Emigrant communities at home maintained strong connections with sojourning Chinese, and local events rarely remained exclusively local for long. Events had repercussions that rippled back and forth across the seas, illustrating the intimately shared historical experiences of people living in multiple locations across a vast water world. The proper geographical framework of analysis—however imprecise and ever-evolving—is the uncharted borders of that maritime sphere within which Chaozhou families collectively dwelled. I refer to that geographical space as maritime Chaozhou and to those kinfolk as translocal families.

Across empires, kingdoms, colonies, sultanates, and oceans, their collective social and economic experiences were translocal as well as transregional. The geographer Tim Oakes and anthropologist Louisa Schein have offered a succinct elucidation of the first term: "translocality means being identified with more than one location." This is not simply a matter of "self-identification," it also reflects how states or other institutions identify people in motion. Translocalism refers to the migration of people as well as to the circulation of capital, ideas, commodities, and disease.[4] Scholars tend to characterize it as a recent phenomenon that reflects the escalating pace of post–Cold War globalization, especially the globalization of instantaneous media communications. The translocal world of maritime Chaozhou nonetheless was driven by centuries of international commerce and labor migration that accelerated in the nineteenth century. The introduction of steamships and telegraphs had equally revolutionary effects on communications across the South China Sea, and in normal times almost as many Chaozhou sojourners returned to as departed from China every year. Like emigrants from other regions of southern China, they tended to travel to the same places, live in close proximity to one another, and establish institutions that reinforced the cultural bond within expatriate communities and with their home villages.[5]

This is a local study in a global context. It will elucidate the entangled history of southeastern China, Shanghai, Hong Kong, and the regions of Southeast Asia to which Chaozhou sojourners traveled after the seventeenth century—including Bangkok and Cambodia on the Gulf of Siam, West Borneo, southern Malaysia, Singapore, and the Mekong delta of Vietnam. As Michael Werner and Bénédicte Zimmerman have shown, entangled history is a methodological approach used in the study of individuals and institutions in a transnational context. Underscoring the complexity of foreign encounters, they assert that culture is not simply transferred from more powerful or wealthy groups to weaker ones or from "cores" to "peripheries," rather all parties mutually affect one another in subtle or profound ways.

Werner and Zimmerman offer useful insights into the transnational scale of analysis in history. This scale, they suggest, "cannot simply be considered as a supplementary level of analysis to be added to the local, regional, and national levels according to the logic of a change of focus." Entangled history on a transnational scale employs its own "space-structuring logic," enabling one to reimagine the space within which historical events take place. One cannot understand the full significance of an event that occurred in a village on the coast of China without considering its impact on a port city on the Malay Peninsula, over 2800 kilometers distant. Global history therefore must be "multiscopic." It must be analyzed across the multiple sites within which historical interactions occur. The transnational scale of analysis enables us to discern how a single event, or series of events, can generate transformations in various locations, transformations that then reverberate back to the original site and produce new changes.[6] Most transnational phenomena nonetheless are "shaped by the specificity of locales," as Katherine Brickell and Ayona Datta have observed.[7] The multiscopic approach enables social historians to focus on the human and local scale within a larger transnational sphere. Migrants may live a global life, but they do not experience it "globally." They encounter it in the quotidian world of the village, port, or colonial plantation. Multiscopic analysis enables us to discern the human experience of global change and thereby determine how disparate local arenas are shaped by similar global processes. It enables the social historian to write global history.

Most scholars of the overseas Chinese experience have argued that the mass migration out of South China in the nineteenth century reflected the empire's social, economic, and political decline. They have attributed the accelerated levels of emigration to large and generalized challenges plaguing the coastal regions, from demographic pressures on land to poverty, chaos in an age of dynastic degeneration, and the "increasing exploitation of peasants" after the 1850s. Moreover, the argument goes, Chinese were attracted to the investment and employment opportunities of the European colonial order, and the imperialist imposition of the treaty port system after 1842 (in the case of Chaozhou, 1858) made it easier for people to depart for those colonies. Chinese have been advancing features of this argument for as long as they have considered the phenomenon of migration out of southeastern China. Wei Yuan, for example, claimed in 1847 that Chinese from Fujian and Chaozhou risked the dangers of travel because "their native country was densely popu-lated and the land was scarce."[8]

The present study does not dispute these well-founded interpretations. Chaozhou itself experienced ten violent antidynastic uprisings in the 1850s and 1860s, and the Taiping rebellion entered its convulsive death throes in its mountainous hinterland in 1866. After 1852 Chaozhou's international port of Swatow (Shantou) also emerged as the major Chinese site of embarkation for poor people who emigrated as contract laborers. They could not afford the price of a steerage ticket.

Nevertheless, Chaozhou's intensifying entanglement with Southeast Asia paradoxically reflected a highly adaptive economic and cultural vitality as well. Access to the territories along the South China Sea alleviated problems big and small: overpopulation on limited cultivable land, natural disasters, violent feuds, and government persecution. Siam, Johor, Singapore, and French Indo-china in particular constituted an expanding frontier for Chaozhouese, provid-ing thousands, and ultimately millions, of people additional territorial re-sources and investment opportunities, a boon that went bust only with the combined impact of the global Depression in 1929 followed by war and revolu-tion in China.

Kenneth Pomeranz accounted for the contrasting modern fates of Europe and China after the mid-eighteenth century in his influential book *The Great Divergence*. Prior to that time, the more commercialized regions of China and Europe were roughly comparable in terms of productivity, food supply, capital accumulation, patterns of consumption, and other attributes of economic dynamism. After a late medieval and early modern heyday, both ends of the Eurasian landmass appeared to have been heading toward a "proto-industrial cul-de-sac." Deforestation, soil erosion, and an intensifying inability to pro-duce the Malthusian "four necessities" of food, fiber, fuel, and building sup-plies on increasingly scarce fertile land threatened the prospects of both East and West. The more advanced economies of Europe—especially the British— nonetheless managed to ward off this looming disaster after 1800 while the Chinese succumbed to it. China, unlike Great Britain, Pomeranz argued, lacked the benefits of colonial expansion, a process that provided access to additional fertile land and resources. The Chinese empire therefore fell prey to ecological disaster and economic underdevelopment.[9]

Pomeranz shrewdly focused on the Lower Yangzi region around Shanghai to make this argument for it was one of the most commercialized and cultur-ally advanced regions of the Chinese Empire and the logical place to explore the divergent fates of the early modern global powerhouses. He nonetheless might have shifted his geographical focus southward after 1750. His inattention to the port regions of southern China—specifically the internationally connected regions of Chaozhou, southern Fujian, and Canton—inclined him to neglect a different Chinese economic prospect. The commercial and demographic expansion of Chaozhouese and Fujianese into Southeast Asia and Shanghai resembled the colonial aggrandizement of Great Britain, Spain, France, the Netherlands, the United States, and Japan. Chaozhouese in particular benefited from access to the land and resources of Southeast Asia because they tended to specialize in commercial plantation agriculture: sugar, rice, and fruit production in Siam; pepper, gambier, and rubber in Johor and Singapore; and, in the twentieth century, rice in Cambodia and Cochinchina (Vietnam). They also engaged in agricultural production in support of other extractive industries like gold mining in West Borneo. A multitude of traders and shopkeepers likewise benefited from the commerce in such items. Historical sources identify these overseas territories as having been underpopulated in the eighteenth and nineteenth centuries.[10] Demographic pressures accelerated back in Chaozhou, but the problem was partially alleviated as the region's workers emigrated abroad and sent remittances to their families. Farmhands from Chaozhou usually worked for employers who hailed from their native place and who benefited from the steady supply of agricultural labor.

Chaozhou's access to the resources of underpopulated lands in Southeast Asia yielded ample supplies of lumber, food, minerals, and other resources, freeing farmers back home to plant profitable cash crops, like sugar and opium, more extensively. Indeed, the Chaozhouese shipbuilding industry was almost entirely offshored to Bangkok in the eighteenth century because access to Siamese lumber made large junk production there more cost-efficient (skilled Chaozhouese shipbuilders ventured overseas with the industry). Coastal Chaozhou and the regions to which local residents emigrated converged economically and socially after this time.

Europeans who espied groups of Chaozhou Chinese living in Southeast Asia in the eighteenth and early nineteenth centuries referred to those settlements as "colonies." In 1834 P. J. Begbie, a British officer stationed in India, for example, called the self-governing gambier planters on the Malayan islands of Riau and Bintang "Chinese colonists." Missionaries referred to the Chinese settlements of West Borneo in 1839 as "the independent colony of Borneo." Colonial officials in India depicted Chinese activities that enmeshed the Siamese economy with that of the China mainland in the 1830s as "colonial." As

late as the 1920s, the Dutch director of the Netherlands Indies Tax Accoun-
tants Service, J. L. Vleming, referred to settlements of Chinese on the island
of Java as "colonies." Even in recent years, Leonard Blussé, a specialist in overseas Chinese history, characterized Batavia (Jakarta) from 1619 to 1740 as "basically a Chinese colonial town under Dutch protection."[11]

From a nineteenth-century European standpoint, Chaozhouese expansion
into Southeast Asia was similar to that of the Western powers in that it shared
some of the characteristics traditionally identified with the colonial project:
commercial elites extracted raw materials abroad. They forged new overseas
markets for the sale of goods and the investment of capital. They wrested control of indigenous territory and provided opportunities for the home country's
"excess" labor supply. J. A. Hobson, the prominent British critic of imperialism, described the arguments of European business interests in favor of colonialism that prevailed in 1902: "We must have markets for our growing manu-
factures, we must have new outlets for the investment of our surplus capital
and for the energies of the adventurous surplus of our populations." Although
generations of historians in the Anglo-American academy have critiqued the
"economic interpretation of imperialism," its logic was compelling to those
who were engaged in the colonial enterprise overseas, and the latter understood Chinese migration to Southeast Asia in the same self-interested light.[12]

Europeans understood that their own colonial project in Southeast Asia
prior to the 1920s was utterly unsustainable without the Chinese. As the former governor of the Straits Settlements, Frank Swettenham, declared in 1906,
credit for the financial success of the colony was due primarily to the
Chinese:

> They were already the miners and the traders, and in some instances the
> planters and fishermen before the white man had found his way to the
> [Malay] Peninsula. . . . They were, and still are, the pioneers of mining. . . .
> They brought all the capital into the country when the Europeans feared to
> take the risk; they were the traders and shopkeepers, and it was their steam-
> ers which first opened regular communication between the ports of the
> colony and the ports of the [independent] Malay States. They introduced
> tens of thousands of their countrymen when the one great need was labour
> to develop the hidden riches of a . . . jungle-covered country, and it is their
> work and the taxation of the luxuries they consume and of the pleasures
> they enjoy [i.e. opium], which has provided something like nine-tenths of
> the revenue.[13]

Europeans also perceived the extent to which their colonies redounded to the benefit of the Chinese. Chaozhouese who returned home after sojourning abroad recounted a joke that was popular among the British in Singapore: in Southeast Asia, "the Europeans raise all the cattle, but the Chinese get all the milk." The joke exaggerated the disadvantages of the Europeans—and antagonized Chinese, who felt that they also did most of the hard work raising the cattle, so to speak—but it reflected British anxieties about the ways Chinese profited from the colonial enterprise without bearing the onus of being "imperialists."[14]

This colonial dynamic was different from that prevailing across the Atlantic Ocean. There was nothing quite like the Chinese mercantile elite in Spanish America, for example. In the South China Sea, "periphery" and "core" or "metropole" and "hinterland," or even "colonizer" and "colonized," were complicated and fungible. Obviously the Europeans and Americans held the preponderant military and governmental power, and a voracious Euro-American market demand led to shifts in the exports of certain commodities—tin and rubber in particular—by the twentieth century. Chinese nonetheless continued to dominate the intra-Asian trade.[15] The rice markets of South China, for example, had as many distorting effects on Southeast Asia as the policies promoted by London, Paris, or Washington. Haydon Cherry has shown how the Chinese-dominated rice trade shaped the prospects of the impoverished floating population of French Indochina, for example. More broadly, Li Tana has argued that the interconnected emergence of Saigon, Bangkok, and Singapore contributed to the rise of heavily capitalized networks of Nanyang Chinese rice traders.[16] What we see in Southeast Asia was a process of Western colonization that advanced Chinese interests almost as much as it did those of Europeans and Americans, mostly because the entire process unfolded across the longstanding translocal spheres of native place groups from Chaozhou and elsewhere in China. As Swettenham implied, British success across Malaya, and most certainly Singapore, was inconceivable without the Chinese. Colonialism in Southeast Asia was a transnational class project as well as an expansion of the European nation-state.

In spite of Swettenham's magnanimous pronouncement, British administrators expressed misgivings about the economic power and demographic heft of the Chinese who emigrated in ever-increasing numbers to "their" colony. They fretted that they were not entirely in control, or, as Governor Frederick Weld observed in the midst of a crisis over the opium farms in 1883, "It is a question of who shall be supreme in this country."[17] This apprehension was not misplaced. Reading the colonial record across the decades of the nine-teenth century, one is astonished by the extent to which the foreign powers served as colonizers fostering Chinese economic interests in the realms of defense, infrastructural development, and supervision of Chinese migration. British colonies were expected to generate revenue to cover their expenses, but much of the cost of establishing the Straits Settlements as a viable polity fell on the home government. During the five-year transition to full colonial status after 1867, for example, the Colonial Office, War Department, and Trea-sury heavily subsidized colonial defense. Even when this transitional period ostensibly ended in 1872, Straits authorities prevailed on these British offices to continue to share in the costs of military operations (in that year, of the £91,595 expended, the colony paid £51,195 and London £40,000).[18]

Moreover, by 1881 only 2,803 male "Europeans" (including Americans) re-sided in the Straits as compared to 143,605 Chinese males. The European figure included 906 British troops.[19] The British military establishment thus consti-tuted one-third of the entire Euro-American male population. The Chinese-controlled opium regime by this point was supplying most colonial revenue, of course, and the heavy military presence contributed to the expansion of British imperial power globally. The British troop and civil servant presence nevertheless was protecting and administering a colony in which the vast ma-jority of Chinese were either making money or helping their compatriots make money. The Chinese Board of Revenue and Board of War back in Beijing certainly did nothing to defend overseas merchants in Southeast Asia. The British, in contrast, fostered Chinese commerce in treacherous waters.

The extraordinary level of British labor inputs into maintaining the Straits was not limited to military defense. Governor Weld proudly itemized the in-frastructural efforts of his government in the 1880s, efforts that included build-ing prisons, hospitals, police stations, and reclamation projects across the major settlements of the colony.[20] The colonial record is bursting with itemiza-tions of expenditures and relentless labor in the administration of lighthouses, sea walls, "lunatic asylums," vaccination campaigns, venereal disease monitor-ing, criminal and civil courts, harbor dredging, and the protection of Chinese migrants.[21] British shippers and merchants benefited from these improve-ments, and the work provided employment to middle-class British expatriates, but the efforts accommodated a far more numerous Chinese business and laboring community.

As the nineteenth century progressed, overseas Chinese in Southeast Asia left the state-building to others. In Siam they loyally integrated themselves into the monarchical order. Elsewhere they let the Euro-Americans bear the burden of constructing colonial states while they continued to dominate the process of resource extraction and commerce in food, lumber, rubber, tin, gold, and other commodities. Networks of Chinese expatriates thrived in the absence of international institutions designed to regulate movement across borders. A common South China Sea port culture evolved out of the Chinese sojourning experience. If the exploits of overseas Chinese constituted "colonialism," it was a translocal type forged informally by Chinese native place groups rather than politically and militarily by a conquering nation-state. This process transformed both Southeast Asia and China itself. The Chinese succeeded in this endeavor because their approach to overseas economic extraction was less expensive and more efficacious than that of the Euro-American variety. Euro-American traditions of economic expansion and power projection were heavily statist, relying on navies, armies, consulates, secret services, and legions of bureaucrats. They also were galvanized by a coercive doctrine of "civilizational uplift." This is a very expensive process by which to achieve economic domination abroad.

The Chinese, in contrast, pursued their interests in Southeast Asia informally after the seventeenth century. Aside from upholding tributary relations, the state was rarely involved in significant ways. Instead, Chinese relied on such institutions as merchant-dominated native place associations, gongsi partnerships, brotherhood societies, business networks, temples, and philanthropic organizations. Not only was this a cheap and effective approach to economic expansion, the process was controlled by those directly involved on the ground. Traditional Chinese institutions of economic extraction were superior to those of Euro-America. They were informal, adaptive, inexpensive, and ultimately more sustainable over the long term. Indeed, these institutions endure in Southeast Asia to this day, whereas the colonial authority of the British, French, Dutch, Spanish, Americans, and Japanese was swept into a vilified historical dustbin long ago.

Colonialism, however, is too limited a term to apply to the variegated experiences of overseas Chinese. Chaozhouese expansion into Southeast Asia and Shanghai reflected less a colonial than a territorial dynamic. By territoriality I do not refer to the jurisdictional basis of modern European states. In European political culture, territory "is an extension of the state's power," Stuart Elden writes; "territory is that over which sovereignty is exercised." Kai Raustiala, who studies territoriality in its legal dimension, notes that it is "the organizing principle of modern government. Territoriality refers to the exercise of power over defined blocs of space." The Westphalian conception of state-hood after 1648 held that "each sovereign state has its own discrete and exclusive territory." Within this system, laws and rights are binding to the territory.[22] The correlation of geographical space with political power also informed the statism of European colonialism in modern Southeast Asia, but it constitutes only one type of human territorialism.

I instead invoke a more primordial idea of territorialism as the "primary geographical expression of social power," as the geographer Robert David Sack has described it. In this understanding, "territoriality is an indispensable means to power at all levels from the personal to the international. . . . In humans [it] is best understood as a spatial strategy to affect, influence or control resources. . . . It is a form of spatial behavior."[23] This conceptualization of territoriality dates back to the Neolithic and developed contemporaneously with the domestication of plants and animals. Territorial claims over time were made by families, tribes, and eventually states in ever-changing, multifarious processes that anthropologists have called "the unfolding of society over a territory."[24]

Territorial domination is often effected through the use of violence, as we see in the battles among Chinese native place groups across the Gulf of Siam. More commonly, however, we witness a spatial dynamic in which local and long-distance migration complemented preexisting orders of residence and political authority. Chinese mass migration fostered newer, nonstatist forms of territoriality in which others engaged in modern state-making while Chinese focused on territorial access, commodity production, and commerce. Chinese territorialism involved spatial strategies designed to appropriate local resources and maximize personal and group benefits without establishing formal governing authority. After the mid-eighteenth century, the economically powerful Chaozhouese in Siam subordinated themselves to the monarchy and gradually assimilated into the local culture. Miners, farmers, and traders from the wider Chaozhou region resided in West Borneo at the sufferance of the local sultan and, after the 1880s, the Dutch. The same can be said of the Chinese planters in Sarawak and the Straits Settlements in the nineteenth century. As the twentieth century progressed, Chaozhouese migrated in increasing numbers to the rice-producing and milling regions of southern Vietnam and Cambodia in French Indochina. In all these cases, they lacked sovereignty over the land, and yet they achieved near total domination of many of the resources and commodities produced in these territories. The very absence of formal sovereignty paradoxically enabled them to achieve unprecedented control over local resources. In its simplest form, Chinese territorialism was resource extraction and commercial supremacy without the establishment of a colonial state. Their power and influence were sustained through a mosaic of familial, brotherhood, and commercial relationships tessellated across the port regions of maritime Chaozhou: Bangkok, Singapore, Saigon, Hong Kong, Shanghai, and Swatow.

This book charts the rise and decline of maritime Chaozhou from the emergence of Chaozhouese polities along the Gulf of Siam in the eighteenth century to the collapse of the global economy in 1929. Part 1, "The Curse of the Maritime Blessing," considers the translocal repercussions of the violent campaigns of the Ming and Qing dynasties to sever Chaozhou from its natural water world from the sixteenth to the eighteenth century. These struggles represented the difference between popular and dynastic conceptualizations of the maritime frontier (*haijiang*) in the early modern era. Ronald Po has defined this frontier as "the sea space adjacent to the Qing empire" and "a 'middle ground' or an in-between space that facilitates the flow of people, ideas, and commodities." Focusing on the Qing configuration of this space, he describes how the dynasty divided the ocean into "inner" and "outer" realms: "the inner sea constituted the empire's domestic seawater, where the emperor could claim ownership of maritime resources." The outer realm was considered strategically important, but also "a capricious domain that lay beyond the purview of administrative governance and economic extraction."[25] The Qing thus understood the frontier as a coastal littoral charted in dynastic cartography and rendered impregnable to threats from the high seas.

This study focuses on the maritime frontier as experienced by southeast coastal populations, whose lives reflected some of the ideas articulated by the pioneering expositor of the role of the frontier in history, Frederick Jackson Turner. Turner did not simply understand the frontier as geographical space, what he called territory that "lies at the hither edge of free land." He instead stressed that it was constantly changing and that frontier making was an ongoing process. It was not a hard boundary, as states were wont to draw; it shifted with the flow of human movement. "It is the graphic line which records the expansive energies of the people behind it," Turner wrote; "It is a form of society rather than an area."[26]

This vividly captures the movement of Chaozhouese overseas. Unlike the Qing, they did not conceptualize the outer realm as territory off-limits to international competition. It was viewed instead as a vital maritime pathway geographically linking the home territory to an ever-expanding frontier of settlement and economic extraction. One is tempted to resurrect the now-archaic use of "frontier" as a verb, as seen in the epigraph to this introduction.[27] To frontier is to engage in a relentless process of territorial expansion, to effect a convergence of the family village with the overseas community. Social fron-tiering constituted a process of geographical expansion that had little to do with the boundary-making of the state, as occurred in coterminous develop-ments in North America.

The frontier expansion of southeastern Chinese villages nonetheless was distinct from the Euro-American variety. In his magisterial global history of the nineteenth century, Jürgen Osterhammel has shown that, in the latter case, "in the nineteenth century, the opposite extreme of 'city' is no longer 'country,' the realm of farming, it is 'frontier': the moving boundary of resource develop-ment." The frontier (or, by extension, the colony) became the "periphery" to the city. It was in the city that "the weapons of subjugation were literally forged." Osterhammel describes the familiar process of European expansion, in which the financial centers of London, Paris, and New York emerged as urban metropoles to expanding peripheries.[28] The difference in the Chaozhouese case is that the "city" in question was not the home port of Swa-tow but the overseas port polities of Hong Kong, Shanghai, Saigon, Singapore, and Bangkok. These dynamic metropoles themselves were economically and demographically incorporated into the expanding Chaozhou frontier. Urban enclaves of modern Chinese development, they simultaneously were embed-ded in the colonial or semicolonial expansion of the European nation-state and made secure by colonial naval power or the Siamese monarchy. The home port of Swatow was never as economically important to maritime Chaozhou as the collective impact of these distant cities. As the political order disinte-grated after 1891, the overseas ports emerged as havens for investment, settle-ment, and banking.

Our story starts with the cataclysmic collision of these contrary perceptions of the maritime frontier, a clash that resounded across the history of maritime Chaozhou. Part 1 illustrates the importance of events in generating and redi-recting large structural transformations in local and global history.[29] These early chapters focus on three developments that reshaped translocal life: the Chinese governmental campaign to forcibly depopulate the Chaozhou coast during the 1660s (which contributed to the emergence of a culture of feuding and fostered an itinerant class of "peasant intellectuals" whose antipathy for the dynasty hardened into a religious ideology); the great victory of the Sia-mese governor Taksim over the Burmese invaders of Siam in 1767 (which led to the enthronement of this half-Siamese, half-Chaozhouese warrior-merchant and the transformation of port polities across the Gulf of Siam into a Chaozhouese economic sphere); and Commander Fang Yao's purge of the brotherhood-dominated villages of Chaozhou from 1869 to 1873. Fang's campaign of rural pacification constitutes the central event binding both early modern and modern maritime Chaozhou as well as parts 1 and 2 of this book. Assuming control of military and even civilian affairs in the region, he slaughtered thousands of "Triads," pirates, and smugglers and drove approximately eighty thousand men into exile in Shanghai and Southeast Asia. This campaign accelerated emigration out of the region in the 1870s. It launched a heavily militarized form of provincial state-building that enabled powerful families to entrench themselves economically. Its sheer brutality temporarily pacified a theretofore ungovernable region and facilitated the participation of Chaozhou's establishment merchants in the capitalist order emerging across the South China Sea. Local communists channeled the deep reservoir of resentments left in its wake into an ideology of class antagonism and revolution in the 1920s.

This pacification campaign in southeastern China was also an important milestone in the history of Shanghai and Southeast Asia. There, locals felt its reverberations without being particularly aware of the event itself. The purge of the underworld element in Chaozhou, for example, led to a dramatic increase in criminality in Singapore after 1869, forcing British administrators to intensify efforts to reform the criminal justice system and formalize colonial rule across the Straits Settlements. The British had been unaware of the causes of the crime wave until 1873, when an investigation into the origins of a riot in Singapore revealed to them the changing social dynamics of the colony.

In Fang Yao's campaign, we witness the transformative power of the local event as its repercussions were experienced across political borders. His military onslaught intensified ongoing trends in maritime Chaozhou, fostering a type of entangled state-building in both Chaozhou and the British Straits Settlements on the Malay Peninsula. Historical incidents that occurred in two ostensibly separate geographical places in fact took place in one social and economic translocal sphere; they were distinct manifestations of the same event and shared mutually transformative consequences. Two states at the early stages of their development—one colonial, one provincial—sought to tame and subjugate the same set of free-wheeling sojourners who long had operated beyond the orb of governmental authority. In so acting, these states became transformed themselves. Entangled state-building is a transnational process in which emerging states approach developmental equilibrium as a result of shared historical experiences and economic trajectories. A multi-scopic analysis of Fang's pacification campaign enables us to witness the inter-crossed processes of state-building between Great Britain's colony in Malaya and the Chinese province of Guangdong, in which Chaozhou is situated. We also discern a larger process of entangled state-building across the South China Sea, a process that the circulation and taxation of opium, the most prof-itable commodity traded in modern Asia, accelerated.

For opium is central to this story. Part 2, "Winning the Opium Peace," shows how the spectacular success of many Chaozhouese merchants after the seventeenth century stemmed, in part, from their participation in the global commerce in this profitable narcotic. Opium was easily transported, and it financially buttressed the trade in other commodities associated with their sojourning experience: rice, sugar, fruit, gambier, and rubber in particular. Chaozhouese trading networks alternated between strategies of cooperation and competition with the imperialist powers across Asia. The remarkable soli-darity with which they operated enabled them to squeeze the British and Americans out of the opium trade in Chaozhou and the burgeoning metropo-lis of Shanghai. Conversely, overseas, they participated in the syndicates that controlled the opium farms and provided the revenues on which the nineteenth-century colonial project in Southeast Asia depended.

The opium trade generated a significant portion of the capital accumulated by the titans of Chaozhouese commerce. This enabled them to diversify their investment portfolios and invest in banking, manufacturing, shipping, real estate, and film. In local biographies published today, they are celebrated as "businessmen" and "philanthropists," and their participation in a now-reviled transoceanic trade tends to be discounted. Of course, the same can be said of the many American fortunes that were forged in the very same commerce: those of the Lows, Delanos, Russells, and others.

The heyday of maritime Chaozhou from 1767 to 1929 reflected more than the role of its sojourning classes in the drug trade, however. An ethos of coop-erative networking, adaptive commercial strategies, and stalwart solidarity enabled them to compete effectively with foreign imperialists at home and abroad. Scholars of imperialism in China have begun to complicate the history of Chinese "semicolonialism," a system in which the Chinese government re-tained political sovereignty but was militarily forced to concede economic privileges and "territorial enclaves" to foreign business interests. While under-scoring the victimization of Chinese by the violent expansion of Western powers and Japan, they point to instances of indigenous agency in shaping the contours of imperialism in such realms as public health, medicine, and business. This scholarship also points to the complexities of the semicolonial encounter across China, though the experiences of treaty ports like Shanghai and Tianjin or the colony of Hong Kong continue to be heavily emphasized.[30]

The present study seeks to contribute to this conversation by illustrating the ways southeast coastal operators successfully resisted and, on occasion, dominated the foreign interlopers. When scholarly attention is shifted to a region like Chaozhou—especially Chaozhou as part of a larger maritime world—the history of imperialism in China appears transformed. The region was "opened" to Westerners as a result of a brutal war, the Second Opium War (1856–1860). Local people nevertheless prevented the British from traveling freely throughout Chaozhou for almost a decade thereafter. To the consternation of foreign merchants, translocal entrepreneurs maintained near total control of the regional economy and disciplined Europeans into conducting business in the Chaozhouese manner. Aside from the shipping sector, they marginalized Euro-American economic power in their home base. In the Lower Yangzi region around Shanghai they drove the foreigners out of the remunerative opium trade. Overseas they dominated the extraction and wholesaling of several products essential to the industrial revolution that was unfolding across the globe and sidelined the British from such industries as rice-milling. British consuls in the treaty port of Swatow protected the local property interests of Chaozhou residents of the Straits who had become naturalized "British subjects" but who nonetheless lived part time in Chaozhou. The British facilitated the emergence of these Chinese as thriving capitalists at home and abroad. Chaozhouese were disdained throughout China for their purported cultural deficiencies: their "violence," "clannishness," and dogged success in business. Unlike so many of their compatriots, however, they competed successfully with the British in the international arena. A scholarly reimagining of the historical geography of southeast coastal China enables one to discern that success and the extent to which the British inadvertently served the interests of their Chaozhouese competitors prior to the 1920s.

Part 2 nonetheless ends with the earlier theme of the accursed blessings of life lived along a maritime frontier. The translocal nature of the economy and family structure—so essential to overcoming the demographic and ecological challenges of the modern era—also contributed to the growing class inequalities of the Chaozhou region. The remittance system in particular exacerbated social antagonisms because families that benefited from the largess of overseas relations thrived while those who lacked such translocal affiliations suffered in comparison. By the 1920s wealth and diaspora were entirely interconnected in areas with significant emigrant traditions, and the class tensions and transforming nature of rural violence in the 1920s and 1930s presaged the larger revolution to come in the 1940s.

The triple impact of global Depression, total war, and revolution in the 1930s and 1940s seriously disrupted the ties between Chaozhou and the lands of the South China Sea. Indeed, a wartime famine prostrated the region in 1943, illustrating the vital necessity of commerce with Southeast Asia, which supplied Chaozhou with a significant portion of its grain supplies. The centuries-long link to a larger maritime world ensured the very survival of the homefolk. Overseas Chinese usually responded effectively to the philanthropic needs of their villages in the wake of such disasters as the deadly tropical cyclone that struck the coast in 1922, but they could do nothing to alleviate the tragedies of war two decades later.

This study focuses on maritime Chaozhou before those disasters struck, when sojourning merchants and laborers alike successfully expanded the geography of their economic possibilities. Here I consider the relationship between an important Chinese sojourning community and the development of capitalism in East and Southeast Asia from the eighteenth to the early twentieth century. Pomeranz was right to point to the ecological challenges confronting the Chinese mainland after 1750, but understanding Chaozhou across its translocal world enables us to see, not a divergence with European modernity, but a convergence in colonized sites that were critical to the industrial revolution and accelerating levels of capital accumulation. Southeast coastal emigrants participated in a Chinese sphere of commercial modernity that adapted to political and cultural transformations. With superior institutions of migration and a masterful application of legal and illegal tactics in their competition with Western imperialists, they emerged among the commercial masters of the South China Sea, serious rivals to the foreign powers before things began to fall apart in the 1930s.

PART I

The Curse of the Maritime Blessing

1767–1891

It was a pertinent and true answer which was made to Alexander the Great by a pirate whom he had seized. When the king asked him what he meant by infesting the sea, the pirate defiantly replied: "The same as you do when you infest the whole world; but because I do it with a little ship, I am called a robber, and because you do it with a great fleet, you are an emperor."

—AUGUSTINE OF HIPPO, 426 CE

1

Pacifying the Seas

IMPERIAL CAMPAIGNS AND THE EARLY MODERN MARITIME FRONTIER, 1566–1684

The maritime people are also the children of the dynasty. If they are suddenly removed, even the birds will sigh, and before they are settled in their new homes, they may flee beyond the sea to join those there. Thus we are really delivering the people into the hands of the enemy.

—CENSOR LI ZHIFANG

CHAOZHOU IS A REGION on the southeast coast of China. It is marked by boundaries. Historically, it was the northeasternmost prefecture of the great, mercantile province of Guangdong. It shared a border with the commercial powerhouse to the north, Fujian province. The circle of latitude known as the Tropic of Cancer bisects the region, and today a marble tower rises forty-five feet above Jilong Mountain to signify the boundary between Earth's subtropical and tropical zones. By the nineteenth century Chaozhou had been partitioned into nine districts (or counties): Raoping, Chenghai, Chaoyang, and Huilai on the coast; Jieyang, Puning, Haiyang (later Chao'an), Dabu, and Fengshun in the interior (map 1). These provinces, prefectures, and districts were administrative divisions, devised by the imperial court far to the north and drawn to establish geographical realities that might subject the area to the unifying control of the central government. The Tropic of Cancer, of course, was invented by international forces far beyond the imperial purview.

Chaozhou is also distinguished by a cultural boundlessness. Speakers of the Chaozhouese dialect and observers of local Chaozhouese religious and cultural practices lived beyond the prefectural border with Huizhou to the south and the provincial border with Fujian. Chaozhou was part of what G. William Skinner described as the "Southeast Coastal macroregion" of China, a macroregion that incorporated parts of three provinces: southern Zhejiang, Fujian, and eastern Guangdong. Macroregions transcended the administrative geography of the central government. They were physiographical expanses formed within the drainage basins of mountain ranges. Distinct and interrelated market economies and cultural patterns evolved within these large territories in premodern times.[1] Chaozhou and the Fujianese prefectures of Zhangzhou and Quanzhou together comprised the economically dynamic "core" of the southeast coast and shared an interconnected social and commercial history at home and abroad.

The cultural boundlessness of Chaozhou extends across the seas. It does not simply lie at the edge of the South China Sea—the Nanyang—it is an integral part of that transnational water world. Culturally and economically, it transcends the boundaries of empire and nation. Chaozhou's maritime history is a chronicle of southeast coastal China as well as Southeast Asia. It is a part of the Southeast Asian "water frontier," a borderland that Nola Cooke and Li Tana describe as "a fluid transnational and multiethnic economic zone."[2] By the early modern era it was a zone increasingly dominated by Chinese merchants from Guangdong and Fujian and politically controlled by an assortment of monarchs, pirates, sultans, and, eventually, European colonialists.

Chaozhou's connection to the sea was a blessing. The profits generated from trade with the Japanese, Southeast Asians (including Europeans after 1514), and Chinese in other regions produced a translocal Chaozhou commercial class that was rivaled in the South China Sea only by merchant networks operating out of southern Fujian and Canton. Common people also thrived along the shore. Peasants avoided some of the constraints of demographic pressures on cultivable land through employment offered by the ocean and rivers: fishing and clamming in particular but also work as stevedores, sailors, shipbuilders, boatmen, and shell harvesters. By the nineteenth century laborers were shipping out in large numbers to work on Southeast Asian plantations and in commercial enterprises owned by sojourning Chaozhou (Teochew) capitalists and remitting a portion of their wages home to their families. Access to the sea enabled Chaozhou people of all classes to participate and accumulate capital in the highly remunerative opium smuggling economy as well. The bounties of the sea theoretically were available to all.

Chaozhou's maritime blessing was also a curse. Over the centuries the coast has been devastated by typhoons and tidal waves. These storms touch ground an average of once every two years, while typhoons that do not directly batter the region but exert a significant impact on agricultural production occur three to four times per year.[3] Moreover, Chaozhou is part of a major delta region where mountain streams cascade into three rivers—the Han, Rong, and Lian—which themselves flow into numerous tributaries before emptying into the sea. These river systems form "alluvial corridors" that carry sediment from inland mountains to low-lying plains. This regenerates farmland and fosters marine industries, but alluvial expanses are subject to occasional floods that torment humans eking a living off the land. It also proves challenging to merchants, who struggle to ensure that harbors do not become submerged by oozing sediment. Alluviation also leads to hydraulic shifts of terrain that wreak havoc on property claims. This ecological instability fostered a good deal of disputation in Chaozhou.[4]

By the late imperial period access to the sea was vital to Chaozhou's fishing and commercial industries. The region constituted one node in an emerging international trade system, and by the Song (960–1279) and Yuan (1279–1368) periods residents regularly embarked on commercial expeditions to kingdoms that now constitute parts of the Philippines, Cambodia, Indonesia, Thailand, and Vietnam. Given the vast distances and necessity of relying on monsoon winds, these sojourners were away from home for long periods of time.[5] This connection to a wider maritime world induced deep unease in central government minds. Officials feared that commercial families might form confederations with coastal power-mongers and foreign entities. They distrusted the cosmopolitan autonomy of maritime culture and sought to co-opt China's profitable international trade. They were frustrated by the ability of criminals to evade the law and sail away to distant lands. From the fourteenth through the seventeenth century, these authorities embarked on periodic campaigns to restrict the region's engagement with its natural maritime geography. The Ming dynasty (1368–1644) launched the first of these efforts with their famous maritime proscriptions. These intermittently imposed interdictions provoked an explosion of "piracy" in the sixteenth century.

After the Manchus conquered China and established the Qing dynasty (1644–1912), they sought to bend the region to their will by driving swaths of the Chaozhouese population from their villages. The coastal evacuation of the 1660s was the most important event in Chaozhou prior to 1869. Because the coast constituted part of the Fujian-Guangdong borderland of resistance to the Manchu invasion after 1644, evacuation processes there were harsher, and lasted much longer, than in other parts of China. Hundreds of villages were destroyed. Untold thousands of farmers, fisher folk, salt workers, and traders were driven inland and left to fend for themselves. Interior regions and coastal villages and towns that were not evacuated unhappily hosted multitudes of desperate, marauding refugees. For much of the 1660s, mass starvation and violent chaos were rife. Then, with a snap of the imperial fingers, coastal inhabitants were allowed to return to their ravaged homesteads. Lineages, depleted of kinfolk, struggled to reclaim usurped land and protect themselves from ambitious predators. Property disputes that emanated from the chaos plagued local courts for decades. With the conquest of the southeast coast, the "four seas of the Great Qing empire had been pacified," as contemporary accounts of the day declared.[6] The most powerful competitors to Qing overlordship had been eliminated, but the violence also induced legions of Chaozhouese to emigrate to Southeast Asia. Many of the refugees from the cataclysmic violence of the Ming-Qing transition proceeded to lay the foundation for the rise of maritime Chaozhou overseas, ironically reinforcing the translocal nature of coastal life.

Ming Precedents: The Buccaneers of the Chaozhou Water World

The violent feuding that plagued Chaozhou in the nineteenth century was, in part, a historically conditioned and logical response to the baleful effects of government campaigns during the Ming and Qing periods. The most commercially destructive effort under the Ming was the ban on maritime travel and commerce, initially imposed in 1371 by the first Ming emperor, Taizu (r. 1368–1398), and stringently revived by his successors in the sixteenth century. Private international trade was banned, and sailing abroad without a permit from the central government forbidden. Transgressors were subject to a range of harsh punishments.

Taizu, ruthless and paranoid, sought to transform his vast and increasingly commercialized empire into an idealized rural autarky in which people remained properly rooted in their villages, respectful of social hierarchy and imperial authority. He envisioned an international order that contrasted starkly with the free-wheeling, commercially interconnected world that had flourished under the preceding Yuan (or Mongol) dynasty. Instead, he and his successors sought to institutionalize a system that was commercially controlled by the imperial bureaucracy and ritually centered on their capital, Nan-jing (after 1421, Beijing). They established what is known in English as the "tributary system" of international relations in which various realms on China's periphery submitted to the symbolic authority of the Chinese throne. Tribu-tary states such as Siam, Korea, Sanfoqi (on Sumatra), and others found that entering into this arrangement not only ensured stable diplomatic relations with the major power of East Asia but also enabled them to engage in a form of duty-free commerce with the Chinese state. Trade relations thus were an extension of diplomacy. Once foreign envoys presented tributary gifts to the emperor, their compatriots were permitted to conduct business at designated points along the Chinese frontier. As Sarasin Viraphol observed, both the Chi-nese and tributary states embraced this arrangement because it constituted a major source of commercial enrichment for their courts.[7]

Chaozhou theretofore had experienced a notable level of development in maritime trade. By the fourteenth century local artisans enjoyed a sophisti-cated understanding of nautical engineering, and the region emerged as a shipbuilding center. Merchants traded along the Chinese coast and across the seas. They sold large quantities of locally manufactured porcelain and other items in Japan and Southeast Asia and returned to China with goods from those faraway lands.[8]

The maritime interdictions dealt a blow to the economy and led to a crimi-nalization of private commerce that transformed merchants into "pirates" and commodities into "contraband." Piracy had not been unknown on the south-east coast, but historians of this period recognize that, in banning international trade, the Ming court begot veritable navies of "pirates," many of whom simply were merchants who continued to traffic privately with foreigners or in foreign ports.[9] This is not merely a modern interpretation. Ming-era observers recog-nized that their government was instituting its own form of lawlessness. As the scholar Xie Jie famously wrote in 1595, "Pirates and merchants are one and the same. When commerce flourishes then pirates become merchants, when com-merce is forbidden, then merchants become pirates."[10] Inevitably concluding that the state's interests were antithetical to their own, coastal traders began to operate beyond the writ of law. As one anthropologist has observed in another context, once people start "doing something illegal . . . they are less likely to feel able to support the government and more willing to do other illegal things."[11] Smuggling, which is trade without state sanction, inculcates in its practitioners contempt for the legal order, a situation that, in the case of China, unleashed violent and predatory opportunism on the coast.

Smuggling constituted the most common form of resistance in Chaozhou. Nan'ao Island emerged as the preferred site for illicit trade. Located off the coast of both Fujian and Guangdong provinces, it was the ultimate borderland hideaway, its many leaf-shaded inlets and tiny harbors providing refuge and opportunities for clandestine activities. In spite of the location of this large island on a naval patrol route during the Ming and Qing eras, it debuted as a smugglers' haunt and piratical base during this period.[12] Opium was among the contraband smuggled into Guangdong in the fourteenth century, and operations off Nan'ao presumably launched the opium-smuggling tradition in Chaozhou.[13]

Local authorities harassed residents whose only crime had been their familial relationship to merchants who continued to engage in maritime trade. In the early fifteenth century, for example, a group of fifty-five Chaozhouese sailed to Java to "trade privately." Most of them probably had been sojourning back and forth between China and that island for years, but their luck ran out in 1444. That year thirty-three of the original sojourners returned to their homeland, probably to import goods and visit kin. Just as they were preparing to return overseas, they encountered an armed force led by the local prefect. Most of the "offenders" managed to evade the authorities and sail over the horizon, but four were captured. They testified that twenty-two members of their original group had decided never to return to China and instead took permanent residence in Java, a development officials characterized as a "rebellious attachment to Java." The captives also must have enlightened the prefect as to the identities of their friends who had managed to escape because, when the prefect reported the incident to the central government, the Zhengtong emperor ordered him to arrest and prosecute their family elders.[14]

It was easier for the Ming to persecute relatives who were left behind rather than stifle overseas commerce. This harassment elicited a good deal of hostility to local officials, and marauders began to target government offices. In 1449, for example, "vagrant banditti" from Fujian who plundered villages in the Haiyang district of Chaozhou "enticed" certain Chaozhou residents to a life of crime on the high seas. They incessantly attacked officials and plundered government coffers.[15] Local treasuries obviously were a lucrative attraction, but the sea ban clearly engendered antigovernmental predation.

Smuggling was endemic throughout the Ming period, but it was a byproduct of an otherwise "normal" system of international trade that was controlled by powerful merchant leagues who were supported by the local population. These families managed to operate relatively unencumbered until the early sixteenth century, when another strong-willed emperor, Jiajing (r. 1522–1567), decided to rigidly reinforce the sea ban, issuing draconian new legislation and dispatching larger naval squadrons to bend merchants to his will. As Kwan-wai So has observed, the emperor was reacting to a steady increase in smuggling along the south China coast. A commercially dynamic economy was emerging at the domestic and international levels as merchants responded to a burgeoning demand for Chinese and foreign products. The foreign predilection for such Chinese commodities as iron chains and cauldrons, silk, bamboo, and lacquerware drove up the price of these items and rendered their exportation too tempting to resist. In spite of the bucolic inclinations of Ming rulers, trade had become "a mainstay of the economy" along the urbanizing eastern seaboard of China.[16]

Intensified interdictions transformed armed-merchant smuggling operations with some violent proclivities into vast piratical confederations that aggressively resisted the Ming civilian and military presence. Thus were born the famous "*wokou* pirates" of the early modern era. Wokou, a derogatory Chinese term for "Japanese pirates," was an anachronistic misnomer for a transnational piratical phenomenon dominated no longer by Japanese but by southeast coastal Chinese merchants whose crews and collaborators included Chinese, Japanese, Siamese, Malaccans, Spaniards, Portuguese, and Africans.[17] The new interdictions, far from suppressing trade, instead ignited an explosion of marauding and smuggling. Commerce was an integral part of the regional economy, sustaining many coastal families. As Ming naval forces threatened the livelihoods of merchants by confiscating their ships, harassing their families, and executing their followers, mercantile forces began to strike back.

The emergence of piratical confederations on the southeast coast represented one stage of historical development before the rise of modern state-building. In areas that have never been fully incorporated into a nation-state, colony, or empire, power-mongers emerge to fill the political void. After acquiring followers, they need to sustain them. In this case, with overseas commerce forbidden, piracy emerged as an alternative revenue source, assuring the allegiance of their dependents.[18] Power accrued to coastal operators who defied the sea bans. This leap from trader to buccaneer was easily accomplished. In this period, commerce required the potential to wield military force, if only to defend one's ships and cargo from predators in ungoverned seas. This force was now wielded in defiance of Ming law.

Chaozhou produced some of the most notorious pirates of the early modern period. Lin Daoqian and Lin Feng were among the more significant of

these adventurers, for their exploits illustrated the profound differences between Chinese and European expansion into Southeast Asia. In spite of their
common surnames, they probably were not related. Officials considered the
younger man, Lin Feng, to have emerged as one of the two successors to Lin
Daoqian by the time the latter fled China in 1573.[19] Here we will focus on Lin
Feng, who was born around 1549 in Raoping district. His rise to prominence
as a merchant-corsair no doubt was facilitated by the fact that he was the
nephew and adopted son of another powerful smuggler-pirate of the Chaozhou
coast, Lin Guoxian. In the 1540s his uncle-father had joined a gang that used
Nan'ao as a base, and upon reaching the age of nineteen, Lin Feng entered the
family business of smuggling, pillaging port towns, and kidnapping men and
women for ransom.[20]

He soon emerged as a ubiquitous force across the Nanyang. From 1568 to
1574 his enormous fleet attacked sites in Chaozhou, Huizhou, Canton, and
Qiongzhou (Hainan), an island off the coast of present-day Vietnam. After an
extended foray in the Philippines, where he tried to wrest control of the islands
from Spain (see below), he established a base in Taiwan in 1575 and renewed
his attacks on various sites in Guangdong and Fujian. Increasingly frustrated
Ming officials dispatched a naval armada in 1576 and bombarded his forces on
the high seas, destroying half his ships, killing or dispersing 1,712 of his followers, and liberating hundreds of people who had been held captive by his organization. Lin Feng somehow escaped, retreating with other survivors to the
"land of the Western barbarians" (probably an island in what is now the Philippines).[21] Exasperated Chinese authorities never did manage to capture him.

Even as Ming attacks kept these pirates on the move, they always managed
to return to their earlier haunts in Chaozhou and Fujian either to smuggle or
to plunder ports. Indeed, one source of the wealth and power of both Lin Feng
and Lin Daoqian was their role as a vital link between the wealthy hinterland
of China and the economies of the South China Sea. They were supported in
these endeavors by their families and friends on the coast. As the Minister of
the Board of War fulminated in 1578:

> The notorious bandits Lin Daoqian and Lin Feng recently fled to islands
> overseas and as yet have evaded Heaven's retribution. Moreover, crafty and
> powerful rich people pretend to be local merchants and collude in welcom-
> ing them ashore. They draw up counterfeit [official] documents, purchase
> contraband . . . and provide the pirates with grain. They also serve as their
> rural guides and just let the pirates have the run of the place.[22]

The geographical mobility of these pirates was predicated on local support in their base areas. Ming authorities well understood the pivotal role such abetment played in the buccaneering triumphs of both Lins, and it is significant that officials contemplated evacuating those supporters from the coast. After inflicting a defeat on Lin Feng in 1576, they were confronted with the vexing task of dealing with his followers who had remained behind. Xiao Yan, an official in the war ministry, noted that if the Ming did not "eliminate" those forces, the dynasty would appear weak. Although Xiao was inclined to execute the lot of them, he suggested that the authorities might consider "securing them in the inland regions."[23] He proposed "civilian" resettlement in the interior as a plausible approach to pacification. A century before the Qing embarked on their own evacuation of the coastal population, Ming officials themselves pondered a policy of resettlement as a means of detaching pirates from their supply lines. It is to the dynasty's credit that, in spite of the havoc wreaked by these adversaries of the Ming international order, officials did not take the drastic measures employed by their successors. Instead, they usually opted for "negotiated pacification," a process in which popular resort to predation was officially forgiven. As Chen Chunsheng observed, however, "pacified pirates" often did not remain pacified for long, and negotiated pacification had its policy opponents in the Chinese bureaucracy.[24]

Lin Feng meanwhile pursued his territorial ambitions elsewhere in the South China Sea. Ming officials reviled him as a "sea bandit." He, on the other hand, fancied himself overlord of Manila and challenged Philip II's colonization of the Philippines from 1574 to 1575. He represented an alternative, almost colonial approach to Chinese economic expansion that was thwarted by the Ming dynasty's own conceptualization of international relations and by the Spanish determination to retain control of the island of Luzon.

The Portuguese explorer Ferdinand Magellan claimed the Philippines for Spain in 1521. By the early 1570s, Chinese merchants were happily trading at Manila with the Spanish, who paid in silver for Chinese porcelain and silks and Southeast Asian products like pepper and cinnamon. Lin Feng encountered two of those merchants on the high seas in 1574. He was astonished by the quantities of gold and Mexican silver coins they transported on their return voyage. They informed him that there was an enormous demand for Asian products in Manila and the Spaniards paid in specie. Lin's captives also relayed intelligence that there were few Spanish soldiers in the port and it was not well-defended. The Chinese corsair beheld an opportunity and set sail for Manila with a flotilla of sixty-two large ships.[25]

As Zeng Shaocong has noted, Lin Feng's confederation was different from those of other Chinese merchants in Manila in one respect: Lin was not simply hoping to make a profit. Having temporarily been driven from the coast of China, he was trolling for a new base of operations, and the poorly defended area around the port seemed ideal. His thousands of followers comprised not only buccaneering merchants but also a number of farmers and artisans, people who would help feed his forces and supply them with goods. All he required was land and a safe harbor, and to accomplish those goals, he needed to eliminate his Spanish competition for mastery of the island.[26] We do not know how Lin Feng perceived the Spanish, but he likely regarded them as similar to his own organization: heavily armed adventurers scrounging for territory and fortune in the uncharted waters of the Nanyang. Did Spanish conquistadors have any more right to these islands than a Chinese marauder? The Spanish certainly thought so, and they considered Lin a presumptuous though menacing upstart. The Augustinian friar Juan González de Mendoza wrote with consternation in his classic 1586 account of this "Chinese rover" that the Spaniards theretofore "did enjoy their new habitation of Manila in great quietnesse . . . [on] Islands that were . . . in obedience to the Christian King Don Philip [when suddenly] they were beset with a mightie and great armada of ships led by the rover Limahon [Lin Feng]." And this Limahon was "determined to go and take the Islands Philippines, and to make himself lord and king over them all."[27]

Lin Feng was not the only pirate threatening Spain's expanding empire across the early modern globe. During their first two centuries as an imperial power, the Spanish were never able to send a sufficient number of troops to staff their colonial forces, and attacks by European pirates were a constant nuisance.[28] When Lin's armada arrived off the shores of Manila in November 1574, there were only seventy Spanish guards on hand to defend the port, though other troops were exploring nearby islands and performing other duties. Lin dispatched a fleet of small ships filled with four hundred "stout and hardy" pirates, commanded by a Japanese corsair named Shōkō or "Master Zhuang" (Zhuang Gong, known as "Sioco" by the Spanish), who stormed the port and set it aflame. The people of the city scattered in terror, shouting "Army! Army! Enemies are coming!" But the army could do nothing. The pirates torched the first barracks they encountered and slaughtered the hapless Spanish troops before they could absorb what was happening. Shōkō's forces fanned across the city and came close to conquering it, but a Spanish officer earlier had espied Lin's fleet as it raced for Manila and managed to get advance word to the Spanish governor (Lavezares), who scraped together enough forces to repel this initial attack.[29]

Three days later the Chinese struck again, this time led by Lin Feng himself commanding a force of a thousand men and heavily supplied by indigenous Filipinos who expected them to drive the Spanish off the islands. The Spanish were doubly besieged when thousands of Mindoro insurgents rebelled in concert with the piratical invasion. They burned the church and convent at Manila and held two missionaries captive. Moros residing in Manila also revolted. But the Spanish had succeeded in reinforcing their defenses in the three-day interim between the two attacks and were prepared for the multiple onslaughts. In spite of the fact that scores of Lin's forces managed to battle their way into the main garrison of the town, the Spanish forces beat them back in a prolonged and bloody encounter in which two hundred Chinese were annihilated (compared to only two or three Spaniards killed). Lin's surviving forces retreated, and when the indigenous rebels saw that they could not rely on Chinese force to defeat the Spaniards, they sheepishly surrendered to the authorities.[30]

The unexpected defeat at the hands of the outnumbered though better-armed Spanish soldiers inclined Lin Feng to seek an alternative site for his base of operations. He retreated north 120 miles and established a settlement near the estuary of the Agno River in Pangasinan. There his forces constructed a fortress and reinforced their control of the surrounding territory. The thousands of Chinese settlers included at least a hundred women and children, and the Spanish perceived the expanding community as something akin to a Chinese colony. Juan González de Mendoza was disconcerted to note that, because Lin's emissaries had convinced the local inhabitants that he had slain most of the Spanish and banished them from the islands, they submitted to Lin's authority, paying him "tribute" and accepting him as "their true and natural lord."[31]

It took the Spanish several months to organize an expedition to expel their rivals from Luzon. By late March 1575, however, they had gathered a force of 256 Spaniards and 2,500 indigenes. These "Spaniards" were better armed than Lin's forces, and they easily won their initial skirmishes with the Chinese pirate, burning almost all his sailing vessels and destroying part of the fort. Successive onslaughts could not dislodge their resolute opponents, however, and the Spanish began to suffer casualties as the Chinese added three additional cannons to the garrison's defense and continued to bombard the advancing army. Realizing that further offensives would only add to their losses, the Spanish decided to lay siege to the fort and starve their opponents out. Without their ships, after all, the pirates' situation was hopeless.

After four months under a hot tropical sun, the Chinese still had not surrendered. They occasionally launched guerilla raids on the idling Spanish troops and somehow managed to keep themselves supplied. Even more remarkably, they surreptitiously gathered pieces of their crippled fleet of ships and hauled them back to their garrison. There, Lin's artisans worked around the clock to construct small but seaworthy craft out of the recycled material. These vessels were completed by August 4, 1575, and Lin immediately ordered his followers to stage a getaway under the cover of night. The Spanish caught sight of the flotilla but assumed the Chinese simply were launching another ineffectual attack and fired a few desultory shots in the direction of the boats. Slowly, belatedly, it dawned on them that this was not the prelude to another battle but the closing act of Lin Feng's Philippine adventure. By then the fort was emptied of the male pirates, while the women and children were abandoned. The Spanish were flabbergasted but could not help but be impressed by the resolute way in which Lin persevered and outsmarted them in the end. González de Mendoza later marveled at an audacious escape "that [had] seemed impossible and caused great admiration amongst the Spaniards."[32]

Some Chinese historians have criticized the Ming for abandoning Southeast Asia to the early modern colonial powers. In his study of Chinese migration to Taiwan and the Philippines, for example, Zeng Shaocong noted that the Ming failed to support Lin Feng in his effort to conquer Luzon. The Ming neither backed his efforts to stake a Chinese claim to the island nor protected subsequent Chinese migrants who were massacred there in 1603 and 1639.[33] Dai Yixuan goes even further, fulminating that the Ming "colluded with the Western imperialists and sacrificed the interests of the Chinese nation." Moreover, he adds, when the Ming grand secretary Zhang Juzheng received the false report that the Spanish had killed the pirate at Pangasinan, "he actually expressed his appreciation to the Spanish colonialists for driving Lin Feng's forces from the Philippines!"[34]

These criticisms illustrate some fundamental differences between European and Chinese approaches to overseas economic expansion prior to the twentieth century. Aside from the periodic extension of China's own borders and the incorporation of Taiwan into the Qing Empire in the seventeenth century, the Ming and Qing dynasties were not inclined to establish formal colonial states in Southeast Asia. They would not send navies to "save" besieged Chinese emigrants or to facilitate the efforts of Chinese capitalists. They would not construe a buccaneer like Lin Feng to be potentially advancing the Chinese imperial cause as, for example, the English queen Elizabeth I understood the efforts of Sir Francis Drake (bearing in mind that Drake spared England as he preyed on the ports of France and Spanish America). Elizabeth condoned Drake's acts of piracy and viewed them as a legitimate instrument of national aggrandizement, not to mention a source of royal revenue. This reflected the practice of "privateering" in Europe and the United States from the sixteenth to the nineteenth century. Privateers essentially were pirates who were sanctioned by the state to attack an enemy's economic interests to destabilize the adversary as well as to share ships and loot with the government. Privateering was essential to early modern war-making and colonial expansion and was a key component of America's successful war of independence against the British.[35] Chinese rulers were capable of cynical pragmatism themselves and were willing to exonerate pirates who submitted to their authority at home. But this approach to international relations was antithetical to the ritualized order the Ming sought to uphold overseas.

Moreover, the Ming accomplished many of their international goals through the use of military might on their borders and diplomacy abroad; they did not need to rely on pirates. Their international system had transformed some tributary states into cooperative allies. When Lin Daoqian escaped to Cambodia and Siam, Ming officials simply requested their counterparts there to suppress him. The king of Cambodia apprehended Yang Si, Lin Daoqian's accomplice, and handed him over—together with gifts of gold, elephant tusks, and beeswax—to the Chinese authorities.[36] At least in the Chinese sources, these Southeast Asian rulers seemed anxious to maintain good relations with the Ming and to fulfill their obligations under the tribute system.

Dai also criticizes Ming officials for having accommodated the Europeans as the Chinese quelled the piratical chaos of the southern coast. In 1554 they permitted the Portuguese to reside in the port of Macao and trade freely as long as they paid a tax and ceased consorting with outlaws. Dai characterizes this as a "collusion" with imperialists that led to the Portuguese colonization of Macao.[37] A Chinese nationalist might take issue with these developments, but the settlement with the Portuguese eliminated a source of support for brigandage in China. It also ensured that the Portuguese operated in China on dynastic terms, reinforcing the government's monopoly on relations with foreigners. Dai, Zeng, and other historians criticize the Ming from the standpoint of modern nationalism, but the dynasty did not imagine international relations from a national perspective but a cosmological one that emanated unilaterally from the imperial court. That the Europeans did not enter into a tributary relationship with the Chinese and would, in time, create a colonial order that undermined Sinocentric diplomacy does not negate the fact that the system enabled the Ming to achieve many of their foreign policy goals in accordance with their political ideals.

Ming international policy nonetheless had a deleterious impact on Chaozhou. Commerce revived after the sea ban was lifted and a system of mercantile licensing was introduced.[38] A century of violence on land and sea, however, inclined the local population to band together in protective and complex social formations. Historians of southeastern China have identified the sixteenth century as a moment when large corporate lineages began to develop and multiply as families defended their homes against marauders. This development is often seen as the precipitating factor in the evolution of a society inclined toward lineage feuding.[39] The insurgencies altered local society and contributed to some of the violent pathologies of late-imperial village life in Chaozhou. The constant threat of attack—not only by pirates but also by government troops ostensibly there to protect residents—inclined families to build heavily armed fortifications around their hamlets, leading to the emergence of enormous "walled villages." Village complexes safeguarded by garrisoned ramparts emerged as an efficacious response to the threat of brigandage. Tanghu township in Haiyang district was one of the more celebrated walled village-market complexes in the area. In 1558 the elders and gentry, led by Liu Zixing, learned that pirates were in the vicinity, so they built protective fortifications and called up young toughs (*yong*) to defend their village militarily. In the end it was the only homestead spared the molestations of predators in the area. Residents learned a valuable lesson and, as the century progressed, single villages built walls and multiple villages collectively transformed themselves into networks of interlocking stockades (*zhai*).[40] Many of the more prominent walled village-market complexes we will encounter again in the nineteenth century—including Outing and Anbu—also emerged at this time.

The construction of fortifications and organization of village armies contributed to the "militarization of rural society," as historians of Chaozhou have shown. These militia were designed to defend life and property from the Ming military as much as they protected the locale from marauders. As time went on, however, even as peasants armed themselves for self-protection, they began to rely on that military power in their conflicts with neighbors or they simply began to prey on the weak, and "the line between 'peasant' and 'bandit' began to blur." As the centuries passed, lineage feuding became increasingly common, and brotherhood societies arose to provide security for their members.[41] The transformed architecture of daily life—the heavily fortified, walled village defended by armed local fighters—was therefore a significant step in the development of a local culture prone to feuding after the sixteenth century. This is not merely the conclusion drawn by modern historians of the region; it was the interpretation of imperial authorities who contended with incessant outbreaks of violence in the nineteenth century. Mao Cheng, the magistrate of Chaoyang district, noted in 1864 that half of the "evils" officials associated with the Chaozhou coast—resistance to taxation, ungovernability of the local population, incessant feuding within and among lineages—could be ascribed to the walled villages that arose in response to the piratical wars of the Ming period.[42] The villages proliferated, becoming a naturalized feature of rural society and rendering the region difficult to govern ever after. Nineteenth-century officials had no difficulty making the connection between the campaigns of the sixteenth century and the troubles of their own day.

The propensity for violence on the maritime frontier thus can be traced in part to the era of sea bans, when coastal inhabitants began to devise protective strategies to deal with the resulting chaos. People understood that the government could not protect them. Indeed, on occasions when Ming officials negotiated pacification settlements with pirates, they actually conferred military ranks on the buccaneers so that, in fact, the local military was led by pirates who had agreed to stop preying on government offices. Chaozhouese learned that they had to protect themselves.[43] That is to say, the Chinese state was instrumental in fostering the violence of the southeast coast during the late imperial period, and these troubles predated the demographic expansion of the nineteenth century.

The local response to Ming policy illuminated a geographical feature of the coastal borderland of which Chaozhou was a part. Access to the sea was a financial blessing for all. But it also constituted the main avenue of escape for violent offenders. No matter how ruthlessly the dynasty patrolled the coast, it could not control the vast ocean. Pirate command was a hydra-headed beast. No sooner did the authorities expel one chieftain than another instantly emerged as a greater threat. Officials could annihilate half a piratical fleet, but the other half would sail away. And then there were the more numerous merchants whose names rarely appear in the historical record who simply continued to seek their fortune abroad in defiance of the interdictions. It was the sea—and their own nautical prowess—that enhanced their capacity to thrive in an illicit commercial order that exceeded the reach of the world's most sophisticated bureaucracy. The Manchus who conquered China in 1644 quickly came to appreciate the ways the maritime dynamics of the southeastern frontier might threaten their own ship of state.

The Coastal Evacuation

The coastal evacuation originated in the violent transition from the Ming to the Qing dynasty. Even after the Manchus ensconced themselves in Beijing in 1644, armed resistance to the new order persisted throughout South China. Zheng Chenggong (1624–1662), better known in the West as "Koxinga," was the most famous and menacing of the opponents to the conquest. Zheng hailed from a commercially powerful family whose native place was Quanzhou, Fujian, just north of Chaozhou. His life experiences were not atypical for the sojourning moguls of the coast. His mother was Japanese, and he actually was born in Nagasaki, Japan. In the wake of the Manchu invasion, his father supported a Ming pretender to the throne but eventually submitted to the new dynasty in 1646. His disappointed son rejected this path and continued in the anti-Qing struggle.

By the 1650s Zheng had established bases across southern Fujian and eastern Guangdong. Qing authorities were convinced that his military success stemmed in part from the support of coastal "traitors" who kept his forces supplied with grain and other goods. Hoping to discourage such popular effrontery as well as assert dominion over the coastal waters, the Qing adopted the disruptive policies of their predecessors by issuing the Maritime Proscription of 1656. Merchants along the entire coast of China south of Tianjin were forbidden to engage in maritime commerce. Foreign ships were similarly prohibited from trading at Chinese ports. These restrictions once again had a deleterious impact on the commercial economy of the Southeast, but they did nothing to stop Zheng's forces. In fact, as Ng Chin-keong astutely observed, the maritime proscription merely enhanced the commercial power of the Zheng organization throughout the southern seas. Their naval power enabled them to continue trading, and their contacts across East and Southeast Asia were obliged to rely on them for supplies of Chinese goods. Maritime trade grew concentrated in their hands. With unrivaled military and financial power, Zheng Chenggong easily ousted the Dutch from their fortress on Taiwan in 1662, and after his death that year, his son and a confederacy of militants transformed the island into an impregnable citadel from which they continued to attack the mainland.[44]

Determined to defeat the Zhengs and subjugate the South, the Qing took the extraordinary measure in 1661 of ordering the evacuation of the population of the coast of China from Zhejiang through Guangdong province—over 1,500 kilometers of coastline. This order (*qianjie ling*) called for local authorities to score a boundary fifty *li* (15.5 miles) inland from the shoreline and forcibly remove the population from the coast to an officially mandated pale of settlement. In 1662 the court singled out Guangdong for special measures, ordering that the residents of all twenty-four of the province's coastal districts from Qinzhou (on the "Vietnam" border) to Raoping (on the Fujian border) be evacuated. In spite of the harsh penalty for resistance—decapitation—many coastal residents, especially fisher folk, defied the order. An outraged court simply redoubled its efforts, ordering the boundary shifted even further inland and expanding the number of districts affected in Guangdong province to twenty-eight. Millions of people in the province were affected, and at least 5,310,000 *mu* were abandoned.[45] This harsh policy was implemented to facilitate the transformation of the southeast coast into a heavily militarized defense zone. The Zheng regime on Taiwan would be detached from its mainland supply lines and more easily quarantined by naval forces. Chaos can be a statebuilder's best friend for, in this case, it forced the Qing to establish a stronger military presence in the region and begin to bring it more fully under its control.

Chaozhou was devastated by the evacuation and other calamities related to the ongoing anti-Qing resistance. The prefecture formed part of the southern Fujian–eastern Guangdong locus of operations for the Zhengs, and the court knew that smuggling networks in the districts of Chenghai and Chaoyang happily supplied anti-Qing resisters with food and other goods.[46] Consequently, evacuation orders were stringently applied and endured in some areas of Chaozhou until 1684, long after the order had been rescinded in the rest of Guangdong province in 1669. Seventeenth-century population statistics are unreliable, and it is impossible to determine how many people perished. Huang Ting, who has investigated genealogical records across the region, estimates that five in ten residents either died or migrated elsewhere. Another historian calculated that the population of the prefecture contracted from 339,805 in 1660 to 188,045 in 1672.[47] These figures undoubtedly reflect the diminished capacity of the state to conduct a census in a turbulent age, but it is clear that tens of thousands of people either died or migrated as a consequence of this violent campaign.

The evacuation formally commenced in Chaozhou in 1662 and increased in intensity by the middle of the decade, but there was enormous local variation in terms of the severity and length of the time people were forced from their homes. To some extent the disparity was determined by the level of proximity to the ocean. The three interior districts of Dabu, Fengshun, and Puning were spared. The districts bordering the coast—Huilai, Chaoyang, Chenghai, and Raoping—were more seriously affected than districts located slightly more inland but accessible to the sea by rivers and sounds that were fairly easy to regulate. Among the fourteen wards of Haiyang, a wealthy inland district that included the prefectural city of Chaozhou, for example, only four wards were entirely emptied of their inhabitants and portions of three others depopulated.[48]

The fact that inland areas were spared the worst does not mean that they were not ravaged by the campaign. Haiyang was located on the Han River, and after one of its wards, Nangui, was evacuated, the neglected embankments collapsed, leading to massive flooding in the region.[49] Moreover, inland districts absorbed much of the population that had been displaced from the coast. Puning, which was not depopulated at all, experienced an enormous increase in population: in 1660 there had been approximately 10,486 households in the district; two years later 51,390 households were recorded; by 1672 the district was home to 91,390 households as a result of the campaign.[50] Refugees desperately resorted to violence in these regions. In July 1669 they gathered into a mob in Paotai, Jieyang, ransacking the town and plundering neighboring villages. Military guards were not prepared to deal with the scale of the violence and lost their weapons in the ensuing melees.[51] Living within the pale of settlement did not protect people from the disruptive horrors of Qing policy.

Not surprisingly, the campaign on the coast was a tale of human catastrophe. Huilai, a sparsely populated district, had been a base of the Zhengs and other pirates. Consequently, the boundary was drawn thirty *li* inland in 1663, and in 1664 the expulsions commenced as villages were burned and fields abandoned.[52] The evacuation from Huilai southwestward into the neighboring prefecture of Huizhou also sparked a mutiny by military forces stationed in the garrison at Jieshi. The uprising was led by Su Li, a native of Raoping who was the regional commander in charge of the garrison and ostensibly responsible for upholding government policy. It is unlikely he had ever been particularly loyal to the dynasty. At the time of the conquest, he and his brother had been leaders of a piratical operation that extended throughout Chaozhou and Huizhou. They operated in league with local salt workers and boatmen and, with a vast fleet at their disposal, were reputed to have been the biggest salt

smugglers in all of Guangdong.[53] Su submitted to the Qing in 1650, and officials, determined to foster his allegiance, appointed him in 1654 to the command of the garrison at Jieshi charged, ironically enough, with the task of
"protecting the coast against pirates."[54] He thus retained his local power while
acquiring the perquisites of military rank. A modus vivendi between the new
dynasty and the old pirate king ensued: as long as he did not rise up against
the Qing, he was permitted to retain his base and continue his commercial
activities. This arrangement ended in 1663, when the boundary was marked in
preparation for the evacuation. Strongly supported by the civilian population,
Su rebelled, and his forces succeeded in slaughtering a good number of Qing
troops before the dynasty quelled the insurrection and slayed its leader.[55]

Su Li rebelled in order to protect his commercial empire. As a military officer, he would not have been evacuated, but the entire population was to be
relocated, and this threatened his interests (indeed, one evacuated ward,
Longjing, was the site of an important salt works).[56] Robert Marks has described Su as a "social pirate . . . who sided with the dispossessed and led his
forces in revolt."[57] Although it is not clear that Su was motivated by altruism,
his fate was intertwined with that of local inhabitants, and he was one of the
few officers in the region who actively resisted the removal of the population
(the other was Xu Long, who, ironically, was the officer who gave Su his
thrashing in 1665).

These salt producers and fisher folk made their living employed in his commercial operations and did not hesitate to join Su in rebellion. They included the
Zhous, a salt-producing household, who had migrated from Hongcheng village
in Raoping, the native place of Su Li. Hongcheng had been producing salt since
Song times, but the salt began to dry up by the seventeenth century, and they
relocated to the salt flats of Jiesheng. At least two members of the family enlisted
in Su's military and participated in the rebellion.[58] What else could they do?
Their village back in Raoping was also being evacuated, so they could not return
home, and it would not have been easy to find work elsewhere given the sheer
numbers of displaced people foraging in the pale of settlement.

The coastal districts of Chaoyang and Chenghai were heavily populated
sites of profound suffering, not only because of the numbers displaced but also
because the violence of the ongoing resistance to Qing authority was so intense there. Chenghai, a wealthy commercial center, was ordered to evacuate
in 1664, and within two years it was seriously depopulated. Approximately
60,282 households were registered there in 1660, and by 1672, four years after the
end of the campaign, there were about 24,104 households.[59] After the military

drove away tens of thousands of people, Chenghai collapsed into chaos. Families scattered, and entire lineages simply disintegrated. As Huang Qiyu recalled, "With the expulsion of our village in the coastal evacuation of 1664, everyone just scattered in all directions. Even after the boundary was opened again, many simply never returned." Some had moved to Puning while others relocated to Qiongshan (Hainan Island)—approximately 600 kilometers away—because they had hoped to continue to engage in overseas commerce. Still others permanently settled elsewhere. "Because of this," he sadly concluded, "they eventually abandoned the lineage."[60]

The Chenghai evacuation was intense but also comparatively brief. This seems surprising, given the district's proximity to Taiwan. But Chenghai was blessed with a powerful and influential elite that had thrown its support to the Qing early on and cooperated with the military. The military-elite complex, which was long to endure in the area, in those days was embodied by Xu Long. Xu was born in Xucuo village in Suwan ward, a ward noted for having produced both scholars and pirates throughout the Ming period. He organized local braves into a coastal defense militia. Relying on the profits of the local fish and salt monopolies to fund his endeavors, he succeeded in driving pirates out of the vicinity.

After the Ming fell, Xu submitted to the Qing, who forthwith conferred on him the naval rank of regional commander of Chaozhou. Now formally part of the imperial military, he found himself in an awkward position when the order came to evacuate Chenghai in 1664. He had thrived as a reliable strongman who ensured order and protected local interests. Now he was expected to deprive farmers, fisher folk, merchants, and salt workers of their livelihoods; drive them into exile; and torch their villages. Rather than comply, he wrote a memorial requesting that the authorities agree to a three-to-five-year delay of the evacuation in the stretch of territory from Nanyang (where his troops were garrisoned) to Nansha village, territory that, not coincidentally, included his own family homestead.[61]

Word of Xu's memorial spread, and his neighbors fervently hoped that they might escape the fate of others in the region. As one denizen of Zhanglin recalled, "Fortunately, we received protection from Regional Commander Xu Long, and we were able to delay our evacuation for a time. . . . All were so grateful for his efforts that the gentry and elders raised money to purchase vacant land . . . on which they would erect a shrine to honor his very birth."[62] Unfortunately, Xu's supplication fell on deaf ears, and the elite never had the opportunity to start construction because they were driven from their homes with the others. Xu nevertheless was celebrated in Chenghai as a man who had the temerity to promote the local interest by truncating the evacuation. Nanyang itself was evacuated in the comparatively late year of 1666—and only after Xu had been recalled to Beijing to join a banner. Residents were permitted to return to their devastated villages two years later. It had been impossible to ignore the order to evacuate, but locals benefited from Xu Long's capacity to delay the inevitable.

Chaoyang, the other district with a substantial coastline, was hardest hit of all. Eight wards (out of thirteen) were completely depopulated in two stages, the first starting in 1662, the second in 1664. In total, the military evacuated and torched at least 186 villages, compelling the now homeless residents to march fifty *li* inland. The agricultural and fishing industries were devastated, a particularly disastrous development considering that people in the district typically made a living engaged in both enterprises.[63] Starvation was rampant. Ji Jichen, a resident of Geyuan village, recalled the traumatic experience:

> On March 16, 1663, Chaoyang Magistrate Xie ordered us to move. The people of [Zhaoshou] ward fled with wild abandon, and thatched huts were burned to the ground. Into the mountains the boundaries were drawn and into the water the stakes were driven [to mark the evacuation border]. There was neither food nor fish . . . and a *sheng* of salt cost a *qian* of silver. Men who lost their livelihoods abandoned their families just to survive: either they sold their wives and kept their sons or they sold their sons and kept their wives, or the wives and sons were all sold. Once these men were on their own, they turned to violence. Fathers did not care for their sons and older brothers could not care for their younger brothers. Alas! In time, the corpses clogged the lanes of the town.[64]

Struggling to survive, evacuees resorted to banditry. As one gazetteer recorded, "After people were driven from their homes, they became utterly impoverished and, as the days passed, they gathered together in response to whistles and shouts and began to plunder the military stockades. . . . Troops campaigned against them and the bandit gangs, now defeated, scattered."[65] Such spontaneous episodes of resistance, usually borne of sheer desperation, were not uncommon. Most (but not all) of the people of Chaoyang were permitted to return to their villages in August 1668, which is to say that they had been forced to fend for themselves for almost six years.

The chaos in Chaoyang was compounded by the fact that an ally of the Zhengs, Qiu Hui, established a base of resistance in 1666 at Dahao, a port in

Zhaoshou ward. Zhaoshou, which was completely surrounded by water, was the only part of Chaozhou to which former residents were not allowed to return after Beijing reopened the border. Ji Jichen recalled the heartbreaking sight of hundreds of devastated villagers weeping at the water's edge, their path obstructed by the military even as other peasants in their midst returned to their homes to rebuild their lives. They were destined to return only in 1684, after the last of the Zhengs surrendered to the Qing.[66]

The perpetrator of this extended misery, Qiu Hui, was a native of Majiao village, near the port. He had thrown in with the Zhengs in his youth and spent many of the intervening years storming the coast of China from their base on Taiwan. He formed an alliance with Dan (Tanka or Danjia), boat-dwelling fisher folk whose hereditary "demeaned" status distinguished them from other Chaozhou residents, who often discriminated against them.[67] These forces continued to attack the Chaozhou coast even after most inhabitants had been permitted to return to their homes in 1669. In February of that year, Qiu's troops raided the port of Haimen and pillaged the villages and market towns of Xiashan and Huanglong wards, running off with considerable quantities of grain. That same year, in a bold strike into the heart of the prefecture, he commanded several hundred vessels upriver into Haiyang. His troops laid siege to Longhu, a walled village filled with influential elites, but the marauders were finally pushed back by Regional Commander Liu Jinzhong (who, at that time, was still loyal to the Qing). Liu ingeniously dammed up the river, forcing many of Qiu's ships to run aground in the mud. His troops captured thirty vessels, but many rebels evaded capture and attacked one hundred villages in the districts of Jieyang, Chenghai, Huilai, and Puning. Qiu's forces kidnapped ten thousand men and women, who were then carried off to Taiwan, where they were sold as maidservants and slaves. Local genealogical records lament the loss of children as young as six, who were never to be seen again.[68]

Qiu Hui's forces absconded to Taiwan in 1680 after suffering a crushing defeat at the hands of a massive army of Manchu and Chinese forces.[69] He remained loyal to the Zhengs to the bitter end and perished in one of the great naval battles that led to the defeat of the Zheng resisters in 1683 and the incorporation of Taiwan into the Qing Empire. Popular accounts celebrate his heroism in this final moment of struggle as he brandished his sword and set fire to his ship's powder kegs just as the Manchu forces clambered aboard.[70] He indeed died valiantly, but his legacy was purchased at the cost of unfathomable hardship back home.

Qiu Hui's escapades remind us that the tribulations of the Ming-Qing transition did not simply end with the termination of the coastal evacuation. Other uprisings and mutinies compounded the calamities, most notably the rebellion in 1674 of Liu Jinzhong, regional commander of Chaozhou and the man charged with confronting pirate kings like Qiu Hui. He arose in sympathy with a more wide-scale rebellion known as the Revolt of the Three Feudatories. It took loyal Qing forces three years of hard fighting to defeat him in 1777.[71] And Liu's mutiny was only one of many violent catastrophes that exacerbated the anarchy of the Ming-Qing transition.

Needless to add, Chaozhou's economy did not thrive during this period. Crops were destroyed, the fishing industry contracted, and commercial networks collapsed as families dispersed. We saw that some merchants who had resided in the commercial center of Chenghai fled the evacuation zone for the relative security of Qiongzhou. They had moved to the island with the explicit purpose of continuing their trade, for it was a major stop on the Japanese and Chinese commercial routes to Southeast Asia.[72] A useful commercial refuge, it was as far south in China as one could sail and distant from the turbulent Guangdong-Fujian borderland. It was not dominated by the Zhengs, so the merchants enjoyed greater autonomy from the sea lords of the South China Sea. Whatever commercial success they achieved, however, would not have redounded to their homeland, for they lost contact with their kin after the conquest years.

Many absconding merchants also resettled along the Gulf of Siam and in what is now Vietnam. The French envoy to Siam, Simon de la Loubère, reported in 1691, for example, that three to four thousand Chinese had been living in that kingdom since the 1680s. Siamese trade was not profitable at that time, for the king monopolized most commercial activity and limited the opportunities of foreign traders.[73] Most of these Chinese had moved to the Bangkok area to eke out a meagre business and to escape the ravages of the dynastic transition in China. Many émigrés hailed from Chaozhou and emerged as the major Chinese native place group in the eighteenth century

Because of Chaozhou's location at the edge of the South China Sea and along the trade routes to the great emporia of what Europeans vaguely called the "East Indies," its residents were subjected to the brutal campaigns of the final two dynasties in Chinese history. Coastal dwellers bore the brunt of these sustained governmental efforts to control commercial activity across a vast ocean. The Ming strove to actualize a Sinocentric ritual order in maritime Asia. The Qing were condemned to forty years of carnage as they lashed the refractory coast to their ever-expanding empire. The greatest challenge to their rule proved to be a transnational governing authority that was more naturally adapted to the realities of the sea. Zheng Chenggong and his allies constructed a maritime empire across an archipelago of islands that had never been incorporated into larger states. Their defiant network guaranteed that the southeast coast remained commercially wired to Japan, Siam, and the port polities in between. Their Fujianese successors continued to dominate that trade into the nineteenth century.[74]

However violent and unreasonable the Qing campaigns against the southeast coast appear to modern minds, they did, in fact, eliminate all competitors to their rule along the Chaozhou coast. They crushed Qiu Hui and Su Li; they defeated the Zhengs, the Southern Ming claimants to the throne, and local mutineers. No significant challenge to their vast dominion appeared again for almost 170 years. This, at least, provided Chaozhouese a measure of relief from two centuries of intermittent brutalization. Chen Chunsheng has asserted that the age of the independent domain along the Chaozhou coast was over, for this scale of "rural militaries" was never seen again after 1683.[75]

The final triumph of the Qing indeed terminated centuries of tumult in the region, but the years of piracy and conquest changed Chaozhou in fundamental ways. The Qing did not eradicate those walled villages. Coastal powermongers forged a commercial order that operated beyond the legal writ of the dynasty. Legions of anti-Qing resisters fled to overseas sanctuaries and participated in the processes of Southeast Asian state-building while their descendants honed a revulsion for the Qing into a translocal religious practice. These dynastic campaigns shaped the history of maritime Chaozhou for generations to come.

2

Back in the World

THE EMERGENCE OF MARITIME CHAOZHOU, 1767–1840

During the Qianlong period [1735–1796], Luo Fangbo of Guangdong traded here [West Borneo]. He was a heroic man who had mastered the martial arts and captured the hearts of the Chinese multitudes. At the time, the local barbarians [Dayaks] often usurped his authority and [Chinese] traders were unable to engage in business peacefully. So Fangbo would lead a mob of fighters and pacify them.

—XIE QINGGAO (1765–1821)

CHAOZHOUESE BEGAN to emerge among the commercial titans and laboring masses of Southeast Asia in the eighteenth century. The triumph of the half-Chaozhou-Chinese king of Siam, Taksin, is the transformative event of our story here. With significant paramilitary assistance from Chaozhouese émigrés, he prevailed over the Burmese invaders in 1767 and reestablished tranquility in the kingdom. Taksin and his successors favored Chaozhouese in particular and facilitated the rise of the fabled Chaozhou (Teochew) junk merchants. Polities along the Gulf of Siam formed a vital zone of maritime Chaozhou, sites of investment and trade, destinations for Chaozhouese labor, and founts of natural resources. Access to land throughout Southeast Asia led to the cultivation of a vast, translocal plantation economy. The eighteenth century represented the beginning of the convergence of Chaozhou's economic fortunes with those of overseas territories. No less than European colonialists, overseas Chinese across the South China Sea enjoyed unparalleled access to the region's bounty.

The rise of maritime Chaozhou coincided with the expansion of the remunerative drug trade in China and around the globe. Chaozhouese merchants and sailors transported opium in sizable quantities at home and abroad. It is not always possible to chart the enrichment of individuals who were never arrested, but profits from the trade clearly enabled Chaozhouese to begin to compete commercially with merchants from Canton and Fujian after the seventeenth century.

The opium trade led to an underground economy staffed by the sort of men who joined sectarian brotherhoods such as the Tiandihui, and the issues explored in this chapter cannot be disentangled from the subject of the next, the rise of brotherhood societies that offered mutual aid to sojourning men. The coterminous emergence of the Chaozhouese diaspora and the expansion of the opium trade were intertwined with that phenomenon. The upsurge of brotherhoods in the middle of the eighteenth century had multiple causes, but this interconnection is commonly overlooked. Chaozhou emerged as a site of emigration at this time, and the increasing visibility of "Triads" back home was intimately connected to the circulation of laborers and merchants across China and Southeast Asia. The proliferation of these sodalities in eastern Guangdong reflected in part the increasingly cosmopolitan experiences of its inhabitants. Their exposure to the descendants of anti-Qing refugees among overseas Chinese undoubtedly rekindled resentments enflamed by four decades of resistance to the Manchu conquest. Many of those who returned to China from abroad had lived for years in polities that were controlled by Chinese leaders of their own choosing, inculcating in at least some of them the idea that there were superior forms of sociopolitical organization to that imposed on them by their Qing overlords. Most significantly, the earliest reference to the Tiandihui in maritime Chaozhou is encountered not in Chaozhou itself but among the Chaozhouese who dwelled overseas. The rise of the Tiandihui was intertwined with the acceleration of the sojourning experience. These developments reflect the entangled history of the South China Sea as well as the extent to which the colonial periphery affected developments in the ostensible Chinese metropole.

Expanding the Geographical Map of Chaozhou

The Qing permitted seafarers to sail overseas after 1683, and the coastal trade expanded internationally. Chaozhou emerged as one node in this wider commerce. In the 1680s and 1690s observers in the Japanese port of Nagasaki recorded that hundreds of Chinese vessels either arrived directly from Chaozhou or had stopped there en route from elsewhere. In 1688 alone, nine fleets of junks arrived from Chaozhou or Nan'ao Island.[1] These fleets carried "local products" from Chaozhou, and the trade fostered the region's recovery from the chaos of the Ming-Qing transition.

Imperial proscriptions against commerce with Southeast Asia, however, intermittently persisted into the eighteenth century. In 1717 the Kangxi emperor prohibited Chinese intercourse with the region and demanded that foreign governments repatriate any Chinese travelers to their lands "so that they may be executed." An edict by the Yongzheng emperor in 1729 decreed that any "undesirable persons" who conducted business abroad should be discouraged from returning home. Historians of the overseas Chinese experience interpret these ineffectual decrees as a manifestation of the court's apprehension that Chinese would encounter malcontents whose families had fled abroad after the Qing conquest.[2]

These fears were not unfounded. Redoubts of anti-Qing Ming loyalists dotted the landscape of Southeast Asia. In the Nguyen kingdom of Cochinchina (Vietnam), for example, Ming loyalists from Chaozhou took refuge in the provinces of Baclieu and Rachgia. These underpopulated regions were situated in the fertile delta plains south of Saigon, and descendants of these exiles prospered as rice cultivators. They were joined by thousands of migrants in the latter years of the nineteenth century, and by the early twentieth century Chaozhouese had settled beyond these areas into Cantho, Soctrang, and Travinh.[3] These latter-day migrants expanded the territory to which the original refugees had absconded.

Qing restrictions, though ineffective, did have a deleterious impact on the rice trade at a time when population growth on the southeast coast increased the need for imports. The court began to recognize that grain deficiencies fostered social disorder and introduced ad hoc adjustments to its policies. Fujianese began to enjoy preferential treatment in the conveyance of rice from Southeast Asia. In 1727 the imperial court granted several firms monopolies over that commerce, and Amoy (Xiamen) emerged as the center of the vital Sino-Siamese rice trade. By the 1750s Guangdong was awarded similar inducements to increase rice imports, but merchants from Canton, not Chaozhou, dominated provincial importation for the next decade.[4] These developments naturally enhanced the longstanding supremacy of these ports in the southern seas.

Chaozhouese often operated in tandem with Fujianese merchants, a relationship that was reflected in such commercial guild alliances as the South

Seas Guild (Nanhai hang) and the Fujian-Chaozhou Overseas Guild (Fu-Chao yanghang), the latter a nine-family enterprise licensed to trade out of Canton by the Guangdong Provincial Customs.[5] The vessels of Fujianese and Chaozhouese active in the coastal and overseas trade were officially referred to as the "Fujian-Chaozhou ships" (Fu-Chao chuan).[6] Chaozhou depended on the Fujianese commercial economy in the seventeenth and early eighteenth centuries. Owing to its privileged status in the Taiwanese and Siamese rice trades, Amoy port emerged as a principal source of rice for southeastern China. Merchants imported twelve to sixteen million pounds of rice annually from Siam alone, and this in turn stimulated a thriving Amoy-Chaozhou rice trade involving three to four hundred junks.[7]

Lacking the privileges of Amoy and Canton, Chaozhou's commercial fortunes were comparatively constrained. By the early eighteenth century, population expansion was transforming eastern Guangdong into a grain-deficient region. The dependence on other markets prevented local traders from responding effectively to periodic crises in the food supply, which exacerbated local disorders and violence. Lan Dingyuan, who served as the magistrate of Puning and Chaoyang districts in 1727, was one in a long line of officials to bemoan the local proclivity for feuding, piracy, and litigation abuse. He ascribed the mayhem to the prevalence of walled and heavily fortified village complexes, where villagers resisted taxation and fought over embankments and water sources. He characterized the mountainous region along the border between Puning and Chaoyang as particularly disordered and was astonished to find that one feud over an embankment in 1727 involved over a hundred combatants from two clans.[8] Although he did not make the connection, it is significant that this borderland had constituted one boundary of the pale of settlement during the coastal evacuation of the 1660s. It endured as a site of disorder throughout the late imperial period and emerged as the main base of the communist insurgencies in the 1930s.

Lan collected the most scandalous cases he encountered in a celebrated legal casebook. Widely consulted by officials, it remains popular reading in China today owing to its titillating accounts of criminal depravity. The casebook was instrumental in disseminating Chaozhou's reputation across the empire as one of the more "violent" regions of China. What is often forgotten, however, is the fact that Lan arrived in Chaozhou during a severe, three-year famine, which surely exacerbated social animosities and disputes over resources. Lan Dingyuan himself reported on the difficulties of provisioning the military garrisons with rice during these shortages.[9]

Chaozhou's rice trade was inadequate to prevent severe crises, though some local merchants managed to deliver domestic grain supplies during periods of pronounced deficiencies. Zheng Xiangde (1659–1739), the progenitor of the commercial empire of the Zheng clan of the Shalong village-market complex in Chaoyang, was one such benefactor in Lan's day. The rise of the Shalong Zhengs is conventionally ascribed to the success of Xiangde, a fishmonger-turned-shipping-magnate from Dongxian village. His childhood had been disrupted by the horrors of the Ming-Qing transition, and, whatever his financial situation was prior to the evacuation, he returned to Shalong a destitute young man. He found work selling fish on a circuit from Haimen port to Shalong. Lin Zhongguang, a wealthy shipper, often purchased fish from Zheng and eventually hired him to carry his goods inland, initially along the waterways of Chaoyang and eventually to Chaozhou prefectural city and Zhanglin port. It was difficult to maneuver large vessels in the shallow passageways of Chaozhou, and transporting goods on behalf of a successful businessman was a breakthrough opportunity for an enterprising man with a small, flat-bottomed boat. Zheng impressed Lin so much that the latter transferred the management of his entire inland business to him. After a few years, Zheng had amassed enough capital to launch his own shipping company. He transported Chaozhouese sugar, porcelain, and embroidery as well as Fujianese tea to Ningbo, Shanghai, and Tianjin and returned with cotton products from the Lower Yangzi region. He amassed a fortune shipping along the coastal trade routes. As Zheng Ruiting has observed, Zheng Xiangde started this business soon after the Qing ban on the coastal trade was lifted in 1683. These commercial "early birds" were meeting a long-suppressed national demand for various goods and the business of long-distance shipping north and south was profitable in those years.[10] Moreover, such enterprising men were not simply getting rich. They were expanding—and linking—the markets of large commercial centers like Chaozhou in the south and Shanghai in the north, pulling the east coast out of the protracted economic slump occasioned by the seventeenth-century crisis. The economic dynamism of the eighteenth century, the so-called era of the High Qing, was generated in part by the energies of coastal merchants like Zheng, who reversed the economic decline of the conquest era.

Having acquired a fortune in the coastal trade, Zheng purchased a scholarly degree and began to invest in landed estates across Chaoyang and in Guilin, in distant Guangxi province. By the eighteenth century his family owned swaths of the most productive terrain in eastern Chaoyang. His spectacular rise from fishmonger to coastal shipper to landowning magnate suggests that he may have sold opium, then a luxury item but nonetheless the most profitable commodity by weight traded along the south China coast. Late imperial fisher folk and fishmongers were among the most common wholesalers and retailers of opium in China.[11]

Whatever the source of his wealth, Zheng was in a position to alleviate the grain scarcities of Chaoyang in 1726. The local gazetteer commended him for his role in transporting enormous shiploads of grain to distribute to the poor.[12] The tribute does not state where he obtained his rice supplies (he never traveled abroad), but the impoverished victims of this prolonged famine apparently would not have survived without these extraordinary efforts at famine relief.

These ad hoc importations of grain never alleviated inadequacies of supply, and social upheavals continued to rock the region. After a disastrous harvest beset the farms near Anbu port from 1747 to 1748, rice prices surged, and merchants began to ship scarce supplies elsewhere to make a profit. The outraged son of a Daoist master, Li Yawan, and his mother "hatched a plot" with twenty-five others to "steal from the rich to relieve the poor." They founded "The Great Kingdom of Li, the Celestial Luminary," and proceeded to plunder various grain-laden junks of their contents.[13] This was a classic Qing food riot in which Li and his followers claimed a right to basic sustenance, and officials grudgingly acknowledged that they represented themselves as Daoist Robin Hoods saving the starving poor from immoral exporters. It was not lost on these authorities that Li established his "Great Kingdom" as an alternative to the "Great Kingdom of the Qing," an implicit critique of the dynasty as unworthy and ineffectual. The protest was one of many that articulated some sort of antidynastic message after the Qing pacified the coast in the 1680s.

If the Qing wished to rule over this area, it was going to have to give the maritime economy of Chaozhou greater leeway to flourish, and the court finally conferred on Chaozhouese the same rice-importing privileges the Fujianese and Cantonese enjoyed. Prior to the 1740s officials feared the deleterious impact both of antidynastic circles overseas and the expanding opium trade along the Guangdong coast.[14] They nevertheless concluded that unreliable grain supplies posed a greater threat to political stability. Importing rice directly from Southeast Asia was one logical solution. Local officials were also determined to fill the granaries and provision the expanding naval forces in the region. Beijing began to offer reductions up to 50 percent in the duty on rice to local importers willing to transport large quantities of grain.[15] From this point forward, Siam became a major source of Chaozhou rice.

Most stalwarts of the Chaozhou junk trade in the eighteenth century hailed from the commercial powerhouses of Chenghai and Haiyang. After 1684 traders from these districts emerged as dominant participants in the north-south coastal trade, establishing a presence in Tianjin, Shanghai, Amoy, Canton, and Qiongzhou. Chenghai natives played a commanding role in the sugar trade of the China coast in particular. By the eighteenth century they were expanding as a maritime network of traders across the South China Sea to Singapore and Bangkok.[16] After the 1740s Chenghai's major seaport, Zhanglin (Changlim), flourished as Guangdong's second most important port (after Canton) and a center of the international rice trade. Zhanglin earned renown as the home of the famous "red-bowed boats" (*hongtou chuan*), junks that dominated the trade between Chenghai and Siam from the mid-eighteenth to the twentieth century. Other ports like Anbu in Haiyang also developed as hubs of the coastal trade connected to international commerce.[17]

Chaozhou's fortunes were enhanced by the reverberations of an important event in the history of the faraway kingdom of Siam: the military victory of Taksin over the Burmese invaders of Ayutthaya in 1767 (Siam was known by the name of its capital, Ayutthaya, from 1351 to 1767). Taksin was born in 1734, the son of a Chaozhou-Chinese father and Siamese mother. His father, Zheng Yong, was a merchant who had emigrated from Huafu village in Chenghai. Like many Chenghai merchants of his generation, Zheng Yong married an indigenous woman and served the Ayutthayan king in various financial capacities, most notably as a tax collector. Because he also controlled the gambling monopoly, he grew quite wealthy and the family became socially prominent. Taksin eventually was adopted by a Siamese nobleman, further propelling the young man's advancement in society. At the time of the Burmese sack of Ayutthaya in 1767, Taksin was serving as the governor of the province of Tak.[18]

By most accounts, Taksin was an unusually accomplished man. Owing to his father's transregional experiences, he was fluent in Thai, Chinese, Malay, and Vietnamese, and he somehow emerged as a favorite of the Ayutthayan king, who bestowed many titles on him. A French Jesuit, Olivier-Simon Le Bon, met Taksin in 1772 and described him as "hardy, courageous, intelligent . . . [and] a brave warrior."[19]

Whatever his personal attributes, he proved the man of the hour during the brutal Burmese onslaught of 1767. Burmese troops pillaged towns and devastated the countryside. After they captured and executed the king at the palace gate, famine and epidemics ravaged the disintegrating Siamese polity. In the face of these challenges, Taksin, alone among the officials of the defunct Ayutthayan state, effectively mustered an army to drive the invaders out of the country. He slowly expanded his base of power and in the midst of this chaos enthroned himself as king of Siam, moving the capital to Thonburi (present-day Bangkok), an area that was dominated economically by Chinese. In spite of the fact that Taksin had usurped the throne, he won many Siamese over because he had proven his ability to defend the kingdom. He also opened the government treasury and purchased supplies of rice from his Chinese commercial backers to feed the starving multitudes. Having restored order and prosperity, he temporarily secured his position against those with a more valid claim to the crown.[20]

Taksin's rise to power was contingent on the support Chaozhouese merchants offered his regime. Because of the pervasive threat from pirates, ocean-going junks were legally permitted to depart China armed with one cannon, eight guns, ten swords, ten sets of bows and arrows, and thirty catties of gunpowder.[21] The Qing, however, could not prevent the purchase of arms elsewhere in the Nanyang, and Dutch Batavia in particular proved a reliable source of foreign weaponry. Merchants from Chaozhou thus were a well-armed force with considerable combat potential, and they constituted a significant branch of Taksin's military during these years. They also supplied him with the food, weapons, and ships necessary to wage war, stabilize his regime, and expand the borders of Siam. Although Taksin identified primarily as a Siamese and relied substantially on support by Siamese officials and soldiers, it is difficult to imagine his many successes absent his alliance with Chinese from his father's native place.[22] Chaozhouese played a critical role in the building of the Siamese state.

Taksin relied on this alliance not only to expel the Burmese and seize power in Siam but also to advance his foreign policy agenda in the borderland frontier of Siam, Cambodia, and Quang Nam (Vietnam). The warfare among these three kingdoms during the 1770s exacerbated the rivalries between two resident Chinese native place groups—Chaozhouese and Cantonese from Leizhou—who had ensconced themselves along the shores of these dominions at the time of the Qing conquest.[23] The turmoil of the Ming-Qing transition generated a mass exodus of southeast coastal refugees to these safer redoubts. Statistical evidence is unavailable, but Chen Chingho has shown that the prolonged migration was so "unprecedented" that it fostered a different sort of overseas Chinese experience in which the scale of their economic enterprises and their services to regional rulers multiplied significantly. Some began to establish political entities that wielded independent military and political authority after the seventeenth century.[24] Mac Cuu (Mo Jiu, 1655–1736), the most notable of these leaders, fled with his "Cantonese" followers from the southern Fujianese battleground of resistance to Manchu rule. He grew wealthy as the developer of silver mines and gambling houses in Cambodia. In 1681, after having served the court in various capacities, he founded the port polity of Ha Tien, which evolved into the premier site of the Cambodian import-export trade.

Chaozhou refugees for their part settled along a coastal stretch of southeastern Siam, centering their activities at Bangplasoi (or Chonburi), Chantaburi, and Trat.[25] Sakurai and Kitagawa have shown that Chinese émigrés successfully ensconced themselves in these territories because a "political vacuum" had emerged along the eastern shores of the gulf as indigenous "land kings" vied for control elsewhere in the region, leaving it open to Chinese market development and political control. That is to say, the emergence of Chinese port polities in the eastern gulf also must be seen in the wider context of Southeast Asian state-building in the eighteenth century.[26] The Macs aligned themselves first with the Cambodian and later the Quang Nam state, while Chaozhouese backed the Siamese.

Chaozhou merchants relied on their sanctuaries in Siam to vie with the late Mac Cuu's son Mac Thien Tu (1710–1780) for control of the eastern shores of the gulf. Huo Ran (Hoac Nhiem)—a trader who was "very skillful in the art of war" and whose forces dominated Kong Island just south of Trat—and Chen Tai (Tran Tai)—who was based in Chantaburi and Trat—battled Mac Thien Tu in the late 1760s as the latter strove to expand his own dominion over the gulf beyond Ha Tien. Mac routed his rivals in these campaigns.[27] Mac was less successful in resisting Taksin's efforts to restore Siamese suzerainty over Cambodia by force. During the course of Taksin's campaigns, another Chaozhou merchant, named Chen Lian (Tran Lien), convinced the king to storm Ha Tien and wrest the prosperous port from Mac control.

Taksin's policy in Cambodia was not uniquely "expansionist," for Siamese kings had been claiming suzerainty over much of Cambodia since the fourteenth century. His agenda was complicated by the rising ambitions of Quang Nam after the seventeenth century as Cambodia became an "arena of competition" between the two powers. Taksin's incursion into Ha Tien nonetheless also was driven by the economic and territorial ambitions of Chaozhouese in eastern Siam. One Japanese historian has gone so far as to claim that "Taksin's early military strategy basically amounted to the unification of [Chaozhouese] powers in the Gulf of Siam."[28]

Taksin personally led the invasion of Ha Tien in 1771, attacking with a force of four hundred battleships and fifteen thousand soldiers while an armada of Chaozhouese junks was commanded by Tran Lien. Mac Thien Tu secured reinforcements neither from the Cambodians (in whose territory Ha Tien technically was situated) nor from the Vietnamese, with whom he was aligned. A mere thousand Leizhou and Cantonese forces collapsed under the onslaught of the more powerful Siamese-Chaozhouese invaders. A victorious Taksin thereupon appointed Tran Lien governor of both Ha Tien and the Cambodian prefecture of Banteay Meas and returned to Siam with his legions, for he feared that his foreign adventures threatened his tenuous political situation back home.[29] Chaozhou-Siamese control of Ha Tien ended in 1773 when the Vietnamese negotiated a resolution of the crisis and the occupying forces withdrew. It eventually was incorporated into the Vietnamese state, but the polity never recovered from the devastation of the Siamese attack and the Tayson rebellion (1772) and went into a permanent decline.

The rise of Chaozhouese commercial power in the Gulf of Siam coincided with momentous transformations in the region: state-building on the mainland, aggressive combat among rising powers, and the intensification of European colonialism. In advancing their own economic and territorial interests, the Chaozhouese engaged in a notable amount of violence. They helped Taksin defeat the Burmese, they buttressed his monarchical ambitions, and they supported his military expansion along the eastern shores of the gulf. From the mountainous heights over Ha Tien, they bombarded the citadel into rubble. To be a member of the commercial establishment at this time did not simply involve the capacity to buy and sell, navigate a ship, ingratiate oneself with whoever was in power in any given locale, or solicit funds to build a temple. It also required the ability to operate as an armed force. We do not know the processes by which these mercantile forces bonded (did they take blood oaths or establish brotherhoods)? We do know that they were forged into a cohesive group by their native place connection, a bond that was reinforced by the quotidian activities of peace and war while living overseas. As Anthony Reid reminds us, state-builders in Vietnam and Siam relied on merchants and laborers from China "to extend their frontiers and their revenue base." In the process, the port of Bangkok emerged as the premier port between Calcutta and Canton.[30] This was a mutually advantageous relationship reflecting the taut entanglement of Chinese in the political fortunes of the emerging states of the Nanyang.

Taksin surely appreciated their stalwart support on the battlefield, but militant solidarity alone does not account for the emergence of Chaozhouese commercial power in the region. Territoriality as a spatial strategy to control resources is not to be equated exclusively with violence and political control; it involves a variety of practices. In this case, Chaozhou merchants acquired a commanding presence in the economy by politically subordinating themselves to whoever controlled the Siamese state. Essential to their rise as the dominant Chinese native place group in Siam were the economic and administrative favors they enjoyed under Taksin and his successor, King Rama I (r. 1782–1809). At the time Taksin took the throne, the Siamese economy was in a state of collapse, and he understood that fostering the foreign trade of the kingdom—especially with China—was the path to recovery. Sino-Siamese trade had a long history, but it increased dramatically after Taksin's coronation, and merchants from Chaozhou were the leading beneficiaries of this expanding commerce.[31] Royal favor transformed Chaozhouese into a privileged economic group in the realm. Aside from placing them in high court and provincial positions, Taksin appointed them as port officials, monopolists, and trade agents who eventually dominated Siam's foreign commerce. Rebels assassinated Taksin in 1782 and King Rama I assumed his throne, but the new monarch retained most of his predecessor's Chaozhouese entourage, ensuring that they maintained control over the treasury, royal warehouses, and tributary trade. This enabled them to continue to dominate Sino-Siamese commercial intercourse, then the most remunerative bilateral trade relationship in the South China Sea, into the nineteenth century.[32] It was during this period that Bangkok began to displace Batavia, a Fujianese commercial stronghold, as a Southeast Asian port.

The transforming fortunes of Chaozhouese are clearly seen in the vital rice trade. Siam's tropical climate and fertile soil are ideal for rice cultivation, and in normal times peasants harvested two crops per year. Contemporary observers marveled that the kingdom was "inferior to no other country in the world" in the production of this calorie-rich grain.[33] After 1767 merchants from the Chenghai district of Chaozhou began to displace those from Amoy and Canton as the dominant millers and shippers of Siamese rice. Sarasin Viraphol has shown that the Qing periodically granted honors to Chinese who imported large quantities of rice from Southeast Asia and that, prior to 1767, Chaozhou natives did not appear among the honorees. For example, in 1758 all seven of the Guangdong rice merchants rewarded hailed from the Canton region and none was from Chaozhou. By 1767, the year of Taksin's usurpation, of the nine merchants so hailed, two were from Canton and seven from Chenghai. Chenghai merchants thenceforth dominated the trade in Siamese rice and permanently surpassed their erstwhile competitors in South China.[34] They no longer were forced to depend on Amoy shippers for their supplies. Moreover, with their grain situation now stabilized, the farmers of Chaozhou were free to concentrate on the remunerative cash-cropping of sugar.

Merchants were not the only class of Chaozhouese to benefit from the favor of Siamese kings in the eighteenth and nineteenth centuries. Taksin hired Chinese artisans and craftsmen to construct his capital at Thonburi. His successor, Rama I, transferred the capital across the river to Bangkok and continued to rely on skilled Chinese labor to build the bustling port city. This led to an enormous influx of construction workers lured from China by the prospect of guaranteed employment.[35] The Chinese population of Siam expanded steadily, from roughly five thousand in the seventeenth century to one hundred thousand by 1830. The majority of those eighteenth-century Chinese were merchants, craftsmen, and laborers from Chaozhou. Considering that the population of Chaozhou at that time was roughly 1,405,180 and that of Chenghai—whence many of those settlers departed—about 90,511, these sojourners represented a significant though unknowable percentage of Chaozhou's population.[36]

Reflecting the increasingly entangled economies of Bangkok and Chaozhou, the Siamese construction industry relied not simply on Chinese labor but also on Chinese building materials. Eighteenth-century observers noted that Chinese ships transported large quantities of brick-clay, encaustic tiles, and especially shell-lime.[37] The Chaozhou coast is a vast alluvial plain under which seashells have accumulated for millennia. Residents of Chenghai specialized in the harvesting of shells and manufacture of shell-lime, for it was situated near the mouth of the Han River and its many silt-depositing tributaries. In two large shell-beds near Swatow port alone, the industry provided opportunities to the owners of 350 single-mast river junks in the nineteenth century. Seven hundred laborers on these vessels collected shells by use of a long, sturdy rod; enormous net-bags; and iron prongs that pried shells loose from the sandy soil and sent them drifting with the current into the nets. The shells were then burned to manufacture a type of lime that was used in construction. These 350 river junks collected enough shells to produce 1,050,000 piculs (69,998 tons) of lime per year.[38] In addition to the shell harvesters, an untold number of people were involved in the manufacture, shipment, and sale of lime. The construction of the urban and commercial infrastructure of Siam thus redounded to the benefit of the Chaozhou economy back home. As the years passed, Chinese also developed the shell-lime industry in Bangkok itself.[39]

Other goods produced and manufactured in Chaozhou were exported to the emporia of Southeast Asia, stimulating the local economy. A junk of 600 tons burthen sailing out of Zhanglin port in 1824 typically carried $70,000 to $80,000 (Mexican) worth of local goods. One junk reportedly transported 31,200 "packages" containing 640,250 pieces of earthenware of varying sizes and types as well as 95 baskets of 20,000 cups. The cargo also included 10,000 floor tiles; 12,000 paper umbrellas; 50 boxes of dried fruits; 100 bales of nankeens; and assorted boxes of sugar candy, gold thread, vermicelli, incense sticks, and dried tobacco.[40] The cargo of this single ship reflected the productivity not only of the agricultural economy but also of the manufacturing shops of the local towns.

This ongoing entanglement can also be seen in the Chaozhou shipbuilding industry. By the latter eighteenth century the large oceangoing junks engaged in the Sino-Siamese trade were constructed in Siam, not only because maritime shipbuilding had begun to shift there as a result of the sea bans of the early Qing but also because Siam had an ample supply of forest timber conducive to the construction of sturdy, long-distance vessels. The British diplomat John Crawfurd observed that the Chinese produced the best ships in all Asia but that, by 1822, the junks engaged in the Sino-Siamese trade were built by Chinese architects and craftsmen in Bangkok (the "ordinary workmen" were usually Siamese). It was cheaper to build there owing to the ample availability of timber brought down the Chao Phraya River from inland virgin forests. Circa 1821 it cost 15 Spanish silver dollars per ton to build a junk in Siam; 16.66 dollars to build in Cochinchina ("Vietnam"); 20.83 to build in Guangdong province; and 30.58 dollars to build in Fujian. These estimates were reaffirmed a few years later by John Phipps, a colonial official in Calcutta and keen observer of East Asian commerce, who noted in 1836 that junks of 476 tons burthen constructed in Siam cost 7,400 Spanish dollars to manufacture while similar vessels constructed in Zhanglin (Chaozhou) cost 16,000 dollars and those constructed in Amoy 21,000 dollars. The vessels manufactured by Chinese in Siam, he asserted, were of "a superior class," inevitably composed of teak and other fine wood products available there.[41] Siam's ample timber supplies transformed Bangkok into a shipbuilding center by the eighteenth century.

All the sailors who staffed the vessels out of Siam and China were Chinese, and by the early nineteenth century most were natives of Chaozhou.[42] In the 1820s a junk of 8,000 piculs (533 tons) burthen required a crew of ninety seamen, for the vessels were cumbersome to sail and required a good deal of manpower. The captain and crew did not draw wages; rather, they were entitled to a certain amount of freight in trade. In the 1820s the captain claimed 100 piculs (13,333 pounds) of tonnage on each journey to and from China as well as a commission of 10 percent of the profits. Each seaman was entitled to 7 piculs (933 pounds) of freight. As one British official observed of these crews, "Everyone is a shareholder, having the liberty of putting a certain quantity of goods on board."[43] This indicates that all crew members were invested in the business of the vessel, and even the humblest sailor, in a sense, was apprenticing as a partner in trade. This was the experience of Chen Huanrong, who was born into a family of modest means in Qianmei village, Chenghai, in 1825. He made his way to Zhanglin at the age of fifteen and found work as a sailor for a shipping firm that sailed the junk circuit along the coast and between China and Southeast Asia. Saving the silver he earned, he eventually purchased a vessel and began to ship goods under his own name. In 1851 he and his brother pooled their capital to invest in a small import-export firm headquartered in Hong Kong called Qiantailong. In the latter nineteenth century his own son, Chen Cihong, would transform the company into one of the greatest rice-shipping firms in all Asia.[44] Nidhi Eoseewong has shown that the business culture of the junk trade enabled small investors to participate in an expensive international venture. They pooled their capital and served as unpaid crew in order to benefit as shareholders. This facilitated the expansion of the capitalist class.[45]

One speculates that the trade in the profitable opium business would have been appealing to a sailor limited to seven piculs of freightage. Sailors and shippers did not advertise this for obvious reasons: trafficking in opium had been outlawed in China in 1729. We do know from British reports that the opium-smuggling operations off the coast of China in the 1820s involved the entire crew: their common interests guaranteed secrecy, and junks departing from Singapore alone inevitably carried eight to ten chests of opium during those years. The Chinese trade in the drug was a commonly observed phenomenon across the region, as seen in European sources.[46]

The passenger trade out of Zhanglin port also was profitable to these oceangoing junks. A single junk sailing in 1822 might carry twelve hundred passengers, and one British diplomat, John Crawfurd, was informed that roughly seven thousand Chinese departed for Bangkok every year. He deemed the passage relatively affordable, referring to the six-dollar cost as "ready money." It nonetheless was about a month's wages for a field worker in Siam.[47]

These passengers sought work as sailors, laborers, artisans, and shopkeepers. As the years passed, even larger numbers secured employment as field hands and mill workers on Chinese sugar and gambier plantations in Siam and further south along the Malay Peninsula. Sugar cane had long been grown in Siam, but its extensive cultivation under a plantation system commenced when settlers from Chaozhou were granted liberal production concessions from the Siamese government in the regions of Bam-pa-soi, La-Kon-chai-se, Bangkok, and Petriu; enormous sugar plantations began to mark the rural landscape.[48] Over thirty such estates were founded in the fertile district of Nakhon-Xaisi, just west of Bangkok. Each plantation employed from two to three hundred Chinese workers. In the area around Petriu, about twenty such Chinese-owned operations could be seen.[49] Crawfurd believed that these enterprises produced some of the "whitest and best sugar in [the East Indies]." All the mills were owned by Chinese, and by the 1820s they were exporting approximately sixty thousand piculs (over eight million pounds) to China, India, Persia, Arabia, and Europe.[50] Expanding production did not simply redound to the benefit of Chinese merchants and laborers. Siamese cultivators also raised sugar cane, and the state garnered revenues of approximately 250,000 baht per annum from the tax on sugar.[51]

Chaozhouese founded estates to produce other cash crops, including black pepper, gamboge, and gambier. They harvested eight million pounds of black pepper annually during the early nineteenth century, though they were obligated to sell two-thirds of the crop to the king of Siam for eight baht per picul. Gamboge, a type of resin used in dyeing, was commonly produced on estates dominated by Chaozhou natives along the east coast of Siam.[52] Siam's sparse population had been decimated by the Burmese wars, and rural laborers and commercial investors from an increasingly over-populated Chaozhou region benefited from their privileged access to the land and resources of the kingdom. In the eighteenth and early nineteenth centuries, at least, these arrangements benefited Chinese of all classes but only the upper classes of Siam itself.

Nidhi Eoseewong, a Thai historian of Chaozhouese descent, has shown that these Chinese fostered the transformation of the Siamese subsistence lifestyle to a market economy. Until the latter nineteenth century, however, this transformation evolved within the traditional "sakdina" system of a social hierarchy dominated by the king and aristocrats, followed by commoners and then slaves. Wealthier Chinese in Bangkok quickly assimilated into the elite ranks, completely absorbed into Siamese culture through marriage and other social and religious practices. Much of the capital generated by the marketization of the economy remained in these elite, Sino-Siamese hands, and the sakdina elite simply became "more bourgeois" as their power shifted from that of status to that of economic domination. In contrast, Siamese skilled workers derived little benefit from the growing economy because their labor was controlled by elites in the form of corvée and other, poorly remunerated, obligations. Commoners and slaves served as a cheap labor pool and as small peasant producers. Almost all the highly paid jobs in skilled labor—milling, sailing, shipbuilding, and the building trades in general—were reserved for the increasing multitudes of Chinese immigrants. In very visible ways, Chinese of all classes reaped the benefits of an expanding market economy.

Nidhi Eoseewong speculates that the Siamese upper classes—intentionally or not—diverted class hatred onto Chinese immigrants because the latter were the face of the market economy: in domestic and international trade, plantation production, and all skilled-labor ranks. This was a particular problem in the countryside, where Chinese commercial elites assimilated more slowly into Siamese culture (often taking two to three generations to do so) and large Chaozhouese settlements remained more recognizably Chinese, organized as they were around their brotherhoods. The Chinese were a privileged group in the realm, and in spite of the fact that they shared much of their wealth with the nobility, they were increasingly identified with "cash wealth in a society where most of the [common] people had none." A deepening ethnic resentment of Chinese occasionally resulted in violence against them. In 1848, for example, when a Chaozhouese "gang" ransacked a sugar plant and killed its owner in Chachoengsao, troops were sent in to quell the turmoil, and legions of locals joined them in a frenzied massacre of Chinese.[53] These resentments did not dissipate and eventually hardened into a pervasive anti-Sinicism by the twentieth century.

Chaozhouese at home and abroad nonetheless continued to benefit from their privileged position across the Gulf of Siam. The thriving port of Zhanglin back home was transformed by the role it played in the early development of maritime Chaozhou. Now a backwater, it was a renowned international center in the eighteenth century, and at least seventy families were engaged in domestic and commercial shipping there.[54] The Cai lineage was among the most prominent in the industry, and it is not surprising that they conspicuously appeared on the list of rice-importing honorees in 1767.[55] They operated a line of "red-bow" junks out of the Southern Society harborage of Zhanglin, where ships engaged in the local and Chinese coastal trade connected with those involved in international commerce (the remnants of warehouses of the Caiwanli firm owned by Cai Yan remain visible today).[56]

The commercial vitality of all ports in the Chaozhou region redounded to the benefit of local villages. Anbu (in Haiyang) was officially designated the main customs port given its proximity to the prefectural capital. Porters from every village in the vicinity gathered to unload goods or transfer cargo from one ship to another on flat-bottomed barges that maneuvered on the shallow, inland waterways. Given the dependence of these hamlets on oceangoing commerce, locals referred to them as "villages of the sea."[57] Some of the most renowned business titans of the Chaozhou diaspora (including Liu Xiri and Guo Yan) had their humble beginnings in the rural hinterland of nineteenth-century Anbu.

I have focused thus far on Chaozhou's connections with Siam, but the region's international trade and migration patterns were rarely bilateral. Several other important nodes in the junk circuit of the South China Sea were involved. Chaozhou ships stopped at most ports in the region and, according to Crawfurd, enjoyed highly favorable commercial perquisites in places like Cochinchina: "the Chinese junks of Chaocheu [sic] are favorites, paying smaller duties" on imports at Saigon, Hue, and Hoi An "than any others," he noted.[58]

Chaozhou natives also established themselves along the Malay Peninsula south of Siam. They had settled there long before the British founded in 1826 the British Straits Settlements, a string of colonial port regions along the Straits of Malacca, including Singapore, Malacca, Dingding, and Penang.[59] Some Chaozhouese pioneers moved to Singapore from either Riau (an island as well as an archipelago near Singapore) or Siam, and by the early nineteenth century the port emerged as an important stop along the Chaozhou commercial routes. Indeed, the British were drawn to Singapore because it already was "on the direct track of the China trade." The mainstay of the agricultural economy across Riau and Singapore was gambier and pepper production on plantations. The owners of these enterprises, and the men who labored on them, were almost entirely natives of Chaozhou.[60]

By the 1840s there were approximately 39,700 Chinese in Singapore. Of that total, émigrés from Chaozhou were by far the most numerous (19,000); followed by Fujianese (9,000); Cantonese (6,000); Hakka (4,000); Straits Chinese from Malacca (1,000, whose forebears long before had migrated from Fujian); and Hainanese (700). Among the 19,000 Chaozhouese, 10,000 were either laborers or planters on the gambier and pepper plantations and 200 were gambier and pepper dealers. An additional 2,000 were "agriculturalists" of varying sorts. Although 3,900 Chaozhou settlers were shopkeepers in urban and rural areas, the majority were employed in the gambier and pepper plantation economy.[61] Southern Malaya, like Siam, was a site of territorial expansion by Chaozhouese.

The most prominent Chaozhouese in Singapore initially established themselves in gambier and pepper production. Gambier was a plant whose extract was used in industrial tanning and dyeing. A gambier-derived paste is also applied to the betel nut leaf and ingested for its mild narcotic effect. Pepper and gambier were cultivated symbiotically. After having been boiled to extract their resin, the residue gambier leaves were strewn around pepper plants to fertilize the soil and protect their roots. Chaozhouese in Singapore exported gambier extract to England, India, Java, Siam, Cochinchina, Cambodia, Borneo, the Dutch East Indies, and, of course, China. Crawfurd estimated that Chaozhou investors on the island of Riau alone produced approximately four thousand tons of gambier per annum by the 1830s.[62] As for pepper, the Dutch and British East India Companies tried to monopolize its distribution in their orbits of trade, but the Chinese created their own system outside of these mercantilist economies, reinstituting production and free trade in pepper at Riau. By the late eighteenth century Chaozhouese agriculturalists had established gambier and pepper plantations across southeastern Siam and Malaya. In the early nineteenth century villagers from the hinterland of the Chaozhou port of Anbu also dominated gambier and pepper production in Sarawak in northwestern Borneo. One, Liu Jianfa, became so wealthy he actually served as the personal banker to the British colonial state there. These Chinese emerged as the leading plantation agricultural producers of Southeast Asia.[63]

Stalwarts of the world of gambier and pepper production included the redoubtable Seah Eu Chin (She Youjin, 1805–1883), a Chenghai native who had earned a living as a clerk on Chinese junks that plied the waters of the Nanyang. These experiences familiarized him with the geography of Malaya as well as with basic commercial practices. He established the earliest gambier and pepper plantations in Singapore in 1823. Fabulously successful in business, he emerged as one of the two most powerful Chaozhouese in the Straits Settlements.[64] In 1837 he married into the family of the other prominent Straits Chaozhouese of his generation, Tan Seng Poh (Chen Chengbao). Tan Seng Poh's father, Chen Yayang, had served as the first kapitan (leader) of the Chinese community of Perak (a northern Malayan state) and was a man whose fortune derived, in part, from his control of the opium farms of Singapore and Johor. His son inherited those farms and emerged as a powerful force in the opium economy of nineteenth-century Singapore. Tan led an opium syndicate that controlled the farms of Riau, Singapore, Johor, and Malacca. Like other

Chaozhouese in the Straits, he also held significant interests in gambier and pepper production.[65]

Because gambier and pepper production was controlled by such Chaozhouese plantation owners, agricultural laborers migrated from Chaozhou to work for them. A similar migratory pattern emerged on Sarawak as well. Businessmen would return to their villages and enlighten rural laborers about employment opportunities overseas. The prospect of working for employers who spoke their dialect and hailed from the same place (and often the same lineage) emboldened them to undertake long journeys to distant lands and accounts for the strong ties of affiliation among Chaozhou sojourners overseas.[66] It also illustrates how modern class formation in maritime Chaozhou was, in part, translocal.

Once ensconced in Singapore, gambier and pepper developers began to expand into Johor, the nearby Malayan sultanate. Chen Kaishun pioneered this effort, establishing a successful settlement plantation in the mid-1840s. Significantly, Chen was also the leader of the Yixing brotherhood ("secret society") of Johor, and when Malays in the district of Muar revolted, Chen raised an "army" of Chaozhou laborers to "pacify" them. The sultan was so grateful, he thenceforth entrusted Chen with all policing responsibilities, conferring on the planter an enormous amount of local authority. That is to say, plantation power was buttressed by brotherhood military might to advance Chaozhou economic interests in southern Malaya. They began to dominate many of the territorial resources of Johor as well.[67]

By 1870 the gambier plantations of Johor employed roughly one hundred thousand laborers, planters, boatmen, and shop owners. As Carl Trocki has shown, the entire swath of territory across Johor, Singapore, and the Riau archipelago could be characterized as a "gambier economy" dominated by merchants and laborers from Chaozhou. By midcentury this economy was "capitalized and controlled" by wealthy "taukehs" (financiers) in Singapore like Seah Eu Chin and Tan Seng Poh. It was supervised locally by *jiangzhu*, "river headmen," most of whom, Trocki asserts, had started out as "secret society chieftains" who led armies of fighters and only later evolved into commercial leaders.[68]

The early expansion of Chaozhouese control over the territory and resources of southern Malaya was predicated on the martial prowess and self-governing efficiencies of the brotherhood society. Ironically, a society that served as a source of development on the Malay Peninsula was deemed a political menace back in Qing China. Sharon Carstens has shown that there were two types of overseas Chinese leaders emerging in the Straits at this time: one, a "wealthy, philanthropically oriented, merchant elite" that tended to live in town; the other, known for "their fighting skills and ability to organize others," who resided in "the highly risky and tumultuous world of the gambier estates of Johor or in the tin mines" elsewhere.[69] This again illustrates the interrelationship of commercial prowess and organizational militancy in the expansion of Chaozhouese territorialism.

The opening of Singapore as a British free port stimulated Chaozhou's translocal trade. The seas were patrolled by the British navy while colonial officials supervised commerce with a light touch. The commentators to *Hailu zhu* (1820), a record of the travels of a Chinese sailor, Xie Qinggao, across the South China Sea in the late eighteenth century, observed that although the British were late arrivals to the port, they "opened the land up, beckoning the merchants from various places to trade and to cultivate the land. They were taxed quite lightly and the port became a meeting place of the sea lanes from all directions."[70]

Laborers also benefited from the colony the British appeared to be launching for the Chinese. John Crawfurd recorded that Chinese laborers in Singapore earned 8 Mexican dollars per month while a Chinese artisan earned 12 dollars. He estimated that the monthly expenses of an urban day-laborer included food at $4.80; clothing at $1.10 and lodging at 20 cents per month. He then deduced that a laborer should have been able to save at least $22 per year ($96 in earnings per year less $73.20 in expenses).[71] These figures do not include other possible expenses, and rural workers in the gambier estates outside of town earned only 3 to 4 dollars per month in the 1840s, though presumably their expenses were lower than those of town dwellers. In contrast, a skilled sugar-press worker back in Guangdong in 1805 earned slightly less than one Spanish dollar per month.[72] In spite of the difficulties of working in a tropical furnace like equatorial Malaya, a laboring sojourn to Singapore might have appeared financially worthwhile to rural workers in Chaozhou at this time.

The Borneo Gold Rush

In 1847 the statecraft reformer Wei Yuan observed that in the previous century, "people from Jiayingzhou [in eastern Guangdong] had traveled into the mountainous areas of [West Borneo] to engage in gold mining. They established their own state, selected their own leaders, and called it a *gongsi*. . . . Every year several junks from Canton and Chaozhou arrive at [Pontianak] port to commence trading."[73] In a nutshell, Wei described the experiences of Chinese in western Borneo. The Dutch and British would lay claim to parts of the island later, but in the eighteenth and early nineteenth centuries the western stretch was dominated by Hakka Chinese gold miners from the wider Chaozhou region. The economy was linked to the commercial nodes of Singapore, Bangkok, Canton, and Chaozhou by merchants from Chaozhou and Canton, and to a lesser extent, Fujian.

Their distinctive form of political organization, *gongsi* (kongsi), has been called "colonies" (by Liang Qichao), "states" (Wei Yuan), "village republics" (J.J.M. de Groot), and "democracies" (Yuan Bingling).[74] Mary Somers Heidhues has described these entities as "religious, economic, and political institutions which acted almost as independent states." Gongsi originated in southeastern China as cooperative partnerships in which participants pooled their capital, each owning a share in the profits of the enterprise. They were depicted by contemporary observers as "economic democracies" for the relatively egalitarian ethos they exemplified: even the humblest miner owned a portion, however small, of the means of production. Each shareholder was entitled to his measure of profit as well as to vote in the election of the leader of each mine. He also was obliged to pay an initiation fee and to perform an oath of brotherhood. In the mining economy of West Borneo, some gongsi were organized into vast confederations of hundreds, sometimes thousands, of miners. Known as *zongting* (literally "assembly halls"), these larger coalitions maintained territorial borders, collected taxes, and attended to the governance of the constituent gongsi through elected leaders. Major decisions were voted on by gongsi delegates to the assembly. Their political and economic activities are emphasized here, but these organizations were characterized by a deep fidelity to the religious cults and temple networks of village China. They venerated the Earth God and shared other rituals that melded them into a religious community.[75] The term "gongsi" actually has a wide range of meanings, and significantly it was used to designate a brotherhood or "secret" society. These gongsi advanced the economic, security, and spiritual interests of the fraternal sodality.

In the 1740s the Malay sultans of Borneo began to encourage Chinese to settle in the western part of the island. These rulers embraced stereotypes of Chinese as hard workers, but, more important, they understood that Chinese mined more efficiently than the indigenous people did. They used machinery, worked in groups according to specialty, and enjoyed access to capital and labor pools. The sultans anticipated larger revenue streams with Chinese in control of the mines. They also hoped that their own monopoly over agricultural production would raise additional income as they sold rice, salt, and other goods to the settlers, but by the 1770s the Chinese were provisioning themselves and came to control the economy and politics of western Borneo.[76]

Luo Fangbo was the most renowned of the gongsi founders. Liang Qichao referred to him as the "king of Pontianak" and extolled him as one of the "eight colonial grandees" of early modern Chinese settlement in Southeast Asia. The historian Luo Xianglin described him as a visionary leader who founded "an independent Republic."[77] Luo Fangbo was born in 1738 in a walled village in Jiayingzhou, a mountainous region in the hinterland of Chaozhou that was populated almost entirely by Hakka. (The five districts that made up Jiayingzhou had been administratively a part of Chaozhou and Huizhou prefectures until 1733, when they were reorganized into a separate department).[78] Luo had academic aspirations but departed for Borneo with several hundred friends and relatives in 1772, probably lured by the prospects, literally, of the gold mines. After serving as a schoolteacher for a time, he began to mine gold himself and eventually founded the Lanfang gongsi. He thereupon embarked on a campaign of economic domination, struggling violently with other gongsi as well as with the indigenous people of the area, the Dayaks, until he gained control of the entire mining vicinity of Mandor. He assumed the official title of Leader of the Great China (DaTang zongchang) and retained authority until his death in 1795. He was succeeded by nine subsequent leaders until 1884 when, after prolonged battles, the Dutch finally managed to occupy Mandor. The European power, however, experienced several military setbacks as it campaigned to bend these settlers to its will, a fact that, in addition to their prosperity, explains the early twentieth-century Chinese fascination with their success.[79]

The demographic makeup of these West Borneo Chinese reflected the ethnic complexity of Chaozhou. Hakka were a subgroup of Han Chinese who spoke their own dialect and lived across a stretch of southern China, largely in mountainous areas. They were the most experienced miners in China, and many pioneers of the gold-mining business were from the mountainous Hakka hinterland of Chaozhou (either Jiayingzhou or Chaozhou's Dabu district). A number of the miners, traders, and rice farmers in eighteenth-century Borneo nonetheless came from the coastal districts of Chaozhou and the neighboring prefecture of Huizhou. Some of these miners were "Hoklo"—or Chaozhouese who spoke Chaozhou dialect—while others were "half-mountain Hakka" (Banshanke), Hakka who dwelled on the hillsides of coastal Chaozhou and

Huizhou. "Half-mountain Hakka," were bilingual and bicultural in the Hakka and Chaozhouese traditions. Although there was occupational diversity on Borneo, in general most Hoklo Chaozhouese were farmers, traders, sailors, and artisans and tended to live in urban areas; Hakka and half-mountain Hakka worked the mines.[80]

Dutch colonial officials conducted a census in 1858 that determined the origins of some Chinese living in the mining regions of Borneo. Looking at their data for the districts of Lara and Lumar, 23.7 percent of the residents of Lara and 30.9 percent of Lumar were from Chaozhou (Jieyang, Huilai, Puning, Chaozhou city, Fengshun, and Dabu—the latter two being exclusively Hakka regions); 26.1 and 21.6 percent, respectively, were from Jiayingzhou; 46.5 and 46.9 percent, respectively, were from Huizhou (mostly Lufeng); and 3.5 and 0.5 percent, respectively, were from Canton. Similarly, the Dagang gongsi, which operated mines just outside of Montrado, comprised mostly half-mountain Hakka from the Huilai district of coastal Chaozhou and the Lufeng district of coastal Huizhou. The dominant lineage groups in that gongsi were surnamed Wu, Huang, and Zheng. The Santiaogou gongsi had eight hundred members, the majority hailing from Huilai and Lufeng and surnamed Zhu and Wen.[81]

I elaborate on these details because, as we will see, these regions of coastal Chaozhou and Huizhou overlap with the major dissemination routes of the Tiandihui ("Triad") ideology into the Hakka and half-mountain Hakka regions of eastern Guangdong. Indeed, dozens of Triads arrested for "subversion" during the first decades of the nineteenth century had the same surnames and were from the same districts as many of these Borneo miners. The regions also overlap with major opium-smuggling routes into the Hakka hinterland of southeastern China. In fact, many Chaozhou shippers already were smuggling opium, salt, and gunpowder into the ports of the gongsi-controlled regions of Borneo during the early nineteenth century. Opium smuggling and sojourning were interrelated phenomena at this time.

The Borneo gongsi raised standing armies and often resorted to violent affrays. Members, in the words of Yuan Bingling, were required to "serve in the militia of the gongsi and to defend the 'republic' with their lives." Some of these campaigns have been referred to as "Gongsi Wars," and although the details need not concern us here, it is significant that the causes of these bloody engagements in Borneo were similar to those back in southeastern China at the same time: relentless battles over territory, water rights, and access to resources.[82] More significantly, in the course of this bloodshed, one encounters the first mention of the Tiandihui (TDH), the anti-Qing brotherhood, anywhere across maritime Chaozhou. Indeed, the earliest references to the organization in Southeast Asia can be found in Dutch sources in West Borneo during the 1770s.[83] In the eighteenth century, for example, the miners of Montrado purchased rice and pork from Chinese farmers who had organized themselves into a brotherhood called the "Tiandihui." The monopoly these farmers exercised over food supplies exacerbated tensions with the miners, and struggles between the two groups ensued. In 1775 fourteen mining gongsi finally organized themselves into a larger confederation, attacking the brotherhood and killing its leader and five hundred of his followers. These TDH adherents were "exclusively agriculturalists," and in addition to provisioning the miners, they did most of the "pioneer work" of opening vast tracts of "barren land" for development. They also militarily resisted Dutch efforts to take control of the island in the nineteenth century.[84]

We do not know enough about this brotherhood to determine whether it had any connection to China beyond the fact that Chinese émigrés had organized it. Although scholars have tended to think of the TDH as essentially an organization for merchants and sojourning laborers, it is clear that even at this early date, settled farming communities were attracted to its organizational style. As we shall see, the same can be said for Chaozhou coastal communities, the homeland of some of these Borneo-dwelling Chinese. By the 1840s the vast majority of farming households in Chaoyang district included at least one member who belonged to a TDH offshoot that rebelled against the Qing, the Double Sword Society.

The vast amount of gold extracted from these mines required attention to security. It is impossible to trace with specificity, but contemporary observers asserted that most of the gold mined in West Borneo was exchanged for silver that ended up in southern China. W. A. Palm, the Dutch East India Company representative in Pontianak, reported in 1779 that Chinese junks arrived every year laden with goods like cloth and hauled away about four thousand reals of gold, roughly the equivalent of forty-five thousand silver dollars (Spanish). By the early nineteenth century the destinations of this gold were expanding to other Chinese-dominated economies, especially Singapore and Bangkok, where the metal was exchanged for opium, salt, tobacco, and textiles.[85] Stamford Raffles, who held various British official positions in Java and Malaya and eventually founded the settlement at Singapore, estimated in 1810 that 3.7 million Spanish silver dollars' worth of gold was produced in Borneo that year. Of that amount, a million went to purchase opium and other commodities in places like Singapore; a million was spent on provisions like food, salt, and oil; 700,000 was remitted to China; and a million was personally carried back to China by Chinese who returned to their homes.[86]

While these are problematic estimates, an enormous quantity of silver was being carried back to China; and not simply to "China" but to specific districts in the Southeast: Chaoyang, Huilai, and Jieyang on the Chaozhou coast; the Lufeng and Haifeng districts of neighboring Huizhou; and Jiayingzhou and Dabu in the mountainous Hakka homeland. It was also transferred to specific lineages: the Zheng, Wu, Huang, Wen, and Zhu of Huilai, for example, and others in Jiayingzhou and elsewhere in Guangdong. This was a significant transfer of capital, which surely offset some the challenges of the demographic expansion of eastern Guangdong in the eighteenth and nineteenth centuries, at least for the families involved. More to the point, there was a lot of gold, silver, and opium to protect.

Maritime Chaozhou and the Early Modern Opium Trade

The practice of smoking opium that took hold in China by the nineteenth century represented the culmination of centuries of transnational commercial intercourse across four continents. First introduced into western China by Turks and Arabs in the seventh century, opium circulated as a commodity in the Ming system of tributary relations with Southeast Asia. By the sixteenth century Java, Siam, and Bengal routinely were offering opium—or "black fragrance" (*wuxiang*) as it was called—as a tributary gift to the emperors. Although the markets of Calcutta historically have been identified as the poppy fount from which the British drew to drown the Chinese in opium, the sultan of Bengal, where Calcutta was situated, had been offering opium to the Ming court since the early fifteenth century, long before the British colonized the region and became players in the global drug trade.[87]

Qu Dajun observed in the 1690s that the tribute missions of the Ming era skirted Guangdong on their way to Beijing, and opium was included in the cargo of the envoys from Siam and Java. These tribute-bearing emissaries surreptitiously engaged in a "private" commerce with merchants in that province.[88] That is to say, opium was a freely traded commodity along the coast of Guangdong during early modern times. Importation of the drug was technically legal under the official tribute system and smuggled as contraband along the coast.

By the 1720s officials were complaining about the deleterious social effects of the opium trade on the coast of eastern Guangdong. In 1728 the regional commander of the Jieshi garrison, Su Mingliang, reported that merchants from Fujian and Guangdong who engaged in overseas trade returned with the drug and sold it for profit. Opium dens proliferated, and youth from "good families" were coaxed into taking the drug by "worthless vagabonds." They lolled around toking opium until they got "as high as if they were drunk." Their youthful constitutions were "fairly robust," and their behavior grew "wanton and evil" and even harder to control. After years of dissipation, however, their health deteriorated and family finances evaporated, and many turned to crime. To address the mayhem at what he considered "its roots," Commander Su called on the Yongzheng emperor to "strictly prohibit" overseas junk merchants from importing the drug. The court thereby "would save the multitudes" and simultaneously reduce lawlessness.[89]

Such expressions of concern about recreational opium use inclined the Qing to outlaw the domestic sale of the drug in 1729, but the expanding commerce with Southeast Asia and overseas travel of sailors, merchants, and laborers sabotaged the effort. Because natives of Chenghai pioneered the region's economic expansion, local gazetteers not surprisingly reported the rise of serious opium addiction by the dawn of the nineteenth century. They explicitly tied local drug problems to the region's accelerating participation in maritime trade.[90]

Opium use was a translocal phenomenon. Seah Eu Chin, the pioneering Chaozhouese gambier planter, wrote in 1848 that most laborers in Singapore had intended to work abroad for three to four years, but only 10 to 20 percent managed to return to China within that timeframe. The rest wasted their income on opium. "After a continued residence here they learn the habit." A larger number of workers managed to return after seven to ten years' residence in Singapore and its environs. Those among the laboring classes who remained after ten years abandoned hope ever of going home. Nevertheless, roughly three thousand Chinese returned annually, and a significant percentage of these men had grown accustomed to using opium.[91] The normalization of opium smoking in southeastern China therefore was not simply due to the increasing importation of the drug. The habit was acquired abroad by sojourners who lived in places where opium was legal and amply available and later returned to their homeland, probably carrying a personal supply.

Chaozhou also emerged as a major site for the domestic cultivation of opium. The Daoguang emperor became so concerned about its widespread production that he issued an edict in 1831 commanding local officials to punish village headmen and lineage elders who participated in or turned a blind eye to its tillage in the prefecture.[92] The edict was ineffectual, and the cultivation of opium became a staple of the Chaozhou economy until 1949.

Chinese sojourners pioneered and dominated early modern opium smuggling into China, but Europeans played a significant role across the South China Sea. The Portuguese and Spaniards were the first Westerners to carry opium into China in the sixteenth century. Opium was the major commodity marketed by the Dutch East India Company, a commercial empire based in Batavia (on Java) and operating across far-flung trading posts in the East Indies, Siam, and Taiwan. The British East India Company (EIC) ultimately gained control of the opium-producing regions of Bengal in 1757 and established a monopoly on Indian-produced drug after 1773.[93]

The EIC did not engage in the smuggling business on the Chaozhou frontier. It instead auctioned its opium supplies in Calcutta to "country traders," private British companies that peddled the drug eastward. Among the latter group, Jardine Matheson emerged as the premier British company in the Chinese coastal trade. It was founded in 1832 by William Jardine and James Matheson, Scotsmen who already had acquired years of experience in the opium markets of Canton. By 1833 it had established an anchoring station at Nan'ao. The local representative and captain of the company ship *Young Colonel*, John Rees, was assisted by Charles Gutzlaff, a renowned Protestant missionary who had mastered the Chaozhou dialect while laboring as a young evangelist in Siam. Gutzlaff's goal was to win converts back in southeastern China, the homeland of his many coreligionists in Southeast Asia. Assisting Jardine with a bit of translation work was the cost of gaining a forbidden entrée to China. Gutzlaff's facility in several dialects reflected the translocal religious dynamics of the maritime frontier, but it also ensured the financial success of smuggling operations.[94]

Chinese compradors and shroffs also were vital to the company's work. They communicated with local smugglers and junk merchants on land and sea, bargained prices, arranged rendezvous points, and assessed the quality of silver being exchanged. The shroffs were particularly essential because the silver exchanged in the smuggling world was comprised of a nonstandardized, nondenominational assortment of silver taels, chopped dollars, silver bits (sycee) and Mexican dollars, and assessing the value of silver content required expertise. Chaozhouese smugglers occasionally tried to fob off bad coins and counterfeit sycee on the unsuspecting foreigners.[95] In some ways, smuggling operations were an entirely Chinese affair that company representatives observed with apprehension.

Jardine Matheson stationed some of its most accomplished Cantonese compradors at Nan'ao. They hosted Chaozhou-area opium brokers on the ship for days at a time, and their entertainment budget was $70 per month (half the monthly food budget). A Jardine representative, H. P. Baylis, expressed some concern about the extravagance of one comprador, Tom the Birdman, as he treated the "Cape brokers" of Chaoyang to banquets of wine, brandy, fowls, vegetables, fish, and eggs.[96] The Birdman, of course, was reinforcing his *guanxi* (friendly connections) with the traders on whom the financial success of the enterprise ultimately depended. Chinese business practice involved personal relationships, reciprocity, and hospitality. Smuggling contraband from ship to shore required trust and loyalty, and Jardine's compradors were forging a professional, and therefore personal, relationship with the traders on the Chaozhou coast. These festive interactions between Cantonese and mostly Chaoyang-area smugglers probably laid the foundation of the Chaoyang-Cantonese syndicate that later constituted the formidable "Swatow Opium Guild" in the port of Shanghai.

Even as the British became more active in the opium trade of southeastern China, Chaozhou merchants who sojourned to Southeast Asia continued to import large quantities of opium, not only into Chaozhou, but also to Canton, Shanghai, Ningbo, and Tianjin. By midcentury Chaozhouese were importing hundreds of chests in a single haul, ultimately driving British smugglers out of the Chaozhou opium market entirely.[97] During this period, unnamed Chinese shippers, merchants, sailors, and travelers accumulated a significant amount of capital in the international commerce in opium.

Whether they acquired their supplies overseas or locally, Chinese merchants dominated the opium trade along the eastern seaboard of China. As Phipps noted in 1836, coastal traders from Fujian and Guangdong purchased opium along the islands near Portuguese Macao and then headed northward toward Shanghai with their large stocks of sugar and other commodities. They returned with goods produced in the north. Chaozhou merchants represented a large percentage of these traders. Among the 846 Chinese junks that operated in the vicinity of Macao before sailing up the coast in the 1830s, 300 were from the Chaozhouese-speaking areas of Chaozhou and Huizhou and 230 from the Fujianese ports of Amoy (80) and Zhangzhou (150).[98] Although these powerful merchants were rarely arrested prior to 1839, one occasionally encounters cases in which wealthy Chaozhouese were apprehended near Macao for having purchased raw opium from foreign vessels.[99]

Needless to add, Chinese were active in the Southeast Asian opium economy itself. Even before the colonial order arose to remap the geography of Southeast Asia—separating "British Malaya" from "the Dutch East Indies," for example—Chaozhouese plantation owners supplemented their incomes by instituting their own opium farms. Opium farms were monopoly concessions for marketing the drug. By 1825 Chaozhouese gambier and pepper producers had founded agricultural establishments across Bintang Island (just south of Singapore). Over thirteen thousand Chinese inhabited five settlements that maintained several opium farms as sources of additional revenue.[100] The Europeans eventually established opium farms themselves, and syndicates of wealthy Chaozhouese occasionally took charge of these profitable institutions that channeled huge revenue streams into colonial coffers.[101]

Chaozhouese merchants, sailors, and laborers had long been involved in the opium trade across Southeast Asia while simultaneously transforming their native place into a major hub in the international commerce in narcotics. And this returns us to the subject of translocal brotherhoods. During this period lodges evolved into protection rackets for the transport and sale of opium and the secure transfer of silver and gold specie. Early "secret society" cases in Chaozhou itself do not mention opium, probably because the authorities were more concerned about the sectarian, ostensibly "seditious," nature of these groups. Hard evidence begins to emerge by the 1830s, when officials were more focused on the opium issue. A brotherhood called the Red Society (Honghui) was reported to provincial authorities in 1840. The syndicate had been organized sometime during the early nineteenth century, if not earlier, to advance the interests of opium dealers in the Hakka areas of the Chaozhou hinterland that bordered Jiangxi and Fujian provinces. Its members wore little red or green woolen buttons as their distinctive mark and hid their opium stocks in bags of salt, carrying them from Chaozhou's Dabu district upriver into Jiangxi province in the interior of China. The society numbered twenty to thirty thousand men along the Guangdong-Fujian-Jiangxi borderland, and local officials claimed they were too afraid to arrest them because they were reputed to have been "fierce and carry daggers."[102]

This "fear" explains why so few details are available to flesh out the connection between the early opium trade and the emergence of sectarian brotherhoods in districts with strong connections to international commerce. Across

Guangdong province, it was common for opium dealers to hire "gangs of protectors" (*dang fanghu*) to ward off busybodies and otherwise incline local officials and commoners to keep quiet about the criminality in their midst.[103] The threat of violence proved a strong inducement to obscure the connection between the opium trade and brotherhood formation.

The opium trade was simply one feature of an emerging, quasi-colonial economy. The offshoring of some of Chaozhou's industries, the inauguration of overseas plantation enterprises, and an ongoing sojourning tradition further entangled the region with the polities of Southeast Asia. In this entangled relationship, there was neither metropole nor hinterland but an increasingly interrelated translocal economy that was dominated by Chinese, often at the invitation of colonizers, monarchs, and sultans. The urban development of ports like Bangkok and Singapore was as vital to Chaozhouese prospects as it was to indigenous ones. The swelling of the maritime frontier also reflected the capacity of Chaozhouese entrepreneurs and laborers to begin to circumvent what Kenneth Pomeranz referred to as an "ecological cul-de-sac." Chaozhouese, like their European counterparts, engaged in their own form of territorial expansion. Land and natural resources may have been diminishing as the population grew back home, but maritime Chaozhou provided the resources, commodities, and work and investment opportunities that enabled its translocal economy to thrive. Chaozhou did not remain trapped in its local ecology in the nineteenth century.

3

Brotherhood of the Sword

PEASANT INTELLECTUALS AND THE CULT
OF INSURGENCY, 1775–1866

Before the ancestral Hall of Wealth and Virtue, we rise up in righteousness.
Exterminate the Qing dynasty! Restore the Ming!

—EXCERPT OF "POEM", 1813

DURING THE EIGHTEENTH CENTURY, maritime Chaozhou emerged as an arena for the organization of sworn brotherhoods, mutual aid societies, and folk sectarian alliances that Chinese and colonial officials characterized as "secret" or "heterodox." These confraternities offered reciprocal protection to sojourning brothers and, eventually, to members of the sedentary population. They constituted an extension of the familial logic of group solidarity to multisurname networks as a means of coping with unpredictable challenges. Brotherhoods enabled individuals to ward off threats, gain financial support, and enjoy a ritualized camaraderie with like-minded fellows. The protective strategy occasionally evolved into a predatory opportunity, however, and the criminal underworld became inflected with the rituals of sectarian fraternities. Criminal gangs bound together by blood oaths were common in translocal Chaozhou by the nineteenth century. By exacerbating the threats posed to the individual, these brotherhoods paradoxically reinforced the necessity of their own existence.

Until recently, scholars accepted the founding legends of the Tiandihui ("Heaven and Earth Society," or "Triads") as historical fact: in the seventeenth century the Kangxi emperor treacherously turned on the monks of the Shaolin monastery after becoming convinced they were plotting rebellion. He burned their temple to the ground and slaughtered all but thirteen monks. The survivors took flight, but most perished on the road, leaving only five to tell the tale of the emperor's perfidy. They joined ranks with others opposed to the Manchu regime and swore an oath to avenge themselves against their conquerors. Thus was born the anti-Qing Tiandihui. Revisionist historians have disputed the reliability of this myth and asserted that the actual founding of the tradition cannot be dated earlier than the mid-eighteenth century, long after the Ming-Qing transition. These scholars also dismiss the notion that men joined these organizations in order to overthrow the Qing prior to the 1850s. Most instead sought to obtain the material and emotional benefits of these sodalities.[1]

An examination of the early history of these societies in maritime Chaozhou complicates this scholarship. Most joined brotherhoods for the reasons alluded to above, and the organizations indeed emerged only after the mid-eighteenth century. The revisionist arguments nonetheless do not explain why an avowedly anti-Qing ideology suddenly arose in southeastern China in 1761 (the ostensible founding year of the TDH in Fujian). Nor do they clarify why anti-Qing sentiment was so central to the rituals, oaths, and identity of these organizations.

Anti-Qing feeling was always latent in this region, coursing subterraneously in the political consciousness of a small number of committed individuals. Literate, usually itinerant organizers articulated a utopian message of opposition to the Qing in spite of the fact that most of their followers simply joined for the benefits of brotherhood. This is characteristic of institutions organized primarily through village and familial networks. Leaders are ideologically committed to the goals of the organization and preserve the integrity of its message. The followers they attract are only vaguely aware of, if not indifferent to, the more profound ideas animating their leaders. Their confessions in court would naturally reflect this indifference and potentially enable them to evade the harsh punishments for sedition. As one anthropologist has characterized the recruiting dynamic of clandestine organizations, "People don't get pushed into rebellion by their ideology. They get pulled in by their social networks."[2]

If anti-Qing sentiment was a negligible factor in mobilization, it remained central to these organizations because it was kept alive by a certain type of individual. Steven Feierman's notion of the "peasant intellectual" elucidates the pivotal role this personality type plays in folk religion and rural politics. Rural life produces a certain type of intellectual, he argues. Most peasant intellectuals begin life as farmers, but "at crucial historical moments, they emerge to organize political movements and, in doing so, elaborate new forms of discourse." Crucial in their evolution as thinkers, they are able to draw on some other life experience—as a trader or worker in a religious community—that broadens their horizons and inclines them to think about the dynamics of power in the wider world.[3] This is an apt description of the people who organized brotherhoods and preserved their discursive and ritual traditions across generations both in Chaozhou and in overseas communities. These individuals infused anti-Qing movements with a sectarian vision in the nineteenth century. They were avowedly anti-Qing even if they lacked the wherewithal to overthrow the dynasty. They also led exceedingly mobile lives.

The rise of the TDH in Chaozhou cannot be disentangled from the acceleration of the sojourning experience and had a major impact on sedentary rural culture. By the 1840s this brotherhood tradition permeated settled rural society and accounts for the explosion of anti-Qing uprisings. These rebellions had multiple causes, but all were galvanized by an antipathy for the dynasty. Across the maritime frontier, metropole and periphery were mutually transformed by the processes of migration.

The Latency of Anti-Qing Sentiment

Qin Baoqi, a pioneering revisionist scholar, identified two broad reasons why brotherhoods emerged on the southeast coast in the mid-eighteenth century. For one thing, as the population expanded, there was an inadequate amount of cultivable land in a region where mountains dramatically sloped into the sea, and many sons were forced to depart their villages to seek employment elsewhere. This "wandering population" turned to mutual-aid organizations and swore brotherhood with others they encountered on their lonely sojourns.[4]

There are no reliable population statistics for Chaozhou prefecture in the eighteenth century. Lin Dehou has shown that in 1730 it had at least 204,401 people, which is probably on the low side. His estimate for 1818, however, 1,405,180 inhabitants, suggests remarkable growth. The demographic challenges would only intensify: by 1928 the population expanded to approximately 4,618,270 people. Chinese scholars have ascribed the large out-migration of the nineteenth century to the fact that an increasing number of people struggled to survive economically on narrow coastal strips of land.[5] Qin writes in this tradition.

Rural families supplemented their incomes with fishing, dockwork, seamanship, and gathering marine products, however. And sojourners remitted large sums from abroad. Laborers who worked the Chaozhouese-owned gambier and pepper plantations of Singapore, for example, remitted anywhere from forty thousand to seventy thousand Mexican dollars to various villages in Chenghai and Haiyang during the early nineteenth century. In 1830 a fleet of ships transported sixty thousand dollars from Bangkok alone.[6] The opportunities of coastal life alleviated some of the problems of population growth, and the lure of remunerative employment inclined local sons to emigrate.

Qin also ascribes the rise of brotherhood societies to the dynamics of the *xiedou* (lineage affrays) that plagued the region. Citing the prefectural gazetteer, he described the phenomenon as one in which "the big clans bullied the little clans and the strong lineages swindled the weak ones. They organized gangs in order to reinforce their own numbers and with extreme boldness fought ferociously."[7] The sworn bond of brotherhood expanded the fighting ranks and facilitated defensive and offensive strategies.

This feuding should not be ascribed to population pressures alone. It was also a repercussion of the evacuation era. Entire lineages either collapsed during the crisis or took years to reconstitute after they were allowed to return to their homesteads. It was not always easy to stake one's property claims, for people in the wards that had not been evacuated naturally began to till long-neglected land. This contributed to a tendency toward property usurpation. The coastal evacuation of the 1660s marked an important rupture in the evolution of the property regime of coastal Chaozhou. Ownership would be determined, in part, by the ability to stake a claim, not simply legally but also physically. Clans weakened by diminished numbers or weak ties to local officials suffered a disadvantage in this environment.[8] Accounts of feuding in other cultures have shown that once a fight over one problem commences, it does not take much to reignite tensions over something else. Feuding feeds on itself and, as time passes, the original cause of disputation becomes immaterial. Endemic feuding creates social orders and personal qualities that encourage more feuding.[9]

The feuding ethos that fostered the emergence of brotherhoods therefore was not simply a response to demographic pressures. It reflected a long, complicated history involving the social repercussions of the maritime bans—including the militarized architecture of villages—an unstable ecology, and the disorderly ramifications of large, predatory lineage formations in an era of limited state-building. By the eighteenth century officials governing Chaozhou found it a challenge to adjudicate quarrels that involved powerful lineages. The situation was not simply one of large, wealthy lineages oppressing weaker parties. Weaker actors occasionally devised imaginative, litigious strategies to attack their powerful adversaries.[10] Brotherhoods emerged as a protective and predatory force in a culture of feuding that was beyond the capacity of officials to control.

Were these sodalities seditious? Building on the work of Chinese revisionists, David Ownby and Dian Murray have argued that the brotherhoods in the TDH tradition should not be referred to as "secret" societies or even adjudged as having been relentlessly anti-Qing. Most were mutual aid societies designed to advance the interests of their members, and other villagers were usually aware of their ritual practices. Moreover, the sectarian uprisings of these brotherhoods usually were precipitated by government persecution or were incidental byproducts of the predatory crime in which some engaged.[11]

These arguments are well substantiated, but when one reviews the criminal case record preserving accounts of Chaozhouese who joined brotherhoods, one begins to question just how attractive these societies might have been to a sojourner. Some individuals clearly felt coerced into joining simply to ward off attacks from the very societies to which they now attached themselves. In 1786, for example, a gang robbed Xu Axie, a peddler from Raoping, while he was attending to business in Fujian. A friend and business associate there advised him to join the TDH in order to forestall future onslaughts and perhaps recover his silver. He did as advised and, miraculously, the silver was returned to him. Evidently, his own friend's "associates" had robbed him and, once he was initiated into their organization, they ceased their harassments. He also received instruction in the hand signals used by the brothers to ward off attacks by others.[12] By his own account, Xu joined simply to get them off his back.

The TDH was a translocal phenomenon, and by the nineteenth century brotherhoods controlled the emigration businesses. They also perpetrated many of the abuses attending the "coolie trade." There were reasons why a sojourner might have been ambivalent about them. Laborers did join mutual aid societies while overseas, of course. By the 1870s over 34,776 Chinese were registered with these societies in the Straits Settlements alone.[13] Many Chinese in Southeast Asia, however, already had family or fellow villagers on whom to rely and had no interest in entangling themselves in brotherhood rivalries. The sultan of Johor, the Malay state closest to Singapore, reported that several headmen of Chaozhouese gambier-producing settlements complained in the

1850s that Singapore-based "secret society" leaders threatened them with violence unless they joined their brotherhoods. One such leader dispatched "well-armed men" over the Singapore Straits to set up branches in these settlements by force.[14] The reluctance to join societies becomes clearer when we turn to oral testimonies from the early twentieth century. Chen Jinhua emigrated to rural Siam. As he recounted, Chaozhouese and Thais were generally peace-loving, "but there were also some very fierce societies. . . . They were constantly fighting. Occasionally people were killed. Very *lihai.* . . . If they lived in a certain area, they formed a gang. That was their territory. Territorial boundaries were how they were divided." If one moved to rural Siam, one was pressured to join a brotherhood, and Chen went to great lengths to avoid doing so.[15] In parts of translocal Chaozhou, it made sense to join for all the reasons the revisionists have identified. Nevertheless, there were as many drawbacks to joining as there were benefits.

As for the discredited notion that these societies were inherently anti-Qing, it remains intriguing that, once provoked, they so often manifested an antigovernment creed. When people declared "exterminate the Qing dynasty and restore the Ming," they must have meant it on some level, even if they did not consider themselves to be the personal instrument of that scenario. Why was this term recited in initiation oaths at home and abroad, and to what extent did it reflect political culture? Resistance to the Qing conquest had been intense and enduring in southeastern China. Considering that the coastal evacuation was memorialized in genealogies as a catastrophe that had decimated their lineages, anti-Qing resentment surely endured among some of the literate population. These genealogies record horrific tales of suffering and loss: kinfolk disappearing forever, corpses strewn along streets and canals, farmers weeping as they were driven from their burning villages. Although such records have enabled scholars to chart a history of a reconstructed orthodox hegemony along the coast, there is something vaguely seditious about their tragic tales of woe at the hands of the conquerors. Even today, Chaozhouese in Thailand continue to vilify the coastal evacuation as one of the worst catastrophes in their history.[16]

After the dynastic transition, Chaozhouese organized or joined rebellions inflected with anti-Qing messages or manifesting fanatical resistance to government forces. In 1721 Du Junying, a native of Haiyang, organized a brotherhood that supported Zhu Yigui's rebellion on Taiwan. Ownby shows that the rebellion was precipitated by mistakes made by insensitive officials. Once the uprising commenced, however, it did not take long for the insurgents—most of whom hailed from Chaozhou and Fujian—to start carrying banners that read "Revival of the Great Ming."[17] Whatever the cause of the rebellion, why did a slogan calling for the restoration of the Ming suddenly come to light thirty-seven years after the Qing had "pacified" the Southeast? Who kept alive such ideas? Some individuals obviously continued to express antipathy for the dynasty. Even if rebels were moved to act by other motivations, a latent anti-Qing feeling had the potential to galvanize a more politicized movement.

In addition to the latency of anti-Qing feeling, TDH organizers were politically committed to its tenets, not that they would confess to such sentiments. Books that reduplicated the orally transmitted, anti-Qing teachings of the TDH were preserved in eastern Guangdong in the late eighteenth and early nineteenth centuries. These books articulated explicitly anti-Qing messages such as "exterminate the Qing dynasty and restore the Ming." People retained them in spite of the fact that possession of seditious material was forbidden. Such people included the peddler Diao Shenghe. He confessed in 1813 that he had "discovered" a book in an "old dilapidated bookcase" in his home in Jiayingzhou. He made several copies of a subversive "poem" discovered therein and carried them on a journey to Sichuan to join his brother, who had opened an inn there. He was arrested in Guizhou, and the authorities discovered the verses on his person. He claimed that he had intended to sell them to people en route "in a plot to defraud them of their money." That is to say, like many criminals brought before late imperial courts, he pled guilty to a lesser crime (fraud) in order to evade punishment for a more serious one (subversion).[18]

Was Diao an ideologically committed sectarian? Was he "anti-Qing"? Officials certainly believed he was after he changed his testimony when caught prevaricating. Beyond that, his family had preserved the book in which the "poem" was recorded, and he obviously was convinced that the journey to Sichuan would be full of people willing to pay good money for a copy. What the officials called a "verse to be memorized" was in fact the familiar TDH oath of brotherhood, and it was indisputably subversive. Diao's version of the oath read, in part:

> We enter the gate of Hong loyally to swear fraternity.
> In the presence of Heaven, we sincerely swear our oath. . . .
> From the Hall of Loyalty and Righteousness,
> We brothers march forth to the center of the City,
> Leading an army of 80,000 troops.

Before the Ancestral Hall of Wealth and Virtue, we rise up in
   righteousness.
Exterminate the Qing dynasty! Restore the Ming![19]

The political message is unmistakable, referring explicitly to the extermination of the Qing dynasty (Qingchao). It also reflects a rural, anti-urban sensibility: armies of men, marching on the city, where representatives of Qing
power resided. Barend ter Haar has noted that references to urban centers in
sectarian oaths reflected identification with the city as a "safe haven" for brotherhoods.[20] Nevertheless, it appears that cities became "safe" only after armies
of Triads had "risen up in righteousness" and conquered them. The written
oath was preserved by people who detested the Qing and were willing to risk
the penalties of censorship laws to preserve and disseminate it generation after
generation. It is telling that, from an entire book ostensibly "discovered" in his
family's bookshelf, this was the particular verse of which Diao made multiple
copies for "sale." If he was not recruiting men into the TDH, he must have
been acting according to the law of supply and demand. He clearly understood that there was a large market for seditious TDH oaths along the migratory
routes out of eastern Guangdong decades before the Taiping insurgencies
of the 1850s.

Diao's world was one traversed by Hakka and Hoklo-Chaozhouese migrants. Versions of his "poem" were not simply transmitted in China but
throughout Southeast Asia.[21] Brotherhoods thrived because anonymous, literate custodians like the Diaos of Jiayingzhou were preserving, copying, and
transmitting their anti-Qing fulminations. Their families had bookshelves;
they themselves could read and write. They had other occupations but were
committed to an enterprise that would overthrow the Qing dynasty as part of
a larger cosmological vision. Most important, they were geographically mobile
men, the peasant intellectuals of rural China.

The fact that Diao was a peddler points to a more mundane reason why
brotherhood members resented the Qing. Many early congregants were itinerants employed as peddlers, porters, boatmen, laborers, and monks. As sojourners from the lower social orders, they were the sort who most consistently were harassed by Qing authorities in late imperial times. I have shown
elsewhere that 62 percent of culprits arrested for distributing and/or consuming opium during the first half of the nineteenth century were sojourners or
migrants arrested outside of their native places. Some 94.8 percent of those
arrested for selling and 85.5 percent of those convicted for consuming opium

were either petty entrepreneurs (peddlers, fishmongers) or members of the lower social orders (laborers, monks, boatmen, sailors, and prostitutes). Sojourners and the rural working classes were more likely to traverse the well-patrolled sectors of the Qing Empire and be subjected to unremitting inspections and petty exactions: they entered city gates, disembarked at piers, and encountered (or skirted) customs bureaus. Government functionaries pawed through their luggage. The places in which they slept and took meals—inns, temples, tea houses—were subject to round-the-clock inspections. These itinerants thus were more likely to encounter the formal legal system and find themselves accused of crimes.[22] The social orders that constituted brotherhoods were constantly harassed by officials and had every reason to despise the government in its routine operations. Even if the majority lacked a fully formed ideology of dynastic opposition, it would not be surprising if they cursed authorities under their breath the second they laid eyes on them.

TDH rituals demonized the Qing because of a longstanding antipathy for the regime. The revisionist arguments regarding sectarian brotherhoods are perfectly valid, and it is clear that their violent eruptions were usually in response to government suppression efforts rather than ideologically inspired efforts to overthrow the Qing for some vaguely imagined eschatological future. But such arguments do not explain why an avowedly anti-Qing ideology arose in southeastern China in 1761 if such ideas had not been percolating in the political consciousness of organizers all along. Anti-Qing sentiment may not have been essential to group mobilization, but it remained an important ritual feature of these societies. Brotherhoods bonded by vilifying dynastic power, contrasting the nobility of the sodality with the unworthiness of the rulers and their minions. It was a way to strengthen personal connections in multisurname brotherhoods whose members gathered together for mutual support, yes, but also in smuggling, piracy, and, eventually, rebellion. Seditious ideas were propagated by motivated individuals who traveled the commercial routes of a translocal economy.

Small-Time Crooks

As we have seen, sectarian gangs like the Red Society were thriving along the opium-smuggling routes of Guangdong by the 1830s. This phenomenon was part of a longer process implicating brotherhoods in the emergence of a transnational criminal underworld across the maritime frontier.[23] Considering that one transmission path of the TDH into Chaozhou was from Fujian, it is not surprising to find initial cases of sworn brotherhoods organized for the purpose of plunder along that borderland in the eighteenth century.[24] These sorts of sectarian-related criminal cases began to appear farther south along the coast after the turn of the nineteenth century.

The first case recorded in Chaoyang is significant because it unfolded in a region that sent many emigrants to West Borneo, where the TDH made its earliest recorded appearance in maritime Chaozhou. In 1802 Zheng Aming convinced Zheng Ayang, a member of a pirate gang, to help organize a lodge of the TDH. As he later confessed, Ayang agreed in order to "avail himself of the opportunity to plunder villages and acquire booty." They recruited several other men who were all surnamed Zheng. At the appointed hour, eighteen initiates gathered at Hongcuo village to swear an oath of brotherhood. Zheng Aming departed soon thereafter but, before leaving, advised the brothers to expand their ranks by starting their own, auxiliary lodges and recruiting more men. The smaller groups could then be organized under a larger confederation. The men complied and swore brotherhood with others among their kin and friends. When Aming returned later that year, the bands gathered in the Tuku area to swear an oath, recognizing Aming as the chief of the Brotherhood Confederation (Zonghui shou), a confederation now large enough "to plunder local villages." Before they could embark on this enterprise, however, the Chaoyang magistrate investigated and sent troops to arrest the pledges. The district city was treated to a bloody spectacle soon thereafter as the organizers were decapitated in the marketplace and their followers were deported to the Manchu penal colony in Jilin.[25]

The case reflected a process in which lodges were constructed out of layers of social networks. This confederation was dominated by two surname groups, the Zhengs and, to a lesser extent, the Xiaos. Of the twenty-two names recorded, nine were Zhengs, including most of the leadership, and four Xiaos. No other surname was repeated more than twice. Zheng Aming drew in as many people as he was able to in the initial oath-swearing ceremony. His confederates then recruited others from their own networks. Their confreres were personally loyal to them, and they, in turn, to the leader of the confederacy. Unlike the wealthier members of lineages in the area, these small-time crooks probably could not draw on large numbers of kin. Small groups of disempowered, socially marginal men nonetheless might gather groups of their own associates to form a league that potentially threatened the community. The capacity to expand exponentially through layers of personal relationships was a hallmark of the Chaozhou criminal underworld. It also mirrored the basic social formation of overseas Chinese from the southeast coast, a formation in which smaller partnerships confederated into a larger union or "general assembly."

The earliest case in Huilai reflected a similar social dynamic. In 1801 a native of Tong'an, Fujian, named Chen traveled to the Mt. Chi area to practice fortune-telling, soliciting clients from home to home. He met with Fang Zhensi, a watchman, and sixty other men surnamed Zheng, Chen, Gao, and Huang and talked about organizing a lodge of the TDH. He encouraged them to change their surname to Hong and to "worship heaven as their father and earth as their mother." Religious issues aside, he also told them that organizing a lodge would enable them to plunder nearby villages because "no one would dare resist us." He compiled a membership register, which he entrusted to Fang, and promised to divulge his full name when he returned for an initiation ceremony.

Chen, like Zheng Aming, is example of the peripatetic true believer who proselytized the ideological message. In her history of the TDH, Dian Murray refers to "Teacher Chen," a man from Tong'an whose given name is never reported and who transmitted the sect into Leizhou prefecture in southwestern Guangdong.[26] "Teacher Chen" is similar to the mysterious Chen in this case, and, if this is the same man, his initiation efforts in Leizhou were decidedly political, calling for the "restoration of the Ming."

In 1802 Fang Zhensi experienced financial difficulties and decided that it was time to gather the group and start raiding villages, but the men were hindered by the fact that they possessed no swords. This indicates that they were probably quite poor and foreshadows their ultimate demise, for an unarmed bandit is a hapless brigand, and one can only imagine the Ah-Q-like quality of their ruminations about robbing their neighbors when those neighbors likely were better armed and organized than they were. They decided to invite a local blacksmith to join the group, and he did his part by smelting weapons in an abandoned temple on Mt. Chi. With that obstacle behind them, they gathered on the mountain to swear brotherhood and to recognize Fang as their "Big Brother." They lit candles and burned incense while Fang and another disciple, Zheng Ahui, raised a pair of newly fabricated cutlasses. Each man drew blood, drank wine, and swore mutual allegiance. The Huilai magistrate meanwhile had gotten wind of their activities and arrested them before they could put their weapons to use. Instead of amassing their fortunes, the leaders were paraded to the execution ground while their followers were exiled.[27]

The case record for this coastal region of Chaozhou involved incidents that exclusively included economically marginal men ostensibly using sectarian ideology as a vehicle for criminal predation. It is impossible to prove but seems obvious that these men were imitating the organizational ethos and ritual practices of others who rarely were arrested and who sojourned as boatmen and peddlers in China, as sailors in the junk trade, or as laborers in Southeast Asia. More significantly, many of the miners and traders who operated the gold mines of West Borneo hailed from these very regions of Chaozhou and were surnamed Zheng, Huang, Zhu, Wu, Cai, and Liu. Some were Chaozhou-dialect-speaking "Hoklos," but most were half-mountain Hakka, bilingual Hakka who dwelled in Chaozhou-speaking areas and tended to live on mountain slopes along the coast of Chaozhou and Huizhou. In this case, the villagers lived near Mt. Chi and probably were half-mountain Hakka, but officials compiling the case record did not bother to identify culprits by their "ethnic" identity. This hilly coastal region as well as the inland Hakka homeland in Jiaying-zhou constituted the native places of sojourning emigrants to West Borneo, where the Chaozhou-connected TDH first emerged.[28] We do not know if Fang's gang had overseas experience themselves, but they obviously were influenced by peripatetic sectarians in their midst.

Hakka-dominated regions of eastern Guangdong were disproportionately targeted in government campaigns against these outlawed sodalities. The dissemination of sectarian organizations is only marginally documented for the Hoklo-dominated areas of the commercialized Chaozhou coast, whereas it is densely recorded for the Hakka and half-mountain Hakka regions of the Guangdong-Fujian-Jiangxi-Guangxi provincial borderland.[29] Hakka were avid participants in brotherhoods, of course, but it is probable that government informants were protecting the dominant, Hoklo subgroup in the region.

The geographical pattern of TDH-related cases that stretch from the half-mountain Hakka regions of the Chaozhou-Huizhou coast into the interior are therefore easily discerned. Intriguingly, these patterns coincide with two opium-smuggling routes into the inland Hakka homeland. During the Jiaqing-era campaigns from 1803 to 1818, for example, TDH cases involving Haifeng, Changle, Yong'an, and Xingning counties were particularly common.[30] These cases map onto the smuggling routes that were reported to provincial officials in Canton a few decades later. One route started in Haifeng city on the Huizhou coast, proceeded north through Yong'an district, then on to the Jiayingzhou districts of Changle, Xingning, and Jiayingzhou city. The second route started in the coastal town of Danshui, then overland to Baozi periodical market, through Huizhou city, and from there on waterways northward to Heyuan, Longchuan, and Yanxia periodical market, "where the Jiangxi dealers [made] their purchases for the southern parts of that province."[31] These likely were the importation routes of the Red Society sectarians.

In contrast, Hoklo smuggling routes that would have originated in Chenghai with its international port of Zhanglin or Anbu port in Haiyang were not reported. These Hakka smuggling routes were reported to Canton by the British who were frustrated by their inability to penetrate the Chaozhou opium market after 1858. They were convinced that they competed unfairly with smugglers and asked Chinese merchants in Swatow to identify the regional smuggling pathways. The British did not identify the ethnicity of their informants, but Hoklos dominated trade and life in Swatow.[32] These informants remained mum about the smuggling routes of their own group and region while they sicced officialdom on their Hakka competitors.

One sees this phenomenon in the Qing anti-opium campaigns of 1839 to 1858 as well, and it is clear that the dominant Hoklo group protected their own at the expense of Hakka whenever the government crusaded against criminality.[33] Although the ethnically subordinate group in Chaozhou was inevitably targeted in official investigations, it is clear that, among all ethnic groups, sectarianism and opium smuggling were interrelated forces that further entangled the economy of southeastern China with that of Southeast Asia.

The Rebellion of the Double Swords

Opium smuggling and the evolution of organized crime reflected Chaozhou's location on the maritime frontier. Frontier societies produce their own social dislocations. A rebellion led by Huang Wukong in Chaoyang in 1844 was a culmination of social trends unfolding since the seventeenth century as well as the opening salvo of an anti-Qing enterprise that would reverberate across the region until the fall of the dynasty in 1912. In particular, it reflected the extent to which TDH ideology now saturated coastal rural communities.

Huang was a laborer from Xialin village. His father died when he was young, and when his mother remarried, he was sent to live with his paternal grandparents. His grandfather, a guardsman in a nearby garrison, instructed him in the finer points of martial arts. After the grandfather passed away, the family found itself in financial straits, and Huang was forced to work as a hired hand for another family. At some point he fell in with a local gangster named Huang Yinsheng, who had organized a brotherhood dedicated to tax resistance. Although Wukong had been the gangster's most trusted subordinate, for some reason he murdered his chief and took over the organization, transforming it into a formidable brotherhood named the Double Sword Society (Shuangdao hui). The initiation ceremony involved the familiar TDH oath and rituals, and he imparted the traditional teachings passed down since the eighteenth century. Huang's subordinates proceeded to form subsidiary lodges, and the ranks of the organization swelled.

Double swords were used in TDH initiations, and Huang undoubtedly had been influenced by local brotherhood traditions when he established his own group. Swords had long lost their symbolic power of imperial legitimation in elite culture, but they remained a potent symbol in sectarian organizations and were essential to the "demonological messianic paradigm" of the TDH. In one myth, a son of the final Ming emperor was rescued by a loyal servant, who also carried away two precious swords associated with the royal family. It was foretold that on the day the Ming prince returned to his people, so too would the swords reappear.[34] The initiation ceremonies of sectarian brotherhoods in Chaozhou incorporated the use of swords, and Huang likewise resorted to these potent symbols of Ming restorationism.

In spite of their religiosity, the attraction of the Double Sword Society was its more prosaic message of tax resistance. Huang instructed his followers to cease paying their land taxes but to avoid plundering villages or killing people. The movement attracted a rural, landowning following. Initially, four entire villages in Chaoyang joined his cause. Eventually, membership expanded by the thousands, most of whom hailed from Chaoyang and Jieyang, and they lay siege to Jieyang district city. When the magistrate led a military force to arrest the brothers, a wider rebellion ensued.[35]

After it was suppressed, Qing officials discovered the extent to which the TDH had infiltrated coastal society. The provincial judge, Kong Jiyin, unearthed the Double Swords' membership rosters and estimated that individuals from "nine out of ten households there had joined."[36] TDH traditions permeated all social levels by the 1840s. It no longer was a sojourning phenomenon ostensibly involving marginal men but a basic characteristic of rural life. Because this was an area populated with menfolk who had sojourned to West Borneo, it is possible—though impossible to prove—that there was a connection between the two organizations. Dutch officials in the East Indies were often puzzled that the brotherhood in its early days was nestled in Chinese farming communities in addition to the more familiar commercial communities.[37] Huang's rebellion reflected the ways the sojourning lifestyle was affecting village life back in southeastern China.

Local authorities now faced the difficult task of apprehending thousands of rebels who were thoroughly ensconced in rural society. The provincial judge thought it unlikely that so many people had been coerced into joining the insurrection; they had participated of their own volition. What was he going to do with all those names? He decided to focus on the ringleaders alone. Huang Wukong was easily captured and dragged away to Chaozhou prefectural city for execution. The authorities subjected an additional three hundred followers to various punishments and then declared that the organization had been successfully "suppressed." No one else was sentenced. Legions of Huang's defeated followers took to the "red-bowed" junks and sailed overseas. Many lived out their days in Singapore, immortalized as "patriotic guardsmen" of the Ming on funerary tablets housed in the Five Tiger Shrine.[38]

The Double Sword uprising was significant in its motives and manner of resolution. It was precipitated by resistance the sectarian rebels took on their own initiative and was not a response to official investigation. They refused to pay taxes and attacked district towns. That is to say, they acted on whatever antigovernment feelings they held. Finally, the sheer scale of the rebel force inclined officials to let many sectarians go free, in spite of the fact that their identities were known. This was in stark contrast to the approach taken during the hunts for brotherhoods decades earlier in which virtually every named individual was tracked down in relentless dragnets. In this case officials essentially would have been forced to declare war on an enormous swath of territory in two districts of Chaozhou renowned for their lineage solidarity.

Most were drawn to the Double Sword Society because of its message of tax resistance. Given this, the rebellion involved taxpaying landowners. While it is impossible to verify that "nine out of ten households" in the region genuinely contributed rebels to the cause (the registers are lost), Kong clearly sensed that individuals from the majority of households joined the brotherhood. Alfred Lin has taken issue with the familiar assertion that the land tax in late imperial China was not particularly onerous. In Guangdong, at least, it was a burden. Copper coins were the daily unit of exchange, but the tax was always paid in silver. After 1713 (the year the Kangxi emperor stoutly declared that the land tax would never increase), the value of copper depreciated in relation to silver. In 1713 the exchange rate was one silver tael per 700 copper cash; by the mid-nineteenth century the rate was one tael to 2,200 coppers. In effect, the land tax had increased threefold in a little over a century.[39]

But why would the problem of taxation suddenly provoke a large, violent rebellion in 1844? The short answer is international affairs and the additional burdens shouldered by farmers on the frontier of an imperialist era. Landowners and commercial elites throughout Guangdong had borne the financial brunt of funding the First Opium War against British forces from 1839 to 1842. As He Zhiqing and Wu Zhaoqing have noted, over 80 percent of the entire cost of the struggle came out of the Guangdong provincial treasury and customs houses alone. At war's end, in order to restore provincial revenues, the land tax was increased.[40] In Chaozhou, at least, farmers resisted these additional exactions.

As we shall see, another likely reason for the popularity of the Double Swords was the violent anti-opium campaign pursued by the Qing between 1839 and 1858. Entire village-market communities along the coast had become heavily invested in the illicit opium trade by the 1830s. The livelihoods of merchants, peddlers, fisher folk, and their relatives across towns and villages were threatened, and recreational opium smokers were subjected to unprecedented harassment by local authorities. The Qing war on drugs from 1838 to 1858 proved deeply unpopular and provoked antigovernment animosity.

Things Fall Apart: The Lingdong Insurrections, 1854–1866

Ten years after the Double Swords were suppressed, the region fell into an intensifying cascade of rebellions that deleteriously affected the commercially dynamic coast. The outbreak of these rebellions in part reflected ongoing demographic challenges in Chaozhou as the population expanded relative to cultivable land. This was not a population that depended exclusively on access to land, however. Most residents along the coasts and rivers relied on a combination of agricultural production and fishing, clamming, and other maritime or riverine enterprises. Peasants in Chaoyang, for example, devoted only half their energies to the cultivation of crops, and the fishing industry had long been a pillar of the local economy. It was one task of women to supplement family income by gathering marine products along the shore.[41] Moreover, the commercial sectors of the economy provided steady work in the ports. Indeed, during the sugar and rice harvesting seasons, it was sometimes impossible for shippers to find enough men to serve as coolies on the docks. The harvests absorbed much of the male labor in the region.[42] Arguments about population pressures do not consider the ways a commercialized maritime economy provided employment outside of agriculture. Demographic pressures were relevant but not determinative.

The emergence of the TDH coincided with the rise of the opium trade in the region, and the Qing "war on drugs" from 1838 to 1858 deeply antagonized coastal lineages that had an economic interest in the business. The governor-general of Liangguang memorialized that opium sellers in Chaoyang, for example, "expressed deep resentment" when they were interrogated by local officials in 1838.[43] Opium dealers, cultivators, and users saw nothing wrong with the recreational use of opium, and governmental harassment seriously antagonized locals.

The most important cause of the upheavals, however, was the fact that they were ideologically detonated by the Taiping rebellion (1850–1866), one of the greatest social cataclysms in Chinese history. Sometimes referred to as a "civil war," its outbreak is a familiar story: Hong Xiuquan was the son of a Hakka farmer whose forebears had emigrated from Jiayingzhou to a village north of Canton in the 1680s. He repeatedly failed to pass imperial examinations and, in 1837, experienced a nervous collapse, taking to his room and writhing in agony as he suffered inexplicable hallucinations. He eventually recovered but continued to be haunted by the experience. A chance reading of evangelical Christian tracts finally enabled him to interpret those nightmares to his satisfaction and begin to propagate a new, chiliastic, anti-Manchu creed combining Christian and popular Chinese religious ideas. By 1844 he was baptizing his Hakka neighbors and smashing statues associated with Confucian traditions. He moved with his flock to Thistle Mountain in Guangxi, where they organized the Society of God Worshippers, transforming the Hakka villages in the vicinity into an enormous religious encampment. These developments coincided with intensifying struggles between Hakka and "Punti" (or "native" Cantonese), and ever larger numbers of Hakka fled to the mountainous redoubt. The embattled community grew militant and religiously fanatical until 1851, when Hong inaugurated the Taiping Heavenly Kingdom, a movement galvanized by a utopian ideology of radical egalitarianism and anti-Manchu millenarianism. In that year the Taipings began their march north, determined not only to overthrow the Manchu demons but to demolish the orthodox, classical order they believed had distorted the historical development of China. They blitzkrieged their way to Nanjing and in 1853 transformed the old Ming capital into their governing seat. For the next decade they devastated much of the prosperous Lower Yangzi region as they struggled with imperial military forces. The Taipings eventually were suppressed in 1866, but the toll this and other rebellions took on the dynasty, and, indeed, the old social order, was enormous.[44]

Although the Taiping movement started elsewhere in China, and prior to 1859 most of its violence occurred in other parts of the empire, Chaozhou was profoundly affected, for it inspired a series of uprisings by sympathetic brother-hoods. These movements were ideological in nature, though natural disasters opened the floodgates to catastrophe. Torrential rainfalls from 1852 to 1854 re-sulted in devastating inundations across the prefecture. Embankments were washed away, harvests suffered, and fishing vessels lost. Provincial authorities delegated a commission to investigate the damage and distribute relief supplies. These commissioners reported that the disaster "did not result in a complete ca-lamity. Relief money has been distributed and funds for repairs handed out. There is no need to offer financial assistance through a temporary remission of taxes."[45]

The decision to insist on tax payment in spite of such devastating losses was a grave mistake. Within months, infuriated peasants, many organized by local TDH brotherhoods, rebelled across the region. Under more normal circum-stances, it is possible that the provincial government might have considered reducing taxes on such a hard-hit region. But Guangdong was under enormous financial pressure during these years. Burdened by the high cost of suppressing the Taipings, it was enforcing tax payments in unprecedented ways, fostering a seething resentment that affected all classes of society.[46]

Chaozhou was beset by insurrection throughout the 1850s and 1860s. Even before the flooding, Lin Yuankai led his brethren into rebellion in Jieyang dis-trict in 1851. Three years later, in Chaoyang, Chen Niangkang of Big Changlong village and Zheng Youchun of Meihua village rose up at Chendian embank-ment. Their movement expanded to include over ten thousand rebels who attacked Huilai and Puning cities. That same year, 1854, Wu Zhongshu orga-nized a brotherhood at Cai Embankment in Haiyang, and within a month they were storming the city of Chenghai and the port of Anbu. After Chen and Zheng were defeated, the remnants of their forces fled to Wu's protection. Now leading a brotherhood army of over twenty thousand, he attacked Chaozhou prefectural city and laid siege to it for weeks. When the Raoping district magistrate marched with troops to defend the city, he was captured. Other rebel forces led by Chen Ashi of Stork Embankment village in Haiyang and Wang Xingshun of Waisha village in Chenghai arose in support of Wu Zhongshu, wreaking havoc along the coast. Not to be outdone, Gu Shengyang led his own brotherhood in an attack on Fengshun city; and Xu Amei and Wu Ading gathered what the government referred to as a gang of "mountain out-laws" that attacked Puning and Jieyang.[47] The violence of these insurrections turned many rural villages into veritable "ghost towns."[48]

Compounding the chaos, the Taiping Heavenly Kingdom began to collapse in the Lower Yangzi in the late 1850s and early 1860s, and remnant Taiping forces retreated south to make their final stand in the Hakka hinterland of Chaozhou. Shi Zhenji, for example, abandoned the main body of Taipings in 1857 when it became clear to him that Hong Xiuquan was planning to assassinate him. Shi had been among the least doctrinaire and most militarily adept of the Taiping leaders, and some of the best troops departed with him, which dealt a serious blow to Taiping fortunes at Nanjing.[49] By 1859 Shi's forces had been forced out of Fujian into Chaozhou, where they lay siege to Dabu city, and Jiayingzhou. Taiping armies devastated the region, slaughtering many of the few remaining officials—including the Jiayingzhou magistrate—and churning enormous waves of refugees fleeing downriver to the coast. Included among those refugees was the entire clan of Huang Zunxian, then a child of ten but a man destined to emerge as a political reformer during the late Qing. The horrors of his blood-soaked childhood instilled in him a lifelong disdain for the governing capacities of the Qing and led him to develop his influential theories of "local self-governance" later in the century.[50]

By 1864 some ninety thousand battle-hardened Taipings led by Wang Hai-yang occupied Jiayingzhou and prepared to fight to the bitter end. Qing forces closed in on him but suffered a devastating defeat in 1865, a rout hastened by the fact that half their number perished in a bubonic plague epidemic in the mountainous region. The military continued to press the offensive, grinding down the Taiping resistance until February 1, 1866, when Wang, the last of the Taiping "kings" to escape from Nanjing, died of a head wound. His vanquished troops shaved their heads and scattered. By February 9 the Qing recaptured the devastated Hakka hinterland of the southeast coast, and a semblance of peace was restored.[51]

The Taiping conflagration ignited the other disorders in Chaozhou. The prefect, Wu Jun, assessed its powerful repercussions in an early report to the governor in 1853. He described the familiar recruitment dynamic for TDH organizations in the region, a dynamic in which a small number of leaders upheld a commitment to the anti-Qing cause while drawing on their networks of less ideologically driven confreres. They exploited the opportunities presented by the rebellion. They infiltrated the militias raised to fight the Taipings because this facilitated the dissemination of their "heterodox ideas" as well as recruitment into their own ranks. "Crafty" sectarians would muster their brothers, who in turn recruited their own disciples from the villages in the area. Indeed, the entire process of suppressing rebellions was having the perverse effect of instigating even more resistance to the authorities. The local gentry and merchants in Chaozhou had complied with Governor-General

Ye Mingchen's command to raise local militias and give combat to various rebel bands that had arisen in tandem with the Taipings. But sectarian brotherhoods simply used this opportunity to "fraudulently establish 'militias' that, in fact, served their own private interests." Once the militias were organized, they broke away from legitimate forces and often gave the latter a sound thrashing. Most problematically, common peasants were recruited into these illegitimate militias and fell under their ideological sway. "Common folk who all along had been listening to the officials now ended up following the rebels." The official process of militia formation led to the organization of parallel forces controlled by sectarian brotherhoods and criminals, who either sympathized with the Taipings or took advantage of the chaos to advance their own agendas.

Moreover, Chaozhou irregulars (*yong* or "braves") had been drafted into the anti-Taiping struggle in Hunan province. Seven thousand of these irregulars were later demobilized, and "almost all of them might be classified as desperadoes with absolutely no prospects who were well-practiced in combat and who treated the regular military with utter contempt." Their return exacerbated disorder in Chaozhou. Prefect Wu managed to arrest one "sectarian chieftain" and his accomplices and, as was common in Qing counterinsurgency, tortured and publicly dismembered them so as to "shock and awe" the population. The prefect, however, was beginning to suspect that this was an inefficacious method of dealing with sectarian movements. By reinforcing the popular conviction that the government "lacked righteousness," it only enhanced the capacity of rebels to recruit men into their ranks. Official violence "simply incited even more disturbances." In making this observation, the prefect discerned the deleterious effect violent government campaigns had on the way common people viewed their own government. It was a rare official acknowledgment that the government itself contributed to a culture of violence in eastern Guangdong. Wu's analysis reflected a dawning official awareness that the state was now competing with the brotherhoods for the loyalty of the Chaozhouese.[52]

Government policies also antagonized commercial elites. The merchants of Chaozhou generously raised large sums to support suppression efforts. In August and September 1857 alone they joined forces with the local gentry to raise 300,000 Mexican silver dollars in support of both domestic counterinsurgency efforts and the struggle against Great Britain and France in the Second Opium War (1856–1860).[53] They nonetheless were violently opposed to the newfangled *lijin* tax, a 4 percent tariff imposed in 1858 on all commercial transactions (half to be paid by sellers and half by buyers). The gentry-led "Public Bureau" (*gongju*) joined merchants in a protest march on government offices in Chaozhou city in 1863. Panicky officials called in troops, and as the crowd fled in a panic, three young boys were trampled to death. This further inflamed popular resentment, and a league of villages was organized for mutual defense against the authorities. Shops were closed, government offices were looted, and the property of the lijin commissioner was torched. Order eventually was restored, but the league was never disbanded.[54]

Merchants were not generically opposed to taxation. In fact, less than a year after this crisis, the commercial guild at Swatow imposed a tax on oceangoing vessels to defray the cost of harbor security.[55] Throughout the crisis they were willing to raise significant revenues as long as they devised and controlled the manner of its collection. They were hostile to efforts to formalize a new system of commercial taxation, and this hostility was driving a wedge between establishment merchants and local authorities. Edward Vincent, a British trader and a long-term resident of Swatow (he married a Chinese woman and had Anglo-Chinese children), reported to his colleagues in Hong Kong that, by 1865, most of the local Chinese he encountered at the port were indifferent to the fate of the Qing dynasty. "The Mandarins of this district," he noted, "are the only people who seem to dread the rebels."[56] This sentiment reflected the ways counterinsurgency efforts antagonized commercial classes.

The story of the Tiandihui in the eighteenth and early nineteenth centuries is connected to the commercial expansion of Chaozhou. Sectarian cases explicitly connected to Southeast Asia became common by the mid-nineteenth century, as we shall see. Chinese officials deplored the deleterious influence of men who had labored in Singapore and elsewhere and become susceptible to the teaching of the TDH. Ironically, European colonial officials who complained about "secret societies" in their own conquered territory attributed the problem to sojourning Chinese who transported their ritual practices from their homeland.[57] Sectarian ideas were kept alive by increasingly cosmopolitan ideologues who circulated throughout their maritime world. These brotherhoods evolved translocally. The earliest TDH-related cases in Chaozhou proper occurred in 1786, but the earliest instance of TDH organization across maritime Chaozhou was recorded in West Borneo in 1775, over ten years earlier.[58] This is not to say that the Chaozhou version of the TDH originated abroad, but that the domestic history of the movement cannot be disassociated from the translocal experiences of Chaozhou sojourners among the laboring and mercantile classes. By the nineteenth century, militarized leagues of men across the maritime frontier organized for the purpose of self-protection, native place solidarity, territorial aggrandizement, and economic benefit but also in solidarity with the Taiping effort to overthrow the Qing dynasty. Provincial officials were aware that these anti-Qing sodalities were now a permanent feature of rural communities along the coast. In the 1860s they decided to do something about it.

4

Qingxiang

PACIFICATION ON THE COASTAL FRONTIER, 1869–1891

Fang Yao . . . is a coercive, talented and clever strategist. He dispels the criminal element and protects the good folk. Troops and civilians alike submit to him in fear. He is fit for the responsibilities of provincial commander-in-chief.

—GOVERNOR-GENERAL ZENG GUOQUAN, 1883

IN DECEMBER 1869 the regional commander of the Army of the Green Standard, Fang Yao, launched a violent campaign of rural pacification along the Chaozhou coast. The bloodiest phase ended in 1873, by which time more than three thousand pirates, rebels, brotherhood leaders, smugglers, and feuding braves had been captured and decapitated. Some villages were cleared of their inhabitants and burned to the ground, while others were forced to pay back taxes and "fines." Tens of thousands of people were driven into exile in distant lands. The provincial officials who sanctioned this campaign referred to it as a *qingxiang*, an effort to eradicate criminal case backlogs, purge the region of its lawless and insurrectionary element, and finally pacify coastal districts that had been beyond the control of the government since the Qing dynasty was founded in 1644.

Fang Yao's campaign of rural pacification was the most significant event to occur in Chaozhou since the coastal evacuation of the seventeenth century. In some ways, it addressed social problems that had been generated by that earlier catastrophe. This was an unusually violent region of China, where feuds and abusive litigation were common and state-building relatively weak compared to other commercialized areas of the empire. Some villages were political entities unto themselves, dominated by single lineages and protected by walls that were almost completely impenetrable. They feuded over property and water rights. They kidnapped for ransom. They preyed on the commercial traffic along the waterways. They profited from the illicit opium trade. They rose in rebellion. Many villages were dominated by the smuggling underworld and fraternal sodalities that were inflected with anti-Qing sentiment. Some had not paid their land tax in over fifty years.

The region emerged as a center of opium importation and cultivation after the drug was outlawed in 1729, and smuggling constituted a way of life for several villages. These economic strategies enabled village power-mongers to dominate and sustain large numbers of poor people who submitted to their authority. It also ensured that these people remained loyal to them rather than to potentially more powerful competitors such as the Qing state or elite organizations. Indeed, underworld networks often subvert the efforts of state-builders to extend central governmental authority into the local arena. Illicit activities become normalized as people are drawn in by their social networks to participate in brigandage or smuggling. The Chaozhou region's intensified incorporation into the global opium economy after the eighteenth century also enabled villagers to diversify their sources of income and, indeed, prosper.

This situation might have gone on indefinitely had Chaozhou not been swept up in the mayhem of violent rebellion in the middle of the nineteenth century. Once the last of these upheavals was suppressed in 1866, the Guangdong provincial government decided to embark on a project of heavily militarized state-building to eradicate, once and for all, the alternative centers of power that had existed outside its orbit of political control. Thus was born the *qingxiang* of Commander Fang Yao. Officials in Canton turned to the scion of a powerful family to subdue the region and to transform the "free trade" in opium into a government-controlled operation for generating revenue. Such campaigns of "bandit suppression" were not unprecedented. What distinguished Fang's enterprise was that it was sustained over an extended period of time. He assumed formal control of the Army of the Green Standard and established martial law in Chaozhou (and, intermittently, other parts of Guangdong) for over twenty years. And throughout those twenty years, the writ of government authority was felt for the first time, if only through the person of Fang Yao and his extended family. In essence, the *qingxiang* in Chaozhou was an enormous, officially sanctioned feud that advanced the interests of the Fangs and their gentry allies at the expense of other powerful families on the coast. Government officials were aware of the ways the Fangs abused their power, but they looked the other way as the commander maintained a semblance of order and embarked on the long process of economic and military development.

The Maritime Underworld of Wang Xingshun

Who was targeted in the campaign? Waisha village, led by the opium-trafficking rebel Wang Xingshun (1814–1857), offers an illustrative example. Wang not only was a true-believing peasant intellectual among Chaozhou area insurgents, he also personified the cosmopolitan mode of the smuggling underworld of coastal China. The statist, capitalist order that governments were building across the South China Sea was predicated on the elimination of the competing global economies in which the Wangs of Waisha participated.

The Wangs were the dominant lineage in Waisha, a walled village-market complex near the mouth of the Han River in Chenghai. Wang Xingshun led a powerful opium-smuggling network and, according to one British trafficker, had a reputation for being "a very bad character." Wang's notoriety presumably reinforced Waisha's monopoly on the opium trade there. Some Chinese importers into Swatow, however, also relied on the village's strong-armed protective services to smuggle their own drug into the large markets of the interior and, when the opium trade was legalized after 1858, those dealers continued to rely on the "Waisha smugglers" to evade the ever-increasing duties on opium.[1] It is possible that the Wangs were Dan (Tanka), socially debased "boat people." In response to a question posed to him in his deposition of 1857, Wang Xingshun noted that his fellow villagers "might be characterized as unsettled boat dwellers" (chuanhu).[2] If so, it might explain their alienation from their more conventional neighbors.

Participation in the global drug trade transformed the village into a formidable political entity in its own right, indifferent to the governing agenda of the Qing. The campaign against the illicit opium trade from 1838 to 1858 (and the heavy taxation of the drug after 1858) proved unpopular in a region where many Chinese families had an economic stake in it. Historical accounts of the upheavals of South China tend to ignore the economic repercussions of the government's drug-trafficking suppression efforts, but they must be factored into the explosion of anti-Qing feeling in Chaozhou at this time.

One Chenghai junk merchant named Wang Wanshun was arrested off the Shandong coast in 1839. He had departed Chenghai on a vessel loaded with sugar and Southeast Asian luxury products, and en route to northern ports he purchased five chests of raw opium from a foreign ship anchored offshore. As he approached Jiaozhou Bay, he was unnerved by the intensity of official security and decided to sell only his sugar there. Just as he turned south toward Shanghai, he was arrested.[3] It is uncertain whether he was related to Wang Xingshun, but the fact that they were Chenghai opium smugglers who shared a surname and generational name suggests a family connection. Either way, Wang Xingshun had generic, and possibly personal, reasons for despising the Qing.

In 1854 Wang traveled upriver to Caitang market town in Haiyang to join Wu Zhongshu, a sectarian who had revolted in support of the Taipings. Popular songs connected to the uprising indicate that Wu, the owner of a gambling den, had been a regular visitor to the Wang household in Waisha. Wang professed a sincere belief in the religious ethos of Wu's brotherhood, which promoted a syncretic mix of folk Buddhist millenarianism and the ritual practices of TDH brotherhoods. Their rebel anthem reflected the goals of the movement: "First we'll snatch Chaozhou, then we'll overthrow Guangdong, then it's on to the capital in support of the King of the Taipings!" Their anger also was fueled by efforts to collect the land tax in spite of widespread flooding.[4]

The two men swore a blood oath, and Wang declared himself commander-in-chief of the Waisha forces of rebellion in July 1854. He organized his men into ten banner battalions, each led by kin or fellow villagers. The fact that the inhabitants of Waisha were involved in the opium trade must also be factored into any analysis of their military organization. Groups that specialize in smuggling and drug trafficking by necessity tend to be "close-knit, cohesive, and ethnically homogenous."[5] Narcotics trafficking involves large sums of money and treacherous maneuvering past government surveillance points. Trust is essential to this enterprise and is forged through years of cooperation. The villagers of Waisha already had a record of collaboration in resistance to Qing policies.

Wang insisted that he believed in the religious teachings of Wu, while his fellow villagers had joined the brotherhood simply because it gave them an opportunity to plunder. Perhaps he was protecting them from the more serious charge of sedition, but his testimony substantiates the explanatory power of network theory as applied to criminal organizations: the leaders are ideologically motivated, but the people they draw into the movement join because of familial or fraternal relationships or because it represents an economic opportunity. As one anthropologist has characterized insurgency in general: popular uprisings traditionally are conducted through "preexisting social networks (village, family, neighborhood or religious party). Insurgent operational art remains fundamentally a matter of aggregating dispersed tactical actions by small groups." Modern insurgencies, he continues, "operate more like a self-synchronizing swarm of independent but cooperating cells than like a formal organization."[6] Wang's operations reflected this insurgency mode, not only in Chaozhou but elsewhere along the coast.

Wang Xingshun and Wu Zhongshu, leading a combined force of ten thousand, attacked Chenghai ten times. "Then, in early September," he later recalled, the great prefect of Chaozhou Master Wu [Jun] led his troops to exterminate us, but I held them at bay from my village of Waisha. After that, the great prefect Master Wu pacified my village, but I continued to resist government troops I don't know how many times, and on 1 December, I led a band of fifty men in an escape to Qundailu [Hong Kong]. The group eventually scattered and I fled on my own to Annam [Vietnam]."[7]

After the rebels vanished, troops entered Waisha and "burned it to the ground." Wang's wife and children were among those killed. Her resistance had achieved mythic proportions by the time a British visitor, John Scarth, reported the nature of her demise six years later: "His wife did not escape and, perceiving she was likely to be taken, collected her children around her and, placing a barrel of gunpowder in the room, when the soldiers arrived at the door, she blew herself and the whole family to atoms."[8] The story is suspiciously reminiscent of the fabled demise of Qui Hui, a Dan (Tanka) who resisted the Qing conquest. As troops clambered aboard his ship off the coast of Taiwan in 1683, he is said to have brandished his sword at them before igniting the ship's powder kegs, killing them all.[9] True or false, the saga of Mme. Wang was a tribute to a woman who heroically perished in the anti-Qing struggle. Indeed, the account might be read as Dan political hagiography.

Wang remained in exile in Annam for two years as he made a living as a peddler. He dispensed with his queue and let the hair around the crown of his head grow out. The queue had been imposed on Chinese males by their Qing conquerors in the 1640s, a somatic manifestation of Chinese submission to Manchu dominion. Cutting one's queue was a political act of defiance. Wang did not confess to these motivations, of course. He merely claimed that barbering fees in Annam were unreasonable, "so I let my hair grow to avoid that expense." While in Annam, he married another woman, and he later assured his interrogators that her family had given him "permission" to let his hair grow. Considering that he had been forced to flee China after leading a rebellion, his interrogator was right to be skeptical.

A Chaozhouese sojourning in the Nanyang easily communicated with those back home. Wang sailed back to Hong Kong in 1856 to join friends in plundering the Canton region. He initially partnered with Zhang Pinghu, a gangster who led a confederation of a thousand sectarians and pirates from native places in every prefecture from Chaozhou to Guangzhou. The water-borne force controlled about fifty fishing smacks, boats designed to keep catch alive and thus fitted with large wells in the hold suitable for stashing loot. Wang insisted that the swashbucklers focused on piracy and had nothing to do with the Taipings. On the other hand, he clearly had not abandoned his seditious commitments. Back in Chaozhou, agents of the Jardine Matheson Company reported that local Chinese traders were apprehensive about messages Wang had been relaying to his followers in Chenghai, assuring them that he was operating temporarily in Hong Kong, but that he was seething with vengeful-ness and planned to "come up with a large force to attack the Mandarins [in Chaozhou]."[10]

Government forces inevitably suppressed this and other confederations Wang organized, but our marauder was never alone for long. He had an un-canny ability to forge alliances on the waterways of Canton—probably because he had spent years purchasing his opium supplies there. By Febru-ary 1857 he had formed his final gang with Chen Baiye and three hundred other bandits. Their small fleet encountered a ferry sailing out of Hong Kong, and they were delighted to unburden her of her cargo. The pirates, however, had made a fatal error. As Wang rued in his confession: "Who'd have thought that the people on the ferry would tell the [foreign] Devils at Hong Kong about it? The Devils were afraid that if their boats got plundered along Hong Kong's trade routes, it would be bad for business. . . . Who'd have thought that the Devils would nab . . . me and seventy-two other guys and hand us over to the Chinese military?"[11] In the end, British naval forces put a stop to Wang Xingshun's four-year stint as a buccaneering rebel.

Meanwhile, back in Chenghai, his village brotherhood had not disbanded. In late 1854 or early 1855 they allied with a leader of the Small Sword Society of Fujian, Huang Wei, and established a base at the Lai Wastelands near Nan'ao Island. It was the perfect hideout, for it was situated along the shipping lanes between Chaozhou and Siam which, by the nineteenth century, was one of the most profitable commercial routes of the South China Sea.[12] After attacking forts in Chenghai and Nan'ao as well as the Tongshan, Xiamen, and Jilong (Taiwan) areas of Fujian, they proceeded to rob fishing boats and prey on commercial traffic, at one point commandeering two enormous vessels and plundering them of their entire contents.[13] This was classic borderland outlawry. "Local" in this case involved four districts in two provinces. In the end they were suppressed by a combined force of the Green Standard Navy and a militia organized by commercial and gentry elites.

The Small Sword Society was a translocal organization. In 1854 they revolted in Shanghai, where they sought "to overthrow the Qing and restore the Ming." Seizing sectors of the city, they burned government offices and assassinated the local magistrate.[14] Moreover, the Small Swords of Shanghai, southern Fujian, and Chaozhou were aligned with their brethren in Southeast Asia. Small Swordsmen in Shanghai hailed the "Gongsi of Righteous Restoration," thus acknowledging their ties to a major Southeast Asian sodality, the Ghee Hin kongsi (Mandarin, Yixing gongsi). By 1876 there were 17,443 members in the Straits Settlements alone.[15] Brotherhood covenant rituals in Shanghai and the Straits derived from those in southern Fujian and eastern Guangdong.[16] They remained unchanged over the course of a century because their organizers maintained the integrity of their texts and practices. Just as Diao Shenghe of Jiayingzhou transmitted these teachings to Guizhou in 1813, others disseminated TDH traditions across the South China Sea. And overseas Chinese periodically returned to reinforce those traditions. Indeed, Chen Qingzhen, the organizer of the Small Swords in Fujian, had arrived from his birthplace in Singapore in the early 1850s to lead the organization in his hometown of Amoy.[17] Sectarian ideology circulated throughout the South China Sea and was kept alive by successive generations of ideologues like Chen, Diao, and Wang Xingshun, cosmopolitan sojourners who traveled back and forth within the boundaries of this enormous maritime frontier. When promoting their agenda in one place grew dangerous, the proselytizers simply retreated elsewhere.

The Rise of Commander Fang Yao

The Wangs of Waisha exemplify the social types targeted in the *qingxiang* campaign: seagoing inhabitants of coastal, walled-villages who had been influenced by sectarian ideas disseminated by translocal sojourners. They had spent years engaged in opium smuggling, piracy, insurrection, tax evasion, and/or crimes related to militant feuding (kidnapping and murder). These were age-old problems, but they had been exacerbated by the socially destabilizing rebellions of midcentury. The succession of uprisings and the government's inability to maintain order inflamed anti-Qing sentiment in the region. Many who participate in rebellions initially do not do so out of fully articulated ideological convictions. Insurrectionary practice transforms political culture, however, as dissatisfied but quiescent peasants experience political mobilization. They march under banners that declare that they are the "loyal and righteous" people who must "overthrow the Qing." In Chaozhou, the doctrines of the ubiquitous brotherhoods were openly articulated and popularized. And the vast majority of people who did not, in fact, rebel experienced an extended moment of monarchical desecration as the dynasty's tenuous hold on power was revealed to all.[18] The Qing may have suppressed the uprisings, but their opponents emerged from the chaos potentially more powerful than before. They could tap into a palpable anti-Qing sentiment that was more pronounced than it had been prior to the 1850s. And the sovereign authority of local troublemakers—pirates, smugglers, heads of feuding lineages—was as unassailable as ever.

Provincial officials were cognizant of this and decided to act. The Manchu governor-general of Guangdong and Guangxi, Ruilin, informed the central government in 1869 that he already had authorized a pacification campaign in Chaozhou. He was motivated by the extraordinary number of criminal cases emanating from insurrections and lineage affrays that had remained unresolved for years. Tax resistance was endemic, and the region was in arrears by at least 200,000 silver taels. Ruilin had devoted years to the suppression of rebellions in the two provinces, and he dreaded the potential of these age-old problems to spark another round of antidynastic violence. He wanted the backlog of cases resolved and the criminal element suppressed in order "to eradicate the sprouts of disorder."[19] That is to say, provincial authorities now understood these problems in a political light, as activities that enhanced the capacity of local power-mongers to organize their followers into armies of rebellion. They resolved to extend governmental writ to the walled villages of eastern Guangdong.

At the onset of the campaign, Fang Yao (1834–1891) was the regional commander of the Army of the Green Standard in Chaozhou. He was not simply a soldier but a scion of the most powerful clan in Puning district. The Fangs claimed to have descended from Fang Tingfan, a prominent official who settled in Putian, Fujian, after the collapse of the Tang dynasty. One of Tingfan's descendants made his way to Puning and founded a new branch of the lineage. The family thrived and established its main ancestral hall in Chaozhou city.

Their familial ties extended across Guangdong and into Southeast Asia.[20] As we shall see, Fang arranged a marriage between his daughter and the son of one of the wealthiest Chaozhouese in the British Straits Settlements. In so doing, the Fangs solidified their position among the powerful, capitalist elite of the South China Sea.

In spite of his pedigree, Fang had acquired little formal education before embarking on a military career. In a communication to the Chaoyang elite, he lamented that he "had grown up in unfortunate circumstances and had never obtained instruction from a village teacher."[21] If his educational attainments were modest, it was not due to financial constraints. Like many powerful lineages in Chaozhou, the Fangs derived much of their income from commercial endeavors. Fang's father, Fang Yuan, had inherited two pawnshops in Puning city (the Yuanyuan and Yuansheng Pawnshops). Other relations also owned pawnshops, indicating that the clan controlled a significant amount of capital in the area. Similarly, sugar was the main commercial crop produced in Chaozhou, and the Fangs were heavily invested in that business. Fang's kinsman, Fang Jiazhi, owned a sugar enterprise in both Swatow (Yi'an tanghong) and in Shanghai (Houan tanghong).[22] Fang hailed from a prominent lineage that had distinguished itself in conventional ways but also had made its mark in the commercial world of the China coast.

He embarked on a military career in 1851, when he helped his father organize a militia of 650 Puning braves to fight the Taipings and other rebels. The younger Fang displayed great aptitude for waging war against insurrectionists throughout the 1850s and 1860s. He came to high official notice in 1856, when Triad rebel forces under Chen Jin'gang laid siege to their militia at Qingyuan. Fang returned to Puning to recruit a thousand more villagers, and then raced back to deliver a smashing defeat to the rebels. Soon after this, he was induced to join the regular military and engaged Taiping and Triad forces in incessant battle in both Fujian and Guangdong. He distinguished himself in the campaigns that annihilated the Taipings in southeastern China from 1864 to 1866. After one such victory in Dabu, the court conferred on him the brevet rank of provincial commander-in-chief.[23]

By 1866 Fang had experienced sixteen years of brutal military struggle against some of the most determined peasant rebels in world history. He also had caught the eye of Ruilin, a Manchu Blue-Border bannerman and a member of the Yehe clan; that is to say, a kinsman of the empress dowager, Cixi.[24] The governor-general had grown impressed with Fang's martial talents and emerged as his major patron in the political world of Guangdong. As the

Taiping threat receded, the continuing disorders in eastern Guangdong and the tax resistance of coastal villages alarmed him.[25] If state-building was the order of the post-Taiping day, the government needed to assert a monopoly on military force and extract greater revenue from commercially dynamic centers like Chaozhou. Ruilin was determined to increase revenues and expel the criminal element, and in Fang Yao he had found the man to do it.

Qingxiang

Ruilin received permission to transfer Fang to the Regional Command of Chaozhou, the home base of the Fang lineage, in 1868. Fang later claimed that the Qing "law of avoidance" preventing officials from serving in their home districts technically had been observed. Throughout the campaign, he officially remained the regional commander of the Nan-Shao-Lian garrison in Shaozhou prefecture and was merely on informal loan to Chaozhou.[26] In 1868 he launched his pacification campaign in the Lufeng area of nearby Huizhou prefecture.

He instantly emerged as a local power-monger himself, the Army of the Green Standard at his disposal, an ambitious lineage at his side, and in possession of a carte blanche from a succession of superiors in Canton. Indeed, such was Ruilin's faith in Fang that he later averred to the Grand Council in 1873 that he had "secretly" given Fang Yao total authority to "strive for thorough results without hesitation until he reached success." This point was affirmed in 1890 by the prefect of Chaozhou, Zeng Jiqu, who claimed that "Commander Fang was granted absolute power over life and death, and he seized and exterminated people . . . for almost 20 years."[27]

Fang declared "strict application of the military mode of adjudication" (*yan shen junlü*), a frontier form of martial law, in February 1869, and the most intense phase of the campaign lasted from December 1869 to 1873.[28] He did not disappoint the authorities in Canton. By 1873 Ruilin and Governor Zhang Zhaodong reported to Beijing on the unqualified success of the enterprise. Thousands of "bandits," "remnants of outlaw gangs," kidnappers, and other criminals had been executed. In the first phase of the campaign, from 1869 to 1871, 288 criminals had been executed in the Chaoyang vicinities of Shalong, Tianxin, Shangdian, Jinpu, and Huayang. Another 234 people were executed in the Jieyang village of Mianhu and its environs; and in Huilai and Puning, 156 men were killed. In the next phase of the campaign, lasting until July 1872, Fang's troops returned to Chaoyang and captured another 272 offenders. By

Fang's own reckoning, the military campaign continued into the mid-1870s and ultimately resulted in the resolution of over a thousand legal cases on backlog; the execution of three thousand "outlaws"; the collection of one million silver taels in tax arrears; and the confiscation of over a thousand weapons, including six hundred cannons.[29] The governor-general and governor deemed the campaign an unqualified success by 1873: "All the captured criminals in each and every case without exception confessed at trial to having plundered, murdered, and kidnapped by force and they were executed on the spot according to law. . . . It was," they wrote, "a moment when impressive military power was displayed and each village upon hearing the news submitted in terror."[30]

Among the executed included Zheng Xitong, the so-called King of Shalong; Zheng Tiaozi, also of Shalong; Wu Atao (of Mianhu); Chen Xieqiao, "the notorious bandit of Chaoyang"; Chen Dumu, the leader of a sworn brotherhood who had slain officials; and Xie Kungang, "the notorious bandit of Chenghai" found guilty of pillage, arson, and murder. Most of those executed were reputed to have participated in the various uprisings of the 1850s; or they had taken property and/or kidnapped, wounded, or murdered others in feuds; or they had engaged in banditry and piracy.[31]

Officials were particularly concerned about the coastal stretch of Chaoyang around Shalong. As far back as the 1720s, a succession of officials had been declaring emphatically that Chaoyang was the most violent district in the empire.[32] This region was a center of opium smuggling and widespread feuding, the most notable of which involved the Zheng lineage. As we have seen, the rise of the Zhengs of Shalong is conventionally ascribed to the success of Zheng Xiangde, a fishmonger who had established a coastal shipping firm in the seventeenth century. His descendants continued to succeed in business and, by the late nineteenth and early twentieth centuries, were commercially powerful in Shanghai, Hong Kong, Siam, and British Malaya.[33] Shalong, simultaneously a township and a village, was situated at the foot of Da'nan Mountain, and the Zhengs benefited from access to its forests as well profits from fishing and salt enterprises. Various Zhengs owned most of the land in this fertile region, and Shalong was considered one of the "richest and wealthiest rural areas of Chaozhou."[34] The translocal business success of the Zhengs naturally enhanced their economic—and therefore their military—power at home.

At the time of the campaign, Shalong was led by Zheng Xitong. Commander Fang was an ardent foe of Xitong and referred to him as "the king of Shalong, a kidnapper and killer who resisted officials."[35] That was the extent of Fang's account of the man he executed without a civilian trial. The Zhengs of Shalong today have their own, folk version of events: Fang Yao established his headquarters in Xiashan ward (a Zheng family redoubt) but "this so-called government office was really established to [collect] and deliver back taxes. Imperial silver was carried off relentlessly until a huge pile filled his halls." The Zhengs continued to resist the payment of what they viewed as an irregular form of tax collection, and Fang sent his troops to "exterminate Shalong." His secretaries advised him that this was a bad idea, for the Shalong Zhengs were renowned for their military prowess.

Like other affluent families in the region, the Zhengs organized a militia to maintain order. The militia's name was "Sunrise over the Shalong Zheng" (Richu Shalong Zheng), and their slogan declared "For thirty *li* in all directions—no rebels!" Their military power enabled them to dominate the other villages in their orbit. This led to the great "Thirteen-Village Feud" of the mid-nineteenth century. The war was launched after a Chaoyang peddler was killed by robbers as he traveled south to Huilai. The Shalong Zhengs used the murder as a pretext to attack Stone Gully village (Shikeng), which they claimed had harbored the robbers. In fact, the Zhengs had long desired to seize the village's stockade. Stone Gully village allied with twelve villages in the neighborhood to resist the Zhengs, and, as expected, the region exploded in violence. Mediators could do nothing to stop it, and officials did not dare to intervene. Eventually the Zhengs triumphed, occupying all thirteen villages and converting hundreds of families into their tenant farmers. "The neighboring villages could not but be terrified of Shalong."[36]

Fang Yao therefore had every reason to target them. They were tax-resisters in a commercialized complex of walled villages who feuded with their weaker neighbors and whose base served as a refuge for any wayward Zheng who ran afoul of the law. Because of this, coastal Chaoyang was subjected to particularly harsh measures during the campaign. Of the 678 men executed in the first two years of the campaign, 288 (over 42 percent) were from Shalong or areas immediately adjacent to it: Tianxin, Shangdian, and Jinpu. The extraordinary violence unleashed on them owed not simply to the fact that the Zhengs had long thrived an alternative power to centralized authority; they also resisted Fang's military forces. Even after his devastating assaults in 1870, they refused to submit, obliging him to redouble his efforts the following year.

He became obsessed with eliminating the "King of Shalong." In the folk version of the demise of the Zhengs, Fang initially cultivated a friendship with Xitong. Indeed, the two men swore brotherhood, and because Xitong was older than he was, Fang recognized him as the Elder Brother. Most of the lineage elders assumed that this was a conventional pacification campaign intended to exterminate rebels and thieves, not locally powerful people like themselves, who were so common on the coast. "The Shalong militia was similar to that of the Fangs of Hongyang [Fang's village]," these men believed, and they were bamboozled by Fang's declaration that "if Shalong and the Fangs of Hongyang joined together, then Chaoyang will be ruled." In this popular retelling, the Zhengs concluded that the campaign simply would solidify a status quo characterized by quasi-militarized, opium-smuggling fiefdoms controlled by commercially powerful landowners like the Zhengs and Fangs. In this imagined scenario, the Zhengs were forging an alliance with another powerful clan.

They were wrong. One day Fang invited the Zhengs to a banquet he hosted at Xiashan to celebrate his mother's sixtieth birthday. He sent eighteen sedan chairs to escort Zheng Xitong, his brothers, and the elders to his headquarters. When seventeen men arrived (one suspicious uncle feigned illness and fled), Fang's troops seized them. He proceeded to enumerate their purported crimes: they had wounded innumerable people in the thirteen-village feud, usurped the land of others, and refused to pay their taxes. He invited them to defend themselves, but their account did not satisfy him. He executed them all on the spot and later destroyed the family gravesites, took possession of all of Xitong's valuables, and shipped them to his family compound in Hongyang.[37] That is to say, having executed the Shalong Zhengs for usurping the property of others, he promptly usurped their property.

There are reasons to believe that the Shalong family lore has historical validity. One missionary who resided in the area between 1880 and 1928, Lida Scott Ashmore, observed in her memoirs that Fang Yao "sometimes . . . would invite leading men to a feast. They dared not refuse. They all knew it was the last food the guests would ever eat. . . . The next day their headless bodies would be lying outside." This reinforces their story, which, indeed, may have been her source of information. It also conforms to Fang's own terse account of how he contended with this powerful family. He arrested Zheng Xitong and his "gang" at his military headquarters in Xiashan, and he executed them.[38]

And what of the Wangs of Waisha further up the coast? Under the leadership of Wang Xingshun, it will be recalled, they had participated in Wu Zhongshu's rebellion of 1854, aligned with the Small Sword Society, and engaged in opium smuggling and piracy. In spite of the thrashing to which they had been subjected in 1855, they continued their buccaneering ways, preying on the lucrative commerce of the ports and upholding a tradition of feuding. Waisha's waterways continued to serve as an important smuggling route, designed to evade the new opium *lijin* tax the provincial government had established to raise revenue during an age of rebellion.[39] As the British began to establish themselves in the treaty port of Swatow after 1858, the Wangs found a new target to harass. They joined an eighteen-village antiforeign league to resist the consular presence, and they succeeded in making the lives of foreigners as miserable as possible. One consul, Chaloner Alabaster, irritably described Waisha as a place where "the Mandarins" had power only on paper, "but real jurisdiction they have none." He also reported that Ruilin had confided that officials had not been able to collect their land tax for over fifty years.[40]

Waisha thus emerged as another campaign target. In July 1869 Fang dispatched troops to summon the village heads to his headquarters and submit peacefully. But, like the denizens of Shalong, the villagers were in no mood to capitulate. One headman was said to have replied airily that it was not convenient for him to respond to the summons, while another "promised an answer in some six or seven years when his [village] supplies would be exhausted."[41] It is unclear whether these villagers were bluffing or they genuinely believed they could withstand a siege by government forces. Fang's annual military assessments commended him for having been a "talented and clever strategist."[42] In this case, the commander bided his time, moving on to Huilai and Jieyang, where he burned defiant villages to the ground and executed hundreds of men. He returned to Waisha as a now-notorious wielder of total violence. Upon his arrival in May 1870 he did not tarry but stormed the hamlet with brutal abandon. Fires burned day and night, and the British consul at the time, William Cooper, grew so curious about the ferocious attack that he proceeded to investigate on a gunboat. As he later reported, Waisha was utterly devastated. Almost a thousand dwellings and temples had been torched, and the few inhabitants who were visible "were in a frightened and subdued state." Significantly, he continued, "Only the houses belonging to the clan Wang have been destroyed, the other 3 clans having at once submitted to authority." The Wangs themselves "fled, . . . preferring witnessing the destruction of their house property to undergoing what they look on as the extortions of the mandarins, in the belief that the present vigorous measures for establishing and preserving order will not be sustained.[43]

The power of Waisha at long last was crushed and the Wangs subdued. Significantly, they chose not submit to Fang's authority and pay the "fines" his troops began to ceaselessly demand. Instead, as Wang Xingshun had done so many years before, they escaped, likely to Shanghai or Southeast Asia, where the vast majority of those who fled the debacle absconded. Unbeknown to them, however, they would not be able to return for a very long time.

Militarization and Legal Procedure

By the time Governor-General Ruilin reported to Beijing in 1873, Fang Yao had accomplished the openly stated goals of the campaign. The refractory villages had been suppressed, the "most notorious bandits and rebels" executed or exiled, and back taxes and "fines" collected. On Ruilin's recommendation, the court conferred on Commander Fang the Yellow Riding Jacket, one of the highest rewards for meritorious service to the dynasty, on October 3, 1873.[44]

One consequence of the campaign was the extraordinary expansion of the power of Fang Yao and his kin. What was supposed to have been a short campaign of rural pacification evolved into the military and economic aggrandizement of a single lineage. The campaign elicited complaints from the very beginning, but the most incisive—and subtly damning—critique of the Fangs' activities after 1869 was written by Zeng Jiqu, the prefect of Chaozhou from 1889 to 1890 and a nephew of the renowned statesman Zeng Guofan. Prefect Zeng was the latest in a long line of officeholders who had been frustrated by the Fangs' usurpation of some of their legal and fiscal prerogatives. Attempts to bring the family to heel—complaining to provincial authorities, informing the central government, beseeching the British to intercede—had come to naught. Zeng took a different approach. He composed a highly nuanced screed, masked as a proclamation distributed to his subordinates, and then turned around and published it in the pages of *Shenbao*—the most influential newspaper in China—on February 10, 1890. As Zeng's critique incorporates many of the criticisms others had articulated over the course of twenty years, it is treated at length here.

At the outset, Zeng dismissed accusations accusing Fang of having abused his authority and personally profited from his campaign, declaring that further complaints against the old soldier himself would be rejected. Zeng thus continued the official tradition of protecting Fang from the political fallout of his violent pacification of eastern Guangdong. By this time, Fang was the commander-in-chief of the Naval Forces of the Green Standard for Guangdong. The second most powerful military official in the province after the governor-general, he had successfully extended his campaign to other parts of

Guangdong and had been defended by virtually every governor and governor-general since the 1870s, including another of Prefect Zeng's illustrious uncles, Zeng Guoquan. In similarly exonerating Fang, Zeng nonetheless used language that can only be read as an implicit critique of this tradition, declaring that Fang Yao had been given "absolute power over life and death and seized and exterminated people for almost twenty years" and had compelled people to pay special exactions that amounted to "several hundred thousands of silver taels." The prefect had no problem with exterminating criminals or collecting revenue, but he believed the process had endured too long and that administrative procedures had been undermined. In the matter of the case backlog Fang ostensibly had resolved, he asked, "What was the name of each criminal executed? Was the case reported to the Board of Punishments? Are those who did not manage to slip past the net of the law still awaiting trial? Where is the money from those exactions actually stored? How was it spent? None of this has been recorded according to law, and no record has been sent to the prefectural or district yamen to be kept for future reference." While acknowledging that his predecessors had determined that all charges against Fang had been proven false, he noted in passing that the militarist had not left an individuated case record that could be assessed by civilian authorities.

Prefect Zeng, however, did not write his proclamation to assail the unassailable Fang Yao. Instead he focused his ire on Fang's self-aggrandizing family, insinuating that while the old man may have been upright, his subordinates and relatives exploited their connection to him to assume extrajudicial power. He fulminated that "the good-for-nothing, low-ranking irregulars (*yong*), as well as the marital connections of the low-life relations of the Fang clan, dare to take advantage of unsettled legal cases at the garrison in order to extort money out of people." The military garrisons had been transformed into alternative law courts, new arenas within which to attack personal enemies.[45]

Prefect Zeng implicitly took Fang Yao to task for failing to control his rapacious family. He charged that "the Fang clan indulged the younger generation of this powerful family in their illegal ways [and] treated the garrison troops as their claws and teeth, resorting to violence and unrestrained rampaging." He identified several instances in which the Fangs exploited their military connections:

The younger generations of the Fang lineage listened to their worthless relations-by-marriage and their friends and used the garrison irregulars like their personal slaves. They supplied themselves through the granaries; they fought over fields; they fought over hills; brawling and fighting with weapons. It would be too difficult to recount [the battles] one by one. . . . Moreover, the troops of the Chaoyang and Puning garrisons used [the campaign] as a screen behind which they could engage in criminal activities, routinely oppress the villagers, and use cottages in which to engage in such lascivious activities as harboring prostitutes and running gambling dens. There is nothing they would not do![46]

The militarization of Chaozhou under Fang was different from the post-Taiping elite mobilization described by Philip Kuhn. The Fangs did not simply control a local militia, they dominated the formal Qing military in Chaozhou. Prefect Zeng's uncle, Zeng Guoquan, had verified back in 1882 that Fang had ensconced his own kin in the officer corps of the Chaozhou Green Standards. Fang's relative Fang Ao had been the brigade vice-commander of Chaozhou since 1870. Another kinsman, Fang Jichun, was the patrol lieutenant of Chaozhou. Fang Chang was a squad commander and Fang Guijun the second squad commander of the Chaoyang garrison; both men also were relations (beyond the five degrees of mourning) of Fang Yao. The Chaoyang gazetteer of 1884 records the unprecedented domination of Puning natives over the local garrison. It was no secret that Fang installed his family and friends in positions of military authority along the coast. Indeed, in responding to various investigations, Fang Yao freely acknowledged that his kin occupied positions of military authority.[47]

Prefect Zeng observed, "Ever since Admiral Fang assumed the seals of office of commander in managing the bandit villages of Chaozhou, every single local, petty military post has been filled by his relatives and relatives of his marital relations. In selecting the relations with whom he was most familiar, his commands could be communicated with great rapidity. It was impossible for them not to oblige him at a moment's notice."[48] That is to say, Fang placed his relatives in local military positions for the same reason Wang Xingshun had installed his own kin as banner chiefs in his rebel brotherhood back in 1854: it was an efficient way to maintain loyalty through the ranks and on up to the commander himself. By the 1880s Fang often was called away to serve in other military capacities, including as a specially commissioned officer to prepare for the Sino-French war. He needed officers personally loyal to him in his frequent absences. However depraved his relatives, they were obedient to his commands.

The prefect nonetheless accused Fang's extended family of having taken over some of the basic functions of government:

They act as though they possess hereditary titles. Even when they officially retire from office . . . these families still rule by force, passing down their positions from generation to generation and, in the end, preside over the routine procedures [of governance], openly accepting the lawsuits of the people. To my disbelief, they preside over court, detaining people and subjecting them to interrogation.[49]

Zeng was disturbed by the Fangs' usurpation of at least some judicial procedures. There was nothing to be done about the thousands of villagers who had been executed as a result of the campaign but, determined to right wrongs, he intended to address the cases of those who may have been victimized by his presumptuous relations. Moreover, "in the matter of those local people who have escaped overseas" because of these judicial shenanigans, he proclaimed, "I have permitted their relatives to compose reports in order to have evidence on which to issue orders about their return."[50]

With that, Prefect Zeng threw down the gauntlet to the military strongman and his conniving kinfolk. Others had complained about all this before, but Zeng was a defender of the prerogatives of civil officials and a stickler for judicial process. Surely the heir to one of the most prominent families in the realm could succeed where others had failed? Apparently not: two months later, he was removed from office and transferred elsewhere. As the British consul wryly noted in an intelligence report to his superiors, "He tried to overawe the powerful Fang family and was worsted in the attempt."[51]

The fact of the matter is that officials in Canton and Beijing were aware of the infamy of the Fang clan at Chaozhou. Chaoyang elites, Fujianese businessmen, local officials, and foreign residents had been reporting on the deleterious effects of the concentration of Fang power for years. In fact, Beijing had been responding to complaints about Fang's family before the qingxiang campaign even had begun, and at least as early as 1863. The Tongzhi emperor in that year issued an edict decrying the wanton murder and plunder of the Chaozhou braves under Fang Yao's command in Gaozhou. The emperor described Fang's younger brother, Fang Xun, as someone who exercised power in "an evil way" and commanded Fang to tell him to cease "this undisciplined harassment of the inhabitants."[52]

An edict issued in the Guangxu emperor's name in 1882 actually condemned some of the very abuses identified by Prefect Zeng. "Brigade Vice-Commander Fang Ao has deceitfully given trouble to rural communities," the emperor intoned, "and the eyes of the big Fangs and the little Fangs are everywhere."[53] He was responding to reports that the Fangs had "mobbed up" and expelled the inhabitants of two Puning villages after years of feuding. Once they were in control of the property, the Fangs changed the name of one of the villages to De'anli village. The emperor ordered an investigation conducted by no less a personage than Governor-General Zeng Guoquan, scourge of the Taipings at Nanjing and, tellingly, the uncle of the scandalized Prefect Zeng Jiqu. Guoquan exonerated Fang Yao of all accusations lodged against him. It is likely that Prefect Zeng was aware of the fact that his uncle shielded Fang Yao from the angry blowback to his pacification campaign, which probably explains why the younger man felt constrained from attacking Fang personally.

Zeng Guoquan, like many provincial officials, believed that Fang's harsh campaign had made him many enemies and rendered him susceptible to false accusations. The charge that his kin had usurped the property of two Puning villages, he determined, was one such unfounded charge. In fact, as he understood it, the land of one of the villages, Forever Peaceful village, had belonged to Fang's kinsman Fang Gaoming. He had fled the chaos of 1854 and simply returned to recover his property after the rebels had been defeated. The other village, Horse Ear Bridge village, was formerly owned by the family of Lin Tao. The Lins had sold the property to Fang Yao, and Zeng insisted that "there is a contract attesting to this" for he had interviewed the relevant officials and local elites. The accusation that Fang's family had usurped the property was untrue. In exonerating Fang, Zeng Guoquan did not countenance the possibility that the Fangs might have bullied their neighbors into selling their village and landed property. Indeed, he dismissed the claim that they had changed the name of the village to De'anli, this in spite of the fact that the village has been known by that name ever since. Today, local historians continue to claim that Fang Yao forcefully drove these villagers away in 1871, razed the village to the ground, and proceeded to build his fabulous estate, eponymously named De'anli.[54] Zeng offered an absolution that local people have withheld for generations.

Zeng reminded the emperor that Commander Fang acted in strict accordance with provincial officials. Fang's kinsmen may have dominated the ranks of the Green Standards, but they ultimately had been appointed by former governor-general Ruilin, who had died in 1874. The campaign was violent because Ruilin had determined that "pacifying" Chaozhou required brutality. Pursuing the backlog of cases through normal legal procedures was impossible because Ruilin had determined that the malefactors could not be brought to court peacefully. Ruilin had decided these things, not Fang Yao.[55] By invoking the name of the Dowager Empress's late kinsman, Zeng Guoquan enabled Ruilin to continue to protect Fang from the grave. Significantly, this memorial was addressed to that very dowager empress, Cixi, who had usurped the throne after 1861. Indeed, the Tongzhi emperor was only thirteen years old when "he" endorsed the campaign in 1869. In fact, imperial sanction of Fang's qingxiang came from the emperor's mother Cixi, who, like the officials who served her, was aware of the many denunciations of the Fang regime at Chaozhou.

Provincial authorities overlooked Fang Yao's defects because he simply was too useful to these beleaguered officials. During his two years as governor-general, Zeng Guoquan had grown alarmed by French aggrandizement in Indochina and almost immediately after exonerating Fang Yao in 1882 dispatched him to Qinzhou in 1883 to defend the border from the Gallic tide. That same year Zeng recommended that Fang be appointed provincial commander-in-chief of Guangdong. He was elevated to leadership over both the land and naval forces of the Green Standards and played a vital role in the modernization of provincial forces and the defense of Guangdong and Fujian during the Sino-French War of 1884–1885.[56] There were years during which provincial officials appeared to need him everywhere at once. In 1884, for example, he was ordered to suppress an uprising of "sectarian bandits" in Huizhou, only to be ordered back to Canton to thwart any possible French attack on the Bogue Forts that safeguarded the provincial capital. Little wonder that the great Self-Strengthener, Zhang Zhidong, wrote of Fang in his annual assessment in 1886: "He has a long-held reputation for being vastly talented. He is skilled in both military and civilian affairs and thus has been entrusted with this heavy responsibility." Another renowned official, Liu Kunyi, had earlier referred to him in 1877 as "a sharp, keen, and capable official . . . and a man of outstanding talent" and, in 1878, as "quite brilliant."[57]

Domestically he maintained the peace in Chaozhou and was busy extending his campaign throughout Guangdong province during the 1880s, "pacifying" bandits or pirates in Huizhou, Guangzhou, Leizhou, Qiongzhou, and on the waters off Hong Kong and Macao. Among his many triumphs, he smashed a transnational pirate "tong," the Lianyitang, in 1889. This gang had been preying on commercial traffic along the sea lanes from Guangdong to Indochina and Singapore for over twenty years.[58] Criminality in the South China Sea was rarely "domestic." Fang Yao participated in an international project of rising states committed to taming the "Wild East" and instituting a regulated commercial order.

Chaozhou was part of that emerging order, and under no circumstances were provincial authorities going to permit this goody-two-shoes of a prefect to welcome home legions of exiled rowdies. As Governor-General Zhang Shusheng acknowledged in his military assessment of Fang in 1881, "Chaozhou has long been a chaotic place and this official has led troops to investigate cases and clear the dockets. In mowing people down, he was tyrannical and although there was no lack of evil deeds and excessively severe punishments, in recent years he has transformed the region from a perilous place to a secure one where theft and violence have diminished."[59] Officials in Canton protected Fang Yao for over twenty years. This was the ultimate source of his power.

Entangled States: Pacification and Opium

Officials appreciated Fang Yao for his martial prowess. His campaign nonetheless had another, unstated objective: seizing governmental control of the lucrative opium trade in order to generate revenue for the provincial treasury. The upheavals of the 1850s inclined several provinces to institute a new levy, the *lijin*, on all commodities, including opium, traded in domestic markets. The lijin on opium was to be distinguished from the import tariff placed on Indian opium after China's defeat in the Second Opium War (1856–1860). The treaty settlement established an import duty of thirty silver taels per picul of opium, which was to be collected on behalf of the central government by the Maritime Customs. The opium lijin, in contrast, was freely devised by Chinese provincial officials to raise revenue and defeat the rebels who threatened the dynasty. It was first imposed in Jiangsu in 1853 and spread to most other provinces by 1860. Thenceforth a "political economy of opium" began to evolve over the course of several decades as the lijin increased and provincial governments became heavily dependent on it.[60] "Opium smuggling" was conceptually and administratively transformed from trafficking in contraband to circumventing the tax regime of the modernizing state.

In 1858 provincial authorities in Canton ordered officials in Chaozhou to commence charging an opium lijin of twenty taels per chest. Local compliance with the new tax in the early years was spotty, and it was more consistently enforced in the treaty port of Swatow than in other harborages.[61] This worked to the advantage of Chinese, who were not restricted to trade at Swatow, as foreigners were. Local merchants nonetheless resisted the creeping expansion of taxation. Inspections were considered intrusive and time-consuming and duties excessive. The Guangdong Provincial Customs had established a "New Chaozhou Customs" on Mayu (Double Island) in 1853 in order to collect revenue along a stretch of coast that had never seen much of a customs presence before. Construction commenced on a new administration building, and when revenuers began to inspect cargo and collect lijin in 1859, a gang stole into the new facility one night and demolished it.[62] When the lijin on all commodities finally was extended inland to the wealthy prefectural city of Chaozhou in 1863, the commercial world exploded in protest. Trade came to a halt as infuriated merchants called a "market strike," and large crowds gathered to protest at the office of the lijin commissioner. Soldiers were summoned, and, after children were trampled in a scuffle, an enraged mob crowded into the building and smashed its interior.[63] The crisis passed, but officials continued to demand an impost that irritated the commercial classes.

The lijin also aggravated local officials. Not only were they forced to contend with angry upheavals, they found it more difficult to demand the traditional sorts of duties—*luodi shui*—that enabled them to pay for their own administrative needs. They benefited neither from the new tariff nor from lijin.[64] Chaloner Alabaster was taken aback by angry comments made by the circuit intendant during a conversation in 1869. The intendant, Zhang Xian, insisted that he, too, reviled the lijin but had no choice but to collect it. Ruilin was known to be "hot upon it" (Alabaster's term) because he believed that the tax would garner a minimum of 240,000 silver taels that year and he was desperate to patch up the provincial deficit. Officials throughout the region understood that lijin benefited the provincial coffers as much as (if not more than) those of Beijing, and the governor-general was right to be "hot" on lijin, for it ended up generating 895,259 taels that year.[65]

Fang Yao was the ultimate enforcer of taxation in Chaozhou, and the pacification campaign was launched in 1869 to coincide with a decision by Ruilin to ramp up collection of the unpopular lijin. The deputy superintendent of customs at Chaozhou had informed the governor-general that the revenues were being "defrauded" and would continue to be so as long as the "turbulent villages on the coast . . . with the protection of the gentry . . . defy the opium lijin."[66] Ruilin decided to embark on a radical change in revenue collection, mandating that all opium imported into Swatow henceforth be taxed at forty taels: thirty taels to the Maritime Customs and ten in provincial lijin. Chinese merchants henceforth were obligated to pay the same levels of import duty and lijin in the traditional ports as was required at the treaty port of Swatow.[67] Knowing that this imposition on the centuries-long opium trade also would be resisted, Canton dispatched several steamships and augmented Fang's troop numbers to ensure that it was collected under threat of military coercion. Alabaster reported that "the [new] fleet, nominally created to check piracy was really solely in being as a means of levying [lijin]."[68] The equalization of the rate paid by foreign and Chinese importers at all ports normally would have incited the usual commercial uproar, but Fang by then had unleashed his campaign against the "lawless" element, torching villages and beheading resisters, and, as we have seen, "each village upon hearing the news submitted [to him] in terror." The major targets of Fang's pacification campaign included some of the leading opium-smuggling centers of Chaozhou, including Waisha and the Haimen and Shalong stretches of the Chaoyang coast.[69] His campaign suppressed them. Fang Yao tamed the coastal villages, ensured the collection of unpaid taxes, and enforced commercial compliance with the lijin on all commodities.

It proved a spectacular success. Throughout the 1870s Chaozhou's treaty port of Swatow achieved supremacy as a center of opium importation and revenue collection. Officials in Canton guaranteed that the rate of lijin on the drug was always far lower than that reigning at neighboring treaty ports. Whenever Fujian increased the tax at Amoy, Guangdong reduced it at Swatow so as to maximize provincial revenues derived from the trade. In spite of its tiny size (its population was 40,216 compared to Canton's 1,600,000), Swatow emerged as the fifth largest generator of treaty-port revenue in China by 1878. Over 45 percent of its total revenue was derived from duties on opium (see appendix).[70]

In Guangdong, opium importation, state-building, and military defense were interconnected manifestations of the power wielded by Fang Yao. His campaign facilitated the incorporation of Chaozhou into the global "political economy of opium." The region was becoming entangled in a European state-building dynamic in colonial Southeast Asia that involved substantial taxation of opium. In Chaozhou itself, this revenue-collecting regime was effected through military violence.

General Self-Strengthening

Fang Yao was Canton's man in Chaozhou. He did not simply keep the peace and ensure the flow of revenue into provincial coffers. He also promoted the Self-Strengthening policies of the day that fostered economic and military development and ideological uplift. Observers of China today will note the similarity to the post-Mao political project, which is fixated on economic growth and a social stability that ultimately is guaranteed by armed force. Indeed, Chinese historical treatment of Fang has evolved over the years from Maoist tirades over the financial aggrandizement of the "local bullies" to contemporary acclaim for a loyal official who fostered domestic tranquility and the strengthening of the nation.[71]

One of his more important enterprises was an ambitious land reclamation and water control project along the Ox-Field Sea, an immense inland bay along the northern border of Chaoyang. The Rong River deposited sediment into this body of water and peasants reclaimed land from mudflats. The local government had been promoting hydraulic improvements there since 1563, but the scale and complexity of Fang's effort starting in 1871 were unprecedented. He imposed a labor tax in the Chaoyang wards of Zhupu and Zhipu, requiring young men to devote 120 workdays to the project. They unhappily constructed sluice gates, irrigation channels, and a canal that ran from the Jieyang border southward to Santian harbor. Between this canal and the bay, they elevated a twenty-kilometer-long embankment. Thousands of *mu* of reclaimed land were added to the tax registers, generating an additional thirty thousand shi (approx. 5.5 million pounds) of grain tax.[72]

Fang pursued other infrastructural projects. He dredged the three major rivers in Chaozhou, which enhanced flood control and improved transport between the economically vital inland areas and the sea. He built or rebuilt aqueducts, dykes, embankments, and bridges and commenced reconstruction of city walls, which had fallen into disrepair after decades of internecine strife. He also erected a new fort in Swatow to protect the harbor from pirates and foreign invaders.[73] These efforts facilitated economic revival and military defense.

They also were astronomically expensive. To pay for them, Fang instituted several irregular fee-collecting systems and called for "voluntary contributions" from landowners and merchants. Aside from his own family, Fang relied heavily on his closest collaborator among the local elite, Guo Tingji (1812–1880), of Guolong village in the Anbu port region of Haiyang. The Guos had long been socially prominent, and by the nineteenth century their financial standing was buttressed by the phenomenal commercial success of overseas kinfolk in the Straits Settlements. Back in 1854, Guo had raised a militia to help suppress the rebellion of Wu Zhongshu.[74] A classic "gentry manager" (*shendong*), he solicited funds as well as supervised many of the construction projects promoted by Fang Yao (and his kinsman, Vice-Commander Fang Ao).

The Guos cooperated with the Fangs in collecting rents on both the northern and southern shores of the Ox-Field Sea reclamation project.[75] Fang Yao forged close ties to the Haiyang landed and commercial elite. The prefectural city of Chaozhou was located there, and the district was the center of political and literati order. Not surprisingly, it was also the beneficiary of many of these infrastructural improvement projects, from flood control and bridges to temples and schools.[76]

Not everyone was enamored of Fang's projects. He wrung enormous exactions out of the local population, and many claimed that he enriched himself at the public expense. In his 1882 investigation, Governor-General Zeng Guo-quan determined that at least one type of exaction, which he called a "multifarious surcharge" (*huahong mingse*), in fact was controlled not by Fang but by the local gentry. They had founded a "Public Bureau" into which they paid willingly in order to continue to fund "bandit" suppression. In Zeng's view, "the families of former bandits refused to pay into it" and reviled it constantly. But Zeng had seen the registers himself: 310,000 silver taels had been contributed; 90,000 had been expended "for the public good"; and 220,000 taels remained. The gentry reassured him about this, he claimed, and "their word was reliable."[77]

How reliable is open to question. Zeng did not identify his gentry sources, but they undoubtedly included the Guos, Fang's partners in promoting the projects. Zeng did not take into consideration that Fang's military power may have made it difficult to do anything but "volunteer" to contribute to the cause. Moreover, Zeng might have seen one set of registers, but there were many development schemes in the works and his predecessor as governor-general, Ruilin, had received imperial permission in 1874 to dispense with formulating "detailed returns of receipts and expenditures" on the grounds that "the funds were raised by voluntary assessment."[78] Fang Yao, in fact, experienced little oversight as he forged ahead on the infrastructural transformation of Chaozhou.

These projects reflected the complementary interests of Canton and the Fangs. Prior to 1949, for example, the reclaimed land along Ox-Field Sea was referred to locally as the "Big Man's land" (*Daren tian*), a reference to Fang's nickname at home and overseas. Fang Yao, Fang Ao, and their gentry colleagues turned parcels of these fields into the sorts of rice-fish farms that were common in southern China and Southeast Asia. Fang collected rents and remitted taxes on these plots to Canton.[79] According to local lore, however, the Fangs otherwise acted as though they owned the property. Fang Yao established a bureau in 1879 to collect rents from the tenants who worked the farms. Although he originally named this bureau the "Hall of Extended Harmony" (Zhihe tang), locals referred to it as the Fangcuo Bureau, or the Bureau of the Fang Mausoleum (*cuo* was commonly used to identify lineage property). Fang installed his kin—initially Fang Jibin, popularly known as Big Daddy Fang Si, and later Fang Sifu—to oversee the collection of rental grain harvested from the paddies. Eventually Fang Sifu transformed the "Hall of Extended Harmony" into a shrimp-processing facility and made a profitable living in the seafood business.[80] Rents, taxes, and public funding were derived from the paddies tilled by tenants, and the tenants presumably benefited from access to reclaimed land. Fang's kin, however, apparently believed the property to be a site on which they could freely build and earn profits in other industries.

Local lore contends that locals opposed this project. Peasants had freely fish-farmed off the shoals that naturally formed in the area for years. The residents of Huayang village, who suffered grievous losses in the qingxiang campaign, were said to have resisted—not the campaign itself but Fang's effort to enclose the land and transform it into a property dominated by elites, the military, and the state.[81] Zeng Guoquan mentioned none of this when he exonerated Fang of charges of usurpation and self-enrichment. Canton created a documentary "reality" that recognized the claims of those who now controlled the territory, but such niceties never extinguished the burning resentments of those who believed they had been wronged and passed their indignation on to future generations.

Fang's insinuation into the economic affairs of Chaozhou extended translocally. In 1871 he took the initiative in establishing in Canton the Chaozhou Native Place Association of the Eight Districts (Guangzhou Chaozhou bayi huiguan). He did not merely solicit contributions from Chaozhou merchants in Canton and Hong Kong to construct the association's building, he directed all who traded in Chaozhou commodities in Canton port to tithe one yuan for every thousand yuan worth of goods they carried. By 1876 he had raised 50,271 silver taels from merchants based in Hong Kong, Foshan, Swatow, and Canton itself. Chaozhouese whose firms were headquartered in Hong Kong paid the preponderance of the contributions, 32,660 silver taels; they also were obliged to "lend" the native place association a further 10,900 taels.[82] Many Chaozhouese merchants had flocked to nearby Hong Kong, and by the 1870s the colony had emerged as the commercial nexus of both Canton and Swatow. The largest Hong Kong–based contributors to this association included the firms Yuanfa hang (Yuen Fat Hong), Qiantailong hang (Kin Tye Lung), and twenty-five other so-called North-South firms (*Nanbei hang*), firms engaged in the international import-export trade between Southeast Asia and China. Yuanfa and Qiantailong had emerged as major Chaozhou-owned rice-trading firms headquartered in Hong Kong, and most of the others probably participated in the rice business, for Chaozhouese were important players in that trade across the Nanyang. Although much of the rice exported from Bangkok, Singapore, and Saigon was initially carried to warehouses in Hong Kong, the consuming markets were in China (Hong Kong and Singapore being major centers of the entrepot trade of the South China Sea). Fang now tapped into the trade of the two biggest rice-importing ports in Guangdong: Canton and Swatow. Although merchants normally organized native place associations on their own, he played the galvanizing role in the formalization of this institution at a time when Chaozhou translocal trade was expanding.[83]

In all his endeavors, Fang Yao represented himself as a great civilizer, designated by the imperial court to bring peace and orthodoxy to a benighted region. In cooperation with local elites, he raised funds to build (or rebuild) four charitable estate schools in Haiyang and five new schools in Chaoyang in 1873 alone. He also raised funds to establish academies throughout Chaoyang, encouraging "locally wealthy families" to offer scholarships so that more locals might pass the civil service examinations. He encouraged the construction of shrines to the worthy forebears of Chaozhou so that people might be inspired to act in ideologically appropriate ways. One shrine, the Manifest Loyalty Shrine (Biaozhongci), was erected to serve as a site where sacrifices might be made to the many troops who had fallen during pacification campaigns from the 1840s to 1870s. The funding for these efforts derived from elite subscriptions and the proceeds from reclaimed lands. Fang Yao had a hand in virtually every project.[84]

Fang was a military idealist. He celebrated the resolve of soldiers guided by the classical tradition. In his view, one could not preserve the moral order without social stability, and the military ultimately guaranteed both. He knew that Chaoyang residents and civilian officials pilloried him for the sheer brutality of the campaign in its early years, but he in turn disdained an ineffectual officialdom. Looking back on his accomplishments in response to one investigation into his behavior in the 1880s, he recalled the "legacy of troubles" bequeathed from one generation to another in Chaozhou:

I personally encountered the bandit-rebels in Chaozhou villages. . . . Merchants could not transport their goods and lawsuits amassed. . . . Local officials were neglectful, calamities deepened, and tyrannical domination and resistance to arrest became routine even as taxes went unpaid. Disputes were never resolved. *And at that time, there wasn't even one or two determined scholars who might energetically have taken responsibility for the region....* I am a man of Chaozhou, and I know its pros and cons. So I . . . assumed the heavy responsibility of empowering the good folk and pacifying the violent ones. Those famous for their murderous evil and who killed without shame were all included in the backlog of cases and they resisted us and did not respect our orders, [so] their cases were decided at the garrisons. Each had resisted paying their taxes, and it was in the garrisons that we devised a way to collect taxes *that the local officials all along should have been collecting themselves.*[85]

He itemized the notorious criminals he had suppressed and then, in a dismissive condemnation of officialdom, practically bellowed, "*In each and every case the civil officials could do nothing and they dared to do nothing!*" It was these ineffectual bureaucrats who handed this mess to the military to resolve. "The order to expel [the riff-raff] was the order of the civil officials, it was not an order presumptuously assumed by the military." And the military did its job. In recent years, the region has experienced "happiness year after year" and the "sound of the savage man has been eliminated.... The culture of feuding has diminished, sufficient taxes are collected, and commercial duties have doubled."[86] The military stepped in when civil authorities failed to ensure the public good.

Chaoyang elites condemned his imposition of militarized rule, but Fang was having none of it. In one message sent to those elites circa 1871 (and republished in the district gazetteer in 1884), Fang acknowledged the disparaging remarks made about him. "Those who offer such critiques say that assuming office should be reserved for the worthy; taking charge of public affairs should be reserved for men of talent. Ever since ancient times, these sorts of men have emerged from their thatched cottages in the countryside and governed this prefecture." Such criticisms, he asserted, did not take into account the fact that civilian governance had declined in Chaozhou. "Those who received posts in the past had been worthies who upheld the law, uprooted the wicked, and [facilitated] the planting of crops. That was the great fortune of the Chaozhouese. But their descendants were not so fortunate."[87] In his view, civilians no longer governed effectively, and his harsh measures were entirely justified by their results.

Fang believed that he was the most recent in a long line of strong, decisive men who had accomplished the impossible across the years of Chinese history. History proved that the suppression of the refractory element was the precondition of a thriving moral order. "Zichan of the state of Zheng relied on violence," he observed, "and thereby made possible benevolent rule." So it must be with Chaozhou. "To use the proper mixture of severity and gentleness is the beginning of governance. . . . I am not a clever man, and how to find the appropriate mix I would not dare to say. . . . I only ask that the gentry disregard my deficiencies . . . and examine into the absence of alternatives [to the course I have pursued]."[88]

Chaoyang elites never did forgive him and perhaps were repelled by his presumptuous identification with the revered sixth-century BCE minister Zichan, whom Confucius depicted as the embodiment of the benevolent official. Nevertheless, Fang surely was thinking of the way Zichan had been described by the Legalist Han Feizi (281–233 BCE) in a familiar tirade against scholarly naiveté:

> The people think their superiors are just being violent. . . . Yu's efforts benefited the entire world and Zichan's efforts preserved the state of Zheng, but both men became the objects of slander. Clearly the wisdom of the people is not good enough to be of any use. Thus to look for worthiness and wisdom when promoting officers, to expect to please the people when governing them—these policies are the sprouts of disorder.[89]

Like the great ministers of classical antiquity, Fang Yao was willing to suffer the slanders of his day, so confident was he that his policies would stand the test of time. How could they not? Feuds, piracy, and rebellions had been suppressed. Rivers were dredged and land reclaimed. Agricultural production soared. Schools and academies were constructed. Domestic and international trade was expanding, and sojourners no longer fretted about the security of their property back home. Surely, in future times, Chaozhouese would look to the prosperity of their age and acknowledge that they owed it all to "Big Man" Fang?

PART II

Winning the Opium Peace

MARITIME CHAOZHOU FROM SHANGHAI TO SIAM, 1858–1929

In pursuing the policy of executing incorrigible criminals without amnesty in the seven districts of Haiyang, Chaoyang, Jieyang, Huilai, Chenghai, Raoping, and Puning, I eradicated the cultural practice of militant feuding. Now those who travel to faraway lands can do so without anxiety about their property [back home], and peasants enjoy the happiness of dwelling in undisturbed security.

—FANG YAO, 1871

PART II

Winning the Opium Peace

MARITIME CHAOZHOU FROM
SHANGHAI TO SIAM,
1858–1929

5

Qingxiang

THE TRANSLOCAL AND TRANSTEMPORAL REPERCUSSIONS OF VILLAGE PACIFICATION, 1869–1975

Man from Chaozhou / Time itself is growing old / The sky above is ash, the road ahead is long / Even the mountains are weary / Even the clouds are weary / There's homesickness in your eyes, in your tears. / Why don't you go home, man from Chaozhou?

—HOU DEJIAN, "CHAOZHOU MAN," 1983

IN TERMS OF THE TRANSLOCAL HISTORY of Chaozhou, the most immediate effect of the qingxiang campaign was a dramatic spike in emigration after 1869. Fang Yao and his forces did not merely execute inhabitants of feuding and rebellious villages. A further goal of the campaign was to force the unruly element to flee into exile.[1] Most of these refugees, possibly as many as eighty thousand, ended up in Southeast Asia and Shanghai. Naturally, the sudden arrival of thousands of men fleeing a campaign against rebels, pirates, smugglers, and swashbuckling braves had significant repercussions. Fang's pacification campaign thus constituted an important event in the entangled history of the South China Sea. In most of these other locations, locals felt its reverberations without being particularly aware of the event back in China. British authorities in the Straits Settlements were puzzled by an upsurge in criminality in the colony after 1869. After a riot exploded in Singapore in 1872, Chinese merchants explained to investigators that the colony had been filling with thousands of desperados whose expulsion from Chaozhou was having a deleterious impact on the social order. Only then did it become clear to colonial administrators that the Straits Settlements had become enmeshed in a violent process unwinding in distant China.

This was a historical event that accelerated ongoing transformations across maritime Chaozhou. Its impact also was experienced deep into the twentieth century and shaped the contours of rural revolution at home and abroad. The campaign was a temporally and spatially boundless event. This chapter will more attentively utilize multiscopic analysis to explore its translocal and trans-temporal impact. Transtemporalism has been proposed as one method in the study of intellectual history, a way to acknowledge the "specificity of historical contexts" even as one stresses "linkages" and comparisons across longer stretches of time.[2] Exploring the long-term repercussions of the pacification campaign enables us to apply the concept of transtemporalism to social history. To understand its peculiar impact requires temporal audacity. Part 2 of this study proceeds chronologically across the late nineteenth and early twentieth centuries. In this chapter a historical event is isolated to explore how it lived on in the social history of translocal Chaozhou. This will involve a series of spatial and temporal leaps from a massive out-migration from Chaozhou to an explosion of criminality on the Malay Peninsula in the 1870s back to the early communist revolutionary movement in 1920s China and onto the Cambodian "killing fields" of the 1970s. These later events evolved in more complicated historical contexts, of course. Tracing a single thread in a larger fabric of human experience nonetheless enables us to perceive the angry resentments that bound three generations together and illuminates the ways a rock song about ethnic Chinese refugees in Thailand in 1983 itself might be the product of a long-forgotten campaign of violence a century earlier.[3]

Normalization of a Sojourning Tradition

Chaozhouese had been sojourning to Shanghai and Southeast Asia long before the campaign. Like Taksin's epochal triumph over the Burmese in Siam in 1767, however, Fang's qingxiang demonstrates how a specific historical event affected broader trends in migration. Periodic suppressions of piracy and uprisings had always sent waves of refugees overseas.[4] The exodus after 1869 nevertheless was qualitatively different from earlier episodes. It is difficult to state with statistical precision how many fled into exile. The Maritime Customs did not begin to routinely record the numbers of passengers departing the port of Swatow until 1869, making it difficult to assess how the initial launch of the

TABLE 5.1. Departures from Swatow, 1869–1897

Year	Passengers departing Swatow	Year	Passengers departing Swatow
1869	20,824	1884	62,551
1870	22,282	1885	59,630
1871	21,142	1886	88,330
1872	37,013	1887	68,940
1873	24,284	1888	65,421
1874	23,046	1889	71,429
1875	30,668	1890	65,427
1876	37,635	1891	59,490
1877	34,188	1892	59,247
1878	37,963	1893	89,700
1879	36,336	1894	75,068
1880	38,005	1895	85,157
1881	30,690	1896	88,047
1882	67,652	1897	67,180
1883	73,357		

Source: CSDQ, 7–8.

campaign affected overall emigration rates. The data collected during the campaign itself are revealing. The year 1872 represented the high tide of Fang's crusade in Chaoyang and Chenghai, when those who had managed to resist the inevitable for a time were finally crushed by the sheer force of military power inflicted on them. Contemporary witnesses confirm that the dramatic increase in emigration from 1871 to 1872 was a result of coastal residents fleeing for their lives. The British consul noted in 1871 that these villagers had begun to emigrate in increasing numbers in 1870 and that many of them were "banditti who . . . feared that had they stayed they might have to answer for their crimes." So pressing was the crush of new emigrants, he continued, that British shippers engaged in the passenger trade found that, for the first time in a decade, they lacked an adequate number of vessels to transport all the desperados trying to escape overseas.[5] As we see in the Customs data, there was a 75 percent increase in passenger departures in 1872 (see table 5.1).

That increase represented only a small percentage of exiles, for Customs statistics included merely the numbers departing on foreign steamers. The vast majority of fugitives escaped on Chinese junks anchored in smaller ports. One suspects that Fang timed the commencement of the campaign (December 1869) to coincide with the shift in the trade winds (the Northeast

Monsoon lasts from October to April), for there were plenty of sailing craft plying the waters of South China in 1869, and travel on those vessels was a more familiar (and affordable) proposition for novice sojourners. It is impossible to cite the number of refugees decamping on junks, but the British paid close attention to the passenger trade, not only because it was a remunerative source of business for British shipping but also because the economic livelihood of their colonies in Hong Kong and the Straits depended on the migration of Chinese. British sources serve as a panoptic eye on human movement across the oceans. One British consul who closely monitored Chinese emigration, Christopher Thomas Gardner, estimated that eighty thousand Chinese had fled Fang's campaign by 1872. A large number of these exiles absconded to Singapore, a settlement off the tip of the Malay Peninsula.[6]

Foreign observers believed that the campaign not only swelled the numbers emigrating abroad, it also led to a change in the geographical and ethnic origins of the typical migrant. As the Maritime Customs reported in 1870, "The districts of [Chenghai] and [Chaoyang], which extend along the coast, [usually] furnish but a small number of emigrants. Boat traffic and the fisheries afford them a sufficient maintenance, and it is calculated that seven-tenths of the population of these maritime districts support themselves by these means." Instead, most emigrants hailed from the Hakka and half-mountain Hakka regions of Chaozhou. "These districts are thickly populated, and the country being poor and mountainous, there are more laborers than can find employment in tillage."[7]

The Maritime Customs was established in Swatow only in 1858, when the town emerged as a treaty port. British expatriates, who staffed the reporting levels, misunderstood the numbers of Hakka fleeing the anti-Taiping counterinsurgency campaigns from that year to 1866 as the "norm" in emigration. In fact, they inadvertently revealed the way military forces shifted their pacification efforts from Hakka to coastal Hoklos in 1869. Fang's campaign nonetheless did inaugurate sustained migration of Hoklos from Chaoyang, for emigration overseas only became routine after 1869. Local people remember the era of Fang's ascendancy as a time when Chaoyang people began to depart for Southeast Asia in significant numbers. Even the Zhengs of Shalong, long involved in the coastal trade, recall the campaign as a moment of accelerated emigration, primarily to Siam, of their kinfolk.[8] The campaign therefore caused some shift in the regional make-up of the typical emigrant in the 1870s.

The Maritime Customs data reveal a gradual increase in the numbers departing the treaty port over the decades. They also reflect the ways specific, though less dramatic, events caused spikes in emigration that contributed to the normalization of emigration. These statistics reflected an increasing willingness to embark on foreign steamers, for routine departures basically tripled over two decades. Table 5.1 charts episodic spikes in the numbers of departures, notably in 1872 (the 75 percent increase as a result of intensified campaigning); 1882 to 1883 (increases of 120 and 137 percent, respectively), 1886 (a 48 percent increase); and 1893 (a 51 percent increase that was more or less sustained through 1896). Most of these accelerations were caused by natural disasters. In the summer of 1882 torrential rainfall led to widespread flooding and significant loss of life. In the fall of 1885 the region again suffered severe flooding that led to the collapse of embankments. The period from 1892 to 1896 witnessed disasters of biblical proportions: flooding during the summer of 1892; a huge (and unusual) winter snowfall and subsequent snow melt that overwhelmed mountain reservoirs; an earthquake and flash floods in the summer of 1894; another earthquake in 1895; and, not surprisingly, a plague of banditry by 1896.[9]

In other words, even as emigration became more common, specific events stand out as having induced people to sail over the horizon to find a better life. Overseas opportunities had long beckoned, but it was these events, at these moments, that compelled them to make the decision to leave. In 1897, to cite another example, two Chaoyang villages—the Chens of Yangfenchen and the Lins of Yangfenlin—waged an enormous feud over water resources that lasted nine years. The lineages collectively lost over 150 relatives to the bloodshed. The battles induced about 100 Chens and Lins to flee "to the lands of the South China Sea."[10] This was an ephemeral event in the history of Chinese emigration to Southeast Asia, but for those who fled, it was a catastrophe that changed their lives forever. They did not flee the generic "disorders" of the southeast coast; they fled the violence of their feud.

The long-term challenges of life in Chaozhou, including demographic pressures and poverty, do not explain why individuals decided to seek their fortunes in a distant land at any given moment. Specific events, small and large, compelled them to make these life-altering journeys. Fang Yao's campaign was the primary catalyst to the dramatic increase in emigration out of Chaozhou from 1869 to 1873. Most of the individuals who escaped were unable to return to their homes as long as he was alive. Subsequent events similarly contributed to spikes in emigration out of the region over the course of sixty years. These accelerations usually diminished in a year or two, but they contributed to long-term, inexorable increases in Chinese migration to Southeast Asia. As the years passed, and even the most humble of émigrés sent remittances home, the financial logic of sojourning appealed to an ever-increasing number of villagers. This contributed to the normalization of overseas migration in rural areas.

The Cultural Anxieties of Male Abandonment

The abrupt escalation of emigration had profound effects on Chaozhou. One repercussion of both the accelerated and long-term, predominantly male exodus from the coast was the distorted gender ratios of many coastal villages as the number of female residents began to exceed that of males. Statistical data is reliable only for the 1930s and will be discussed in chapter 8. Suffice it to say here that a target of pacification like the village-market complex of Shalong was majority female by the twentieth century.[11]

The precipitous expulsion of tens of thousands of men was devastating to women who were left behind. Many of these women became responsible for abandoned children and elderly in-laws and worried that they would never see their spouses again. Adele Fielde, a missionary stationed in Swatow, recorded the lamentations of one such woman:

> My husband was an upright and affectionate man. . . . We had 3 children, and my husband was fond of them, good to me, and very filial to his old mother.
>
> 10 years ago, when I was 25, General Fang subdued the clans, burned the houses of those who would not desist from feuds, and severely punished many as a warning to the rest. As my husband had been engaged in supplying the combatants with powder and shot, and as his neighbors chose to put him forward to receive the punishment that must be dealt out to someone in our village [i.e. substitution], and as he had not money with which to pay a fine, he fled to Singapore, whereupon General Fang banished him for 12 years. When he went, he was greatly grieved at parting with the children, and knelt down and did obeisance to his mother. My youngest child was 10-months-old when he went. He has been gone for 9 years. I wish he could secretly come and see me and the children, and then go back undiscovered by his enemies. Some who were banished and who returned too soon have been caught and beheaded, [however].[12]

While the woman painted a glowing picture of moral rectitude on the part of her husband, the account of conjugal affection was sincere and she obviously suffered in his absence: "I pray every day that he may live to come back," she said. In the end, what kept her from committing suicide, as did one of her unhappy sisters-in-law, was her conversion to Christianity and the prospect of having "a heaven to go to."[13] Her children, however, grew up without ever seeing their father, and they knew exactly who the villains in their family drama were: the Fangs.

In the wake of the campaign, popular hysteria was inflamed in 1871 by rumors that women—especially those under the influence of foreign missionaries—were poisoning food and well water with the "powder of the immortals." The rumor initially arose in the British colony of Hong Kong, the first stop for many fleeing Fang's campaign. It quickly spread via placards to Chaozhou communities in Canton and eventually back to Chaozhou. One such placard posted in Jieyang claimed that these women advised people "to mix the powder into their dumplings and, after paying adoration to the Spirits and Heaven and Earth, the entire household was to eat them together. The powder was said to dispel disease and ensure eternal youth." Once eaten, however, people's stomachs swelled "like drums" and they died. As a consequence of these rumors, people began attacking vendors of food as well as Chinese Christians, the ostensible source of the problem.[14]

Food panics were nothing new. Indeed, there was a long history of accusing others of poisoning wells in the context of feuding in Chaozhou.[15] This instance, however, clearly reflected male anxiety about the vulnerability of women left behind in a social whirl of roaming males, missionaries, and unpredictable violence. The dockyards of Swatow were teeming with men. Republican-era censuses recorded 15,311 males and only 10 females there.[16] This reflected the port culture of the city, peopled as it was by long lines of stevedores loading and unloading ships and "Swatow sailors" who served as hands on sailing vessels. The last view departing males had of their homeland was of those bustling wharves, with their armies of single, laboring men, the infamous "rootless rascals" of late imperial times. The numbers of these itinerant laborers had increased with the commercialization of the coastal economy, and the settled population deemed them a sexual threat to the familial order. Concern for the women left behind surely preoccupied departing men and was reflected in the rumor mill of the Chaozhou frontier.

The sojourning sons of Chaozhou's emigrant communities sent remittances home and alleviated the financial concerns of their families, but anxieties about these absent males never dissipated. Whether the menfolk had escaped the wrath of Fang or simply departed to seek opportunities, those left behind felt their absence. Many migrants never managed to return—or returned only after an extended period of time, leading to a palpable sense of loss and despair which the magistrate of Chaoyang identified as an important feature of "Chaoyang culture." He noted, "[Men] go abroad and after many years never return. Their families pray to the spirits and promise to be virtuous. They invite sorcerers to inquire into [their situations] . . . all to no avail."[17]

Finally, people in Chaozhou were cognizant of the abuses suffered by coolies who went overseas. Many migrants were poor, agricultural laborers who could not afford the cost of overseas passage. Some who departed for the Straits sailed as "credit ticket passengers," travelers who relied on "coolie brokers" to pay for their tickets with the understanding that they would work off the price of their passage for six months. This normally was not a problem as long as the broker arranged employment with agents of the gambier and pepper plantations or other industries controlled by Chaozhouese. Credit ticket passengers nevertheless were more likely to be the victims of abuses overseas for, if employment could not be immediately secured for them, underworld characters who controlled the trade locked them up in stiflingly hot buildings or ships until jobs were found. It was not unusual for these laborers to be shipped against their will to other places, including the dreaded Deli on Sumatra. This was a particular fate of emigrants from Chaozhou, for passengers from Amoy and Hong Kong always paid their own way after 1852. Horrible stories about the unlucky fate of many sons of Chaozhou circulated on the home front, exacerbating the disquietude of the region.[18]

Translocal Repercussions

Like other events in Chaozhou's history, the significance of the qingxiang can only be fully appreciated in its larger, translocal context. Fang Yao's rural pacification was an important episode in the history of the South China Sea, and one most clearly sees this in the British Straits Settlements. For one thing, the dramatic increase in emigration to Singapore generated an equally dramatic increase in the price of steerage passage on steamers to that distant port. In November 1871 a ticket cost $4.50 per person. By October 1874 that price had nearly doubled to $8.00 per person, and by October 1875 the price had increased to a range of $8.00 to $10.00.[19] There may have been other factors involved, but the laws of supply and demand surely enabled owners of passenger lines to take advantage of the market for steerage passage to Singapore.

The laws of supply and demand operated in other ways. The sudden arrival of thousands of men fleeing a campaign in Chaozhou had an immediate impact on Chaozhou-dominated sectors of the Straits economy. Most notably, it affected the wages of agricultural labor in gambier production. The leaves of the gambier plant can be processed into an extract with a variety of industrial uses. By the early nineteenth century its production on plantations in the Straits was almost completely controlled by Chaozhouese merchants, and migrant laborers from that region preferred to work for employers from their native place.[20] Prior to the campaign, a new hire in the Singapore labor market was offered approximately $6.00 per month to pick gambier; by the spring of 1871 wages for work on gambier plantations had plummeted 33 percent to $4.00/month.[21] A dramatic increase in the supply of labor resulted in a decline in wages offered in this sector of the Chaozhouese translocal economy.

Another ramification of the mass exodus out of Chaozhou was a surge in criminality in Singapore and Penang after 1869, and the burgeoning levels of crime induced the British to reform their policing system and continue to formalize colonial governance. Reliable statistics relating to crime rates in the Straits began to be recorded only after 1870, so there is no chart to which one can point in order to demonstrate a rise in lawlessness. One nevertheless can find numerical evidence for this upsurge by closely inspecting the colonial budgets, specifically the data for "projected" and "actual" expenditures for 1869 through 1872. There were large discrepancies between the *budgeted* amounts for the police and jails for 1871 and 1872 and what was *actually* spent. In particular, expenses for food rations and clothing for prisoners and apprehended suspects were much higher than had been anticipated. For example, the figure projected in 1870 to be spent on jails in 1871 had been $16,000; the actual expenditures were $20,460, a 21.7 percent discrepancy. This was the largest discrepancy in the entire budget and one that had not been encountered in previous budgets. A memo explaining the gap was attached to these figures in the 1872 budget: "Rations for Prisoners at House of Correction proved to be underestimated in 1871 *owing to an increase in Police prisoners which had been accidentally omitted from supplementary estimates in 1871, so added here.*"[22] The miscalculation resulted from an increase in the costs associated with feeding an unexpectedly large number of inmates.

By 1871, when colonial authorities computed the "estimated budgets" for the administration of the police, prisons, and convict departments for 1872, they began to plan for much higher expenses than they had been forecasting prior to 1870. In 1870 they had predicted that the budget for "rations for prisoners" in the Houses of Correction in Singapore in 1871 would be $7,000. The actual expense for rations in 1871 turned out to be $10,000, or an unexpected increase of almost 43 percent in the consumption of food. When the authorities in 1871 computed the "estimated expenses" for rations in the Singapore Houses of Correction in the 1872 budget, they increased the estimate to $10,000.[23] This statistically illustrates that colonial authorities were adjusting to the reality of an increasing number of criminals after 1869.

Anecdotal evidence also demonstrates that these authorities contended with an increase in criminality. Thomas Scott, a member of the Legislative Council for the Straits Settlements, for example, remarked at a meeting in May 1871 that a recent spate of gang robberies and kidnappings was actually part of a larger trend toward "a general and greatly increased prevalence of . . . crimes and breaches of the law." "*The Government,*" he continued, "*are aware that crime is on the increase* and they are prepared to take steps for reorganizing the police with a view to check it."[24]

Ironically, at this very same time, the British consul back at Swatow had been reporting to his superiors in the Foreign Office that under the martial law imposed by Fang Yao, "many of the most notorious among the leaders of gang-robbers [in Chaozhou] have departed for Shanghai or Singapore." He also observed that, as a consequence, "of late a great decrease is observable in the prefectural city in the number of thefts and robberies."[25] In the entangled world of the South China Sea, Chaozhou's loss was Singapore's gain.

Deluged by crime, colonial officials embarked on a major reform and expansion of the policing capacities of the Straits. Among various recommendations made in 1871, they called for an increase in the number of police inspectors as well as the appointment of ethnic Chinese as police officers. This latter reform was deemed vital because the police force as then constituted was unable to address the challenges of surveilling the criminal underworld without trained officers who could speak the various dialects of the immigrant groups in the colony.[26] The demographic realities of Singapore motivated this line of thinking. By 1872 Chinese expatriates already constituted 62 percent of the total male population of the settlement.[27] Maintaining order was inconceivable without an increase in the number of officers conversant in the nuances of Chinese culture. Colonial authorities promulgated the "Police Force Ordinance" and the "Penal Code Ordinance" that same year and devoted the next several years to refining the legislation.

Significantly, within a year the Legislative Council decided to abandon the very reform that had seemed so essential back in 1871—training more Chinese police—because Chinese advisers to the council strongly opposed it. Tan Kay Seng, a Straits-born Chinese who had served as an interpreter for the police and the Supreme Court for thirty-two years, opined that Chinese in the Straits could not be relied on to arrest members of their own native place groups: "The Hokkien [Fujianese] constable would take up a Taychew [Chaozhouese] Criminal, but a Hokkien could not take up his own countrymen. . . . They would not apprehend men of the same society as themselves. They all belong to the Secret Societies." If a feud ever broke out among the two groups, as they frequently did, "the Chinese could arrest a few of the opposite Society, perhaps, but not their own."[28]

The personal identification of a villager as from Chaozhou or Fujian was enhanced by the act of migration, and such identification was reinforced by the tendency to reorganize brotherhood affiliations along native place lines. This was a departure from the tendency back home to organize sodalities across the provincial line between Fujian and Guangdong. The antagonistic relationship that evolved between Fujianese and Chaozhouese in the Straits undermined the prospect of hiring Chinese as police inspectors. Most of these sojourners belonged to brotherhoods that prohibited members even from informing officials of a brother's transgressions, much less arresting him. In the end, the government opted for a force that was supervised by British nationals and largely staffed by ethnic Malays and Klings (Singaporeans of Indian descent), who were deemed more dependable in the enforcement of colonial law.[29] Significantly, back in Chaozhou, when British merchants were attacked by villagers after the treaty port of Swatow was "opened" in 1858, they organized a police force of "night patrollers" to protect their lives and property. That force also was staffed entirely by Malays.[30] Across parts of maritime Chaozhou, Malays were emerging as a transnational police force protecting British interests.

In this fashion, the British devised legislative reforms to address the crime wave in the Straits. Nevertheless, it took governing authorities a while to comprehend that they were swimming in the waters of a specific event that was drifting from across the sea. For it was not generic "Chinese" or "Straits" criminality surging in the colony but Chaozhouese criminality. Only with the outbreak of urban violence in late 1872 did officials to begin to investigate what was going on in the Chinese community and reevaluate the changing social dynamics of the colony.

In 1873 the Legislative Council appointed a committee to investigate a riot that had unsettled Singapore in October 1872. The disturbance was not the usual conflict among Chinese native place groups but the result of a simple problem that had gotten out of hand because there were so many recently arrived, unemployed "rowdies" from Chaozhou loitering about. Investigators concluded that the riot had been precipitated by a "misunderstanding" between Chinese street hawkers (specifically those who sold cooked food) and the fledgling police force. Colonial authorities had passed legislation back in 1860 to regulate street hawking to reduce impediments to traffic and improve the sanitary conditions of the roadways. Apparently, no attempt had been made to explain the legislation—in Chinese—to the hawkers. In 1872, when the police—without acting in concert with mediators or effectively articulating their policies—decided to start enforcing these rules more stringently, the hawkers sensed that they were being treated disrespectfully, noting that "traveling cook shops" had provided meals to Chinese on the Malay Peninsula for years without incident. Some patrolmen were so intransigent, the hawkers later testified, that they would badger a man who even put his basket down for a brief rest before moving on. Increasingly agitated, they complained to Chinese business leaders, and on October 29 they took to the streets in peaceful protest against the indignities to which they had been subjected. Unexpectedly, however, the demonstration exploded into violence as mobs suddenly attacked the police with stones and drove them away. Law enforcement slowly lost control of the situation, and a larger rabble took over parts of Singapore. There was some vandalism, and several shops were plundered.

At the height of this émeute, some of the most prominent Chinese business elites of the colony were harassed. The carriage of Chen Chengbao, an opium farmer and gambier plantation owner who at the time was the wealthiest Chaozhouese in Singapore, was attacked by the mob, but he escaped unharmed. The windows of the home of the eminent Cantonese merchant, Hu Xuanze, were also smashed (Hu, or "Mr. Whampoa" as the British called him, was a member of the Legislative Council and the only Chinese on the Executive Council in the nineteenth century). As the violence intensified, this apprehensive elite prevailed on the government to call in troops to suppress it. They claimed that the rioters were not afraid of mere police officers and would defer only to armed might. As Chen later testified, "The Chinese would look upon a soldier as they would a tiger, and therefore would be afraid."[31] Military force in the end was applied and order restored.

During the official inquiry into the cause of the riot, Chinese witnesses from the commercial and laboring classes testified that events back in Chaozhou were deleteriously affecting the Straits Settlements. Intimately informed about conditions in their home villages, they made the connection between the mass exodus of criminals from Chaozhou and the discernible increase in the number of robberies and kidnappings overseas. Business elites watched with alarm as the Straits filled with these notorious fighting men and underworld characters, men who now were only marginally employed and who, in their view, had exploited the hawkers' peaceful demonstration against the police as an opportunity to pillage. They insisted that the hawkers had played little role in the violence for they were actually "a harmless . . . kind of people" who indignantly protested what appeared to them as unreasonable limitations on their trade. Instead, almost all the rioters were "samsengs" (fighting men) and the "rowdies of the town, who took advantage of the dissatisfaction amongst the hawkers . . . to riot for the purpose of looting and theft." In other words, the street hawkers demonstrated; the samsengs rioted.[32]

The British finally understood the causes of the upsurge in crime. "The number of 'Samsengs,' or fighting men, in the Straits has during the past two years very sensibly increased," investigators reported. "*This is due to the fact that the Mandarins of late years have been clearing out hordes of rowdies and bad characters who have infested a district (Tay Chew) [Chaozhou], near Swatow.* Numbers of these roughs," they continued, "having escaped with their lives, have been brought to the Straits by sailing and steam vessels, and are now infesting this Colony with their presence. These men, accustomed to live in their own country by plunder and violence, bring with them the lawless habits they have acquired. They have no ostensible mode of gaining a living."[33] In the entangled world of translocal Chaozhou, Fang Yao's solution was now the problem of the British, who ramped up their efforts at police reform.

The crime wave in the Straits began to abate by 1874. Increasingly professional law enforcement probably maintained order more effectively. Certainly by 1887, the inspector-general of police, Samuel Dunlop, was lauding the efficacy of the police, noting that, because of their efforts, "life and property in the Colony are infinitely more secure in 1887 than they were in 1872." In spite of the fact that immigration to the Straits increased during those years, per capita violent crime had diminished. "The difference," he asserted, "is the service of the police force."[34] In his view, the reforms implemented to address the surge in criminality had improved the government's capacity to maintain order.

Back in 1874, on the other hand, Dunlop had identified more significant economic reasons for the diminution in the level of violent crime. "The

demand for labor," he reported, "has relieved the Settlements of a large portion of its criminal class. Crime consequently has diminished very consider-
ably." The need for workers farther north along the Malay Peninsula and on
Sumatra in the Dutch East Indies, he continued, "led to the withdrawal of
many of the [fighters] belonging to the Secret Societies."[35] In other words,
continued migration elsewhere along the Straits of Malacca solved some of
the social problems that had been unleashed in the colony by the pacification
campaign back in China. Or, more to the point, employment opportunities
enabled these men to apply their energies to more conventional economic
pursuits, transforming them from freewheeling challengers of dynastic authority in China into a compliant labor force in the harsh plantation economies of Southeast Asia.

This is a salutary reminder that these migrants were not innately violent or
oriented toward crime. Most were poor and had been dependent on village
power-mongers back home for their livelihoods in the smuggling, pirating, and
feuding enterprises of the coast. They had been forced to escape to colonial
economies that could not immediately absorb the tens of thousands of refugees fleeing the campaign. The gambier and pepper economy in particular
suffered from an oversupply of labor. These men were unable to find gainful
employment, yet they could not return home without risking execution, so
they spent their early days in the Straits contriving protection rackets or relying on their brotherhoods for sustenance and companionship. Within a few
years, they managed to find jobs and start their lives over again, traveling ever
more deeply into the tropics of Southeast Asia, no doubt wondering if they
would ever see their villages again.

Fang's campaign was not the only development that inclined the British to
formalize colonial control. The Larut Wars (1861–1874) between Hakka and
Cantonese brotherhoods and their Malayan allies, for example, unsettled mining regions near Perak. Years of intermittent violence inclined the British to
sign the Pangkor Treaty of 1874 which, in establishing a colonial "Resident"
for the Malay States, began the process of increasingly direct British oversight
of Peninsular Malaya beyond the settlements of Malacca, Singapore, Penang,
and Dingding. These sorts of events illustrate the historical interconnection
between southern China and Southeast Asia and, in the specific case of Fang's
campaign, the interconnection between provincial state-building in China and
colonial state-building in the Straits. The Larut Wars, after all, were a geographical extension of the battles between Cantonese and Hakka that had fueled the
Taiping upheavals back in China.[36] The situation on the peninsula reflected

the complicated social geography of Chinese migration. The expanding south-eastern frontier of all Chinese native place groups was transforming the political dynamics of the colony.

The Temporal Boundlessness of a Historical Event

Fang Yao died in the summer of 1891, twenty-two years after launching his campaign of rural pacification. With the passing of such a ruthlessly effective commander, social disorders again began to afflict the Chaozhou frontier. The Fangs remained predominant in Puning, but they never again enjoyed the same control over the military as when their patron administered the Green Standards.[37] Chaozhou returned to its old ways. Violent clan fights rocked the social terrain, a phenomenon locally attributed to the disappearance of "the firm hand of General Fang," and pirate attacks from Swatow to the Vietnamese border intensified.[38] In the first decade of the new century, brotherhood rebellions again disturbed the tottering Qing dynasty, and by the second decade the inland customs bureaus that regulated domestic trade were routinely looted and robbed.[39]

The abortive uprisings were connected to other trends across maritime Chaozhou. Chinese Singaporeans committed themselves to the nationalist cause and by 1905 were aligned with Sun Yat-sen's Revolutionary Alliance. They dedicated themselves to overthrowing the Manchus, establishing a republic, eradicating the imperialists' treaty port system, and promoting the equalization of land rights.[40] The many Chaozhouese Singaporeans who resolved to wage revolution back home included Lin Shouzhi, who had been raised in the Anbu port area of Haiyang and, after joining his wealthy father in Singapore, emerged as a leader of the alliance; Zhang Yongfu (Teo Eng-hock), a Straits-born Chinese whose grandfather had emigrated from Raoping; Xu Xueqiu (Koh Soh Chew), the son of a Haiyang merchant who energized the cause; and Chen Yunsheng (Tan Huan-seng).

Even before the establishment of the Revolutionary Alliance, these men were organizing clandestine revolutionary cells back home. In 1904 they printed and distributed five thousand copies of Zou Rong's anti-Manchu screed, *The Revolutionary Army*. Xu Xueqiu established a base of operations in Haiyang and began to organize brothers in the Three Dots Society, who proceeded to recruit others beyond Anbu port. They were particularly successful in organizing TDH-affiliated laborers who were constructing the Swatow-Chaozhou railway. Meanwhile, Xu, whose family fortune had enabled him to purchase the official rank of taotai, relied on his "status" to ingratiate himself with the magistrate and receive permission to organize a self-defense militia of four hundred men.[41] In so doing, he adopted the tactics of Taiping-era brotherhoods, who organized militias ostensibly to uphold the orthodox order but in fact were dedicated to its destruction. He and his fellow subversives, however, were imbued with the revolutionary fervor of twentieth-century nationalism.

By May 1907 the revolutionaries had extended their clandestine activities into Huanggang, a port long considered a "flourishing center of the Three Dots Society."[42] The ever-watchful magistrate and officers in the local garrison grew suspicious as preparations for an assault on Chaozhou city progressed, and they called for additional military support from the regional commander at Chaozhou, Huang Jinfu. He dispatched a squadron of troops to investigate. After marching into town, the soldiers proceeded to harass a group of women enjoying an opera performance in a market square. When two men intervened, the troops arrested them, and the mood in town turned ugly. Xu Xueqiu at this time was overseas, and revolutionary leadership had been left in the hands of the Three Dots' chieftains, Yu Jicheng and Chen Yongbo. Knowing that the uprising had been imminent anyway, they decided to act while locals were riled and before the military was reinforced. On May 22 they prematurely launched an uprising in Huanggang. Leading a contingent of seven hundred brothers, they captured the town's garrison and easily took control of the port. The squad commander surrendered while the commanders of the Huanggang garrison and the barracks in nearby Zhelin were captured and decapitated, their bloody heads rammed onto poles and displayed in the marketplace.[43]

In spite of these victories, time was not on the side of the revolutionaries. They simply were not prepared to take on the prefectural army, and their allies in other locations could not act quickly enough in their support. Commander Huang rushed to the scene with two thousand troops and, after pitched battles, the so-called Huanggang Uprising (or Teochew Revolt) was crushed on May 27, less than a week after hostilities had commenced. Approximately two hundred rebels were killed, but most escaped to fight another day.[44]

The suppression of the rebellion in 1907 produced the familiar spike in emigration out of Swatow. In combination with the defeat of revolutionary upheavals in nearby Huizhou, emigration increased by 40.5 percent that year, well above the norm of the first years of the twentieth century (table 5.2).

In the twentieth century, affluent Chaozhouese in overseas enclaves once again voyaged home to galvanize the traditional brotherhoods. The revolu-

TABLE 5.2. Departures from Swatow, 1898–1909

Year	Passengers departing Swatow	Year	Passengers departing Swatow
1898	70,716	1904	103,202
1899	86,016	1905	93,645
1900	93,460	1906	102,710
1901	89,538	1907	144,315
1902	104,497	1908	112,061
1903	129,539	1909	84,246

Source: CSDQZ, 7.

tionary impulse in this sense marked a continuity with an older political tradition in which peripatetic, southeast-coastal frontiersmen proselytized their convictions at home and abroad. Now, however, they fused the longstanding antipathy for Manchu rule with the modern ideology of nationalism. This reflected a new phase of Chaozhou history in which intellectuals, armed with some Western ideas, devoted themselves to modern nation-building on the rubble of revolutionary destruction. The Ming would not be restored. Instead, "racially" Han Chinese rule would be reinstated through the establishment of a republic. Xu and his colleagues in Haiyang recruited their neighbors with promises to "topple the Manchus and restore Han Chinese rule" (*dao Man fu Han*), thus transforming the subversive slogan that had long reviled dynastic, rather than ethnic or "racial," enemies.[45] This time they were not thwarted. After the failure of the Huanggang Uprising, Huang Jinfu launched his own qingxiang campaign from 1907 through 1908, extending his quixotic pacification efforts beyond the districts of Raoping and Haiyang to coastal Chaoyang and beyond; all to no avail, for the Qing were soon toppled by forces elsewhere in China in the Revolution of 1911.[46] There would be no Yellow Riding Jacket for Commander Huang.

In light of the developments that transpired after 1891, it is difficult to argue that the era of Fang Yao's pacification had not long been over. The problems that Fang had contained from 1869 until his demise plagued the region once again, exacerbated by the fact that, after 1916, the fledgling Republic of China (1912–1949) disintegrated into the chaos of warlordism. After a devastating typhoon in 1922, piracy became so endemic around Swatow that the port barely functioned. A confederation of corsairs dominated the waters off Nan'ao, Chaoyang, and Jieyang, their ranks augmented by thousands of demobilized warlord soldiers. Trade shut down almost entirely in 1923 as merchants in the interior refused to ship goods to port for fear of robbery, and traders outside of the region began to frequent more peaceful centers along the coast. Predation had a serious impact on the coastal economy and undermined the revenues of the Chaozhou Customs.[47] It was as though Fang Yao's campaign had never occurred.

There nevertheless occurred a series of flashing epilogues to the qingxiang and its inextricable connection to the South China Sea, reminding us that local events reverberate not only across space but across time as well. It is impossible to understand twentieth-century history without reference to it. Back in 1890 a frustrated Prefect Zeng Jiqu expressed contempt for the ways in which the Fangs had aggrandized themselves in the region. "Who knows where the long-accumulated effects of these evil practices will lead?"[48] We now know the answer to that question. Long after the dynasty that Fang had salvaged was overthrown in the Revolution of 1911, and even as the republic that replaced it disintegrated into the chaos of warlordism, the remarkable ascendance of the Fang clan began to assume new political meanings. Shortly after the founding of the Chinese Communist Party in 1921, radical organizers in eastern Guangdong began to interpret Fang's pacification campaign not as an unreasonably ferocious effort to impose order but as the most recent and significant phase in the entrenchment of "feudal," gentry control over rural Chaozhou. The Fang lineage's absurdly dominating presence in Puning city and its rural hinterland came to symbolize the absurdity of the social structure of the entire southeast coast and, indeed, of China itself. In spite of the fact that Chaozhou was full of far wealthier gentry and mercantile families, communist reportage in the 1920s focused obsessively on the Fangs of Puning. Fang's campaign and its aftermath buttressed the argument for class warfare and rural revolution, a revolution intended, literally, to "defang" the local elite.

In 1922 communists like Peng Pai began to organize a rural revolutionary movement in northeastern Guangdong. The effort culminated in 1927 with the establishment of the Hai-Lu-feng Soviet in his native Huizhou, just south of Chaozhou. These developments most directly affected Huizhou, but the communists also established small organizations in the Chaozhou districts of Huilai, Puning, Jieyang, and Chao'an (formerly Haiyang).[49] Not surprisingly, communists of the era vilified Fang control over Puning, which they attributed to the legacy of "Big Man Fang." By the 1920s, they noted, of the twenty thousand residents of Puning city, over half were surnamed Fang. "Out of four doors in Puning, three are owned by Fangs, and not a single word of the common people will ever reach a government office," went a popular saying. Those ten thousand Fangs were heavily armed with hundreds of guns of Western manufacture, which they used to dominate town and countryside. They monopolized government positions beneath the rank of magistrate, including the police force and mayor. They were detested collectors of an ever-proliferating number of "fees" needed to keep various weak, Republican-era governments and militaries afloat, and Fang Yao's son, Fang Tingzhen, was said to have relied on this money to send his own son to school in Beijing. Fangs also dominated the educational profession as principals and teachers in the public schools, "propagating the ideology of familism" (*jiazu zhuyi*) to the next generation.[50]

Communists depicted Fang's heirs as classic "evil gentry and local bullies" who demanded money from struggling cultivators in the countryside by claiming (falsely, in the communist view) that the peasants' grandfathers had long been indebted to their own grandfathers. If peasants resisted these "unjust debt" repayments, the Fangs would beat them up and wrest thousands of yuan from their victims.[51] Fang Yao's own father and other kin had been pawnbrokers in the district city, so it is possible that peasants outside of town had owed money to them at some point, and the dunning for repayment of debts contracted years earlier was deeply resented. In these accounts, peasants who had endured such harassment now were inspired by the communist-affiliated Haifeng Peasant Association to address rural problems. They requested communist assistance in organizing an association of their own "to resist the oppression of the Fang clan."[52]

Violence erupted between peasants affiliated with the peasant unions and various Fangs in 1925 and 1926. But the communists of this period were far too weak to overthrow the dominant lineages of Chaozhou, supported as the latter were by their kin as well as the local military.[53] Landowners and merchants organized their own militias to resist the demands of these associations. The Fangs in particular rallied a formidable force of supporters, including the Fangs of Tuyang village who, since the early nineteenth century, were the toughest marauders in the area.[54]

The communist movement in Huizhou culminated in the establishment of the aforementioned Hai-Lu-feng Soviet in 1927. Local Communists rose up after Chiang Kai-shek launched a bloody purge of communists from the Nationalist Party. The soviet was not long-lived. The counterrevolutionary forces of the Nationalists crushed it in 1928, a mere four months after its founding. Compounding the disaster, an abortive communist uprising three hundred miles north of Chaozhou in Nanchang in August 1927 was repulsed, and battalions of the Red Army fled south, hoping to use eastern Guangdong as a staging ground for conquering Canton. Days after their arrival near Swatow, they were almost totally annihilated. As one frustrated party cadre later reported, they had no base of support among the majority of peasants and laborers in Chaozhou, and yet the Red Army marched into it anyway. "How could it not be defeated?"[55] The communists scattered into the mountains and across the seas as the peasant associations collapsed.

Scholars of the soviet movement tend to depict the Fang lineage of thirty thousand individuals in city and countryside as one formidable, counterrevolutionary entity when, in fact, it was as riven by political disagreements as any other clan in Chaozhou. Many Fangs actually joined the Peasant Association in Puning, for example.[56] Moreover, the most prominent communist to hail from the region, Fang Siqiong, better known as Fang Fang (1904–1971), was related to Fang Yao and born in the same village of Hongyang. Communist biographies of Fang emphasize that his family was among "the poor and weak branches" of the Fangs and "had been oppressed by officials and gentry bullies alike."[57] Fang helped organize the Hai-Lu-feng Soviet and continued his underground activities in Guangdong, Fujian, and Jiangxi beyond the 1920s. Needless to add, his kin were scandalized by his radicalism and plotted to assassinate him. When he got wind of this, he is said to have laughed, "I'm rather partial to the name 'Fang' in spite of them. In fact, from here on out, I am going to call myself Fang."[58] He became famous under this adopted nom de guerre.

The scholarship also tends to minimize the enormous suffering of the local population as communists and counterrevolutionaries of all stripes waged their battles in their midst. After the suppression of the Hai-Lu-feng Soviet, many communists fled to a new base established on Da'nan Mountain, which loomed over the borderland of Puning, Chaoyang, Huilai, and Jieyang. From this haven, they launched guerilla attacks against Chiang Kai-shek's Nationalist armies but were finally defeated in late 1935 after Chiang launched a military offensive against them.[59] Puning was hard hit by these developments. A traveler's guidebook in 1933 described an economy devastated by military violence. Gentry and merchants focused their energies on security measures and had virtually nothing left over to invest in education and other social services (those in Chao'an, which was not terribly affected by the turmoil, spent 260,000 yuan per year on education alone). Only the opium poppies were said to thrive in the district; they were cultivated in abundance in spite of government proscriptions.[60]

Living through this violence was terrifying. Financially comfortable peasants were constantly harassed in the countryside, and this was a period when

TABLE 5.3. Departures from Swatow, 1917–1937

Year	Passengers departing Swatow	Year	Passengers departing Swatow
1917	69,375	1927	222,033
1918	57,416	1928	211,977
1919	83,518	1929	no data
1920	109,318	1930	123,724
1921	135,675	1931	80,202
1922	136,680	1932	36,824
1923	133,122	1933	44,858
1924	152,064	1934	56,293
1925	131,092	1935	130,766
1926	83,974	1936	91,157
		1937	68,661

Source: CSDQZ, 8.

such families moved permanently to Swatow or emigrated.[61] The bloodshed did not spare any class, however, and, not surprisingly, emigration spiked dramatically (table 5.3).

The spike in emigration in 1920 was occasioned by warlord Chen Jiongming's occupation of Swatow that year and Nationalist efforts to defeat him thereafter. It was sustained by other events: alluvial shifts along the Han River which led to feuding over land in 1921; the horrific typhoon of 1922, which killed over thirty thousand people; and the fighting and struggles associated with communist agitation and counterrevolutionary suppression.[62] The truly significant increase occurred in 1927, when the number of departing passengers exploded to 222,033, an unprecedented escalation of almost 165 percent that was sustained through 1928. This exodus reflected both the cumulative effects of the Northern Expedition of Chiang's Nationalist armies to defeat local warlords and unify China as well as the violent suppression of the Hai-Lu-feng Soviet. The final acceleration in passenger traffic occurred in 1935, a year in which Nationalist forces finally annihilated the guerillas of Da'nan Mountain. Emigration out of Swatow port increased by over 132 percent in that year of intense warfare, the second largest spike in the history of the port.

Some emigrants were communists, but not the majority. There had only been 560 party members in Puning, for example. There were many more partisans in Huizhou—11,500 in Haifeng alone.[63] Many partisans who survived the 1928 onslaught did not go abroad but fled into the mountains to continue the struggle, however. Peasants who had supported the party probably constituted a significant percentage of those fleeing for their lives. Communist records show that during the "counterrevolutionary" suppression efforts in Puning from December 1927 to January 1928, over a thousand Puning peasants fled to Southeast Asia because they feared that their landlords would take revenge on them now that the movement had been crushed.[64] Those who were politically active, however, cannot account for the 564,776 refugees during these three years. The vast majority fled the violence of political warfare.

Included among those victims were members of the Fang clan of Puning. The family suffered immeasurably in these upheavals. Fang Yanshan (Png Yen San) was one such unfortunate. His family lived in the district city, where his father was the principal of Puning Middle School. As he explained in an oral interview decades later, they departed for Singapore in 1927, when Yanshan was thirteen years of age, "because our lineage was really unharmonious and . . . the area was very chaotic." Their troubles stemmed from one fact:

> We had produced Big-Man Fang. . . . The whole area was surnamed Fang, about 30,000 of us. . . . This powerful surname ate the little surnames; this powerful lineage ate the little lineages; the powerful [Fang] kinsmen ate the little kinsmen. Because of this, those direct descendants of Big-Man Fang themselves became the biggest family around. My father, a school principal there, did not get along with them. Plus there was also the matter of the [Nationalist] party purge [of leftists]. He couldn't do anything else but to escape to Singapore.[65]

His father undoubtedly had obtained his position on the strength of the family connection, but his experiences revealed that many Fangs themselves resented Fang Yao's branch of the family; his progeny lorded it over their own relatives. Yanshan's family was caught in the middle of this struggle:

> The political situation was not good and our relations with our kin also were not good. At the time, my father was a teacher; he lived in the academic world; he knew many of these leftists. So my kin said that my father was a leftist. . . . There was one named Fang Fang [the communist leader]. In the past he had been my father's student. Fang Fang . . . was part of a hostile faction. So, at the time, my father went to Singapore first. . . . And not long after that, I escaped myself.[66]

The precipitating factor in their departure had been a family quarrel over the father's connection to Fang Fang. An intellectual in a rural township, Yanshan's father probably listened sympathetically to the leftist critique of the status quo in Puning. But the family was in an untenable situation. Yanshan offered a vivid description of what it was like to be a Fang in Puning during these years:

> It was chaotic back then. We were robbed. Our home was robbed by people from other villages. This is because we [Fangs] in Puning and people from other villages—townsfolk and out-of-towners were in the middle of a *xie-dou* [armed feud]. People were killed for 2 or 3 years. *At that time, if the communists heard that your name was Fang, they'd just kill you.*

When the interviewer asked why that was, Yanshan replied, "Because they [figured] if we were named Fang—they'd say that we built up our lineage by bullying other people. *When the communists rose up, they aimed directly at the Fang lineage.*"[67] Like Fang Yao's campaign back in 1869, the communist insurgency in this region resembled an enormous lineage affray, only now the Fangs were targeted.

Yanshan noted that it was unusual for people like his family to emigrate prior to this time. "We had land, we had gravesite property. My father had a job as a school principal. And for that reason, we ought not to have wanted to go abroad." Among the Puning Fangs, at least, it was only "people without resources who went abroad in those days." But the tide had turned. Their enemies were driving untold numbers of Fangs overseas. It should be noted that some members of the family already had emigrated abroad for commercial reasons. Yanshan had a relative in Annam (Vietnam) who had grown "very wealthy" in the cloth business and invited him to live with him. Instead, he fled to Penang to work in the shop of another relative.[68]

The Fangs were not alone in fleeing the chaos. Boats were packed with refugees of all sorts. This book opened with a snippet of the life of Chen Jinhua of Yueling village in Puning. His large family owned 15 *mu* of land, which was sizable for Chaozhou but not unusually so. The Chens produced ample food for their needs and owned a fruit orchard. They also had relatives overseas. For all of these reasons, he observed, "when the communists came, they claimed we were rich."

In 1932 he and his older brother decided to emigrate to Siam "because things were very bad. The communist base was [nearby] at Da'nan Mountain." While they traveled to port, they were seized by communist insurgents who asked what they were doing. The quick-witted Jinhua told them he was going to Swatow to work as a laborer, and they left him alone. His brother, however, told them he was a peasant, and they beat him up and singed his back and chest with the incense sticks he carried in hopes of praying at a temple. When an interviewer asked Jinhua why he was spared and his brother not, he replied,

If you lived in Swatow, it meant you did not live in a rural village. It meant that you could not possibly participate in the Communist Party. My fourth older brother told them he tilled the soil. [So they asked him,] "Are you participating in communism?" [And he said,] "No." And when he said "no," they beat him, beat him severely. . . . They beat him till he cried and then could cry no more. It was a horrible situation. So we in China at the time were in a pitiful situation. There were many such unfortunate people, many who were beaten to death, many who were injured as the result of beatings.[69]

Chen articulated the dilemma of many who lived in the midst of these battling armies: "This is why I went to Siam, because of this situation. There was nothing you could do. Because of this, our large household of twenty or thirty or so, all of us escaped. There . . . was no way we could stay. . . . We lived in suspense the entire day. We were terrified the Nationalist army would come, and we were terrified that the communist army would come. . . . So we all fled."[70]

He fled to Siam; his brother to Chao'an district city; another brother to Penang; the father to Singapore; and other relatives escaped to Cambodia, Singapore, Penang, and Siam. "The whole family just scattered." His entire family-village (*jiaxiang*) comprised a thousand men, and all departed: "our entire village dispersed," except for the women. The steamer that carried him from Swatow to Bangkok was filled with about fifteen hundred passengers, almost all of whom were escaping the chaos of Chaozhou.[71]

The Chens may have been wealthier than Jinhua was willing to admit. His mother had given him twenty silver dollars when he departed (the passage to Bangkok was eight yuan in those days), and his sister's husband owned a sugar plantation in Siam; he also had kin with business interests in Penang. But the family did not appear to have been among the elite who had benefited from Fang Yao's campaign. They did not own vast properties along the Ox-Field Sea. They seemed to be "middle peasants" with adequate resources and overseas connections, but local communists proceeded to treat them as they had the Fangs, as emblematic "evil gentry."

The emigration waves propelled by these upheavals had their usual impact on the shores of Southeast Asia. In 1928, for example, the Legislative Council of the Straits Settlements was compelled to issue a new Immigration Restriction Bill "to restrict or prohibit the flow of undesirable immigrants." Colonial authorities feared that hordes of revolutionaries were arriving from the

"Swatow district" and constituted "a possible source of social and moral danger." The colony suffered strikes and bombings, leading to intensified police surveillance. The Immigration Bill was one of several legislative items (including amendments to the Banishment Ordinance, the Arms and Explosives Ordinance, and the Seditious Publications Ordinance) that exacerbated political, mostly anticommunist, repression in the Straits.[72] The colony once again was awash in the sociopolitical troubles of southeastern China.

An unprecedented number of refuges took residence in Cambodia (French Indochina). Migration of Chinese to Cambodia had been holding steady at 2,000 per year, but during the 1920s it accelerated. In 1905 about 170,000 Chinese resided in Cambodia; by 1941 that number had grown to 300,000. Most of these immigrants hailed from Chaozhou, and by the early 1960s, 75 percent of all Chinese in Cambodia were natives of that region. Almost all hailed from Jieyang, Puning, and Chaoyang, the districts bordering Da'nan Mountain. Significantly, prior to the 1930s Cantonese had predominated as the largest Chinese dialect group in the country, but Chaozhouese began to displace them in the late 1920s.[73] The great migration thus transformed the overseas Chinese community of Cambodia.

It also transformed Cambodia's rural economy. Most Chaozhouese moved to small towns in the countryside. By 1967 almost all rural shopkeepers in Cambodia were Chaozhouese; they constituted over 90 percent of the rural Chinese population there.[74] As W. E. Willmott observed, Chaozhouese shopkeepers "constituted the primary link between the Khmer [Cambodian] peasant and the outside economic world." He noted that some French observers depicted these shopkeepers as "exploiters" of those peasants, but this denigration reflected the typical bias of the French against the Chinese in Indochina. Even French scholars who were disdainful of the Chinese, such as Jean Delvert, acknowledged that, without these entrepreneurs, the Khmer "peasant doubtless would be hampered . . . in securing his subsistence." Those "boutiquier villageois," Delvert wrote, "lived in symbiosis with the peasant." They purchased crops and supplied peasants with commodities that were not easily obtained in the countryside: pots, salt, matches, jars, ploughshares, and so on. Khmer producers usually could not pay for these goods in cash. Instead, they paid in paddy, maize, and other produce later, at harvest time.[75] Delvert emphasized that this system transformed Cambodian peasants into consumers in ways that had not been common before the migration of Chaozhouese. He also noted that the shopkeepers themselves purchased their wares on credit from wholesalers and that both wholesalers and retailers were exposed to significant financial loss if the harvest was bad or the peasant otherwise was unable to pay for the goods. In fact, many shopkeepers "were themselves quite poor." They usually were the impecunious, distant relations of more commercially successful families located in Phnom Penh or other cities.[76]

A small number of Chaozhouese grew affluent and influential. Even less surprising, some of those success stories were immigrants from the Hongyang area of Puning named Fang (better known by the pronunciation of their name in Chaozhouese, Pung). Fang Qiaosheng (Pung Kheav Se), currently the wealthiest banker in Cambodia, hails from a family that fled Puning during the political traumas of the Republican era. Like Fang Yanshan, his parents had been schoolteachers in the district city and resumed that profession upon moving to Cambodia. Finding their salaries inadequate, they switched careers, founding the Vegetable Market Company (Caishi gongsi), which sold plant and vegetable seeds. After that business began to thrive, they branched into book-printing and manufacturing. By the time Qiaosheng was born in 1946, the family fortune was secured, and the Fangs emerged as leaders of the Chaozhou community in Cambodia.[77]

Fang Qiaosheng's other relations fared even better. His uncle, Fang Bingzhen (Pung Peng Cheng), was a wealthy businessman and close adviser to Prince Sihanouk. Among other positions, he served as the secretary general to the Throne Council from 1960 to 1970 and as the *chef du cabinet* during the prince's exile in Beijing from 1970 to 1975.[78] His wife achieved prominence in her own right. Tong Siv Eng was elected to the National Assembly in 1958 and became Cambodia's first female minister in 1959. Aside from serving as the minister for social action from 1959 to 1963 and minister of health from 1963 to 1968, she was a leading advocate for women's rights.[79] From this we see that at least some Puning Fangs thrived in exile during their short respite from communist persecution.

Rural shopkeepers were lumped together with these more distinguished elites and reviled as "class enemies" during the bloody rule of the Khmer Rouge from 1975 to 1979. Roughly 50 percent of the ethnic Chinese population of Cambodia (now Democratic Kampuchea) was decimated in the "killing fields" of Pol Pot's regime. Out of a total Chinese population of 430,000 in 1975, about 215,000 died from execution, starvation, and mistreatment. It was, as Ben Kiernan has noted, "the worst disaster ever to befall any ethnic Chinese community in Southeast Asia." When considered in tandem with communist policies banning the Chinese language or any expression of cultural difference, the extermination of half the Chinese population was, quite simply, genocide.[80] The vast majority of victims were Chaozhouese, most of whom either had escaped communist persecution or fled counterrevolutionary retaliation back in China or simply sought a better life in places where battling armies were not a scourge on the land. They had fled the cataclysms of revolutionary China only to discover that the struggles were being waged elsewhere across maritime Chaozhou. Fang Qiaosheng's father perished in the terror, but Qiaosheng managed to flee with his family, first to Thailand (where a number of Puning Fangs lived) and later to Canada. His aunt and uncle ended up in France. Once again Fangs fled a communist insurgency that targeted people like them, one generation after another rising to the heights of Asian politics, only to find themselves running for their lives to ever more distant lands.[81]

The atrocities of the Cambodian "killing fields" constituted distinct historical events and generated their own ghastly repercussions. Does it make sense to connect the experiences of Fang Yanshan, Chen Jinhua, Fang Qiaosheng, Pung Peng Cheng, and hundreds of thousands of unnamed refugees to another violent, long-forgotten event that had transpired in Chaozhou a century earlier? The larger historical context must be factored in, and the following chapters will expand on that context. Historically isolating one event nonetheless enables us to discern just how Fang Yao's campaign from 1869 to 1873 reverberated across time and space in distinctive echoes of triumph and horror. Peasants were beheaded in a village in Chaoyang, and the criminal justice system of a British colony across the seas was transformed. Children grew up without ever encountering their exiled fathers, and a rage simmered beneath the surface of an ostensibly pacified society. Revolutionary utopians focused their ire on a long-dead commander's descendants, and, in a reversal of roles, his kinfolk were driven overseas, only to find themselves engulfed yet again by waves of revolutionary calamity.

One cannot understand the structural transformations of maritime Chaozhou without considering the pacification campaign of Fang Yao. Such transformations were more complicated than a single event and certainly were not the mere consequence of the actions of a "great man," even a "Big-Man" like the admiral of Guangdong. Modern state-building in the wealthiest province of China in the latter nineteenth century nonetheless was extended to its second largest commercial region through the martial violence and tax-collecting relentlessness of the pacificator of eastern Guangdong. The post-Taiping elite aggrandizement so characteristic of China in the decades before the revolutionary era was effected in Chaozhou, in part, by the development schemes pursued in the shadow of the Fang-dominated Army of the Green

Standard. Chaozhouese emigration was accelerated by Fang's expulsion of the turbulent element that so often had defied officialdom. Most important, the decades of militarized social order around the ports of the region facilitated commercial enterprise and further contributed to the emergence of Chaozhouese among the masters of the South China Sea. Fang's campaign facilitated the development of capitalism across maritime Chaozhou even as it sparked the flame of revolutionary destruction to come. At home and abroad, Chinese and European state-builders were taming the Wild East and regulating an international trade order that benefited the establishment merchants of the south China coast, further entangling China and the colonial powers in a political economy of opium.

6

Narco-Capitalism

RESTRAINING THE BRITISH IN SHANGHAI, 1839–1927

> At the bottom of every great fortune without apparent source there's always some crime—a crime overlooked because it was done respectably.
>
> —HONORÉ DE BALZAC

A LOT OF PEOPLE got rich in the opium trade in China: British, Americans, Parsis, and, of course, Chinese. Prior to 1858, when the sale and recreational use of the drug were illegal, fortunes were made by smuggling. The south China coast was the most cosmopolitan arena for contraband trade in modern history. The British imagined they made life easier for Western interests when they fought two wars with the Qing—the First Opium War, 1839 to 1842, and the Second Opium War, 1856 to 1860. The treaties and conventions that concluded these wars "opened" fifteen Chinese ports to foreign trade (including Shanghai in 1842 and Swatow in 1858) and, after 1858, imposed a de facto legalization of opium on China.

They have been justifiably maligned by historians for making all this happen. They forced open treaty ports and along with other imperialist powers transformed them into semicolonized metropolises intended, at least, to suit the needs of foreign capital. When attention is shifted to translocal Chaozhouese, however, one sees that the British did not always prevail in the age of legalized opium. The British profited handsomely by shipping opium from their colony in India to Shanghai and Hong Kong and were planting a significant stake in the Shanghai economy by the twentieth century. After 1858, however, merchants from the Chaoyang district of Chaozhou dominated the commerce in this narcotic at Shanghai and ports along the lower course of the Yangzi River. These traders increasingly marginalized the British in the most remunerative trade in China. They also succeeded in checking the expansion of British interests during the nineteenth century. Unique among their Chinese contemporaries, they competed with and often triumphed over the imperialists both in that port and, as we shall see, back in Chaozhou itself.

Vast fortunes were made in the opium trade across maritime Chaozhou in Shanghai, Southeast Asia, and back home. The capital derived from the opium trade enabled Chaozhouese to branch into less stigmatized enterprises— banking, real estate, manufacturing, and film. Opium undergirded capitalist accumulation. In this, Chaozhou opium magnates were no different from other titans of nineteenth-century international trade. Some of the wealthiest families in the Anglo-American world experienced a similar path to financial enrichment. After accumulating profits in the opium traffic, they reinvested the money in other endeavors that required significant capital inputs. This is the story of the Jardine Matheson Company of Scotland and David Sassoon and Company of Baghdad (by way of Bombay). An astonishing array of American elites enhanced their fortunes by selling opium in China: Perkins, Forbes, Delano, Low, and Russell, among others. The grandest American opium-running syndicate of them all, Russell and Company, has been called "America's Jardine Matheson." Founded in 1818, the company emerged among the three biggest opium dealerships on the China coast.[1] Opium eased families into affluence across the nineteenth-century globe.

Marketing opium was one way to accumulate the capital necessary to invest in modern enterprise and enabled Chaozhouese to compete on an equal playing field with foreign imperialists. Zheng Yibin, a businessman in Shanghai in the late nineteenth and early twentieth centuries, believed that participating in the opium trade was the most efficacious way "to overcome the monopolistic associations of the foreign powers."[2] The Chaozhou opium clique for a time challenged and triumphed over those foreigners.

Recreational opium use was a popular homosocial practice in China prior to 1949. It was also universally considered a legitimate medicine. Most of those arrested for smoking opium during the Qing "war on drugs" from 1838 to 1858 claimed to have been treating an illness, and even addicts asserted that their initial foray into abuse had been for medicinal purposes. It was said to cure stomachaches, disorders of the vital energy, and an assortment of other, often serious maladies including malaria and dysentery. Doctors prescribed opium as standard treatment for various illnesses (indeed, an opium purchase occasionally was described as "filling a prescription"). Criminal cases reveal a popular lore that opium was an effective treatment for diseases that otherwise had no remedy. If the drug did not actually cure these afflictions, it alleviated their symptoms.[3]

Because smoking opium was popular, the trade was profitable. We have seen how participation in the global commerce in the drug enhanced the power of heavily fortified villages back in Chaozhou. The opium trade produced a similar dynamic translocally. It undergirded the economic power of Chaozhou merchants in Shanghai in particular. It also enabled these merchants to financially assist their families back home, thereby strengthening the ties of lineage and village across vast distances.

The Emergence of the Chaozhou Syndicate at Shanghai

Chaozhou merchants were involved in international and coastal opium trafficking long before the "treaty ports" were opened, as we have seen. Similarly, the involvement of the Chaozhou bang ("Swatow Guild") in the Shanghai opium trade predated the British "opening" of that port in 1842. Chaozhouese themselves have elided this history. Writing in 1965, the former opium merchant Zheng Yingshi (b. 1901) relied on the "oral tradition of [his] forebears" to describe how Chaozhou brokers—and his clan, the Zhengs—emerged among the dominant opium dealers in Shanghai. According to this tradition, "prior to the Opium War, England and America were the earliest chieftains of narcotics dealing. . . . After the Opium War, Shanghai became an important base for imperialists to open and promote the sale of opium in China. So the Chaozhouese who were living in Shanghai became important opium sellers on behalf of the imperialists. Because of this, some of them became extremely wealthy and the richest tycoons of the Shanghai Bund."[4] This is a somewhat misleading account of the rise of the Chaozhou clique. His branch of the Zhengs indeed served as brokers for Jardine Matheson in Shanghai in 1843, but Chaozhouese had been selling opium in that port for at least two decades prior to that date (and probably earlier). This is not to exonerate the British for having smuggled opium in flagrant disregard of Chinese law but to clarify how the British transformed a longstanding Chinese coastal business.

The British relationship with Chaozhouese was forged years before the Opium War in Chaozhou, not in Shanghai. During the 1820s Jardine Matheson established a station off Nan'ao. The island was ideally situated at the junction of two great commercial provinces, Fujian and Guangdong. More important, it lay on the shipping route linking Southeast Asia, South China, and Shanghai. It was a convenient site for merchants to purchase opium en route to northern markets.

Sugar was the leading commercial crop produced in Chaozhou in the nineteenth century, and Shanghai was its premier market.[5] Merchants traveled to the villages that produced various grades of cane and purchased the crops outright. In some instances they extended credit to producers and collected the cane at harvest time. They then transported it to local ports, where mill workers extracted sugar and loaded it onto ships bound north. The ships returned to Chaozhou laden with cotton and Manchurian beancake. The latter was the primary source of fertilizer utilized in eastern Guangdong, and Chaozhou was its largest market.[6]

No commodity traded across maritime Chaozhou was a stand-alone product; the commerce in all goods was interconnected. The Chaozhou opium trade operated across Asia in a symbiotic relationship to that of sugar, beancake, rice, cotton, gambier, and pepper. Opium was distinctive because its trade by far was the most remunerative by weight. Including opium made the entire coastal trade more profitable. Exporting products like sugar was essential to the vitality of the Chaozhou economy, of course, but this more conventional trade also served as a useful cover for the commerce in contraband.

Shippers associated with the junk trade from Chaozhou to Shanghai were major customers of the Jardine Matheson opium station off Nan'ao during the 1830s and early 1840s.[7] These merchants did not need to rely on the Jardine dealers there. They already participated in a wider coastal trade that brought them down to the opium markets of Macao and Canton. But sugar merchants otherwise found it convenient to strike deals with foreign smugglers along the way. As the Jardine ships cruised the coastal waters, they often encountered a "fleet of junks" heading north, and inevitably one or more of the vessels would approach them to bargain over an opium purchase. One such fleet passed a Jardine ship, the *Colonel Young*, on February 14, 1838, and a junk hailed them to purchase fifty chests of opium for $27,660 Mexican dollars and sycee. Because the merchants feared that a Chinese naval patrol was monitoring them, they arranged the exchange of silver and opium to take place ten miles northward.[8] Hauling aboard multiple chests laden with opium and silver on the open sea was time-consuming and dangerous, but the mobility of both parties facilitated surreptitious transactions.

Serendipitous encounters were common, but junk merchants were not always inclined to leave purchases to chance. More typically, they would send someone on long boats to track down the Jardine vessel and instruct them where to meet the fleets to transact business. They usually left a deposit of $30 to $100 (Mexican), which they occasionally sacrificed if they managed to arrange a better price with some other smuggler. The ships would rendezvous at the agreed on site after performing prearranged signals, and the Chinese handed over the silver. After the shroffs determined that the silver represented a mutually agreed on value, the Jardine representatives relinquished the opium. In the event that the Chinese navy bothered to patrol the area, the parties would meet at a predetermined alternative location.[9] This rarely happened, however, for the Green Standard naval forces stationed at Nan'ao were routinely bribed. In fact, during the height of the anti-opium campaign in 1839, the Jardine representative, H. P. Baylis, reported that local "mandarins" sailed out to his ship to inform him that "a man of high rank is expected in the vicinity for the purpose of ascertaining whether there actually are so many [foreign] vessels at [Nan'ao], as have been reported. They therefore wish us to go away for a time that he may be enabled to send in a statement to the effect that we have all left." Baylis complied.[10]

When we last considered British opium smuggling off Chaozhou in the 1830s, Tom the Birdman and other Cantonese compradors for Jardine Matheson were wining and dining local opium brokers. Who were these brokers? It is impossible to identify by name the shippers and brokers who participated in this commerce; Jardine did not trade and tell, but they did refer to "Cape brokers" with whom they regularly conducted business and who frequently approached them from the Chaoyang port of Haimen.[11] Much of the rest of their business came from junks traveling past what the British called "the Cape of Good Hope." This was the northeastern shore of Chaoyang, across from Swatow, at the maritime entrance to the Ox-Field Sea. Chaoyang merchants were active in the lucrative sugar trade to Shanghai and were in a financial position to make large purchases of opium. For example, on March 30, 1838, Baylis reported to William Jardine that a fleet of thirteen junks that had just cleared the cape on their journey north had purchased 334 chests of Malwa opium and 55 chests of Patna for a price of 132,000 taels of silver sycee; they cleaned him of his entire stock.[12] This was an enormous outlay of capital reflecting the resources of the wealthier merchants who traded in northern ports. The district magistrate complained to provincial authorities in 1838 that Chaoyang sugar merchants engaged in opium smuggling, noting that "there were very wealthy villages there that produced sugar, and prosperous merchants set sail for the high seas from such ports as Dahao on the pretext of selling sugar but in fact to smuggle [opium]."[13] The connection between British smugglers and the sugar and opium dealers of Chaoyang was well established back in Chaozhou in the 1830s, long before Shanghai was opened as a treaty port. In fact, it may have been forged earlier, farther south in the Canton area, for merchants from Chaoyang were habitués of the foreign opium depots of Lintin in the 1820s.[14]

Chaozhou-area merchants had dominated the Guangdong sugar trade into Shanghai since at least the early eighteenth century. Not only did they control the export market out of Chaozhou, they also monopolized the trade out of other sugar-producing regions of Guangdong like Enping.[15] By 1759 these traders had organized their own huiguan or "native place association" in Shanghai, the Native Place Association of the Eight-Districts of Chaozhou. Huiguan were fraternal orders organized by sojourning merchants from the same native place. They performed a multiplicity of roles—trade association, philanthropic order, site of social fellowship—and engaged in a variety of activities: temple-building, lobbying, charitable work, and facilitating the burial or repatriation of merchants and laborers who died away from home.[16] Native place associations constituted the principal institution buttressing the expansion of the southeast coastal economy into other territories.

The Native Place Association of the Eight Districts of Chaozhou was organized around three *bang* or confraternities of natives from particular districts: the Chaoyang-Huilai bang, the Haiyang-Chenghai-Raoping bang, and the Jieyang-Puning-Fengshun bang. Merchants from Chenghai, Haiyang, and Raoping appear to have dominated Chaozhouese shipping into Shanghai as well as the association for much of the eighteenth century. Chenghai natives also had pioneered the economic connection with Siam, and Chenghai and Haiyang natives dominated Chaozhou life in the Straits Settlements in the early years, so their commanding presence in the commercial world of Shanghai is not surprising.[17] Operating out of Chenghai's international port at Zhanglin and Haiyang's port of Anbu, they enjoyed an early advantage in maritime trade. Chinese observers in Shanghai believed that these merchants collectively supplanted the Fujianese as the most important shippers in the port by the mid-nineteenth century.[18]

As the decades passed, merchants from Chaoyang district began to displace the stalwarts of Chaozhou's commercial circles in Shanghai. This can be seen in the construction of a new building to house the native place association in 1811. The Chaoyang-Huilai group, which specialized in the marketing of sugar and tobacco, made the largest contribution to this project by far.[19] The fact that they eclipsed the powerful merchants of Chenghai and Haiyang in manifesting their philanthropic chops—one of the more important institutional activities of the merchant—was due to their ongoing participation in the profitable opium trade. As Bryna Goodman has shown, the Chaoyang-Huilai group felt obliged to deny that they had traded in opium in Shanghai prior to its legalization in 1858. The fact that everyone else in mercantile circles believed that they were implicated in the illicit trade aggravated tensions within the larger organization and inclined the Chaoyang-Huilai bang to form their own association, the Chao-Hui Huiguan, in 1839.[20] It is unclear why merchants from Chenghai would have engaged in such gossip considering that Chenghai merchants also smuggled opium, as we have seen. Chaoyang sugar merchants involved in the coastal trade nevertheless had a long history of opium trafficking. As early as 1814 they appeared in the criminal record as significant wholesale purchasers of raw opium.[21] As they were major customers of Jardine Matheson back in Chaozhou, it was natural that they emerged as opium dealers in Shanghai prior to 1842.

The Chao-Hui Native Place Association was dominated by Chaoyang natives from the beginning. Seventy-two businesses contributed to its founding in 1839. Total donations amounted to 73,661 silver taels, and the Huilai group (two donors) contributed only 19. In fact, by 1866 few Huilai merchants operated in Shanghai, and none contributed to the rebuilding of the association in that year. The original name, Chao-Hui Native Place Association, was retained as a courtesy and to affirm the continuing "friendship among local communities" back home and in Shanghai itself.[22] After the 1860s the Chao-Hui bang comprised only Chaoyang natives.

The Desheng firm contributed the largest amount to the founding of the new association, 6,420 taels. It was owned by the Guos of Tongyu, one of the three surname groups that dominated the Chaoyang clique in Shanghai. Little is known about the Guos who pioneered the opium trade, but they were said to have gotten their start during the Daoguang era (1821–1851) and by the latter nineteenth century were assuming leadership roles in the association.[23] One leader of the younger generation, Guo Zibin (1860–1932), was born a peasant but eventually departed for Shanghai, where he apprenticed himself to an opium firm. After years spent learning the business, he established the first of many companies, the Guo Hongtai, which specialized in the sale of raw opium in Shanghai and along the Yangzi River. A shrewd businessman who attended to all aspects of his trade personally, he amassed an enormous fortune derived entirely from opium. His Chinese biographers claim that he came to regret the role he had played in the trade and remorsefully began to diversify his investments. After 1914 he successfully branched into textile manufacturing, rice milling, and modern and native banking. They also identify his generous philanthropic endeavors. A leading board member of the Chaozhou native place association during the Republican period, he contributed extensively to charitable causes that assisted the poor in both Shanghai and Chaozhou. By 1923 he had sponsored the establishment of at least six schools in Chaoyang, Swatow, and Chao'an (Haiyang). In 1925 he donated fifty thousand silver dollars to Fudan University in Shanghai to establish a psychology department.[24] The extent of his philanthropy was remarkable, and it is little wonder that his biographers tend to overlook his role in the opium trade, for he probably contributed more to the welfare of people in Shanghai and Chaozhou than did any government office of his day.

Guo's life trajectory from opium magnate to legitimate businessman to philanthropist accords with those of the second major surname group to emerge among the Chaoyang syndicate, the Zhengs. They owned the Zhengxia Ji company, which contributed the third largest sum to the founding of the Chao-Hui Native Place Association in 1839: five thousand taels.[25] The few sources that address the company's early years claim that the Zhengs who founded the company followed Jardine Matheson into Shanghai when the city was "opened" to foreign trade after the First Opium War ended in 1842. It is clear, however, that the company already was well established in the trade before the British gained access to the city.

Zhengxia Ji was founded by Zheng Jiechen (also known as Granddaddy Zheng Si), a native of Shangyanding village in the Chengtian township of Xiashan ward. His son, Zheng Rangqing, also traded in opium, while his grandson, Zheng Zhengqiu (1888–1935), an ardent nationalist, avoided the family business like the plague and channeled some of its fortune into a new industry, film. He was the founder of the Shanghai motion picture studio Bright Star Films (Mingxing dianying gongsi) and a pioneering director of some repute.[26] The three generations of Zhengs manifested the family patterns of the Chaoyang clique. The older generation made their fortunes in the opium business while the younger generation branched into more "legitimate" endeavors.

Zheng Jiechen was something of an underworld character, surrounded by blackguards and martial arts experts. This aura of the big-time gangster apparently impressed British traders and inclined them to partner with him after they arrived in Shanghai.[27] Zheng was no "running dog" of the imperialists, however. In fact, he was sued by British opium interests in 1879 for leading a syndicate that strong-armed foreigners out of the drug business in Zhenjiang, a port town on the Yangzi that had been forced open in 1860. He appeared in court, arrayed in the attire of one who had purchased high official rank, and listened placidly as his British competitors complained that their witnesses (three compradors) were too afraid to appear in court because "they stated that they were in danger of their lives at the hands of the Swatow men." In the end, Chinese officials decided in favor of the syndicate (see below).[28]

How he emerged as a leader of the Chaoyang merchants is unclear, but he already was thriving in Shanghai by 1839. Zheng Yingshi, whose father traded opium in Swatow before moving to Shanghai, claims that other families surnamed Zheng among the Chaoyang group in Shanghai essentially "availed themselves of their connection to Jiechen to join the opium business."[29] What was the unspecified "connection" that undergirded the rise of the Zhengs in a syndicate that dominated the Lower Yangzi opium market? They all came from Xiashan ward in Chaoyang and shared a common surname. The Zhengs of Shalong were part of this extended network, and it is possible that they recognized (or claimed) some form of kinship with the Zhengs who owned Zhengxia Ji as well.

We know more about the Shalong Zhengs in Shanghai than we do the putative leader of the syndicate. Their rise is conventionally ascribed to Zheng Xiangde, the seventeenth-century fishmonger-turned-shipping-magnate. I speculated that his spectacular success as a merchant and landowner might, in part, have derived from the opium trade. Speculation aside, his business took him to Ningbo, Shanghai, and Tianjin, and sometime between his demise in 1739 and the emergence of the Chaoyang group in Shanghai in the early nineteenth century, the Shalong Zhengs began to traffic in opium. One suspects that they may have been treated to fine wine and cuisine courtesy of Tom the Birdman. Their leader back home, Zheng Xitong, most likely made his fortune in the trade, and he was powerful enough to emerge as a special target of the violent state-builder, Fang Yao. Fang, who coined the moniker "King of Shalong," envied Xitong's enormous complex of mansions, which he characterized as "a palace."[30]

The Shalong Zhengs were among the dominant players in the Chaoyang syndicate. They were congeries of families who hailed from Shalong, a township complex of markets and villages near the Chaoyang coast. They established four family firms in Shanghai and the Lower Yangzi: Renji, managed by

Zheng Jianming (who later became a force in the Chaozhou Native Place Association); Baocheng, directed by Zheng Shiren; Baotai, managed by Zheng Shibu (the younger brother of Shiren); and Yongkang, led by Zheng Yaochen. Collectively, they exerted considerable power in Shanghai.[31]

Zheng Yaochen, born in the late 1870s, was an emblematic figure in their story. Like many in the Chaoyang clique, he was said to have come from a humble background and moved to Shanghai to seek opportunities and perhaps to evade persecution by the family nemesis, Fang Yao. His English was good enough to be hired as a translator by the Baghdadi opium magnate Silas Hardoon, and he rose to the rank of comprador for Hardoon and Company. Hardoon was one of the major foreign firms that imported Indian opium into Shanghai after the port was opened in 1842 (the others were David Sassoon and Sons, Jardine Matheson, and Russell and Company). Hardoon himself was one of the more interesting figures among the Shanghai expatriate community. Like many Jewish families, the Hardoons had fled persecution in Baghdad for the security and opportunities of Bombay. There, Silas was taken under the wing of a leader of the Baghdadi Jewish community, David Sassoon. Sassoon had built a successful triangular business shipping Indian cotton and opium to China and Chinese goods to London, and Hardoon assumed responsibility for Sassoon's real estate and opium interests in Shanghai in 1868. He eventually branched out on his own. Like many Baghdadis who operated in the orbit of the British Empire in the East, he became Anglicized in speech and dress. By the twentieth century he was one of the wealthiest men in East Asia.[32]

Hardoon's true interest lay in Shanghai real estate, but, like many others, he raised the necessary capital through the opium trade. Zheng Yaochen, his comprador, operated the company's narcotics operations and succeeded spectacularly. It did not take Zheng long to follow Hardoon's example and break away from his mentor to start his own company. He purchased the Yongkang Company from a Ningbo businessman and relied on profits in the opium trade of Shanghai and Zhenjiang to amass an extensive real estate portfolio throughout the Lower Yangzi. The company reached its height between 1910 and 1922, possessing over five hundred properties in Shanghai, Suzhou, Jiujiang, and Zhenjiang. They also branched into banking, investing in a native Chinese bank, the Jukang qianzhuang. An influential figure in the Shanghai Chaozhou Native Place Association, he reputedly possessed over one million silver dollars in his later years.[33] By the time the opium trade was outlawed in 1917, he no longer needed it.

Most of the other Shalong Zhengs had similar experiences. They departed for semicolonial Shanghai during the early Guangxu era (1870s–1880s). Some initially served as compradors for the big foreign importers before establishing their own firms, while others established businesses with family money. They used their opium profits to expand into other sectors of the Lower Yangzi economy, notably banking, real estate, and construction. They also branched into manufacturing, pooling their capital to establish the Hong Yu Silk Factory and the Hong Zhang Weaving and Dyeing Works.[34]

Like their forebear, Zheng Xiangde, they invested in land back home. In 1916 Zheng Yaochen built an enormous estate in Xixi village named "Six Miles of Auspiciousness." The brothers Zheng Shibu and Zheng Shiren similarly possessed extensive landholdings. These properties were managed by local kin.[35] Having amassed fortunes in Shanghai, these ostensibly poorer relations among the Shalong Zhengs began to adopt the landowning manner of country squires themselves.

They also contributed to the development of their native place. Indeed, the history of modern education in Chaoyang and Swatow reads like a parable of the philanthropy of the Shanghai opium syndicate: in 1920 Zheng Qiting and Guo Zibin established the Shantou Great China Middle School in Swatow; in 1921 Zheng Jianming established the Qidi School to provide free public education in Swatow; Zheng Qinchu, Zheng Yousong, and Zheng Guokai established public schools in Shalong, Chaoyang, and Swatow during the 1920s; and so on.[36] This was a chaotic period in Chaozhou history, with warlording armies struggling for power and a fledgling Communist Party challenging the social order. The largesse of these once-poor relations began to transform the infrastructure of Chaoyang. Their very success, however, proved an inducement to others to leave. As one local chronicler observed, "It was influential in encouraging other people from Shalong to go to Shanghai and make a living."[37]

There were other, negative, inducements to depart for Shanghai. Although the most violent phase of Fang Yao's campaign had ended in the 1870s, relations between the Shalong Zhengs and Puning Fangs did not improve thereafter, and there occurred several subsequent altercations between the local military and Shalong residents.[38] Moreover, Canton instituted provincial opium farms in the 1870s. In 1875 the provincial treasurer sold the right to collect the opium lijin for five years across Guangdong to a merchant named Huang Jinyuan for an annual charge of 420,000 Mexican silver dollars. In 1880 the farm was transferred to another merchant, Li Yuheng, for 900,000 silver dollars per year. In 1886 the Opium Lijin Office farmed the right to collect the lijin tax in both Swatow and Amoy to a company headed by Cai Boqi for a sum of 1,200,000 silver dollars.[39] These monopolies, controlled primarily by Cantonese networks, undermined Zheng interests in Chaoyang.

Because some Shalong Zhengs served as opium farmers in Jiangsu province, it made sense for enterprising kin to travel north to Shanghai (which was in Jiangsu) and seek their fortunes there. This was particularly the case for educated men. Chaozhouese merchants in Shanghai depended on literate scholars from home to maintain records and contend with the complexities of running a business in a treaty port.[40] Geographical mobility enabled Chaoyang opium traders to transcend the challenges they confronted in their native place and expand their interests into the semicolonial world of Shanghai.

"Guilding" the Imperialists

The Zhengs of Chengtian and Shalong, the Guos of Tongyu, and the Chens of Chengtian dominated the opium trade in Shanghai and the Lower Yangzi until 1927. Other families from Chaoyang were also drawn to the business, and they worked closely with Cantonese, who tended to serve as compradors for foreigners. The preponderance of one native place group in the most profitable business in Shanghai during the latter half of the nineteenth century is striking. Chaoyang natives purchased raw opium from importers. They sold raw opium at the wholesale and retail levels. They processed opium into paste and sold it to dens and shops. They transported Indian opium from the International Settlement to other sectors of the city. They transshipped the drug to other Yangzi River ports. Their work was institutionally facilitated by Chaozhou native place associations, which served as branches of the business.[41]

Their power was not simply commercial, it was political. Merchants associated with the Chao-Hui Native Place Association controlled the collection of opium lijin, the duty on domestically traded opium, from 1858 to 1887. This privilege transformed them into a formidable force reviled by the British in Shanghai for decades. Backed by a century's worth of knowledge of local markets as well as by legions of their compatriots, they were more effective farmers of this tax than any official, which is one reason why provincial authorities conferred the monopoly on them. The other reason was that Chaoyang opium merchants in Shanghai loaned the government 400,000 silver taels during the Taiping upheavals, and in return they were permitted to farm the opium and sugar lijin.[42]

A system evolved wherein Chaoyang merchants purchased Indian opium from foreign importers who sold their stocks on "receiving hulks" anchored at port. These foreigners paid the import tariff established by the Shanghai Tariff Conference in 1858. When the Chaoyang clique sold their supplies to other Chinese merchants, the latter paid lijin as well as other imposts (in 1879 in Jiangsu, the lijin was 20 silver taels per chest while supplementary charges ranged from 1 to 3.25 taels).[43] This system financially benefited the syndicate, for they received a percentage of the lijin collected and monopolized the domestic sale of imported opium.

The syndicate ruthlessly defended their turf. As one vice-consul at Shanghai, Clement F. R. Allen, observed, "Complaints have been more than once preferred against the Guild for threatening violence, and actually assaulting Chinese who are not members of the same [native place] society, who have ventured to buy opium [directly from foreigners]." On the other hand, Allen continued, the Chaoyang syndicate also ensured that smuggling was minimized. "I am justified in saying that no opium is smuggled into Shanghae, nor owing to the proceedings of the Guild is it possible to smuggle the drug past the inland [customs] stations, as the inland tax [lijin] is commuted before it leaves this port."[44] By outsourcing tax collection to the Chaoyang clique, officials maximized the revenue collected.

Historians have noted the futile British struggle to overcome the economic power of what they called the "Swatow Opium Guild" in Shanghai and the Lower Yangzi.[45] During the 1870s the Indo-British firm of David Sassoon and Sons established a branch of their business in the treaty port of Zhenjiang, 250 kilometers upriver from Shanghai. They shipped several chests of opium every month and began to undercut the business of the syndicate by selling below market price. In so doing, they also undermined the revenues of Jiangsu province, for the Sassoons did not collect lijin from their customers. In 1878 the syndicate decided to act. They established a heavily manned "picket" around the Sassoon warehouse in Zhenjiang to monitor those who entered and threatened a two-thousand-tael fine against any Chinese merchant who did business with the firm. Sassoon was rendered "taboo" within commercial circles, and their business in the port dried up. The company appealed to the circuit intendant, asserting that their treaty rights of free trade at the port had been violated. The intendant, responsible for maintaining revenue streams, was not sympathetic, opining that the British simply did not understand that the port was experiencing a trade depression. Sassoon and Sons, old hands in trade, saw the writing on the wall and sold their Zhenjiang branch property to twenty-six members of the Chaoyang syndicate for 22,300 silver taels.[46]

This was one of many squabbles between British and Chaoyang merchants, and foreigners learned to avoid antagonizing them. In the lexicon of British commerce in China, a new verb emerged: "to guild," as in "Bradley and Company have little fear of guilding now that they [no longer express] interest in Steamers northwards."[47] It was used in reference to the boycotting and ostracizing in which Chaozhouese collectively engaged to defend their interests, not simply in Shanghai but in other ports. One British Parsi was so unnerved by what had transpired in Zhenjiang that he actually requested a Chinese colleague to write a letter to the effect that he had never shipped opium there on his own account "in order that he might show the letter to the Guild and stave off their resentment."[48]

By 1879, however, two British merchants, T. W. Duff and D. M. David, no longer could abide this state of affairs and famously sued the Chao-Hui Native Place Association for having violated the free trade rights enshrined in the Treaty of Tianjin by excluding them from marketing opium in Zhenjiang. Duff and David argued that their exclusion represented a "conspiracy" hatched by the Chaoyang opium clique to monopolize the trade. "Swatow men," they alleged, aligned with the Chinese compradors of Western firms to dominate the wholesale market in both Shanghai and Zhenjiang and to monopolize the collection of opium lijin. As Duff testified, "the Swatow men . . . hold the whole opium trade of [Zhenjiang] in their own hands. . . . In fact the treaty port of [Zhenjiang] is entirely closed to foreign trade in this import . . . and it is [all] through the great influence of the Swatow Guild." They estimated that they had lost ten thousand silver taels in business since 1878 and sued in the Shanghai Mixed Court for that amount.[49]

The lamentations of these merchants reflected just how vital the opium trade continued to be in foreign commercial calculations. Indian opium remained the one foreign item Chinese purchased in sizable amounts. The British had imagined that opening multiple treaty ports after two wars would transform their fortunes, but these "Swatow men" refused to respect the stipulations of the unequal treaty system. Zhenjiang, located at the intersection of the Yangzi River and the Grand Canal, was an important market for the re-export of opium out of Shanghai. Roughly one-third of all Indian opium imported into Shanghai was re-exported to Zhenjiang, a trade the Chaoyang merchants exclusively controlled.[50]

The "Swatow Opium Guild Trial," as it was called, collapsed just as the plaintiffs finished presenting their arguments. The British consul and vice-consul, who represented the interests of Duff and David, took umbrage at the

Chinese circuit intendant's comment that the plaintiffs had not proven their case and stormed out of the courtroom. The lawyers for the Chaoyang syndicate, W. V. Drummond and R. E. Wainewright, then proceeded to eviscerate the case the consulate had set forth. They denied the accusation that the Chaoyang dealers had established a "monopoly" at Zhenjiang in its technical sense, and even if this were true, there existed similar "capitalist monopolies" as well as trade organizations in England after all. The businessmen from Chaoyang did not "conspire" to control the market, they simply were better organized and more familiar with the territory and cooperated more readily with their fellow Chaoyang natives than British did among themselves. The consul had presented no evidence that the Chaoyang merchants had broken the treaties or that the Chinese government had given them a monopoly on the opium trade. Moreover, their clients had not prevented the British from trading with anyone. The fact that foreigners felt intimidated by "the Guild" was irrelevant. These fears were grounded in the fact that Chaoyang merchants would cease to deal with them if they were crossed. Chaoyang merchants were free to do business with whomsoever they pleased, and considering that the Chaoyang merchants were "the largest customers" of the foreign merchants at Shanghai, "it had been unwise, as a matter of business policy, to quarrel with them" in the first place.

Drummond added that the so-called Swatow Guild was not a guild at all, but a native place association, a fraternity that represented twenty to thirty thousand laboring and commercial sojourners from Chaoyang in Shanghai, among whom only two to three hundred were engaged in the opium business. Merchants from Canton and Chaoyang similarly had organized a native place association at Zhenjiang (the "Canton-Swatow Club"), but it was open to all merchants from those regions and did not exclusively advance the interests of opium traders. There was, in fact, no such thing as a "Swatow Opium Guild" in Shanghai, Zhenjiang, or elsewhere, and, at any rate, the treaties did not prevent Chinese businessmen from entering into any sort of combination they chose.[51]

The defense was disingenuous, for the "Swatow Guild," the foreign term for the Chao-Hui Native Place Association, was dominated by the Chaoyang opium and sugar merchants who led and funded its operations. Moreover, these merchants controlled the Chaozhou native place associations along the lower reaches of the Yangzi River. As Zheng Yingshi, an opium trader, recalled, "It can be said that all commercial centers that had a Chaozhou native place association were also regions to which the power of the Chaozhou opium clique reached. Each area's Chaozhou native place association became a hotel for opium merchants."[52]

The opium merchants of Chaoyang aspired to a monopoly over the domestic trade. Western accounts of these Sino-British tensions ignore the fact that the right of the clique to collect opium lijin was not restricted to Shanghai or Zhenjiang. These merchants had been appointed the opium farmers for Jiangsu, in which these ports were located. They collected lijin on domestic sales of the drug and transmitted the government's share every month to provincial authorities. It was a major source of government revenue from 1858 to 1887.[53] They surely understood this right in terms of the traditional authority accorded other monopolistic enterprises, like salt and iron. They had a financial stake in squeezing out commercial operators who did not have the obligation to transfer lijin to officialdom. It is not surprising that they posted the "Opium [Lijin] Tax Office" sign right next to the sign that read "Chao-Hui Native Place Association." The fact that the British consul failed to "prove" that such a state-sanctioned arrangement existed reflected his lack of competence compared to that of a barrister like Drummond, who seized on this failing with relish.

In monopolizing the business, the Chaoyang clique manifested the tendency toward exclusivity and domination evinced by other major players in the global opium trade. It goes without saying that the production and sale of Bengal opium was a colonial monopoly in British India. The revenues were existentially vital, and without them, "India would be insolvent." The British Straits Settlements farmed out exclusive control of opium sales to Chinese syndicates. The colony depended heavily on revenues from these monopolies to sustain itself.[54] Similarly, provincial authorities in China conferred monopolies on Chinese merchants to ensure reliable revenue streams.

Moreover, the British themselves strove for monopolistic control of the import trade in China. Back in Chaozhou, from the 1830s to 1850s, representatives of Jardine Matheson periodically struck deals with their major British competitor, Dent and Company, to maintain an opium-smuggling duopoly in a fruitless effort to drive out other foreign competition. They manipulated the price of Indian opium to seek the largest possible share of the market.[55] In Shanghai the company continued its efforts to thwart competition. In 1886, during the course of a Sino-British dispute over lijin, the directors of the Lijin Office and the "Swatow Opium Guild" proposed to four British importers a mutually beneficial arrangement. If the British acceded to a resolution on Chinese terms (involving joint collection of lijin), the Chinese Lijin Office promised to guarantee that all Indian opium carried into Shanghai on foreign bottoms would be required first to pass exclusively through the receiving "hulks" of those firms only: those of Jardine Matheson, David Sassoon and Sons, E. D. Sassoon, and Cowasjee Pamanjeethi Framjee (a Parsi firm).

The Chaoyang clique essentially offered to extend the monopolistic structure in the Chinese domestic business to an exclusive group of importers, and these parties were amenable. William Keswick, the director of Jardine's operations in Shanghai, emphasized that the firm was willing to make significant concessions in return for an oligopoly in the foreign importation of opium. As he noted in correspondence with the lawyer for the Chaoyang syndicate, W. V. Drummond, "Before agreeing to this we shall require from your clients sufficient guarantee that no further hulks than the existing four will be permitted at this port, and that. . . . Opium cannot be landed direct from [an] importing vessel, but must be first passed through one or other of the present four hulks." The other parties also expressed willingness to enter a deal as long as they enjoyed an oligopoly.[56] The deal fell through when the British could not agree on the specifics (relating to the expiration of the arrangement and the amount of dividend each party would receive for collecting lijin) and the Parsi company could not arrange to have their partners in Bombay accede in a timely manner. The negotiations nonetheless demonstrate that the Chinese were not uniquely committed to monopolies over the trade.

The Swatow Opium Case of 1879 manifested the effectiveness of the native place association as an institution projecting commercial power in distant places. In a culturally diverse treaty port like Shanghai, one adaptation they made was to the realities of the legal system. In the International Settlement, a "Mixed Court" had been established over which the foreign consul and the local Chinese magistrate both presided. Given the infiltration of British legal culture into the system of dispute resolution, Chaoyang merchants did not simply depend on Chinese officials to promote their interests, they hired a British a barrister-at-law, W. V. (William Venn) Drummond. The Chaoyang clique relied on several legal experts, but Drummond was their most consistent consigliore in Shanghai. The son of a Highgate parson, he was called to the bar at Lincoln's Inn. After practicing in Hong Kong, he arrived in Shanghai in 1872 and over the next four decades enjoyed a highly successful career.[57] His name appears frequently in the records of the Mixed Court, and he almost invariably won his cases. He prepared his witnesses well, relied on his own interpreters, and shredded his opponents' arguments with finely honed reasoning.[58] British consuls resented the ways Drummond advanced the legal interests of the Swatow Opium Syndicate against those of their British competitors. As Chaloner Alabaster, British consul at Shanghai, lamented in 1885 during the course of one legal imbroglio, "As regards the Mixed Court . . . there is greater difficulty as Mr. Drummond is doing his utmost to prevent things working smoothly. . . . But it is the object of Mr. Drummond and the Syndicate to ignore me altogether, and as the [Chinese officials] seem entirely under their dictation, I do not yet see my way clearly to a solution of the difficulty."[59] It was as though British diplomats had not considered the possibility that Chinese would rely on a British lawyer to compete on an equal footing with British subjects and thereby triumph in their legal disputes. This is one of many instances in which the Mixed Court and consular courts, which the British had insisted on instituting in the treaty ports, served Chinese as much as British interests.

Narco-Patriotism

Because they collected opium lijin, the Chaoyang clique's interests in Shanghai coincided with those of the provincial government, which depended on these imposts as a revenue source. From 1869 to 1885 the Jiangsu treasury garnered 2,235,004 silver taels from the opium lijin alone.[60] The syndicate profited from fees derived from lijin collection as well as from their monopoly on the marketing of opium. This income defrayed the costs of maintaining a literal army of "lijin runners" to enforce duty collection, prevent smuggling, and otherwise protect the business interests of the syndicate. One presumes that most of these runners were themselves from Chaoyang, not only because that fit the cultural pattern of sojourning—merchants established themselves in a trade and laborers from the same region followed—but also because the native place associations controlled the employment of migrant labor in the port of Shanghai, relying on labor contractors (*baotou*) affiliated with these organizations to recruit workers in a variety of occupations.[61]

British consular officials deprecated these runners, viewing them as violent enforcers of the narco-power of the Swatow Guild. The runners constituted a "private police force" that enabled the syndicate to harass their Chinese and foreign competition, and Alabaster endeavored to "check their pretensions." In his view, "the Syndicate who farm the collection are . . . using their position to obtain a monopoly of the trade . . . and harassing independent dealers by surrounding their establishments with spies and watchers, making descents upon them ever and again, seizing and questioning their agents and generally worrying them."[62]

Alabaster's fulminations were expressed in the context of an ongoing dispute between the British and Chinese authorities as to whether the Chinese in the International Settlement had any "right" to collect a tax to which the British Crown had not acceded. Essentially, it was a clash over which nation had ultimate sovereignty over the section of Shanghai in which most foreigners had chosen to live. By aggressively asserting the taxation authority conferred on them by the Chinese state, the merchants of Chaoyang extended the writ of that state. And they put the British on notice that they were determined to triumph in this struggle. As Alabaster warned his superiors in the Foreign Office, his "earlier hopes that the Lijin Syndicate would abandon their attempt to levy lijin on opium consumed in the Settlement have not been fulfilled, and . . . I am informed by their legal adviser they intend pushing the question, to use his words, to the bitter end."[63] The syndicate, backed by a battalion of lijin runners and assisted by their British lawyers, challenged the quasi-colonial sphere the British had been building since 1842.

Alabaster asserted that his predecessor, P. J. Hughes, had agreed to "allow" the syndicate to issue "tickets" that enabled the runners to operate in the International Settlement because he thought the system would prevent the smuggling of Indian opium. But even as Hughes agreed to the system, "he foresaw the danger of allowing an independent police force in the Settlement and the necessity of imposing checks on their actions."[64] There already was a police force in the Settlement, of course, the Shanghai Municipal Police, established in 1854 under the authority of the British-controlled Shanghai Municipal Council and composed of British, Irish, Sikh, and, later, Chinese officers. By "independent," he meant "independent of British control." When Hughes agreed to a system in which the runners collected lijin and monitored the opium market, he had presumed that they would "cooperate with the foreign police" and operate "with the assent of the [British] Assessor in the Mixed Court." The syndicate did neither, and Alabaster characterized this as "trying to run roughshod" over his authority.[65]

It should be added that Alabaster bore a special animus toward Chaozhouese. As consul in Swatow in 1869, he had railed incessantly about the militant resistance of coastal villagers to the British presence. His diplomatic career was almost derailed after he overreacted to peasant attacks on a British naval patrol by arranging to have their village bombed (the so-called Cockchafer Affair). After having been chastised by Lord Clarendon, the secretary of state, he was deeply resentful, feeling that the Foreign Office simply did not understand his "difficult situation" in having been posted to a violent region where the peasantry "had the reputation of being invincible."[66] He characterized Chaozhou as a place where "clan fights, private murders, gang robberies, systematized blackmail and everything oppressive and wrong that existed in Europe in the darkest ages have flourished in the villages thickly scattered in this N.E. corner of Kwangtung from time immemorial."[67] Alabaster's subsequent request to be transferred to Shanghai was granted, and how disconcerted he must have been to discover that his greatest antagonists in the port were sojourners from that very corner of Guangdong. He did not refer to his earlier travails in his accounts of Shanghai's Chaoyang clique in the 1880s, but it is unlikely they were far from his mind.

The British dispute with the opium syndicate was a test of the legal status of the International Settlement of Shanghai. Was it to be treated as a semicolony, or was it to remain a sovereign part of China? Chaoyang merchants obviously were motivated by economic self-interest; they did not express a political agenda in public (though it is unlikely they were very pro-Qing). Nevertheless, they resisted the consolidation of British authority in the city, counteracting the creeping expansion of British control so commonly seen elsewhere across the British Empire. The government had offered them a monopoly on the collection of opium lijin. The Chinese had every right to impose a tax on domestic commerce and every right to send runners to enforce Chinese law. Judging from the fulminations of British consuls, this assertion of Chinese sovereignty was deemed an unnaturally aggressive resistance to the British understanding of how the treaty system was supposed to operate.[68]

Banking on Change

Chaoyang merchants increasingly diversified their investments when it became clear that the trade in Indian opium would become illegal after 1916. This is seen in the expansion of Shanghai's native banking industry, a trend in which the Chaoyang syndicate played a significant role. Of the 120 native banks (qianzhuang) established in the city from 1912 to 1926, 33 were founded by Chaoyang natives, all of whom had made their fortunes in opium during the nineteenth and twentieth centuries. Collectively they invested 2,076,400 silver taels in these financial institutions during this period.[69]

Their investment in new banks was unprecedented. From 1843 to 1895, arguably the heyday of the syndicate, they invested in virtually no new banking enterprises in Shanghai. From 1896 to 1911 they were involved in the founding of two native banks, a mere 3.7 percent of the total.[70] The fact that over a quarter (27.5 percent) of all native banks founded from 1912 to 1926 were capitalized entirely by Chaoyang opium traders indicates that they diversified their portfolios after the founding of the Republic of China in 1912, when it became clear that opium once again might be outlawed. They also were responding to the increasingly shrill, nationalistic outcry against the culture of opium use in China and sought to "improve their status" as the trade became socially stigmatized.[71]

The wealthiest Chaoyang merchants invested in more than one bank during this period. The Xinyu Native Bank, for example, was founded in 1915 through a partnership led by Chen Qingfeng, Guo Zibin, and Zheng Jianming, who moved into the financial sector even as they branched into textile and tobacco manufacturing, real estate, and other businesses.[72] Xinyu probably owed its success to the fact that it was founded by leaders of the three dominant Chaoyang lineage groups in Shanghai. Not only were these men prominent in Shanghai business circles, they had high social standing among—and lineage, marital, and village links to—dozens of other Chaoyang families in the city. Prior to 1937 the native banking structure of Shanghai continued to be heavily organized around native place; Chaozhouese tended to invest in banks together as a group, as did natives of other places in China like those from Shaoxing, Ningbo, and Suzhou.[73] The Xinyu Native Bank, like many of the other Chaoyang-affiliated banks, catered to the entrepreneurial and investment interests of small businessmen from Chaozhou in particular and contributed to the ongoing viability of Chaozhouese interests in the Lower Yangzi region.

Chinese native banks were small-scale by international standards but significant in the context of early industrial Shanghai. They financed domestic commodity flows and offered a secure source of credit in urban and rural areas. They functioned as commercial banks, conducting financial exchanges, issuing cash notes, and offering discounts to the business community. Unlike modern banks, they did not expect merchants to put up security for their loans, considered insulting in a business culture in which one's reputation in a local market system was a form of collateral. Native banks were essential to financing regional trade networks in the Yangzi River valley. Foreign banks began to appear in Shanghai after the 1860s, but they lacked branch services in the inland areas, leaving the native banks in control of indigenous money markets. Foreign banks, however, increasingly issued "chop loans" to these smaller banks, which turned around and lent money to Chinese merchants, an investment dynamic that enhanced the prosperity of the native banks by increasing their capital power.[74] By establishing these banks, Chaoyang merchants diversified their own business interests, but they also contributed to the prosperity of the regional economy prior to World War II.

Finally, the Shalong Zhengs collectively were significant participants in this turn to native banking. Of the 2,076,000 silver taels initially invested in these banks, they put up 700,000. Zheng Jianming, for example was a founding partner in the Xinyu, Xincheng, Xinfu, and Renyuan Native Banks (he was also chairman of the board of a modern bank, Huatong Bank). He initially invested at least 174,000 silver taels in these firms. Zheng Yaochen, Zheng Yousong, Zheng Shibu, and Zheng Qiting also invested in native banking during this period.[75] This underscores the continued prosperity of a lineage that stoutly resisted the rise of Fang Yao back in Chaoyang. The geographical mobility of the Zhengs enabled them to shine in another corner of translocal Chaozhou, far from the shadows cast by their enemies back home.

Back to the Future

The clout of the Chaoyang opium syndicate did not end in 1887, when responsibility for collecting lijin was shifted to the Imperial Maritime Customs. For one thing, Chaoyang natives continued to receive monopolies over incidental sorts of taxation over opium. In 1895, for example, provincial officials conferred the authority to collect a tax on processed Indian opium ("paste") in Jiangsu. Zheng Rangqing of the Zhengxia ji firm was deputed to act as director of the bureau charged with collecting this impost of twelve silver taels per chest of processed opium, just as his father (Jiechen) earlier had served as a leader of the syndicate responsible for collecting lijin on imported raw opium. The bureau for the collection of the new tax, the Processed Opium Tax Bureau (Yan'gao juanju), was headquartered at none other than the Chao-Hui Native Place Association.[76]

For another thing, they continued to thrive in the opium trade. In 1906 the Qing government announced a plan to eradicate the trade in both imported and native Chinese opium within ten years. Chinese opium prohibition, however, turned out to be as effective as the roughly coterminous prohibition of alcohol in the United States. Market demand simply drove the trade back to the underground economy that had flourished prior to the 1850s, and the illicit trade flourished. After the Qing were overthrown in 1912, nationalist revolutionaries established the Republic of China and declared their intention to abolish the trade forthwith. A delegation of Chaoyang merchants led by Zheng

Zijia traveled to Beijing to meet with the new minister of finance, Liang Shiyi, to request that Yuan Shikai's new government adopt a "go-slow" policy of prohibition to give those invested in the business time to transition to other endeavors. The minister scrupulously responded that "the present government is a revolutionary government and opium absolutely will be proscribed." The merchants nonetheless intuited that the minister was open to "persuasion" and arranged to have their Indo-British colleagues in the Foreign Medicine Guild (Yangyao gongsuo) offer him an enormous bribe. Liang's tone notably softened. He permitted the syndicate to continue to sell opium as long as they paid Yuan's government a special "seal fee" of 2 *jiao* per *liang* of opium. Throughout the remainder of Yuan's term (1912–1916), the merchants paid the "seal fee," and, as Zheng Zijia's son later recalled, "the sale of opium remained an open and legal business."[77]

By this point, most of the British and American houses had abandoned the heavily taxed import trade to a small number of Indian and Baghdadi importers (the so-called Yangyao gongsuo, which included David Sassoon and Co., E. D. Sassoon, S. J. Ezra, and Edward Ezra). The Zhengxia Ji, the Guoyu Ji, the Li family firm of Liwei Ji, and other, smaller firms continued to sell Indian opium. These foreign and Chinese companies agreed to deal with one another exclusively and exclude interlopers (the agreement was formalized by the establishment of the Shanghai Opium Merchants Combine in 1913). They convinced the Shanghai Municipal Council to recognize them as the exclusive purveyors of Indian opium in the International Settlement. They entered into a similar agreement in 1915 with the provincial governments of Jiangsu, Jiangxi, and Guangdong, which recognized their monopoly on Indian opium until 1917 in exchange for payment of an additional fee per chest of opium. This oligopoly enabled them to inflate prices and maximize profits as the 1917 deadline approached.[78]

The disintegration of the Republic into warlordism after 1916 complicated their efforts to remain dominant in the business. To transport opium out of Shanghai, they were forced to pay various "protection fees" to local militants. Moreover, warlord armies elsewhere in China fostered the production of native opium as a revenue source, further exacerbating the already crippling competition Indian opium faced from cheaper drug from Sichuan, Yunnan, Guizhou, Rehe, Gansu, and Xinjiang. The French smuggled Yunnan opium from their colony in Indochina, which bordered that province. The Japanese shipped "frontier opium" (*biantu*) from Manchuria to the ports of the eastern seaboard. The Chongqing Opium Merchants, who operated as agents for

Sichuan officials, specialized in an east-west commerce whereby they shipped Sichuan opium to ports downriver and carried foreign munitions on their return voyage. These and other aggressive commercial players undermined the Chaoyang network.[79]

Chaoyang merchants adapted to changing circumstances after the British banned Indian opium exports to China in 1917. Noting that the Japanese had nurtured a small market demand for Persian opium (*hongtu*), several decided to traffic in that variety. In 1920 Zheng Yibin, a comprador for a Norwegian company, passed through Iran on his way home from Europe. He purchased a supply and contacted several Chaoyang merchants upon his arrival in Shanghai. They agreed to go into business with him, raising one million yuan to form the Xinyuan Company. Zheng, now the director, returned to Norway to purchase a two-thousand-ton steamer he christened the *Asian Treasure* (Yachen). He procured five hundred chests of Persian opium in Iran and hastened back to Shanghai, only to find that the British authorities in the International Settlement refused to cooperate. He turned to the French, who controlled their own sector of Shanghai, the French Concession, and permitted him to establish the business there. After decades of operating out of the British-controlled Settlement, the Chaoyang syndicate (twelve large family firms and forty smaller companies affiliated with Xinyuan) decamped to the French Concession to promote the "red opium" market."[80]

The company subordinated itself to the boss of the French Concession underworld, Du Yuesheng (a Jiangsu native), and continued to overcome obstacles. In the end, however, they were undone by their own success. Other merchants perceived that there was a demand for Persian opium and began to enter the business themselves. They flooded the market and drove the price down. Those affiliated with the Xinyuan Company determined that the only way to guarantee profits was to invite virtually every other Chaoyang merchant in Shanghai who had a continuing interest in the trade to join them. They reorganized their company into a larger entity, the Gongping Company, still headed by Zheng Yibin but now capitalized with ten million yuan invested by the new partners. Zheng was flush with confidence or, rather, overconfidence. The firm proceeded to import an astronomical supply of Persian opium, only to discover belatedly that the new stock was defective and could not be processed into the paste that the Chinese consumer preferred. It could not be sold. Zheng desperately tried to reason with his Persian suppliers, but the latter were not amenable to negotiation, and the Chaoyang company lacked the capacity to "guild" foreigners in a distant land with little stake in the Chinese economy. Ultimately, the company was forced to unload the opium for a tiny fraction of its original price on the Japanese, who refined it into inexpensive "medicine balls" to sell in local shops. Gongping never recovered from this debacle and eventually went bankrupt. The smaller firms were hit especially hard and family fortunes were lost. Zheng Yibin, devastated, died soon thereafter.[81]

The collapse of the Gongping Company extinguished the economic power of the Chaoyang opium syndicate in Shanghai. Individual actors continued to trade, but the network as a formidable, monopolistic force was finished. They had survived the termination of their monopoly over lijin collection and adapted to the challenges posed by a disintegrating political order. They could not withstand a business setback that stemmed, essentially, from their inexperience in Persian opium as a commodity, however. It is impossible to imagine someone like Zheng Jiechen seriously misjudging the quality of an Indian opium shipment back in the 1860s, and one can only imagine the mutual recriminations that tore Gongping asunder. Even if they were to regroup, they faced stiff competition from traffickers in cheaper, domestically produced opium. Their strength in the nineteenth century—a knowledge of and monopoly over Indian opium—became a source of their weakness after 1917. And, unlike their erstwhile adversary in the drug-dealing underworld, Du Yuesheng, they did not have a personal connection to the strongman emergent, Chiang Kai-shek. Soon after his Nationalist forces entered the city in 1927, the generalissimo established the Opium Suppression Supervisory Bureau (OSSB) and placed at its head the mobster who had helped him crush the labor movement in Shanghai, Du.[82]

Even after Du's Green Gang established their own monopoly over the trade, Chaoyang natives continued to play a role. Bureaucrats assigned to the OSSB consulted such retired opium magnates as Zheng Shouzhi, who advised them on the finer points of generating revenue. In appreciation for his mentoring, the Nationalist government appointed him the Shanghai bureau chief of the OSSB. Another stalwart of the old Chaoyang network, Lu Qinghai, was appointed bureau chief of the OSSB in Hubei. These men received a "share of the spoils" of an opium business that fronted as a suppression bureau.[83] They may have been subordinate to Du, but their business experience was valuable to the Nationalists, who were desperate for stable revenue streams.

The connection of Chaoyang merchants to the trade endured until World War II. When the Japanese occupied eastern China in 1937, they severed Shanghai's communications with Sichuan, Guizhou, and Yunnan, the main sources of the city's opium by then. Chaoyang merchants in Shanghai contacted their colleagues in Swatow to arrange a new supply route, and Swatow reemerged as a fount of Shanghai opium from 1937 to 1939. Zheng Yingshi, who managed an opium-processing firm in Swatow, made most of the local arrangements with the cooperation of the police and the Swatow Customs. After Swatow itself was invaded in 1939, he shifted his operations to Xingning, in the mountainous hinterland of Chaozhou. Opium supplies became unreliable, however, and that business collapsed as well.[84] Ironically, in the end, the Zhengs resorted to the old Hakka smuggling routes of the nineteenth century.

Capital Accumulation and Imperialism

The Chaoyang syndicate channeled profits from the opium trade into other businesses. In this they were no different from other international players in the nineteenth-century commercial world. Jardine Matheson, a legendary conglomerate of businesses in East Asia, accumulated a colossal amount of capital from marketing opium and, on the strength of that income, expanded into insurance, milling, shipping, and other businesses. After the 1860s, when they were forced to the margins of the trade, they concentrated on these other enterprises. Opium, however, had made it all possible.[85] Similarly, Abiel Abbott Low (1811–1893), a descendant of one of the early settlers of Salem, Massachusetts, made his fortune as a partner in the leading American opium-trading firm, Russell and Co. He returned to the United States to establish his own business, A. A. Low and Brothers, invested in the installation of the first transatlantic cable and, along with Collis P. Huntington, built the Chesapeake and Ohio Railroad. He served as president of the New York Chamber of Commerce. A major landmark in that city, Low Memorial Library of Columbia University, is named for him.[86] Low's biography is an American version of that of Guo Zibin. They made their original fortunes in opium; they offered important service to commercial organizations; and they are celebrated in local histories as philanthropists and businessmen, their drug-dealing pasts furtively dropped into footnotes or, in the case of Low, ignored. Indeed, the role of the opium trade in the rise of American capitalism is an almost completely unexplored historical topic.

In Chinese narratives of the trade, Chinese participants are derided as "traitors," people who cooperated with foreigners and flung their society into the dungeon of the opium den.[87] This is understandable. Foreigners and Chinese alike transgressed the laws of the Qing, and their continued smuggling led to the outbreak of the First Opium War in 1839, which inaugurated the unequal treaty system and a "century of humiliation" at the hands of imperialists.

There is another way to view the Chinese who were involved in the opium trade, however, a perspective that points to their significance at this moment, and this place, in modern history. They amassed capital in a trade in which south-eastern frontiersmen had been involved since late medieval times. The trade was profitable because opium was the Chinese recreational drug of choice, just as imbibing equally addictive alcoholic beverages emerged as the Anglo-American way to unwind. Unlike foreign participants in the trade, however, the Chaoyang syndicate channeled their profits to benefit Chinese economic interests: those of their families, their native place, and the Lower Yangzi. They invested the money in banks and factories; they built schools and hospitals; they contributed a phenomenal amount of disaster relief to a home region constantly beset by natural calamities. Their financial support of the needy outstripped the support that any Chinese state managed to provide prior to 1949.

The Chaoyang syndicate also played an important role in thwarting the expansion of British power in the Lower Yangzi region during the nineteenth century. The fulminations of British merchants in Shanghai attest to this. The opium wars had been fought to "open" the Lower Yangzi in particular to British commerce. When the diplomat Rutherford Alcock advised the British Foreign Office on what to demand from the Chinese as the Second Opium War was winding down in 1857, he opposed an increase in the number of treaty ports already opened to British trade in 1842. He believed such an expansion would simply add to the administrative expenses of the Foreign Office without offering much payoff to British commercial interests. Instead, to achieve Great Britain's goal of bolstering trade in a cost-efficient and profitable way, it made more sense to concentrate on the five port regions already opened and seek treaty rights that would facilitate British penetration of hinterland economies. He emphasized the importance of focusing on Shanghai and expanding British interests into the Yangzi River valley, with its dense population, commercial vitality, and numerous ports.[88] In the end, he lost one battle—commercial lobbyists insisted that eleven more ports, including Swatow, be "opened"—but won another: many of the new ports, including Zhenjiang, were located along the Yangzi, which enabled the British to operate in the riverine interior. As one British observer noted years later: "The most important feature of the new arrangements was the effective opening of the river Yangtze."[89]

And yet, in the most remunerative trade of nineteenth-century Shanghai and its hinterland, opium, the Chaoyang network hindered their progress at every turn. They permitted the British to haul Indian opium to the shores of Shanghai, but no more than that. They were far more effective in blocking the expansion of British interests than any contemporary Chinese military corps, commercial clique, or high-minded literati movement. These merchants did not ineffectually wag their angry ink brushes against the winds of imperialism and war. They uniquely contended with British power in the nineteenth century. They did not have a navy at their side, but they did not need military force. They frustrated the British at Shanghai with commercial power, the cohesive practices of the guild brotherhood, and a formidable determination to protect their economic turf and thereby ensure that the Chinese benefited from the profits of the opium trade. They left more than one infuriated British merchant muttering, "The Guild and its connexions now [have] the whole opium trade in their own hands."[90]

In the Swatow Opium Case of 1879, the British articulated highly expansive interpretations of the treaty system, interpretations predicated on a sense of vast commercial entitlement in the ports of China. The Chaoyang syndicate of Shanghai shrugged off the stipulations of six treaties signed with foreign powers. Their own interpretation of those settlements prevailed. They even defeated the British in the juridically hybrid Mixed Court system the British had imposed on China. They found themselves the best English barrister in Asia, and together they crushed their opponents in litigation. After the agitated British consul stormed away in frustration, the Chinese taotai officiating at court proudly proclaimed that "this was a Chinese court, and that he would proceed to hear the case alone."[91] In exercising their lijin-farming rights in the Lower Yangzi, these merchants upheld the sovereign power of the Chinese government to tax commodities as it saw fit and in spite of strident, foreign opposition.

From the eighteenth to twentieth centuries the British colonial project in India depended on the export of opium to China. Colonial authorities in South Asia, British consuls in China, and government officials in London anxiously watched the sun set on the Indian opium market in China. They also marveled that the two great commodities whose intertwined trade so marked modern Sino-British relations—Indian opium and Chinese tea—began to decline in interrelated ways at the same time: just as native Chinese opium displaced the drug produced in South Asia, South Asian tea began to eclipse that of China in international markets.[92] In the twentieth century British fortunes in Shanghai were salvaged by the emerging imperialist on the East Asian stage, Japan, which won the right for all foreign powers to commence building factories in China after its victory in the first Sino-Japanese war in 1895. British direct investment in China increased in subsequent decades, and they gained a foothold in the manufacturing sector of the economy.[93] Like so many other Chinese businessmen, Guo Zibin the textile manufacturer was never going to compete with the British in the ways that Guo Zibin the opium magnate did. Nevertheless, Guo Zibin the sojourning cook from Chaoyang became a manufacturer, a banker, and a highly lauded philanthropist after a career in an opium trade that the British made legal but were unable to make their own.

7

"This Diabolical Tyranny"

DISCIPLINING THE BRITISH AT CHAOZHOU, 1858–1890s

Considering how this locality has grown during the past ten years, one cannot but be sanguine as to its future—so far, at least, as Native interests are concerned.... It is difficult to be equally hopeful as to the concerns of Foreigners in Swatow.

—C. LENOX SIMPSON, COMMISSIONER OF CUSTOMS, 1891

CONVENTIONAL HISTORIES of China record that Chaozhou's maritime port of Swatow was "opened" to foreign trade as a result of the Chinese defeat at the hands of the French and British during the Second Opium War (1856–1860). The treaties that terminated this war—the Treaty of Tianjin (1858) and Convention of Beijing (1860)—opened Swatow and ten additional ports to Western trade and permitted foreign travel to the interior of China, among other stipulations.[1] As Zhao Chunchen has shown, however, it was the Americans, not the British, who opened the port to foreigners. In 1858 the British, French, Russians, and Americans signed separate treaties with the Qing, but the renewal of hostilities between Chinese and Franco-British forces in that year invalidated the agreements among those belligerents while the Americans ratified their treaty with the beleaguered Qing court. The Xianfeng emperor issued an edict on November 9, 1859, commanding local officials to "open" Chaozhou to the Americans.[2]

If the Americans technically opened Swatow to foreign trade, the British emerged as the dominant Western presence after their military victory in 1860.

The British had assumed that, with legal ingress to Chaozhou, they naturally would emerge as powerful players in the regional economy. They did not. Coastal villagers did not take kindly to the alien intrusion, and British nationals could barely manage to travel into the hinterland of Swatow port. The British also were forced out of the only sector of the Chaozhou import economy into which they ever had managed to make inroads, the opium trade. British steamers began to displace Chinese junks as a mode of commercial transport, but the cargo on board was primarily Chinese-owned. British merchants were also subjected to stringent "guilding" whenever they tried to alter the commercial dynamic of the economy. They had performed their historical service to Chaozhou merchants: supplying junk traders with drug on the latter's trek north; trafficking in opium with local smugglers; and, of course, waging wars that ultimately led to the de facto legalization of the opium trade after 1858. Those merchants, however, thwarted British expansion into the regional economy.

The British consulate in Swatow also served Chinese interests more effectively than those of their own nationals. Most plaintiffs who lodged civil accusations in the consular court were Chinese, not British, and British consular and naval authorities dutifully captured and punished British culprits who cheated or assaulted local people. Chinese officials, on the other hand, could barely be bothered with the profusion of British legal complaints the consulate sent their way. The consulate itself was transformed into an institution that protected and advanced the interests of overseas Chaozhouese. These Chinese had become naturalized British subjects in the Straits Settlements and in Hong Kong, yet their wives, children, parents, and other kin continued to reside in Chaozhou. The British Consulate in Swatow emerged as a transnational institution that reluctantly served the needs of Chinese who made most of their money in the colonies the Europeans built and maintained. The sun never set on the British Empire, and it beamed brightly over their Sino-British subjects.

Chaozhou Lessons: Resisting the British

The treaties China signed in the wake of the Second Opium War did not specify that they were establishing a treaty port at Swatow (Shantou) which, aside from serving as a base for the opium and coolie trades, was not a significant commercial town in 1858. The accords instead opened the prefectural city of Chaozhou, the commercial and administrative hub of the region, located on the Han River about thirty-five kilometers from the coast. Foreigners hoped to access the prosperous interior, including Anbu, Chaozhou city's main port. British consular officers also expected to have access to influential prefectural officials who were not always inclined to make the journey to the coast. The deepwater harborage around Swatow nonetheless was conducive to steam shipping, and the town emerged as the modern seaport of eastern Guangdong. By 1862 its status as a "treaty port" was formalized in law. The lure of Chaozhou city as a political center and of Anbu, Zhanglin, and Huanggang as dynamic ports of trade, however, did not subside. In fact, most trade at Swatow was conducted by agents for larger firms in the towns beyond.[3]

Chaozhou was a culturally cosmopolitan region filled with returned sojourners of all classes who had resided overseas. John Scarth, who lived in South China from 1847 to 1859, was surprised to encounter peasants who were fluent in foreign languages. As he recalled, "The people of [Chaozhou] . . . are very friendly to foreigners. This may arise from many of them having been abroad. . . . It is curious to be addressed by a labourer in the fields in the Malay language. He sees a foreigner and thinks he should know that foreign dialect. Numbers of the people here speak Malay."[4]

Returned emigrants were not the only multilingual people in Chaozhou. Members of the Chaoyang opium clique in Shanghai had become fluent in English while trading at Swatow and got their start in the larger port serving as translators and compradors for foreign firms. The crews of British ships that plied the South China Sea tended to be multinational, but by 1874 most of the sailors on vessels that worked the coast of China were natives of Chaozhou.[5] As we have seen, local sailors predominated among the crews of junks sailing between China and Siam. Chaozhouese were accustomed to dealing with foreigners, and there is ample evidence of their friendly hospitality to visitors.

The violent opposition to the British presence in Swatow during the 1860s therefore was not a manifestation of cultural xenophobia but of patriotic resistance. Popular hostility had been growing since 1852, when a riot against the coolie trade at Amoy drove the business southward to Swatow. Abuses in this trade were legendary, as local traffickers kidnapped and sold peasants to foreign shippers who transported them to labor-hungry colonies in Southeast Asia, the Caribbean, and South America.[6] By the 1860s Swatow was the center of "credit ticket" emigration, a system in which extremely poor laborers who could not afford to pay for their passage departed on credit. This obliged them to enter into indentured servitude to pay off the cost of their overseas journeys. The system was often oppressive, especially at colonial ports like Penang, where coolies might be shipped against their will to plantations in the Dutch East Indies.[7] Most laborers willingly traveled to Southeast Asia to seek employment, but routine migration was shadowed by tales of horrible crimes that fostered antiforeignism.

Chaozhouese also violently resisted the British consular presence, a struggle that might be characterized as an informal extension of the Second Opium War. On July 6, 1860, the first British consul, George W. Caine, arrived at Double Island, a site of opium smuggling and illicit foreign residence in the 1850s. Caine, the son of an old military man who had served as the colonial secretary of Hong Kong, disembarked from a warship to the cacophony of a seven-gun salute. Another burst of gunfire rang out as he hoisted the Union Jack atop the building that was to serve as a temporary consulate. With this display of martial fanfare, Caine triumphantly declared the treaty port of Chaozhou "open."[8]

Caine's optimism was premature for, within a month, angry placards reviling the British in apocalyptic terms appeared across the region, and antiforeign violence became a way of life. It would take almost a year for the British to secure themselves at the seaport of Swatow and an additional nine years of stonings, cursings, and mob attacks before they could travel safely and routinely to the prefectural capital at Chaozhou. An eighteen-village anti-British league led by the walled village-market complex of Outing harassed them in Swatow, while examination elites mobilized angry throngs in other towns.[9] A classic case of asymmetrical conflict, the British navy was unable to "perform" its maritime power and awe the Chaozhou populace. The prefectural seat was miles inland on the Han River, and the waters were too shallow for large steamships. Caine repeatedly begged his superiors to dispatch a British force to force residents to recognize the treaty arrangements, but the Foreign Office did not oblige.[10]

Some of the opposition was instigated by merchants who were adamantly opposed to the establishment of the Imperial Maritime Customs at Swatow. These merchants were not anti-British per se. British smugglers attested that they had experienced nothing "but kindness and civility" from Chinese merchants prior to the opening of the port. This changed markedly, they noted, with the establishment of the Maritime Customs.[11] Merchants resented the intrusive and time-consuming inspection regime along a stretch of coast that had not seen much of a customs presence theretofore. They conflated it with the British, and at least one military officer referred to Caine as the "Hoppo" (customs superintendent).[12]

Opposition to the official British presence was fostered by the examination elite, and their motivations were decidedly political. A placard plastered across the city of Chaozhou in August 1860 illustrates their vengeful and nationalistic frame of mind:

> The British—whose disposition is like dogs ... or the beast that devours its mother—thrust themselves forward ... snorting violence and murder. ... They destroyed our sea defenses, stole the guns and valuables of our provincial city [Canton] ... and reduced its shops and houses to ashes.
>
> ... Is there anyone with blood and life in him in considering all this who does not long to ... strip the skin off them? Let us ... sweep this alien miasma clear away, forging our spears and vowing enmity till the stinking brood is driven off. ... Now we hear that the devil chief [Caine] proposes to wander upcountry and gaze upon our own prefectural city of Chaozhou. How opportune for our desire *to wipe away humiliation (xuechi) and avenge our quarrel*!
>
> ... They do not know that we Chaozhou men are universally recognized as warlike and resolute above all others. ... Heretofore if we felt dislike [for a neighbor], we took revenge; *how much the more should we act in a national feud (guochou)*?
>
> ... If fathers and older brothers summon their sons and younger brothers ... we might muster millions of men. ... Were every alien soldier to come, how could they stand against our valor? ... The disgrace of ten-odd years would be wiped out. ... *To slaughter the rebellious aliens on behalf of their nation (wei guojia)* ... would it not show that the people were brave, that they knew their duty.[13]

This declaration of opposition to the British exuded the spirit of twentieth-century Chinese nationalism: the characterization of wars and unequal treaties as a national "humiliation"; the yearning to extirpate the shame; the identification of village and town with the larger nation-state. In spite of its inflammatory depiction of the invaders as devils and beasts, it is not an expression of hatred for hatred's sake. The placard itemizes the crimes the British indeed had committed against the Chinese, including the unjustified declaration of war and the devastation of Canton. Elsewhere in the screed, the authors decried British opium smuggling, the drain of silver from the economy, the foreign "threat" to womenfolk, and the loss of Chinese territory. These were not manifestations of provincialism but expressions of outrage over imperialist depredation.

As Paul Cohen observed, twentieth-century Chinese nationalists rebuked their compatriots, not for having suffered humiliation at the hands of foreigners but for their "failure to recognize humiliating acts as humiliating," for their lack of national "consciousness."[14] The anti-British fulminations of the Chaozhouese in 1860 were among the earliest manifestations of a discernibly "nationalist" discourse in China. Their arguments were distinct from those of the elites who had resisted the British near Canton during the First Opium War (1839–1842). Frederic Wakeman depicted those earlier Cantonese pronouncements as lacking in "national identification" and enmeshed in the particularistic loyalties of village and sib.[15] Chaozhouese resisters to foreign incursion were entangled in those particularisms as well, but they interwove them with the nation-state (*guo*). Thinking nationally but acting locally, they fought to reverse the humiliation of wars and treaty making. This surpassed the vague "protonationalism" commonly seen elsewhere in nineteenth-century China.

Most anti-British propaganda in Chaozhou was anonymously authored by an elite-dominated "Peace Preservation Bureau" (*bao'an gongju*). Originally organized to facilitate the pacification of the countryside, it evolved during the 1860s into an organization dedicated to the promotion of Fang Yao's economic development projects.[16] The most influential members resided in Haiyang district, home to much of the domestic and overseas commercial elite. The bureau was led by a retired magistrate named Qiu Buqiong. Qiu had obtained *juren* examination status in 1804 and held a number of important posts during his official career. He also assisted local troops in suppressing the uprisings of Huang Wukong in 1844 and Wu Zhongshu in 1854. By 1860 he was over eighty years of age, and local officials were a little in awe of him. Other influential Haiyang elites—including the *juren* Wang Ze and Wang Huanzhang—helped Qiu manage the bureau. Huang Qiyu, who did not possess exam status but reputedly was the wealthiest man in Haiyang, was another leader.[17]

The bureau became deeply committed to the anti-British struggle and effectively mobilized the countryside. It rallied every village in Chaozhou to establish local branches and physically resist the foreign intrusion. Coastal villagers hurled stones at the unwelcome guests at every opportunity and on occasion fired cannon balls at British naval ships. "Armed mobs" prevented British delegations from entering the city gates of the prefectural city.[18]

The British persisted in their efforts to uphold their treaty rights but could travel inland only when accompanied by a veritable army of Qing troops. After one such visit in 1865, Caine reported to his superiors that an angry mob had driven his group to take refuge in the circuit intendant's headquarters, where, he complained, "to all intents and purposes we were prisoners." The bureau fabricated ingenious placards on this occasion. One, fraudulently posted under Caine's name, declared that the consul had come to propagate the Christian tidings. He called on all residents of the city to "gather yourselves at [the intendant's office] and hear the gospel preached. To each [listener] will be presented a copy of the Sacred Book of Jesus as well as seven mace of foreign silver." Given the antipathy for Christianity among large sectors of the population (especially at a time when the quasi-Christian Taipings threatened the southeast coast), the placard was designed to maximize the chaos of Caine's visit. Compounding the threat, vagrants and beggars who crowded into town undoubtedly would have been disappointed to learn that the "promised" charity was not forthcoming. The desperate intendant, backed by the belligerent crowd, finally prevailed on the British to abandon their diplomatic effort. Caine's interpreter, R. J. Forrest, indignantly recalled that they were then forced to pass through "one of the densest mobs I ever saw. The people showed every sign of hostility, hooting, reviling, and throwing stones. I am certain that had it not been for our large guard we should never have got to our boats."[19]

Such resistance persisted until the end of the decade, when the violence subsided. In December 1868 diplomats finally managed to travel to the city unmolested, and a British merchant, Thomas Richardson, established a branch of his business there. Two months later Caine's successor as consul, Chaloner Alabaster, finally reported to the Foreign Office in 1869 that he had returned "from a successful trip to Chaozhou." As he noted in his dispatch, "My trip a year ago would have been madness."[20]

That his foray into the interior coincided with Fang Yao's qingxiang campaign was not coincidental. Governor-General Ruilin had been under pressure from Beijing to resolve the crisis, and the statesman Ding Richang, a native of the Fengshun district of Chaozhou, was sent to negotiate with the gentry. He may have convinced them that their agitation ran counter to the spirit of dynastic revival that was drifting across China. On the other hand, Fang already had embarked on his pacification campaign in nearby Huizhou, and they may have been unnerved by the violence unleashed there.[21] One way or another, they taught the British some powerful lessons about running roughshod over the people of Chaozhou. It was the first of many such lessons the British were to endure.

Marginalizing the British: The Case of Opium

One goal of the treaty settlement was to facilitate British commerce in Chaozhou. Prior to 1842 the British enjoyed certain advantages—including superior shipping technologies and a monopoly over Indian opium production—and their smuggling businesses thrived. By the mid-nineteenth century, however, Chinese importers drove the British out of the only trade in which they had enjoyed success. After establishing a colony in nearby Hong Kong (in 1842) and strong-arming the Chinese government to accede to the de facto legalization of the trade (in 1858), their advantages receded, and British opium dealers in Chaozhou found themselves hoisted on their own colonial petard.

Picul for picul, opium was the most valuable commodity imported into Chaozhou in the nineteenth century, and one focuses on it as an example of British economic marginalization not simply because it is a more absorbing subject than, say, beancake fertilizer. The latter, which was shipped from northern China, was used to enrich the sugar cane fields and was the second most important import item during these years, but an item whose value did not come close to matching that of opium. The trade statistics from 1867 illustrate the point. In that year, 7,516 piculs of opium were imported at a value of $3,627,000 (Mexican). At the same time, 1,308,154 piculs of beancake were imported at a value of $2,406,356.[22] That is to say, in spite of the fact that 174 times more beancake than opium was imported into Swatow, the total value of the opium was far greater.

British merchants could not compete with Chaozhouese, who dominated the commerce of Swatow. During the 1840s the narrative of the British opium trade shifted from stories of successful salesmanship to defensive grousing about the relentless "combinations" of "Swatow merchants" who were "taking over" the import business. Their Chinese competition regularly sailed from nearby Hong Kong straight into Swatow and then to ports along the inland waterways of Chaozhou. Foreign dealers began to abandon the old smuggling station of Nan'ao for Double Island and eventually Swatow itself, to little avail.[23] Their Chinese competitors relentlessly undersold them, charging $10 to $25 less per chest than dealers associated with Jardine Matheson.[24] They were willing to accept lower profit margins to expand their market share.

Chaozhou importers also enjoyed an effective network of partners along the coast. After 1842 some of the "Swatow dealers" who formerly had purchased from British smugglers now obtained their stock directly from Hong

Kong. There they were represented by agents like Li Chung, a Chaozhouese who was well informed about Hong Kong prices and adept at selecting finer grades of Malwa and Patna. He would send market information on fast-boats to Swatow, ensuring that the Chaozhou dealers were as cognizant of market conditions as any British national. The Parsi dealers in Hong Kong also sold them drug below the Hong Kong market value, which enabled them to pass their savings on to their customers in Swatow.[25] Needless to add, the opium farm in Hong Kong had passed from British to Chinese hands in 1845, so Chinese controlled much of the opium now pouring into mainland China. Approximately 75 percent of all opium produced in India passed through Hong Kong, and until the late nineteenth century the colonial economy was utterly dependent on the transshipment of opium to China.[26] Colonial authorities were not finicky about who sold the opium as long as the commerce thrived.

Foreigners also suffered disadvantages when silver dollars and sycee were in inadequate supply, rendering it difficult to pursue commercial transactions at Swatow. The problem was seasonally alleviated when Chinese junks returned with specie from their commercial adventures in Southeast Asia or when Chinese vessels engaged in the beancake-sugar-opium trade arrived from northern ports. Most of this silver ended up in inland areas distant from Swatow port, however.[27] There was a thriving banking industry in the region, but Chaozhou city, not Swatow, was its center. Chinese importers had access to highly capitalized opium dealers operating in the wealthy interior markets. Jardine representatives were always chagrined to report that Chinese lorchas departing from inland ports routinely sailed past them laden with silver dollars and sycee from a Chinese bank in the prefectural city—sometimes carrying as much as $200,000—and bound for the Hong Kong opium markets.[28] Branches of the government bank at Canton were established in Swatow and Double Island after 1858, but Chaozhouese and Cantonese continued to monopolize the silver supply.[29]

The opium market in Chaozhou prefectural city was controlled in part by resident bankers there. Throughout the 1850s Jardine's agents at Swatow reported the arrival of lorchas bursting with opium that had been purchased with sycee advanced by these bankers. The financiers not only profited from their share of the trade, they charged a high premium for advancing sycee to the traders as well.[30] They also prevented the British from penetrating the market in Chaozhou city. When the shroff for Dent and Co. carried opium directly in that town in 1853, the bankers organized a "boycott" of the firm.

Jardine agents, witnessing the results, decided it was best to cede that enormous market to the Chinese.[31]

This again underscores the complementarity of the banking and opium industries along the China coast. In the case of the Chaoyang opium syndicate in Shanghai, the profits derived from the drug trade were reinvested in banking in the twentieth century. Back in Chaozhou, a reverse dynamic was at play. To control the silver supply in Chaozhou was to control the wholesale trade in opium between Hong Kong and eastern Guangdong to some extent. By shipping silver to Hong Kong (to speculate or to purchase goods), they essentially took much of the metal out of circulation in Swatow and left foreign importers scrambling for customers who could pay for opium with silver.[32] Hsin-pao Chang once speculated that the rise of the powerful Shanxi banks was related to the expansion of the opium trade in China. They were the sole medium through which revenue was remitted from Canton to Beijing, and their services facilitated foreign trade at that port. Because opium constituted over half the total imports at Canton when most of those banks commenced operations (circa 1820), he noted, "the banks' fortunes [at Canton] were necessarily connected with the opium trade."[33] One need not speculate about the banking and opium industries in Chaozhou. Wholesaling the drug required significant capital in the form of silver. The wholesaling import trade in Chaozhou city expanded with the backing of the banking industry, which underwrote large purchases in Hong Kong. The banking industry was implicated in the growth of the opium business in southeastern China.

The native banking industry in Swatow itself developed during the latter half of the nineteenth century. The Maritime Customs reported in 1906 that one thing that distinguished Swatow from other commercial centers was the fact that locals maintained control of the port's banking industry and thwarted the expansion of the Shanxi banking system there. "It keeps the bulk of its banking business in the hands of its own people," the Customs observed. "The combination amongst the local merchants is so strong that, of the powerful [Shanxi] banks, who have forced their way into every other mercantile community in the country, only one—the great [Weitaihou] firm—has succeeded in holding its own here." Aside from that establishment, only the Haiguan bank, which was responsible for remitting government revenue to the provincial capital, and one other Cantonese bank had survived in the local economy. All other banking houses—eighteen of which had been founded in the 1890s and ten of which had endured over a longer period of time—were "purely local establishments."[34] The capacity of "Swatow merchants" to maintain control of their banking industry attests to their solidarity as a commercial network but really can be ascribed to their participation in the opium trade. These merchants acquired capital that enabled them to sustain a local banking industry that was almost completely independent of the Shanxi networks that otherwise dominated banking across imperial China.

Finally, prior to 1869, the British suffered from disparate levels of taxation. Foreign importers were forced to pay the treaty tariff of thirty taels on opium, but Chinese simply avoided the "treaty port" at Swatow and landed their opium at smaller ports, where local authorities maintained a lower level of taxation. During the 1860s roughly 90 percent of trade in all goods between Hong Kong and Guangdong was with ports that had not been opened by treaty. The diversion of trade to other ports did not undermine the commerce of Chaozhou as a whole, simply that of the treaty port on which the British had placed their hopes, Swatow. The British were excluded from those ports even as the trade expanded, and a frustrated consul at Canton, D. B. Robertson, complained, somewhat ludicrously, that "the Chinese are becoming their own importers."[35] Fang Yao's militarized regime ensured that Chinese importers began to pay higher levels of lijin tax on their opium after 1869, but by then they had driven foreigners out of the market.

British dealers lamented their marginalization even as they grew resigned to their fate. By 1873 Jardine's agent, Edward Vincent, sounded the death knell of British trade in most commodities in the region: "The apparent dullness of our market is merely because Foreigners are excluded from participating. The Chinese are evidently doing a good business, [however]." In 1879 the British consul at Swatow reported a fact long obvious to all: the opium trade at that port was "now entirely in Chinese hands."[36] It should be added that most of the opium imported into Swatow was not consumed there. It was reexported to Jiangxi and parts north, contributing to a healthy import-export economy and, of course, to government revenues.

Disciplining the British

What of the commerce in other commodities at the port? In 1868 British consul George Caine drew a detailed, vividly colored map of eastern Guangdong. He identified areas of robust sugar production and charted the locations of large deposits of natural resources essential to industrialization: iron and coal in Jiayingzhou and Dabu; lead in Bingcun and Sanheba; and so forth.[37] This was classic colonial cartography, an effort to visualize the local terrain in order to control its resources. The British had big plans for penetrating the regional market, but, aside from shipping, those plans came to naught. The Chinese maintained control over the import and export of all commodities.

Marginalizing foreign business did not undermine the Chaozhou economy, and Swatow continued to develop into a modern port in the nineteenth century. In the aggregate, at least, the region was not becoming "impoverished." In fact, despite its small size (only 40,216 native and foreign residents in 1891), Swatow routinely ranked fifth among treaty ports in terms of aggregate trade and customs revenue generated during the late nineteenth century. It was exceeded only by Shanghai, Hankou, Tianjin, and Canton, all of which were far larger in population (see appendix). In the eighteenth century the Chaozhou Customs collected an average of 33,000 silver taels per annum. By the 1870s the Maritime Customs at Swatow was collecting from 740,671 to 842,962 haiguan taels; in 1891 it collected 1,644,573 haiguan taels.[38] The port's dominant position in the opium trade—third, after the top importers, Zhenjiang and Shanghai—was a factor in the outsized role it played in the national economy. In 1875, for example, Zhenjiang imported 11,758 piculs of opium, followed by Shanghai at 10,699 piculs and Swatow at 10,185 piculs.[39] Chaozhouese, of course, dominated the trade at those two ports as well.

Increasing revenues reflected the soaring value of Swatow's import-export trade in almost all commodities. The total value of its trade in 1866 was 11,341,431 haiguan taels; by 1886 it was 21,329,627; and by 1895 it was 26,984,558 haiguan taels. Sugar was the major commercial crop produced in and exported from Chaozhou. In 1863 the total value of the sugar exported from the region was £567,393; by 1888 it was £1,004,424.[40]

The enormous coastal trade, especially in sugar and beancake, accounted for the bulk of imports and exports, and foreigners were marginalized in that commerce. Statistics from 1889 tell the story of continued Chaozhou domination of their port. Of the £2,885,929 worth of trade with other treaty ports on foreign bottoms alone, £2,842,095 worth belonged to Chinese merchants and only £43,834 to all foreign merchants combined.[41] Swatow was not Shanghai, and foreign traders in the region adapted to their status. British shipping agents, for example, usually gave precedence to the sugar shipped by Chinese. When the local agent for Jardine Matheson, Edward Vincent, discovered that he would be unable to load both a small Jardine and a large Chinese shipment of sugar to Shanghai, he bumped the cargo of Jardine, his own partner. "To shut out the Chinese sugar now would only prevent my ever being able to collect freight for you [as a shipper] again," he explained.[42]

Chaozhouese retained control of their Chinese sugar markets, and those domestic markets expanded in the late nineteenth century. The cultivation of sugar cane in Sichuan was abandoned as that province turned its agricultural land over almost entirely to opium poppy cultivation. The ports along the Yangzi that used to purchase their sugar from Sichuan increasingly turned to Chaozhou supplies, which were transshipped via Hankou and Zhenjiang. Exports to these two ports combined increased from 291,498 piculs in 1883; to 449,409 piculs in 1884; to 528,798 piculs in 1885.[43] A broadening of Chaozhou's *domestic* markets thus helped to soften the blow of growing competition from Javanese and Philippine sugar. Their share of international markets beyond Hong Kong declined, but their Chinese markets were large enough to satisfy most production. In 1880, for example, 218,000 piculs of sugar were shipped to foreign ports (90,000 piculs to Hong Kong alone). That same year, however, Chaozhou merchants exported 1,035,705 piculs of sugar to Chinese ports. We do not have specific data for exports in Chinese-owned junks and lorchas, but in 1880 those vessels made roughly a hundred trips to Hong Kong carrying an approximate total of 250,000 piculs. Hong Kong was an emerging market for Chaozhou sugar, indicating once again the extent to which that colony served as a nexus in the trade of maritime Chaozhou. British traders, however, were almost entirely excluded from this commerce with "their" own colony.[44]

Sucheta Mazumdar has charted the decline of sugar production across most of Guangdong province in the early twentieth century, attributing it to global competition from places like Java. When Chinese smallholders no longer received an adequate price for their cane, they began to plant other cash crops, and sugar production plummeted.[45] This occurred in Chaozhou as well. The Chaozhouese sugar trade specifically was undermined by the transformation of their major market in Shanghai, which began to turn to cheaper Southeast Asian varieties in the very late nineteenth century and then abandoned Chaozhou sugar during the 1921 to 1928 period.[46] As we shall see, however, most of that Javanese sugar was exported by *Chinese* who had offshored production to Southeast Asia. Here I simply observe that Chaozhouese merchants prevented British capitalists from dominating their economic turf in the nineteenth century.

The economic story of the latter half of the nineteenth century was one of commercial prosperity in the aggregate. Customs officials and foreign consuls in Swatow often referred to "the growing prosperity of the people" by the late 1870s.[47] The dynamism of the commercial classes being a given, they attributed the expansion of trade to the salutary effects of Fang Yao's pacification campaign and development projects. Cultivable land increased, waterways were banked off, and peasants grew confident they could sojourn overseas in peace. The dramatic doubling of beancake fertilizer imports during the latter 1870s was represented as both cause and effect of a more prosperous society: more land was turned over to cash cropping and sugar cane production soared; peasants thus could afford to apply more fertilizer to their crops; and the enriched soil produced abundant harvests in return.[48]

Chinese officials also asserted that coastal Chaozhou had become more prosperous in the late nineteenth century. The magistrate of Chaoyang remarked on the good fortune of the district in 1908, attributing it, among other things, to the enormous remittances that were sent from laboring and commercial sojourners in Siam, Indochina, Shanghai, and elsewhere. "Many millions of dollars (jinqian) have been sent and the region is wealthy and populous."[49] Roughly 930,562 emigrants departed the port of Swatow from 1870 to 1889, and those sojourners reliably sent money to their families.[50] Not only did this alleviate population pressures at home, it constituted a steady influx of cash earned abroad.

This impression of general prosperity exacerbated British commercial frustrations. They were particularly perplexed by their inability to penetrate the cotton market with their cheaper product. The initial challenge stemmed from the fact that cotton had been one of the commodities interwoven into the coastal trade since the seventeenth century. Chaozhouese transported sugar and opium to northern ports and returned with cotton and dyed cotton piece goods from Suzhou and Shanghai, goods that they sold not only in Chaozhou but in Leizhou, Qiongzhou, and other southern ports.[51] After Swatow was opened, importers continued to purchase northern Chinese cotton, probably because a portion of the coastal trade was marked by barter. Even during the 1860s, when the commercial dynamic began to change, native cotton was preferred. In 1868, for example, 47,408 piculs of Chinese cotton valued at $1,114,088 were imported into Swatow. That same year, 33,713 piculs of cotton valued at $707,973 were imported from Hong Kong.[52] In spite of the fact that the Bombay cotton available in Hong Kong was priced on average at $21 per picul and that of northern Chinese varieties at $23 per picul, the Chinese product prevailed. In 1869 Chaloner Alabaster marveled that Swatow was almost unique in the world in resisting inexpensive British cotton in favor of a more expensive "native cotton cloth."[53] Chaozhou merchants eventually yielded to the market logic and began to purchase Bombay cotton in Hong Kong in larger quantities. By 1885 Bombay-produced cotton yarn was supplanting the native item; indeed, it represented approximately 85 percent of the total import in cotton yarn that year.[54] This transformation redounded to the benefit of the British colonies in Hong Kong and India, but Chaozhouese, not British, merchants carried the cotton goods from colonial Hong Kong. The British were almost completely shut out of the trade. As the British consul reported in 1878, commerce in "cotton and yarn . . . is largely (I may say chiefly) in Chinese hands."[55]

British efforts to change the commercial dynamics of the port were in vain. Unlike Amoy or Fuzhou, where foreigners gained a foothold in tea exportation, or Shanghai, where they dominated the International Settlement, the British could not make significant inroads into the commodity trade at Swatow during the nineteenth century. As N. B. Dennys and W. F. Mayers observed in their famous exposé of the treaty ports of China in 1867, the trade of Swatow was so dominated by Chaozhouese and Singaporean Chinese that few Europeans decided to settle there.[56] The various trials of Thomas William Richardson, the lead partner of Bradley and Company and a man who did decide to reside in Swatow, illustrate the challenges. Like other foreign firms, Bradley had been muscled out of the opium trade, but they thrived in shipping and were especially active in the Chinese passenger trade to Southeast Asia (a trade that the Chinese commercial guild of Swatow, Wannianfeng, shunned). Richardson's efforts to advance more profitably into the commodities trade were less successful.

One could recite a litany of setbacks he suffered, but a resolute "guilding" at the hands of local merchants taught him a lacerating lesson as to who ruled the waves of Chaozhou. Among his many roles, Richardson served as the Swatow agent for the Union Insurance Company, a British maritime insurance firm founded in Canton in 1835 but headquartered in Hong Kong after the First Opium War.[57] Chaozhouese understood the advisability of insuring their valuable cargoes and purchased policies from Richardson and other agents at Swatow. In 1874 a British steamer loaded with Chaozhou sugar foundered near the port of Jilong, Taiwan. It had been bound for Shanghai but detoured to the island because coal prices were cheaper there. Several merchants had insured their cargoes through Union Insurance, but because the vessel had deviated from its direct course to Shanghai, the company refused to honor its policy and compensate them. Their customers were infuriated, not only because coastal steamers routinely stopped at Taiwan to stock up on coal supplies but also because several of their colleagues who held policies with other insurance companies were promised compensation. Richardson, who was merely the agent for the firm, was obliged to enforce the policy.

Established circa 1866, the Wannianfeng (or "Swatow Guild") was the guild for all Chaozhouese commercial traders in the port except those in the tea trade (who tended to be Fujianese) and those who ran emigration hongs.[58] It was a dominant force in the region, and when outraged members learned of the perfidy of Union Insurance in the fall of 1874, they met and resolved to execute a total boycott of Bradley and Company, a firm that was heavily involved in shipping and therefore dependent on Chinese patronage. The guild did not make a public announcement. They did not berate Richardson. They did not stage protests or engage in any sort of performative hullabaloo. They simply spread the word that any Chinese who wanted to do business at the port needed to boycott Bradley completely, and the business of the firm quietly evaporated.

With Union's permission, Richardson desperately offered policyholders half compensation, but by then merchants insured through other companies had been fully compensated and the guild demanded full payment for those insured by Union as well. Union agreed to this, but on the condition that they sign a power-of-attorney to authorize the insurer to sue the owners of the steamer. The merchants would brook no conditions for full payment and continued their boycott. Richardson turned to his consul, who was told by local officials that the guild had assured them that no "combination" was in effect against Bradley at all, the market simply was slow at that moment. Richardson knew full well that he was being "guilded," however, because the market in fact was thriving as usual, and the coolie brokers had told him in late October that they were being pressured to boycott him as well. This posed a serious threat to Richardson's business, for it was heavily involved in the passenger trade to Hong Kong and the Straits Settlements, and late October represented the beginning of the "emigration season" at Swatow.[59]

Richardson managed to obtain a copy of the resolutions guild members had agreed on at a meeting. The document stated that Bradley and Company stood alone among insurance agents in refusing to compensate the sugar merchants for their loss. Its "greed for gain" therefore was to be punished. The guild decided to issue red-colored notices stamped by all Chinese firms declaring that business with Bradley in its entirety—whether the hiring of go-downs, chartering of vessels, or shipment of cargo—was to cease starting on October 3. The guild also consulted a lawyer (zhuangshi) in Shanghai to determine the finer points of the legal issues involved, especially how English law defined "loss" (because some of the sugar salvaged from the shipwreck had suffered deterioration but remained marketable at lower rates, and it was unclear whether the policy covered that sort of loss). Whatever the uninsured loss amounted to, no one shipper would be forced to bear an undue burden, they declared: "The loss will be averaged among the shippers according to the extent of their shipments. Let the loss fall on all and not on one only!"[60]

One can see how the Swatow Guild maintained its esprit de corps. They attended to practical matters and relied on Shanghai lawyers. They determined that one firm's loss was a *collective* loss, to be spread among all the firms affected by the disaster—as long as they otherwise received the full insurance payment. Demou was the firm most affected by the problem of deterioration, and it would always remember how its brothers came through in a time of disaster. It reflected an awareness that enterprises that shipped cargo across treacherous seas were constantly threatened by calamities, and the generous company this time might be the distressed firm the next. The agreement was a way of keeping everyone's business afloat and maintaining solidarity in the face of a common enemy. This was an exceptional business practice and constitutes another reason for their insuperable command of their commercial turf.

Chaozhou solidarity was also ensured by disciplined adherence to group decisions, decisions usually made by larger firms. Having settled on a plan, the guild mandated that "no dissenting voice will be allowed to be heard."[61] The group was expected to maintain strict solidarity in boycotting Bradley. No one dared to break ranks, which proved key to their success in the dispute with the insurance company. Richardson's business was collapsing, his Chinese employees victimized by false accusations at the yamen courts, and he found that the consulate could not help him in this commercial squabble, for guild members did not take the consulate seriously. As he informed the consul, "The remonstrances made by you to the authorities were at this meeting treated with ridicule and contempt—and the importance and influence of the British consulate jeered."[62]

Richardson could do nothing but submit to the authority of the guild. "We were forced to feel our inability to cope with such weapons as were being directed against us," he complained, "we had to surrender." His company paid the remaining sum of $27,510 out of its own pockets. "The power thus wielded by an irresponsible guild is boundless. The only remedy against abuses of such nature will be found in a force sufficiently strong to exact a heavy indemnity. . . . Diplomacy . . . here completely fails." If they were allowed to continue in this vein over every grievance they had with a British firm, he averred, "every dispute will be solved by recourse to this diabolical tyranny," and the British will always lose.[63]

Richardson, the hapless man-in-the-middle of a power play between the Wannianfeng and Union Insurance, vented furiously after suffering his "unconditional and mortifying surrender." His assertion that only brute "force" could significantly check the silent, guilding discipline of these merchants nonetheless is revealing. One can see how much more effective was their "diabolical tyranny" than the hubristic shelling of a port by the British navy, the sort of warmongering that indeed had given foreigners access to this region but could not be used on a daily basis to British commercial advantage. The guild exercised a commercial authority that was "boundless"—to use Richardson's word—incontrovertible at home and extending to their connections in Shanghai and their ability to affect the passenger trade overseas. Their power emanated from a solidarity that was effective precisely because of its ethereal nature, its absence of physical force, its boundlessness. They practiced a commercial *wuwei*—nonaction—which in doing nothing all is accomplished, ensuring that "all things are in order," as the Daoist classic intoned. The natural order of the port was the Chaozhou way—mutual accommodation when it seemed advisable (relying on dependable British steam shipping), otherwise ruthless Chinese control of their territory. This episode revealed the inner strengths of the guild and the weakness of British merchants in confronting it. What must have antagonized Richardson most of all was the fact that the Chaozhouese were entirely in the right in their confrontation with Union Insurance. Anachronistic as the comparison may seem, anyone who has ever struggled with an insurance company cannot but cheer these merchants as they triumphed over a profitable corporation attempting to pettifog its way out of honoring a policy. They had paid their premiums, played no role in determining the route taken by the steamer, and refused to "remain on hold" as instructed by their insurance broker.

This territorial bravado was not limited to the mercantile classes alone. Workers also exerted a level of autonomy that was surprising given the economic changes across the South China Sea. Jardine Matheson, for example, established a sugar refinery at Swatow in 1880 and almost immediately experienced labor trouble. The local engineer they sought to hire refused to work for the unspecified wages offered, which were lower than those paid in Hong Kong. The manager of the Swatow plant was forced to request that the chief engineer from Jardine's Hong Kong operations be sent, but he too would only work for Hong Kong wages. He also demanded a two-week advance in pay and, on being refused, threatened to wreck the refinery's machinery. Fearing that he might incite other workers into striking, the manager complied with the request.[64] He also had problems recruiting less skilled laborers. He wanted to pay most of the twenty-five workers $5.00 per month for the hard work of digging ditches and lugging coal and bags of sugar but could not procure an adequate force because the headman of the village from which they were hiring demanded better pay. The manager insisted on the original offer, which would limit the total cost of labor to 1.5¢ per picul of raw sugar, as opposed to what would have been the 3¢ cost per picul if the headman's wishes had prevailed. Eventually the manager succeeded in working around the headman but was forced to contend with a sullen labor force. The refinery struggled for a few years and failed in 1886.[65]

Jardine Matheson sought to establish a European style of management over the labor force, a force whose pay was to be measured against other costs and, ultimately, profits. They struggled, however, with the labor system maintained in Chaozhou. For one thing, because sugar workers were part of a larger translocal labor force in Hong Kong, Java, and Siam, they understood that the wage offered by the refinery at Swatow was less than that offered elsewhere. Indeed, as we have seen, skilled laborers already were emigrating to work in overseas sugar mills. Jardine presumed that the company was being reasonable, considering that the cost of living was higher in Hong Kong. From the standpoint of these laborers, however, it would not be much trouble to sail to Hong Kong or the Straits for work. Considering that the wage for a less-skilled field hand on a gambier plantation in Singapore or Johor was $6.00, it made little sense to take employment with Jardine. As a labor force, they at least had options.

The villages adjacent to ports also dominated the labor supply in a territorial manner and seized the opportunities afforded by economic development. The inhabitants of Shawei (Swaboe), for example, were dominated by the Li clan, who owned much of the land that evolved into the modern port of Swatow. They spent the 1860s in a multivillage league that opposed the establishment of the Imperial Maritime Customs and resisted the British presence. By the 1870s the violence had abated and the villagers adjusted to the expansion of the port by monopolizing dockworking jobs.[66] This evolved into the normal system of labor supply for much of the region. The most powerful village in the Anbu port area was Maling, a hamlet dominated by the Chen and Yang lineages. Labor services at the train station at Anbu were controlled by these two families after 1903. As Wang Changrui, a resident of another village, recalled, "People from other villages were unable to get jobs [there]. It was as though a private gang had drawn a border."[67] In his view, these lineages succeeded because they had large numbers of males, a reality equated in the region with the capacity to advance one's interests.

The Maritime Customs was forced to comply with this order. A family named Wu controlled all boatmen's positions at the customs station at Paotai on the Rong River. In 1922 the Customs finally attempted to break this monopoly by transferring thirteen Wus to other stations and refusing to replace a deceased boatman named Wu with another man named Wu. In the end, the deceased simply was replaced by his adopted son, who was surnamed Lin.[68]

British merchants could not make the labor system conform to their needs. The seasonal, migratory, and almost completely rural labor supply occasionally made it difficult for British shippers to hire a sufficient number of workers to load steamers, demonstrating their inferior status in the hierarchy of employers. In 1874, for example, the Jardine agent reported a delay in a ship's departure because much of the port's labor force had been diverted to cutting new paddy in the inland rice fields and was not available to load cargo. He was obliged to wait until that more important work was completed before he could adequately staff his stevedore line.[69]

Why in the world did these British persevere? For one thing, even a shaving of the trade at the second largest commercial region in Guangdong and the fifth most lucrative treaty port in China was worth the effort. Bradley and Co. stayed the course into the twentieth century, serving as agents for the Hong Kong and Shanghai Banking Corporation, the Peninsular and Oriental steamship lines, and various insurance companies. By 1908 they finally managed to invest in the local coal industry, among other interests.[70] More important, Swatow remained vital to the spectacular British success story across the South China Sea: shipping. Indeed, British merchants had demanded that Chaozhou be opened as a treaty port because they discerned great potential for their shipping industry along its coastal waters. Chaozhouese recognized the superiority of steam shipping, which liberated commerce from the trade winds and proved a more reliable mode of transport in unpredictable waters. These advantages gradually induced them to resort to foreign vessels. British shippers also dominated the passenger trade to Hong Kong and Singapore because, in an effort to discourage the business, Chinese officials slapped a $200 tax on Chinese-owned vessels engaged in the trade.[71]

Junk shipping constituted the rare example of a Chaozhou business that was sidelined by British competition. Its decline nevertheless was gradual. In 1880 sixty-six seagoing junks with a capacity of two thousand to ten thousand piculs were still active in the coastal trade out of Swatow because such vessels continued to have their appeal. For one thing, they offered more "lay days" at coastal ports, a practice that facilitated barter exchanges necessitated by the chronic shortage of silver.[72] Sixty-six junks constituted a small percentage of the enormous fleets that had plied the waters of Chaozhou earlier in the century, but the junk trade persevered. Moreover, single-masted junks thrived, not simply because they were better suited to maneuver in the shallow waters of a river delta but because they played a vital role in the local economy. On the shores of Chenghai alone, 350 single-mast junks were engaged in seashell harvesting. The shells were processed to manufacture lime, which was used in the construction industry. In 1879 approximately 1,050,000 piculs of lime were produced annually at this site with an estimated value of $262,500.[73] These smaller junks offered work opportunities to hundreds of men and women. Customs reports in the early twentieth century continued to refer to a "declining" junk trade that never seemed to disappear entirely.[74]

The triumph of British shipping, though disruptive, did not devastate the Chaozhou economy. Seamen on the old junks transitioned to steam, and, as we have seen, the majority who worked on steamers plying the coastal trade were Chaozhouese with long experience at sea.[75] Moreover, the commerce at Swatow in steamers and sailing vessels expanded after 1860, and dockworkers increasingly found employment. Judging from the lamentations of foreign shippers, it was difficult to staff a boat-loading "coolie line" during harvest season. The triumph of British steam over Chinese sail was a singular British success story, but the larger Chaozhou economy absorbed the blow in the nineteenth century.

The Sino-British Consulate

The British Consulate was established at Swatow to attend to the needs of British traders in the region. Its success in this regard was limited. In contrast, the extent to which the institution served the interests of Chinese in Chaozhou, including the diaspora Chinese of Southeast Asia, is remarkable. The consulate more consistently advanced the legal claims of local Chinese plaintiffs against the British than it succeeded in resolving the dilemmas the British confronted.

One sees this in the consular court records. Under the extraterritorial arrangements of the treaty system, British consuls acted as district judges, responsible for adjudicating civil and criminal cases involving British subjects. Registers of legal judgments were reported semiannually to the British Supreme Court at Shanghai.[76] Judging from these brief communications, the principal judicial duty of the Swatow consul was to discipline legions of rowdy seamen who manned British ships. The cases record the familiar nuisances endured in port towns or on ships at sea: drunk and disorderly conduct, assaults, and insubordination. Although the majority of offenders hailed from the British Isles, the record reflects the cosmopolitan diversity of those who labored on transoceanic British steamers: Chinese, Malays, Dutch, Arabs, Americans, and Javanese, among others.[77] The consulate's "Police Sheet" for 1864, for example, records that the majority of those charged (fifteen out of twenty-four, or 62.5 percent) hailed from the United Kingdom, and all but one of those lodging accusations had British names.[78]

Chinese plaintiffs resorted to the consulate to seek justice in civil or criminal matters involving British subjects. From 1867 to 1886 a total of seventy-seven civil disputes were adjudicated at the consulate in Swatow and reported to the Supreme Court at Shanghai. Seventy-four of those cases reveal enough information to enable us to discern the national identities of the plaintiffs. Thirty-eight involved plaintiffs with Chinese names lodging accusations against men with British names. Of those thirty-eight cases, the British consul judged in favor of the Chinese plaintiffs in thirteen cases; seven were withdrawn or dismissed; and seventeen cases do not reveal information on any decision rendered.[79] That is to say, just over half the civil cases involved consuls addressing the complaints of Chinese in civil matters. The British Consulate evolved into an institution in which Chaozhou residents might obtain justice in their disputes with British subjects. This is not to say that the system worked perfectly to address the needs of Chinese litigants. On occasion British businessmen might declare bankruptcy and disappear into their vast empire.[80] Consuls were determined to validate the system of extraterritoriality, however, and worked diligently to bring their compatriots to justice.

British sojourners were often displeased with this turn of events. John Stott, master of the steamer *Jessie MacDonald*, took umbrage when the consul, Robert Forrest, accepted the charges of several Chaozhou residents who complained that Stott's ship had departed in June 1876 with a number of unpaid bills. Stott owed the tailor San-ju $60.64 for clothes supplied on captain's orders to crewmembers. He also owed Wangki $15.60 for sampan services to the ship and an unspecified amount to a local man for ship's ballast. When Forrest decided in favor of the aggrieved Chinese and ordered Stott to compensate them and pay court costs, Stott turned "very violent and abusive . . . and used language and threats which ought properly to have resulted in his incarceration." In the end, Forrest compelled Stott to pay the sums he owed by withholding his ship's papers until payment was rendered.[81]

One suspects that this was not the first time the blustering Master Stott had abused local businesses as he sailed from port to port. He obviously assumed he could get away with double-crossing the Chinese with whom he did business at Swatow. He might have succeeded had there been no British Consulate with the authority to detain his ship indefinitely until he met his obligations, and the fact that the consulate accepted the Chinese version of events enraged him. He believed a British institution abroad was meant to serve British interests, and it was through such cases that British nationals came to believe that the "normal" judicial dynamic in the consulate at Swatow was one of Chinese accusing British. Paul King, who worked in the Maritime Customs Service in Swatow and was frequently called on to serve as an assessor to the court, reminisced that cases there usually involved Chinese plaintiffs charging British defendants.[82]

The record for criminal cases is also significant. The Swatow consulate reported a total of 447 criminal proceedings to the British Supreme Court at Shanghai from 1867 to 1886. The majority involved masters of British ships punishing miscreants among their multinational crews for a variety of infractions, from assaults and murder to drunkenness, indebtedness, sodomy, and even insulting the captain's wife while aboard ship.[83] In disciplining British seamen, the consulate constituted a transnational court that disciplined the unruly element in port and across the Britannic maritime world.

The consuls also punished British for committing crimes against Chinese. Of those 447 proceedings, only 204 include the specifics. Among those cases, 20 involved Chinese plaintiffs accusing British subjects of various malefactions. The consul ruled in favor of those plaintiffs in 10 (or 50 percent) of the cases, while the others were either withdrawn (4), dismissed (4), or the judgments were not reported (2). This is an admittedly limited record, but it indicates that local Chinese made use of an institution that addressed the transgressions of the highly mobile British population that passed through Chaozhou.

The consular record was in stark contrast to the experience of the British Consulate in lodging accusations in Chinese government offices on behalf of British subjects. The legal record is incomplete. Consuls did not report every instance of disputation to their busy and often exasperated superiors. They generically complained year after year about the dilatory Chinese response to their plaints, and annual trade reports routinely included comments such as "the authorities . . . did not during the year shew much diligence or interest in questions of debt referred to them."[84] This claim is substantiated in the limited statistical record in consular correspondence with the British minister in Beijing from 1860 to 1890. Excluding numerous missionary-related cases (which often involved Chinese Christians accusing other Chinese), incidents involving attacks on British consular and military authorities, and occasional piratical attacks, roughly forty cases were reported. Of that total, five (12.5 percent) were addressed and resolved by local magistrates or by the circuit intendant or prefect in Chaozhou, while the resolution of five cases remains unclear. The magistrates otherwise proved unresponsive (by British lights) in approximately 75 percent of the cases. Twenty-eight of the total cases involved unpaid commercial debts (involving promissory notes or business obligations for goods delivered). Three of those debt cases were resolved by Chinese officials (though the British creditors were never paid anything near the amount owed, and the cases took years to conclude) and the resolution of five debt cases remain unclear. Twelve cases involved criminal matters (mostly robbery and assault, but also two cases of murder and attempted murder). Two of those cases were resolved by the Chinese authorities.[85]

Some Chinese magistrates did not mask their resentment of the British and were disinterested in making the lives of their uninvited guests any easier than necessary. In reviewing these decades of case reports, however, one also must consider differences in nineteenth-century British and Chinese legal practice. Chinese magistrates tended to delay judicial proceedings in civil disputes because resort to the formal courts by one of the parties often galvanized disputants to intensify their efforts to resolve their differences through mediation, ultimately rendering formal adjudication unnecessary.[86] They were disinclined to respond with alacrity to British accusations in civil disputes.

Moreover, magistrates in Chaozhou were accustomed to a system in which the Wannianfeng (Swatow Guild), led by representatives of twenty-four leading firms in the region, resolved most commercial disputes among themselves. Customs officials characterized the guild as "a chamber of commerce, a board of trade, and a municipal council . . . which possesses a power to enforce its rules that many a government might envy." This guild was governed by regulations and practices that served as a form of "commercial law" that was binding on all Chinese merchants in the region. One regulation mandated that firms that failed to pay their debts "in full" would be "boycotted" by the others if they attempted to establish their businesses again.[87] Reputations for probity and reliability mattered in a port like Swatow, and the local deadbeats were known to all in spite of the far-flung nature of everyone's business interests. Credit in Chaozhou was extended as "long credit," credit extended over a long period of time. Such practices required enduring personal connections as well as institutions that facilitated long-distance trade—the native place associations in particular. These trade organizations worked reasonably well for Chinese merchants, but not for the British. As Chaloner Alabaster fumed in 1869, "The Chinese creditor [is] generally able to obtain settlement of debts owing to him through the guilds or the Mandarins," but the foreigner had no institutionalized means of compelling debtors to meet their obligations. When they absconded to their villages, Chinese creditors could "appeal to the sense of justice of the people. But when a foreigner is concerned the villagers among whom the debtor has taken refuge are always convinced that their countryman is in the right."[88] This ongoing problem inclined foreigners to opine that the Chinese "needed" European-style commercial law, but the Chinese did not feel compelled to change their mercantile order to suit British needs.

Compounding the problem was the transnational nature of the business life of foreigners and Chinese. What was a British consul to do when encountering debt cases involving Chinese who traded along the Chinese coast, used property in Shanghai as collateral for a loan contracted in Hong Kong, and then absconded to rural Chaozhou when their business faltered? What was he to do about a merchant who owed money in Swatow but fled to Saigon when his firm collapsed?[89] Collecting debts across the vast sea was challenging. British consulates, like colonial courts, were supposed to serve as loci of British law, but they were not adequate to monitor a transnational economy. In 1871, 242 European merchants in the Straits Settlements wrote in frustration to colonial authorities that "the mass of the trading classes are people who flock here from other . . . countries." If a trader failed, he could simply abandon his obligations and remit his cash homeward. "To leave Singapore is a matter of no difficulty—a boat in ten minutes time takes him across the river to the foreign territory of Johor, or he crosses over to Rhio in a few hours . . . and finds his way back by a circuitous route to his native land. Once in . . . China, Siam, Sumatra . . . or even in British India, the . . . debtor is almost absolutely free from the pursuit of justice."[90] Indebtedness in a transnational context was different from the context in which the population remains settled. It was not simply the proximity of the sea that enabled people to abandon their obligations. It was the human geography of constant circulation that made it possible to disappear into different jurisdictions. A debtor floated across borders and became less accountable to any one authority in spite of the fact that numerically he had more authorities with which to contend.

The British constructed a global network of colonial and consular courts, but for the system to work in Chaozhou, they needed Chinese officials to engage in more formal approaches to commercial regulation. More to the point, they worried that problems relating to debt recovery undermined their trade interests. As Alabaster reported in 1869: "Another grave disadvantage under which foreigners lie is the insecurity of all contracts . . . with Chinese [and] the unwillingness of the mandarins to enforce foreign claims against native debtors. If a Chinese has a claim against a foreigner every remedy existing in our courts is freely and fairly offered him. . . . But if the case is reversed a lengthy correspondence is as a rule necessary . . . and unless the Consul . . . is extraordinarily energetic and persevering no attempt is even made to do justice."[91] Consuls were obliged to engage in endless "prompting" of officials over the course of years. In one case involving the bankruptcy of a Chaozhouese firm in Singapore in 1864, the owners returned to their village in Haiyang, leaving over $24,000 (Mexican) in unfulfilled promissory notes. Tasked with recovering the sum, George Caine communicated with Chinese magistrates, prefects, circuit intendants, and governors-general on twenty-four occasions.[92] If Caine had been Chinese, the authorities would have reviled him as a pettifogger. It was easier for British consuls to attend to the few cases presented to them, of course. Chinese officials were burdened with many more responsibilities. What we see in this realm of law, however, was the clash of two legal cultures and the reluctance of Chinese to change their procedures simply because the British asked them to. As a practical matter, this meant that Chinese plaintiffs were more likely to gain satisfaction in the British Consulate than British plaintiffs in Chinese courts. If the comments of Alabaster and others are to be believed, these practices undermined British prospects in the region. In Chaozhou, even the deadbeats performed a historic service to the nation.

Transnational Citizens

The British Consulate at Swatow provided invaluable service to Chaozhou (Teochew) Chinese who worked in British colonies. The early consuls were slightly flummoxed by Chinese who claimed the rights and protections of "Her Majesty's British subjects" but appeared in the attire and hairstyle of Chinese nationals. The Supreme Court of the Straits Settlements nevertheless determined that "all persons of Chinese race born in a British Possession [were] in strictness, according to English law, British subjects. [But] children of Chinese parents who were never naturalized or were born Chinese subjects [were] not entitled in China to be considered or treated as British subjects."[93] Some Straits Chinese obtained British citizenship, and the return of such naturalized subjects to China exacerbated tensions between the British and Chinese governments, for the latter would not countenance the notion that a Chinese residing in China was not "Chinese." Qing officials also continued to fear the subversive tendencies of Sino-British sojourners. The British minister in Beijing, Rutherford Alcock, was sympathetic to the Chinese complaint that British naturalization hobbled efforts to check anti-Qing criminality. He issued regulations throughout the 1860s restricting various prerogatives of British citizens of Chinese descent in China itself, declaring in 1868 that all Sino-British subjects must "discard the Chinese costume and adopt some other dress whereby they may readily be distinguished from the native population." Those who ignored this regulation would relinquish rights to British protection in court.[94]

Historians have shown that overseas Chinese adopted multiple citizenship claims in order to protect their property in a time of political instability at home or to participate in the commercial opportunities afforded foreign colonialists. Peter Thilly, moreover, has demonstrated that the Japanese promoted such claims in a form of "citizenship-based imperialism" that extended Japanese jurisdiction over transnational Chinese business networks.[95] British consuls at Swatow nonetheless firmly believed that "well-to-do Chinese" were, in fact, in great need of protection by the British government. These individuals, one noted, were "looked upon by the people [in Chaozhou] hardly as fellow-countrymen, but rather as fit persons to be subjected to imposition and extortion" by villagers and officials alike.[96]

Wealthier sojourners tended to apply for naturalization and proactively obtain the protection of the consulate. In 1879, for example, only seven Chinese registered as British subjects whereas 28,048 Chinese disembarked from ships arriving from foreign lands that year. Most migrant laborers did not qualify for citizenship, and those who did were probably unwilling to pay the $5 registration fee.[97] Of the seven registrants, five were merchants and two were commercial clerks. Most could speak English, and four had been inserted into the British jury lists for Swatow.[98]

The Liu brothers, Liu Mingyi and Liu Changyi, were the most significant among these registrants. Sons of the founder of a major rubber enterprise in

Singapore, Changyi was renowned throughout the colony for transforming the firm, Rong Feng, into one of the leading companies in the Straits. The family also participated in syndicates controlling the opium farms and later invested in the modern bank that served Chaozhouese interests in the Straits, Hong Kong, and Bangkok. They were an affluent and influential overseas Chinese family.[99]

Although both were born and resided in Singapore, they occasionally returned to Chaozhou, probably to their village of Liulong in Haiyang. Several of Changyi's children were born in Chaozhou and he identified with his native place. Nevertheless, his registration as a British subject was not simply a cynical ploy to protect his assets. He had studied at the Raffles Institution, an elite Anglophone academy in Singapore, and was to be elected an officer of the Straits Sino-British Business Association in 1900. Like many Chaozhouese, he was both a cosmopolitan colonial subject of the British Empire and a devoted son of his village.[100]

As such, he endeavored to protect his properties in Chaozhou. In 1879 he registered the deeds to a 486-*mu* plot of real estate he had purchased about three miles from Swatow for 1050 silver taels. The vast stretch of property included a lagoon as well as dams and sandbanks. He intended to rent the lagoon and adjacent areas to tenants, primarily for the purpose of fishing. The consul, William Cooper, was reluctant to act without instructions from the ambassador, for he did not want to take responsibility for assets in rural areas beyond the port. In this case, he felt that it might be "inexpedient that British offices should become concerned in the disputes and complications which may easily arise about a property of this kind."[101] He did not elaborate but probably dreaded being dragged into landlord-tenant disputes. We do not learn how this request was resolved, but Liu expected the consulate to serve his interests.

This was one of many tactics this sojourner adopted to protect his possessions in his native place. Another, more intriguing, stratagem was to arrange a marriage between his son, Liu Bingyan, and the daughter of none other than Commander Fang Yao.[102] We know little of the personal relationship between the Singaporean capitalists and the military strongman, though it is likely that the property Changyi registered in the 1870s was located on land reclaimed along the Ox-Field Sea and that Fang's Self-Strengthening enterprise was 1,050 taels richer as a result. Fang presumably kept his eye on his in-laws' estates as the men worked overseas. A quintessential "translocal family," the Lius relied on the "great pacificators" of Guangdong and distant Malaya, colonial authorities promoting their commercial endeavors in the Straits while the Swatow consulate secured their interests back home.

Registration had a downside, for it rendered Sino-British subjects vulnerable to lawsuits in the consular court. In 1880 one Chinese firm charged Ye Gaoyang (Yap Co Ghiong) with an unspecified offense involving a sum of $99. The court decided for the plaintiffs. Yap, a naturalized British subject born in Penang, had registered at the consulate in 1876 as a clerk for "Khoo-Teang-poh and Co. of Penang" and claimed the extraterritorial rights of a foreigner. He also appeared on the 1880 Swatow Jury List, indicating that he spoke English and was trusted to assess cases involving British subjects.[103] Although he lost his case, it is unlikely Yap ever doubted the wisdom of registering, especially given the nature of his company's business at Swatow, the coolie trade. Khoo Teang Poh (Qiu Tianbao) descended from a commercially powerful, Fujianese family in Penang. His brother, Khoo Thean Tek (Qiu Tiande, or Tan Tek), was the leader of a major Fujianese "secret society" in Penang and owner of two enormous coolie depots there. Colonial officials identified the brotherhood as one that posed "a danger to the public peace," and Thean Tek as "the head and front of all offenders in Penang," and someone who transshipped unwilling coolies from Penang to Deli, Sumatra.[104] The younger Khoo, Teang Poh, ran the Swatow end of the business, regularly shipping laborers to Penang. Given that both Khoos had been leading agitators of the Penang Riots of 1867 (a series of battles waged among Chinese dialect groups) and that Thean Tek had been found guilty of abetting several murders in the course of the riots, it is curious that the consuls back in Swatow embraced their employee as a juror.[105] It is possible that the consulate did not make the connection. On the other hand, the British, who stoutly defended the coolie trade and exaggerated the effectiveness of the regulations they had imposed on it, did not always understand what was going on beneath the surface of their global self-interest.[106]

The "emigration business" in Chaozhou was hazardous. Falsely or otherwise, brokers were accused of various crimes. Merchants engaged in any branch of the trade were not welcome to join the Wannianfeng guild at the port. The military boss of Chaozhou, Fang Yao, was an ally of the guild and shared that body's antipathy for the credit ticket system. The two most powerful Chinese forces in the region (the guild and the military) were unremittingly hostile to coolie emigration businesses. British citizenship protected their interests and liberated men like Yap to operate in a transnational enterprise that had many detractors in China.

In contrast, local brokers were constantly harassed and not a few were executed by Fang. Zheng Asi, a passenger broker from Dahao, Chaoyang, was one hapless victim. In October 1875 a disgruntled former client, upon arrival at Singapore, falsely accused him of having kidnapped and sold him abroad. The client arranged for a friend back in Chaoyang to inform Fang of the "offense," whereupon the commander, without consulting civil officials, immediately beheaded Zheng in January 1876. British authorities in Singapore eventually determined that the broker had been falsely accused, but by then he was already dead and, as a Chinese subject, beyond the reach of consular protection anyway.[107]

Conclusion

Chaozhouese triumphed over their imperialist adversaries in the nineteenth-century as merchants maintained control over trade and workers set some of the conditions of labor. Commercial dynamics would shift in the twentieth century, especially as the sugar industry declined. In the meantime, however, they maximized their advantages and prevented the British from gaining a foothold in the economy.

British imperialism had an impact elsewhere in China, of course. And, indeed, some of the story told here is a tale of Chaozhouese contributing to the expansion of the British Empire in different ways: facilitating the sale of Indian opium, hauling Bombay cotton from Singapore or Hong Kong to Chaozhou and Shanghai, and contributing to the economic vitality of Hong Kong. As John Carroll has reminded us, however, Hong Kong was as much a Chinese colony as a British one.[108] They were not simply abetting British colonialism, they were maximizing the commercial interests of capitalists who were predominantly Cantonese but also Chaozhouese and Fujianese. One might say the same of the Straits Settlements, where Chinese from Chaozhou and Fujian predominated. The Colonial Office in London in the 1890s was flabbergasted to learn that it could not even shift the currency of these colonies from the silver dollar to something based on the gold standard because the Chinese, who dominated the economies of both places, simply would not countenance it. London hoped to promote colonial trade with countries whose currencies were gold-based. As the chief justice of Hong Kong, James Russell, testified in 1893, however, Chinese dominated the trade of Hong Kong, and the colony was an extension of the Chinese economy. "Hong Kong must have the same currency as at the open ports of China," Russell testified, because "the ports are Chinese, and silver is the Chinese standard . . . and the [British] merchants living in the open ports must conform to their ways if they want to do trade." Witnesses from the Straits similarly emphasized that the colony was merely part of "a very large silver-using area" dominated by southeastern Chinese. The Colonial Office had difficulty accepting that Hong Kong's trade with China should be accommodated over its trade with London, but William Keswick, the director of Jardine Matheson in 1893, noted that changing the basis of the currency to suit London was ill-advised because the economy of Hong Kong was thoroughly integrated with the ports of China.[109] Chinese merchants preferred silver and that was that. At the dawn of the twentieth century, Chinese commercial power in the South China Sea continued to outweigh that of the British colonial state.

In marginalizing the British, Chaozhouese did not inhibit the integration of their port region with the modern global economy. As the nineteenth century progressed, Chaozhou was increasingly integrated into that economy, but their spheres were Shanghai and Southeast Asia, not that of the colonial metropole of Euro-America. They did not need access to European markets and resources. They had entrée to European colonies, and integration with those sites enabled them to maintain commercial dominance. Needless to add, the obstructions experienced by the British at Swatow were not avenged in Hong Kong or the Straits Settlements. Indeed, the British welcomed Chaozhouese business, facilitating the expansion of Chinese interests across the South China Sea.

8

Translocal Families

WOMEN IN A MALE WORLD, 1880S–1929

The special characteristic of the emigrants from our land is that they do not
accept economic support from our country. Each voluntarily migrates to the
colonies [of Southeast Asia] and initially encounters obstacles but, in the end,
they thrive. As for their lives overseas, just as before, they are able to make a
marriage match from their old village and become a large-scale collectivity
[*da guimo de tuanjie*].

—MUTUAL AID SOCIETY OF SHANTOU OVERSEAS
CHINESE IN THE NANYANG, 1934

SOJOURNING MERCHANTS and laborers maintained a connection to
Chaozhou. They were members of translocal families, families whose intimate
lives were collectively lived across vast territories. One cannot understand
their experiences with reference to a single place: family history unfolded in
multiple locations. Poorer households might only have maintained the bond
when sons sent remittances in support of parents, wives, and children. Some
workers lost contact with their villages entirely, but even in those cases the
demographics of family life were played out translocally. Emigrant villages
back home were transformed into majority female sites, reflecting the gender
dynamics of only one node of familial territory. When one factors in the predominantly male experience of sojourning and incorporates data from across
Southeast Asia, the families again manifest the conventional Chinese sex ratios
of males numerically exceeding females by far. Family life in maritime
Chaozhou was a "large-scale collectivity."

Prior to the twentieth century, women who lived conventional lives stayed at home, in Chaozhou. They cared for children and in-laws and upheld the conjugal family's claim to territory in the village. Translocalism was a familial strategy in which women continued to cultivate roots in the ancestral land while males gained access to the resources and work opportunities of distant colonies and treaty ports. Some women who emigrated in the nineteenth century did so to engage in sex labor, exploiting an overseas market of male laborers who left their families behind and otherwise lived in predominantly masculine worlds. Conventional female emigration increased after the fall of the Qing in 1912, but only significantly so in the 1920s with the rise of communist insurgencies and anticommunist counterinsurgencies. Even then it was difficult for male sojourners to countenance the idea that the conjugal tie to the family village might be undone.

The history of the sojourning working classes of both sexes was one of circulation across borders. As W. A. Pickering, the "protector of the Chinese" in the Straits Settlements, observed, "The line of demarcation between Immigrant and Emigrant [in Singapore] is . . . extremely fine, as a coolie may be technically an immigrant at 9:00 a.m. and . . . become an Emigrant at 9:30."[1] This mobility made it difficult for British authorities to ensure that individual Chinese fulfilled colonial economic agendas rather than their own.

The Demography of Translocalism

Women in Chaozhou lived conventional lives in the late Qing period, and contemporary sources celebrated their industriousness and virtue. "They rarely ventured out in public if they lived in town nor did they get calluses on their hands and feet [from farm labor] if they lived in rural areas," the prefectural gazetteer for 1893 assures us. The magistrate of Chaoyang reported in 1908 that "Chaozhouese practice strict separation of men and women. When women go out the gate it is the custom to wear a veil over their faces." But even when they gestured toward propriety in this manner, the unemployed idlers who wandered the district city would "laugh at the women and annoy them" when they dared to venture beyond the home.[2]

These sources acknowledged that most women worked. Aside from caring for their families, they engaged in spinning, weaving, embroidering, sandalmaking, and operating wells. Some labored outside of their villages. Women who lived in mountain areas gathered firewood, and it was not uncommon to encounter "women peddlers carrying goods on poles slung over their shoulders," the Chaoyang magistrate observed, slightly aghast, "but you would never see that in the [district] city." Women who lived by the seashore gathered marine products to make ends meet.[3] Like men, women benefited from opportunities that did not involve access to farmland. The mountains and sea offered alternative sources of income.

The treaty port of Swatow was a site of mass in-migration during the latter nineteenth and early twentieth centuries. Very few people were "from" Swatow, and the port was something of a ghost town during the Chinese New Year, when people traditionally journeyed to their hometowns to celebrate the most important holiday of the lunar calendar.[4] By the 1940s it had become a modern city of 176,304 residents, 93,087 of whom were males and 84,217 females. Significantly, however, only 16,805 of those residents identified the city as their native place. Some 157,993 residents had moved from other places in Chaozhou or Guangdong province, and 1,457 hailed from other provinces in China.[5] The city itself had been expanding into rural areas, transforming cropland into urban space, but over 90 percent of its inhabitants were from somewhere else.

As in other treaty ports, formal educational opportunities for women slowly expanded in the early twentieth century. By 1919 thirty-six schools were educating 3,716 students: 2,865 males and 851 females (80,000 people lived in the city at the time). Nine of these schools were exclusively devoted to the education of women. One school, the Swatow School of Obstetrics, trained women in Western medical approaches to pregnancy and childbirth. The Chaozhou Overseas Chinese Industrial Arts Council founded the Overseas Chinese National Primary School of Industrial Arts (Huaqiao gongye guomin xuexiao), an institution that offered three years of heavily subsidized training in skills relevant to the industrialization of the economy. Thirty-eight boys and nineteen girls between the ages of eight and fourteen enrolled, indicating that women were expected to participate in the modern work force. By the 1920s women indeed were engaged in industrial labor. Workers in some sectors of paper manufacturing, such as tinfoil pasting, for example, were almost entirely female.[6]

These changes had an impact on some women, but the majority were not directly touched by such transformations at this stage. The phenomenon that significantly affected their lives was the intensification of emigration. Between 1900 and 1928 approximately 3,306,397 Chinese sojourned overseas from Swatow. Chaozhou was not "emptying out," of course. During the same span of time, 2,203,982 travelers returned to Swatow. Departures thus exceeded returns by 1,102,415. The figures indicate that, during any given year, large numbers of people were absent from their villages, particularly in the wake of catastrophic events. In 1927 and 1928, for example, a total of 434,010 passengers departed Swatow (222,033 in 1927 and 211,977 in 1928). The chaos and bloodshed associated with the establishment of the Hai-Lu-feng Soviet in 1927 and the counterinsurgency campaigns of the Nationalist armies inclined many to flee during those years. In contrast, only 83,974 had departed in the previous year, 1926.[7]

The twentieth century witnessed an escalation of departures from the region, a great migration that had been building since the nineteenth-century. Such an exodus—almost exclusively of men—had profound effects on Chaozhou society. One repercussion was the "distorted" gender ratios of some coastal villages as cumulatively millions of men traveled abroad and their wives, parents, and children remained at home. In the natural world, about 105 boys are born for every 100 girls. Those numbers even out by the adult years, and women tend to outnumber men in old age. In the sex ratio dynamic of late imperial and Republican China, however, males typically outnumbered females by roughly 20 to 30 percent; these ratios were largely the result of female infanticide.[8] The demography of coastal Chaozhou, in contrast, was anomalous to that prevailing elsewhere in rural China. Some villages and townships (*zhen*) in Chaoyang were 60 percent female by the Republican period. By 1940 approximately one-third (32.1 percent) of such entities there were majority female (45 out of 140 counted in a census). The entire population of Chaoyang was 49.57 percent female by 1940. In Chenghai district, 31 out of 119 villages and zhen (26 percent) were majority female. The entire district was 47.97 percent female. In contrast, only 2.6 percent of the villages in Fang Yao's home district of Puning were majority-female (1 out of 36 villages counted. The entire population of Puning was 46.2 percent female, however). Majority-female villages were found in eight of nine districts (table 8.1).

The districts with fewer majority-female villages nonetheless had significant percentages of women residing there by contemporary Chinese standards. The Hakka district of Dabu experienced the lowest female-to-male ratios in Chaozhou, and it did not have any female-majority villages, yet the population there was 45.06 percent female (table 8.2).

Chenghai and Chaoyang had the largest number of female-majority villages and townships and the largest percentages of women in general. These two districts happened to have borne the brunt of Fang Yao's pacification campaign. The sex ratios of some of targets of the campaign are striking. Shalong, for example, was 53.9 percent female. Its gender disparities (2,098 more females than

TABLE 8.1. Percentage of Majority-Female Villages and Townships, by District, 1940 (unless otherwise noted)

District	Majority female villages and townships (%)
Chaoyang	32.1
Chenghai [1933]	26
Chao'an (Haiyang) [1946]	20
Jieyang	14
Raoping	13
Huilai [1941]	12
Fengshun	3.2
Puning	2.6
Dabu [1928]	0

Source: Percentages culled from data in CZZ 2005: 2147–2212.

males out of a total population of 26,404) account for almost 24 percent of the total gender disparity in the entire district of Chaoyang. Local lore identifies the campaign as the major factor in the transformation of Chaoyang into an emigrant district, and male migration thereafter became common. The vast majority of these émigrés ended up in Siam (as of 1958, there were 23,687 overseas Shalong natives, and 21,257 of them resided there), but other Zhengs sailed to the Straits, French Indochina, and the Dutch East Indies.[9]

On the other hand, Chao'an (Haiyang, prior to 1914) was populated with wealthy elites who had cooperated with Fang's development efforts, and yet it ranked third among those with female-majority villages. Clearly the most important factor shaping the gender ratios in all three districts was their long tradition of overseas travel and their proximity to the busiest port of embarkation, Swatow. By 1905 there were at least sixty "sojourner inns" (kezhan) catering to the needs of laboring emigrants in the area.[10] The geographical ease of migration and the fact that sojourning elites offered locals employment overseas explain the disparities in gender ratios.

The prevalence of women in these villages raises hope that female infanticide was not routinely practiced. Unfortunately, that was not the case. One simply needs to explore the demography of Chaozhou in its translocal dimension, for maritime Chaozhou in its overseas sites was heavily male, and multiscopic calculation brings the approximate numbers back to the conventional, majority-male figures of pre-1949 China.

The immigration statistics compiled by the British Straits Settlements illustrate the gendered dynamics of migration. The colony depended heavily on

TABLE 8.2. Percentage of Males and Females, Chaozhou Districts

District	Year	Males (%)	Females (%)
Chaoyang	1940	51.1	49.9
Chenghai	1933	52.03	47.97
Chao'an	1946	51.7	48.3
Jieyang	1940	52.9	47.1
Raoping	1940	52.1	47.59
Huilai	1941	53.1	46.9
Fengshun	1940	54.29	45.71
Puning	1940	53.8	46.2
Dabu	1928	54.94	45.06

Source: CZZ 2005: 2147–2212.
Note: There are problems with the data: some were gathered during wartime, and some districts
(Chaoyang) have more detailed data than others (Dabu). They nonetheless were collected by Chinese
police officers conducting a census (see Hong Kong, Public Record Office, HKMS202-1-10, 29).

Chinese (as laborers, investors, and the chief consumers of the monopoly
opium on which revenues depended), and the British assiduously recorded
the numbers arriving in Singapore. Statistics for 1878 highlight the heavily male
world of Chinese migration. In that year a total of 58,643 Chinese arrived at
Singapore (1,824 of whom were women). Of that total, 23,466 arrived from Swatow, 102 of whom were women, less than 1 percent (0.43 percent) of Swatow passengers. Some Chaozhouese women must have arrived via Hong Kong rather
than Swatow. The majority of Chinese women who arrived in Singapore traveled
first to that colony. The Hong Kong data do not differentiate Chinese passengers
by their native place, but presuming that many of these females hailed from
Chaozhou would not change the ratios significantly. Of the 21,100 total passengers
arriving from that colony, 1,688 (or 8 percent) were female.[11]

The 1881 census figures for the Straits Settlements (now Singapore, Malacca,
Penang, Province Wellesley, and Dingdings) reinforce this analysis, portraying
a colonial society that was heavily male across all national groups except for
the native Malays (table 8.3).

This snapshot underscores the masculinity of foreign life. The Chinese had
the lowest percentage of females among groups with a significant presence:
17.6 percent female. Indeed, because the Chinese constituted the largest portion of the population at 41.1 percent of the total (and 62.3 percent of the settlement of Singapore), much of the gender imbalance can be ascribed to them.
The census recorded data for people from twenty-one other lands and reinforces the statistical picture of a predominantly male world focused on com-

TABLE 8.3. Straits Settlements Population (selected), 1881

Total population	423,384
Male	281,687
Female	141,697
Total European and American population	3,483
Male	2,803
Female	680
Total Malay population	174,326
Male	86,701
Female	87,625
Total Tamil population	37,305
Male	28,535
Female	8,780
Total Chinese population (all dialect groups)	174,327
Male	143,605
Female	30,722

Source: CO 275/25 (1881), 268b.

merce, plantation production, and resource extraction. The indigenous Malays alone manifested scientifically natural gender ratios in which females roughly equaled the number of males.

Each settlement recorded data by Chinese native place. Here I focus on Singapore, the largest settlement by far. The figures reinforce the idea that the British were building a colony for the Chinese, who constituted 62.3 percent of the total population. The mass migration out of China led to the demographic displacement of every other group, including the ostensible "Euro-American" colonizers (1.9 percent) and local Malays (15.8 percent).[12] The data in table 8.4 also underline the point about the demography of Chaozhou.

The heavily male ratios for all Chinese immigrants are similar. The Straits-born Chinese, who descended primarily from Fujianese, in contrast had remarkably natural gender ratios, probably because they were among the wealthiest people in the colony and therefore not driven in desperation to infanticide, but also because many of these long-term residents had intermarried with Malayans and assimilated more tolerant attitudes with regard to girl children.[13]

Of all Chaozhouese in Singapore, only 7.49 percent were female and 92.51 percent male. The sex ratio was 100 women for every 1,233 men. This gender dynamic was replicated in other settlements. In Malacca, for example, 3.3 percent of the Chaozhouese population were female and 96.7 percent male.[14] Across Malaya there was a notable imbalance of sex ratios among

TABLE 8.4. Chinese Population by Native Place, Singapore, 1881

Total Chinese population	86,766
Male	72,571
Female	14,195
Fujianese/Hokkien	24,981
Male	23,327
Female	1,654
Chaozhouese/Teochew	22,644
Male	20,946
Female	1,698
Cantonese/Macaos	14,853
Male	9,699
Female	5,154
Straits-born (from all native places)	9,527
Male	4,513
Female	5,014
Hainanese	8,319
Male	8,266
Female	53
Hakka	6,170
Male	5,561
Female	609
Native place not stated	272
Male	259
Female	13

Source: CO 275/25 (1881), 308.

Chaozhouese in the 1880s, and thus we thus begin to see the process by which emigrant communities back in Chaozhou became majority female or had larger female populations compared to villages elsewhere in China. At any given time, the vast majority of migrants absent from Chaozhou were men, which led to anomalous percentages of women back home. If we consider these villages in their translocal context, however, they were not majority-female at all.

These imbalances are seen in other lands to which Chaozhouese migrated, albeit with less specificity. G. William Skinner estimated that Chinese women constituted 2 to 3 percent of Chinese migrants to Siam from 1882 to 1892. Approximately 177,500 Chinese arrived in Bangkok during that decade (99,400 departed, presumably for China). Women thus constituted 3,550 to 5,325 of those 177,500 migrants to the kingdom. Women increasingly departed for Siam

TABLE 8.5. Chinese Population of British Malaya Relative to Other Populations, 1921

Total population	3,358,054
Male	2,061,622
Female	1,296,432
Total European population	14,954
Male	10,048
Female	4,906
Total Malay population	1,651,051
Male	843,703
Female	807,348
Total Indian population	471,666
Male	335,485
Female	136,181
Total Chinese population	1,174,777
Male	848,776
Female	326,001
Total Fujianese	380,656
Male	261,741
Female	118,915
Total Cantonese	332,307
Male	227,341
Female	104,966
Total Chaozhouese	**130,231**
Male	**102,160**
Female	**28,071**

Source: Census, British Malaya, 1922, 148 and 186.

in the twentieth century, but they were always far outnumbered by men.[15] Most Chinese residents of Siam hailed from Chaozhou, but sex ratios cannot be processed with native-place precision. Nevertheless, it is clear that counting sojourning males in the aggregate brings the sex ratios back to the "normal" range seen elsewhere in China.

Chinese women migrated in slightly larger numbers after 1911, and their percentage of the overseas population increased. By 1921, for example, Chinese female immigrants constituted 15 percent of Chinese immigrants to the Straits, up from 3.1 percent in 1878.[16] Chinese males, Chaozhouese in particular, nonetheless continued to predominate deep into the 1920s. The 1921 census for what was now "British Malaya" bears this out. The statistics in table 8.5 also show that the British continued to build a colony for the Chinese.

By 1921 females represented 38.4 percent of the Chinese population, a significant uptick from 1881 (17.6 percent). Chaozhouese women, however, represented only 27.4 percent of the Chaozhouese total, indicating that they were less likely to migrate than women from the two other major Chinese groups, Fujianese and Cantonese. In spite of the increasing number of women, Chaozhouese men constituted almost three-quarters of that native place population, and the overseas experience continued to be heavily male.

The major discrepancy between the censuses of the 1880s and 1920s was the diminution of Chaozhouese as a percentage of the total Chinese population of British Malaya. Throughout the nineteenth century they had vied with the Fujianese for numerical supremacy and far outnumbered those from Canton. Although their numbers were not insignificant, by the 1920s they had fallen behind the other groups, this in spite of the fact that emigration out of Chaozhou had increased. There were complicated reasons for this, but the most important was the decline of pepper and gambier plantation agriculture in the twentieth century. This had been a major sector of Chaozhouese investment, and the majority of nineteenth-century Chaozhouese were rural laborers who worked the pepper and gambier estates of Singapore and Johor (Indeed, many of those laborers were poor, "credit ticket" passengers who were obliged to work in indentured servitude for a period. This is one reason why their numbers increased relative to the better-off Fujianese, who paid their own way but arrived in smaller numbers). Chaozhouese merchants in the Straits began to abandon this sector for real estate, rubber, rice, and banking. They came to dominate the rice and fruit trade in particular, and laborers inclined to work in Chaozhou-dominated economic sectors either continued to migrate to Siam or, increasingly, made their way to French Indochina. Chaozhouese completely supplanted the Cantonese as the majority native place group in Cambodia during the 1920s, constituting 75 percent of overseas Chinese there by midcentury. This led to a coterminous reduction of their share of the Straits population.

Wherever they traveled, sojourners left behind villages with more females than was the norm in China. Visitors to the Hakka hinterland of Chaozhou in the 1920s were surprised to see numbers of women working in the fields and even as stevedores in the waterways connecting the East River to Swatow and Canton. Communist general Zhu De ascribed the large number of female laborers to the region's tradition of male emigration. "This was the first time I had ever seen physically strong and emancipated women in China," he declared. "Forced to shoulder every responsibility, they had become emancipated from the ancient tyranny of fathers, husbands, and in-laws."[17] Although it is not clear that wives of sojourning men were as liberated as the general claimed back in 1927, demographic realities indicate that women were destined to play a role in the looming revolution. Already in the 1920s, many provided essential services to the rural movement in the region. They helped found Peasant Leagues and participated in combat in the Peasant Self-Defense Corps. They served as stretcher-bearers who conveyed wounded comrades to villages beyond the reach of the Nationalists and carried supplies to beleaguered communist forces. They also acted as communication scouts among dispersed units of fighters.[18]

Demographic realities had other repercussions. Reporting on field research he had done in the emigrant village of Fenghuang ("Phoenix") in Chao'an district in 1923, Daniel Kulp revealed that villagers in the area expressed concern that "sexual irregularities" had been "increasing" owing to the intensified migration of husbands over the decades. Such irregularities included tabooed sexual intercourse between local men and their sisters-in-law, aunts, nieces, and cousins. Other scandals involved men cavorting with their neighbors' female kin and maidservants.[19] No mention was made of homosexual relationships, a topic about which it is difficult to find detailed information. Tze-Lan D. Sang has noted that public discussions of female sexual intimacy were becoming more common in the 1920s, but evidently these farmers were not participating in them.[20]

Details of a world in which wives remained at home, caring for their husbands' parents and children and spinning cloth or collecting seashells, are otherwise elusive for the prewar years. We do know that it was not an entirely lonely existence. Emigrant communities were characterized by female storytelling and ballad-singing gatherings, and the more educated among them participated in reading circles.[21] Social life outside the family was sororal, and these activities made the long years bearable, and perhaps more fun. Most, however, missed their absent husbands. Zhu De shared one communist-inspired ballad titled the "Ten Entreaties," which attested to their difficulties: "My beloved you are not so far away! / Take your quilt and return to your native home / Do everything to join the revolution / ... Workers and peasants, hand in hand / You take the rifle, I take the sword."[22] Although the lyrics reflected Zhu De's own radical sympathies, they attest to a desire for the husbands' return.

Marriages in Chaozhou were not always happy, of course. Divorce was rare, and there were few socially acceptable ways to escape a bad marriage. Male emigration emerged as a solution to connubial turmoil. The husband and his relatives continued to accept responsibility for the abandoned wife and children, but the daily stress of living in bitter matrimony was mercifully at an end.[23]

TABLE 8.6. Ages of Chaozhou Males in Singapore, 1881

Age	Number
0–15	147
16–20	616
21–25	2,565
26–30	3,710
31–35	3,704
36–40	2,901
41–45	2,513
46–50	1,494
51–55	1,195
56–60	631
Over 60	789

Source: CO 275/25, "Report on Census of Singapore, 1881," 237–38.

Translocal Marriage

In the late nineteenth century many male Chaozhouese left China after they were married. This can be discerned from the data relating to their ages in the Singapore census figures for 1881 (table 8.6).

There were a small number of youths under twenty—most of whom were probably born in the colony—and of older people over fifty-five—reflecting the high death rates of Chinese laborers as well as the fact that many returned home after years of toil. There was a dramatic uptick in the numbers of males older than twenty, and the vast majority ranged in age from twenty-one to forty-five. The norm apparently was to depart between age twenty-one and twenty-five and to work abroad during their prime laboring years.

Why twenty-one to twenty-five? Most departed China with the permission of their elders and clearly were deemed old enough to journey to a distant land. More important, the mean age for male marriage in southern China was 20.7, and many of these men would have married and produced one male child.[24] That is to say, their parents would have permitted them to depart as long as they had fulfilled their filial obligations. If they perished at sea or succumbed to the tropical illnesses of equatorial Asia, their sons, raised at home by mothers and paternal kin, would continue the male line.

Thousands of émigrés to the Straits in these years, however, sailed as "credit ticket passengers," and one cannot simply assume that they had married before departure. They could not afford the price of passage and instead relied on "coo-

TABLE 8.7. Contract Labor Arrivals in Singapore by Place of Origin (selected), 1883

Place of Origin	Number	Place of Origin	Number
Teochew (Chaozhou)	4,672	Boyanese (Baweanese)	711
Hui Chiu (Huizhou)	2,681	Hainanese	495
Hakka	1,255	Malays	378
Hokkien (Fujianese)	1,023	Javanese	156
Cantonese	926		

Source: CO 275/29 (187–93b), PLCSS, 6 May 1884, "Annual Report of the Chinese Protectorate, 1883."

lie brokers" in the Swatow area to make travel arrangements. Ultimately the ticket would be paid for by agents representing gambier and pepper plantation owners at Singapore, and the traveler would be obliged to work for about six months to pay off the loan. Emigrants arriving from Swatow constituted the bulk of those traveling in this manner. In 1883, for example, 10,249 credit ticket passengers arrived in Singapore (out of a total of 112,261 Chinese). Chaozhouese constituted the majority of contract laborers, about 45.6 percent (table 8.7).

Many Huizhou sojourners also would have hailed from the Chaozhou-speaking regions of that prefecture. Most contract laborers were too poor to purchase a ticket using family resources, and their families might not have been able to afford the costs of a traditional marriage. Among the 33,536 passengers who arrived from Swatow in 1883, at least 14 percent were such laborers, and presumably many were not married. The vast majority of Chaozhouese immigrants, however, paid their own passages.

By the 1930s the average age of male emigrants from Chaozhou decreased. Chen Ta conducted field research in southern Fujian and eastern Guangdong and found that 37.9 percent of males departed between the ages of ten and nineteen, and 46.6 percent departed between twenty and twenty-nine.[25] In the 1880s youths under the age of twenty did not normally emigrate, otherwise their numbers would have registered more significantly in the census. This age reduction probably reflected the normalization of sojourning by all classes of men. It is also likely that parents decided to spare their sons the dangers of the political turmoil of the 1920s and 1930s, dangers that included impressment into forced labor on behalf of warlord militaries or the threat of physical assault by communists who targeted families with overseas connections. As we have seen, Chen Jinhua and the other men in his village fled the violence of Puning in 1934. At age twenty he ended up in Singapore, but other relatives migrated to Cambodia, Siam, and Penang. Under chaotic circumstances, considerations of age did not apply, though most older people did not go abroad.[26]

If the men were not married before departing, their families eventually arranged a marriage back home. Chen Jinhua offers a vivid picture of this process. He initially headed for Siam but later settled in Singapore. After a few setbacks he obtained steady work and managed to acquire some savings. He thereupon sent a photo of himself to his mother, who remained in Puning. He was her favorite child, and she managed to find a pleasant, illiterate villager for him. After she showed his picture to the woman's family, they agreed to the betrothal. All the arrangements, including the payment of the dowry, were made in China. Chen played no role in the matter and never saw his new wife before the day she arrived in the colony. The fact that he was employed and saving money presumably enhanced his marriage prospects back home.

Chen's mother escorted his bride to Singapore, something that would have been unthinkable in the 1880s but was not uncommon by the 1930s, especially in a family with multiple overseas contacts. He had an income and lived a secure distance from the violence of Puning. His mother probably hoped that he would produce a son sooner rather than later and that agenda was better fulfilled in the tranquility of Singapore. This arrangement nonetheless generated other problems, for there was no one back home to care for his mother once she began to decline several years later. He returned home to build a new house and to secure a concubine who would care for her. His new partner upended those plans, however, when she "wailed like a baby and said she wanted to come to Singapore too." This created new complications because colonial authorities would permit a Chinese man to bring a second wife to the colony only if the first wife signed a statement of approval. Chen's first wife was inconsolable. She had agreed to the second marriage only because the plan had been for the second wife to care for his mother back home (which enabled her to avoid that fate herself). She too "wept like a baby," but in the end she agreed to the emigration of the concubine. Later, when asked by his interviewer whether they all "lived in peace" after she moved in, Chen sighed, "no."[27]

Chen's dilemma reflected more than the unhappy prospect of dwelling abroad with two feuding women. Even in turbulent times, sojourners usually left their wives and small children at home. It was cheaper to sustain them in the family village rather than in Southeast Asia. More significantly, their wives, parents, and children perpetuated their personal ties to the village and their family claim to land. Wang Chunquan explained in an interview why his great-grandfather never brought his wife and children to Singapore even after he began to make money as an umbrella-maker in the mid-1880s: the whole idea of sojourning was to "return to the root," to return to China. The men hoped to go home someday and "you did not want to lose your connection to the village . . . if you brought your wife to the south, it *would be as if to say you did not love your village, that you wanted to flee it.*" Instead the great-grandfather continued to send money to his family back home, hoping one day to save enough to build a big house with thirty rooms, one in which his entire family someday could live together.[28]

Even under the violent circumstances of the 1920s and 1930s, women were expected to remain in their husbands' villages. As Chen Jinhua recounted, "At a time when people are fleeing chaos, the men are the first to go. Women do not flee. Women might temporarily flee to a secure place for a spell. After a while, if the situation isn't urgent, and if there aren't any bandits about, then they dare to return." Despite repeated inquiries by the interviewer, Chen could not imagine a situation where one would not want the woman to return to the man's village. Even after the Japanese invaded Chaozhou in 1939, women were expected to remain in the village. In normal and abnormal times, "the husband was in Singapore and the wife in China."[29] This was one way to maintain a claim to village land.

Sojourners feared weakened kinship ties if one did not maintain a physical presence in familial territory back home. Wang Changrui recalled that it was expensive to travel back to China, and once there, one had the expense of living several months in China while not working overseas, so only the wealthy returned home frequently. His own branch of the family, which lived in Singapore, returned to his village in Chao'an infrequently and slowly "began to lose the family branch mentality."[30] Extended absence from the village potentially reduced lineage identifications.

C. F. Remer related the life story of a typical sojourning businessman. Raised in a village near Swatow, his father brought him to Siam to learn the family business in 1900, when he turned seventeen. Two years later he was sent back to his village to be married. After three years and presumably the birth of a son, he returned to Siam to help run the firm. After that—from age twenty-two to age fifty—his life cycled between two places, but for every four years he lived in Siam, he devoted only one year to village life with his wife. He retired to the village at age fifty, when his own son assumed responsibility for the business in Siam.[31] This information, conveyed to Remer by a younger family member, indicates that the couple were together for only 20 percent of their married life before the husband returned home permanently. Significantly, Remer, an economist, related the story as he pondered whether the remittances sent by a man who lived primarily in Siam should be considered a "foreign investment" in Chaozhou. What he was describing, of course, were the complexities of translocal married life or, what the Chinese called *liangtou jia*: "family on both ends."[32]

Financially secure émigrés usually contracted a second marriage in their overseas communities.[33] Polygamy was useful in diaspora. Sojourners sent remittances home, simultaneously improving their families' living standards as well as maintaining the emotional and territorial bonds of the village. The secondary, overseas wives ensured that these men enjoyed family life even as they benefited from access to overseas colonial resources. The wives left behind, of course, lost the routines of conjugal life.

They did, however, enjoy close relationships with their children. Chen Jin-hua's mother was the major influence in his life. It was she who gave him twenty silver dollars so that he could move to Siam; his mother told him where and how to find his brother, who was already living overseas; his mother arranged his marriage back in China and brought the wife to Singapore. He was very close to her. As he acknowledged, "Because I was the baby of the family, my mother was extremely fond of me." Indeed, in spite of the fact that his older brother was responsible for her needs as a matter of custom, it was Chen who took it on himself to obtain a second wife to ensure his aging mother's well-being.[34] As we have seen, this second wife ended up moving to Singapore herself. Chen's devotion to his mother, however, was an expression of the close parental bond mothers and their children forged in a social context in which so many fathers played more distant roles.

Female influence can be seen in other ways. The prominence of maternal and other female relations in the social networks of sojourning Chaozhouese males in the twentieth century is encountered in many of the oral interviews preserved in the Singaporean archives. Commercial families often married into other commercial families, reflecting a marital networking tactic for families in diaspora. This ensured access to intricate circuits of mutual assistance in multiple locations and was roughly comparable to the practice in which Chinese gentry families married into other gentry families back in China.

Liao Zhengxing (1874–1934) founded one of the great gambier and pepper businesses in Singapore in the nineteenth century. He eventually branched into rubber and in 1907 was a founding investor in Sze Hai Tong Bank, an institution that catered to Chaozhouese. A director of the Singapore Chinese Chamber of Commerce, he was one of the most influential men in Singapore, and yet he had very humble beginnings. A native of Haiyang district, his father died when he was young and his family fell into straitened circumstances. His family permitted him to emigrate to Singapore to work in a shop owned by his wife's relatives. It was through that connection that he got his foot in the door of the Chinese commercial world of the colony.[35]

Similarly, when Wang Changrui moved to Singapore in the 1930s, he and his father lived in a warehouse belonging to an import-export business managed by his maternal uncle, Chen Chuliang. They met the uncle back in Swatow and swore brotherhood with him. Once in Singapore, they assisted him in the wholesale end of the business, shipping Chinese imports throughout Malaya.[36] With this maternal connection the Wangs got their start in the Straits. Significantly, however, they felt obliged to formalize the family connection by swearing brotherhood with his mother's brother, reinforcing a bond that was not entirely "real" in the absence of this ritual act. One would not have engaged in that formality with a paternal male relative, though it was a common practice in transnational, fraternal organizations.

Commercial families also had the financial resources to maintain multiple families in different locations, usually in the native place and in the ports where their businesses were headquartered. Gao Manhua, the founder of Yuen Fat Hong, the great Chaozhou rice-trading firm, was emblematic of the wealthiest sort of overseas merchant. He had nine sons with five wives living in Chenghai, Hong Kong, and Bangkok, which also happened to be major rice emporia.[37] This family dynamic reinforced the Gaos' network of personal connections in commercial nodes across the South China Sea.

These families benefited from access to international markets and foreign commodities, but the multiplex household structures also led to complications, especially as modern communications improved and social mores changed. We see this in a lawsuit Low (Liu) Soon Wah lodged against her nephews in the colonial courts of Singapore in 1931. Soon Wah was born in Chaozhou, probably in the family village of Liulong, in 1877. Her father was Liu Xiri, who had retired to his native place in the late 1870s after building the most successful gutta percha (rubber) business in Singapore. The company expanded under the management of his sons, and by the time Soon Wah was born, they were among the wealthiest families in the Straits. They struggled during the Depression but remained socially prominent, with interests across Malaya, Siam, and Borneo.[38] Xiri had at least two wives, for half of his nine children—including his immediate successor Liu Changyi—were born in Singapore and had taken British citizenship, and half were born in Chaozhou—including the commercial wizard Liu Kunyi and, of course, Soon Wah.

At the heart of Soon Wah's lawsuit was her claim that she and her four sisters were entitled to a share of their father's estate. In 1884, when she was eight years old, she asserted, her father had made a verbal declaration that he wanted his daughters to inherit equal shares with their brothers. He died that year without leaving a will, however, and his surviving sons continued to manage his properties and businesses back in the Straits. They supported their sister financially, but she received nothing near the amount to which she would have been entitled as an equal partner in a thriving business. By 1931 she was living in Singapore herself. Her brothers had all died by then, and she might have felt more comfortable challenging the younger generation. After multiple suits and appeals, she triumphed over her nephews and won her share of her father's estate in 1933.[39]

What inclined Low Soon Wah to sue her kin in a colonial court almost fifty years after her father's demise? It is possible that her nephews had reduced the amount of support they funneled to her from properties held in trust. Their businesses suffered during the Depression, and they may have introduced unwelcome austerities. The date of the lawsuit is also significant: 1931. New laws governing inheritance had gone into effect in the Republic of China in that year. The revised civil code gave daughters equal property rights for the first time in history, though in practice families continued to operate according to "the logic of family property."[40] These laws affected wealthy families in particular, and it is possible that Soon Wah was inspired to act as a consequence of transforming legal notions in China itself.

If she was galvanized by the spirit of reform in China, in the end, she obtained justice in Singapore, site of her family's success. Her father had died intestate and, under British law, such circumstances led directly to probate court. Probate established her equal claim to the patrimony, and eventually an appellate court ensured her victory. That is to say, the woman left behind in Chaozhou successfully claimed a share of her father's estate by relying on the services of a British court. Colonial authorities upheld a legal system that addressed the multifarious needs of southeast coastal Chinese.

Working Women

A small number of Chaozhouese women emigrated overseas, and, as usual, British colonials provided useful statistical information about their experiences. The female employment data in the Straits Settlements Census of 1881 did not make distinctions by native place. The authorities seemed interested in the topic primarily as it related to males, who tended to organize into the dreaded "secret brotherhood societies" on that basis. The information for Chinese women as a whole nonetheless is revealing. Here the focus again is on Singapore, the largest Chinese-occupied settlement (table 8.8).

As in China itself, the majority of women in Singapore led quiet, conventional lives as wives, mothers, and daughters. Of the 14,195 women in the settlement, 11,392 dwelled in the domestic sphere of the family. Service as a maid was also an employment option, though the vast majority of Chinese servants were men (12,586). Most women did not work outside of the home, and one suspects that those few who operated commercial businesses had inherited them from deceased husbands; indeed, the operations would have enabled them to continue to reside overseas in spite of the demise of their spouses.

Women in the domestic sphere constituted the majority of Chinese women, but the next largest category of occupation was "Profession not stated"; 1,960 women in total. Most of these women surely were prostitutes, and it is unclear why the census did not comment on this. Colonial officials otherwise were obsessed with the state of the brothels. They assiduously investigated the immigration of prostitutes, registered their names and addresses, monitored their health for any sign of venereal disease, and fretted that the "secret societies" monopolized the industry. They also determined that the majority of prostitutes in nineteenth-century Singapore came from Chaozhou and Canton.[41]

As in port regions around the globe, prostitution was common back in Chaozhou. One feature of the business along the coast was its waterborne character. Veritable fleets of Chaozhou "boat ladies" plied their trade along the Han River and at sea. The floating bordellos of the more refined courtesans were referred to as the "six-canopied vessels" (liu peng chuan). Lin Dachuan, a poet and scion of an old Haiyang literati family, celebrated their beauty and sophistication, recounting somewhat stylized stories of fabulously attractive women with a come-hither gleam in their eyes begging scholar-officials for a nice bit of verse.[42] These women were renowned outside of Chaozhou. The great poet and gadabout Yuan Mei referred to their "six-canopied vessels" in his poetry collection, Suiyuan Poetry Talks (1788). The historian Zhao Yi, on the other hand, conveyed a few less captivating details, including the fact that many of the prostitutes were younger than fifteen years. They were sold to the brothels as children and coerced into sex labor by the time they turned thirteen or fourteen. Zhao pointedly remarked that whenever high-ranking officials came to Chaozhou on business, they invariably repaired to the boats to

TABLE 8.8. Occupations of Chinese Women, Singapore, 1881

Domestic occupations, total	11,710
Wives	7,036
Girl children	4,356
Servants	318
Professional occupations, total	23
Actors, artists, musicians	14
Physicians, surgeons, dentists	4
Schoolmistresses	3
Civil service	2
Commercial occupations, total	30
Boarding house keepers	4
Butchers and pork-sellers	2
Cake-sellers	6
Hawkers	2
Merchants and brokers	2
Pig-dealers	4
Poulterers	4
Ship-chandlers, shopkeepers, general dealers	6
Agricultural class occupations, total	5
Fruit cultivators	1
Gambier and pepper planters	3
Market gardeners	1
Industrial class occupations, total	459
Barbers	1
Confectioners	8
Laborers	14
Dressmakers and seamstresses	426
Washerwoman	1
Unclassified occupations, total	1,977
Profession not stated	1,960
"Lunatics"	13
Prisoners	4

Source: CO 275/25, "Return of Occupations," 240–42.

drink and make merry. He also believed that this tradition of floating brothels had originated among the Dan people of the Pearl River area around Canton and spread to Chaozhou during the eighteenth century. Roughly half the prostitutes who plied their trade along the Han River were Dan, the socially debased "boat people" of the south China coast.[43] The expansion of prostitution in Chaozhou coincided with the commercial recovery of the economy in the eighteenth century. The growing ranks of sex workers probably reflected an already impoverished boat people adapting to new opportunities, though the phenomenon may have been exacerbated by a process in which people lost access to land and were obliged to live on water.

Nan'ao, long a piratical and smuggling haunt, was also a center of the regional sex trade. The intensifying commerce with Southeast Asia in the eighteenth century coincided with the rise of seaborne prostitution. Floating bordellos cruised toward the island to rendezvous with sailors returning from their journeys. Charles Gutzlaff sailed on one Chinese junk from Siam to China in 1831. The ship did not have a permit to stop in the ports of Zhanglin or Anbu, so it anchored temporarily off Nan'ao to offer its seamen the opportunity to visit their families. The Pomeranian missionary, who had learned Chaozhou dialect in Siam, stood aghast at the ensuing spectacle:

> As soon as we had anchored, numerous boats surrounded us, with females on board, some of them brought by their parents, husbands, or brothers. I addressed the sailors who remained in the junk and hoped that I had prevailed on them in some degree to curb their evil passions. But, alas! No sooner had I left the deck, than they threw off all restraint; and the disgusting scene which ensued might well have entitled our vessel to the name of Sodom. The sailors, unmindful of their starving families at home, and distracted, blinded, stupefied by sensuality, seemed willing to give up aught and everything they possessed, rather than abstain from that crime which entails misery, disease, and death. Having exhausted all their previous earnings, they became prey to reckless remorse and gloomy despair. As their vicious partners were opium smokers by habit, and drunkards by custom, it was necessary that strong drink and opium should be provided; and the retailers of these articles were soon present to lend a helping hand.[44]

Gutzlaff seemed the only man on board embraced merely by "gloomy despair." He was soon fated to abet the Jardine Matheson Company in its opium-smuggling enterprise at Nan'ao, however, and hardly in a position to condemn Chinese sailors and their female companions who enjoyed the drug. He nonetheless reminds us of the interconnections among the opium, gambling, and prostitution businesses in the vicinity of the island, not to mention elsewhere along the South China Sea. Nan'ao had never been well regulated, and its location along shipping routes made the enclave an ideal site for surreptitious pleasures.[45]

Chaozhou prostitutes were remarkably peripatetic. Their "flowery boats" were well-known in the vicinity of Canton. The memoirist Shen Fu (b. 1763) recalled a visit he and his cousin made to the "singing girls" on the Pearl River, participating in a local custom euphemistically referred to as "paddling around" (*da shui wei*). His cousin, a merchant well-acquainted with the demimonde of the provincial capital, described the Chaozhouese as "dolled up like immortals." Shen, however, was a native of Suzhou with a decidedly literati taste in women and deemed them slightly bizarre. They wore their hair in bangs with the sides turned up in tufts like a servant's coif. Many wore trousers and did not have bound feet (which indicates they probably were ethnically Dan boat people).[46]

Chaozhou prostitutes sojourned beyond the waterways of Guangdong to the flowery world of Shanghai. There they operated on land, staffing over thirty-six brothels throughout that burgeoning metropolis in the nineteenth century.[47] Like other Chaozhou businesses, the sex industry thrived in this northern treaty port. By the twentieth century prostitutes circulated regularly between Shanghai and Swatow. Local literati were not pleased with their influence on women across the region. The prefectural gazetteer lamented in 1893 that "Chaozhou women now imitate the streetwalkers who travel back and forth on ships between Swatow, Suzhou, and Shanghai. They doll themselves up and travel into the remotest villages and towns in their bare feet to give [other] women scandalous hairdos."[48] The Depression hit Shanghai hard, and many of that city's streetwalkers headed home to Swatow in the 1930s.[49] As we shall see, the economic collapse had a deleterious impact on all migratory laboring classes.

Given their seagoing traditions, many Chaozhouese prostitutes not surprisingly ended up in the Straits Settlements. Women were not permitted to depart alone from the ports of South China, but Chen Chengbao, the most prominent Chaozhouese in the Straits in the nineteenth century, claimed that "secret society" members smuggled women aboard oceangoing vessels on the high seas off Swatow to evade inspections at the port. Women, dressed in men's clothing, were hauled aboard in large baskets, he averred. Most women, however, were simply smuggled out of Chaozhou a few at a time into the nearby British colony of Hong Kong, where they were free to travel internationally.[50]

Given the profits of the sex trade, young girls were imperiled by their mere residence on the Chaozhou coast. Kidnapping was a problem, but child-selling was more prevalent, and the proximity of the sea ensured that the most vulnerable might easily be transported abroad, where they knew no one. Upon arrival they were sold either to the brothels or into a form of indentured servitude that might include sexual obligations. The story of Lin Qiumei (Janet Lim) is a compelling example of the latter phenomenon, known by the Cantonese term *mui tsai* or "little sister" system (Mandarin: *meizi*). The system operated as a type of informal charity in which financially secure families took in abandoned girls as servants in exchange for a promise to arrange a marriage for them when they came of age. The custom had its darker side, however. Qiumei was born in Hong Kong in 1923, but her family returned to her father's village in Chaozhou when she was an infant. The father died six years later, and an uncle she had never met returned from Singapore to take control of the family properties. Her mother eventually remarried, and the new family moved to Swatow to enable her stepfather to find work. Unsuccessful in that endeavor, they decided to return to his village. En route they stopped at a large house teeming with women and children, and her mother told her that she and her husband were depositing her there while they settled down but would retrieve her in three months. A few weeks later the proprietors of the house told her they were taking her to her stepfather's village. She joyfully boarded the boat in Swatow expecting to reunite with her mother, but a week's passage later, someone shouted "there's Singapore!" Her mother never told her she had been sold, and Qiumei never saw her again. At eight years of age, she did not know what else to do but obey the female trafficker who accompanied her. "Call me Aunty," the woman said. She complied, which is how they slipped past the British inspectors.

She was sold to an "old man" for $250 dollars. Abandoned by her mother, transported thousands of miles away, she moved about her household chores "like a machine." Her master was a wealthy landowner, a drinker, and an insomniac. His wife lived a few miles away, and he roamed the female quarters at night to select a maidservant to share his bed. He finally began to hound Qiumei, but she always managed to hide in the nooks and crannies of his estate. He even recruited his wife to assist him in these nocturnal quests. She found Qiumei hiding in the rafters and tried to dislodge her with several hard pokes of a sharp pole. Neighbors heard her nightly screaming and began to gossip, but the harassment continued. On one trip to inspect his plantations in Johor, she broke free of him as he pawed at her.

The couple grew frustrated with the youngster's refusal to submit and deposited her with a kindly widow who might calm her down and clarify her obligations. The widow took good care of her and even promised to let Qiumei marry one of her own, friendly little boys when she grew up. But the child needed to understand that the old man had purchased her because he liked to have sex with young girls in the belief that nature would thereby "grant him a longer life and [help him] remain strong and healthy." It was his wife's idea that they "import" girls from China for this purpose. Technically his second wife, she sought to remain on good spousal terms by supporting his "health" regimen. When Qiumei turned eighteen, as was the practice, he would provide a dowry and arrange a suitable marriage. The widow sympathetically told the girl the facts of her new life, sighing that "only the gods could save [her]." Apparently they did, for almost immediately an ordinance restricting the *mui tsai* system was passed, and she was required to register with the authorities. A Chaozhouese-speaking woman who worked for the Office of the Chinese Protectorate removed her from the household and, at ten years of age she was placed in the Poh Leung Kuk (Office to Protect Virtue), a refuge for women fleeing prostitution and coerced servitude. That year there were 423 other admissions, almost all of whom had been brought to Singapore as orphans, singers, or prostitutes. Eventually the British compelled her master to pay her $700, and she enrolled in a Church of England boarding school where she not only received an education but, in her words, "a home, security, affection, and personal guidance."[51]

Prostitution was a big business in the Straits, and Qiumei's ordeal reflected the demand for female sexual labor in a predominantly male colony. In 1876 a total of 1,335 prostitutes were registered in the settlement of Singapore alone, and Chinese women, numbering 1,174, constituted 87 percent of them. Colonial inspectors did not specify their native place but did observe that the vast majority had immigrated from Chaozhou and "Macao," a term they used to refer to "Cantonese."[52] Cantonese sex workers served only Chinese, whereas those from Chaozhou catered predominantly to Chinese but also to men of other nationalities. Chaozhouese prostitutes were not more "cosmopolitan" than their Cantonese sisters. They served non-Chinese only in those neighborhoods where they shared the business with Cantonese (for example, the areas around Victoria Street). In those areas where Chaozhouese monopolized business (the areas around North Bridge Road and New Bridge Road), they catered to Chinese men only, indicating that they were subordinate in some way to laborers from Canton.[53]

The life of prostitutes in Singapore was not easy. Some were known to have been beaten or denied adequate nutrition if they failed to generate income. Others contracted sexually transmitted diseases, although, because of the inspection regime, they usually received timely treatment in hospital. On the other hand, their mortality rates did not appear to be noticeably higher than those of other Chinese. They also earned a fairly decent living compared to their working-class brethren. Each prostitute earned approximately $20 per month circa 1876. That was over three times what a typical Chaozhou agricultural laborer on a pepper and gambier plantation earned during the same period ($6 per month). The women nonetheless were obliged to reimburse the amount the brothel owners had paid for their purchase (usually $300 to $400 for a "good-looking" woman; less for a plain one). They also had to compensate the owner for various living expenses. Prostitutes were known to complain that they had difficulty saving money.[54]

In spite of these problems, brothels offered a semblance of family life for the women and the men they served. British inspectors were surprised to discover that many children inhabited the Singaporean institutions. In 1876 one bordello was found to house ten prostitutes, twelve children between the ages of twelve and sixteen, and twenty children under the age of twelve, which is to say there were more children than adults living in the facility. According to Chinese interviewed by colonial officials, most of the adults were orphans who, at the age of six and upward, had been purchased from brokers in China and brought to the colony to be raised as prostitutes. As children they sang songs to entertain the clientele, but they began serving the men sexually after they reached adolescence. Some of the children were boys, and British inspectors suspected they also engaged in sexual labor.[55]

The sexual exploitation of children bothers a middle-class sensibility, but in multigenerational prostitution, at least, this was the only world they knew. They may have been purchased, but they called the madams "mother." Many, born in Singapore, were the offspring of prostitutes or brothel owners. A Chinese tailor who was interviewed by British inspectors attested to this, asserting that he did not think it was "a bad thing," nor did he advocate removing them (as some officials advocated) because "it is the custom that descendants of prostitutes should follow their parents' business and therefore I see no harm in their remaining."[56] In spite of the fact that prostitution had been criminalized in China in 1723 and such hereditarily debased households statutorily liberated from their caste-like status, the custom endured through the generations.[57] The tailor understood that this was how a certain class of the poor adapted to their circumstances. It is possible, moreover, that many of the prostitutes were themselves married. Trafficking in women was "absolutely central to the marriage system" of China, Matthew Sommer informs us. In a society with such lopsided sex-ratio imbalances, peasants adopted strategies to market the sexual labor of female relatives. Polyandry (a practice in which a woman took additional husbands in order to sustain the existing conjugal family) and wife-selling (a practice in which the existing family was broken apart) were common survival strategies.[58] Males also prostituted their female relations in the Straits. Indeed, officials found it difficult to prosecute some brothel keepers who beat their employees because the latter were reluctant to press charges against their own kin. Females prostituted their daughters as well.[59]

Virtually all adult female prostitutes in the 1870s and 1880s were recorded upon arrival "as coming [to Singapore] to join their husbands, and the procuresses are described as their mothers or as coming to join their sons in this Colony."[60] Whether or not they were telling tales to gain entry, it is clear that the business was a family affair to some extent. As we saw in the waterborne traditions off Nan'ao Island, it certainly was a familial practice back home in Chaozhou. Margery Wolf's fieldwork in Taiwan showed that villagers tolerated women who turned to prostitution to support their families. As long as they engaged in their business elsewhere, they were accepted and, indeed, were considered "filial" daughters who sacrificed a "normal life" for the sake of their families.[61] Given the fate of impoverished women in China, many gamely exploited their most marketable skill in the vast world of the sojourning multitudes. For every Qiumei who ran to the police station to resist her destiny, there were many more girls and women who chose not to, this in spite of the fact that it was understood even by an eight-year-old that the British would offer them a path out of sexual servitude. Liberated, at least, from the constraints of paternal kinship, they were sustained instead by the sororal communities they forged.

The men who patronized Singaporean establishments purchased sexual intimacy. One nevertheless can imagine them enjoying the comforts of socializing in a quasi-familial setting. Even the disapproving British officials acknowledged that the younger children acted as servants to the elders. They sang to the men for entertainment and "helped contribute to the revelry of the brothel."[62] Having young children serenading them, scampering around, and likely referring to them as "Uncle" must have been part of the appeal. However inadequate, it must have been a fleeting experience of home life for all concerned.

Prostitutes eventually left the brothels to marry. The "Protectorate of the Chinese" reported that forty-nine women did so in 1884.[63] On the other hand, marriage itself was fungible. As James Warren has shown, most women who departed the brothels did so as concubines—a legal partnership that lacked the social status of married wife—and it was common for working-class couples to live together without formally marrying. Many women, he noted, were abandoned when their lovers returned to China alone.[64]

Prostitutes were integrated into the larger female world of the Chinese diaspora. Hairdressers and dressmakers served women in both the conventional domestic and sex-working worlds. Literati back in Chaozhou certainly construed hairdressing in the 1890s as something suspiciously connected to the trade. Some of the 426 professional dressmakers and seamstresses recorded in the 1881 census probably were retired sex workers. A legal case illustrates the intertwined lives of some of these women. In 1890 Chan Ah Luk left the Straits to take work as an ayah (maid) to a Chinese family living in Dutch Sumatra. She left her three daughters with her sister-in-law, Li Ah Yi, a seamstress and hairdresser who lived in Penang. Part of Li's business involved dressing the hair of several prostitutes who lived on her street.

One day the Penang inspector of brothels noticed the eldest daughter, a sixteen-year-old named Lam Tai Ying, standing on the pathway of a brothel talking to a prostitute. He took custody of both Lam and her guardian and sent them to the Penang "protector of the Chinese." The British decided that the girl was being "trained for immoral purposes" and, per the stipulations of the Women and Girl's Protection Ordinance of 1888, removed Lam "to a place of safety," in this case, a Catholic convent. The ordinance mandated that any woman under the age of nineteen who lived in or "frequented" a brothel "shall be deemed to be a girl who is being trained for immoral purposes." The circumstances seemed to reflect the statute, although both women testified that Lam had merely accompanied her guardian as the latter fixed the hair of brothel employees.

When the mother learned that her daughter had been placed in a convent, she returned to the Straits and took legal action, demanding a writ of habeas corpus to force the protector to return her daughter. The case was appealed to the Supreme Court, where her lawyer argued that neither the daughter nor the sister-in-law had been interrogated under oath, and no cross-examination that might counter the narrative being constructed by the protector had ensued. The Court agreed and returned Lam to her mother.[65]

The case offered no details about the family life of Chan, Li, and Lam. Who and where was Lam's father? His existence is never mentioned, and Chan is never identified as a widow. Was Li herself married? Reference was made to the women's status as "in-laws," but no clarification was made in the record. Considering the preponderance of males in the Straits, there is a startling absence of menfolk in the lives of these women. One wonders if Chan or Li had done a stint in the brothels and then moved on to other forms of employment.

Speculation aside, the case reveals the interrelationship between working women and the world of prostitution in a sojourning context. A woman in the British Straits Settlements obtained employment in a Dutch colony a boat ride across the Straits of Malacca. She needed to place her children somewhere, and her in-law was available. As a seamstress and hairdresser, Li operated at the intersection of the conventional and unconventional worlds. There were so few sojourning women of means, and so many prostitutes, a hairdresser would naturally serve the latter among a limited clientele. Drawn into the orbit of the brothel, they were subjected to the surveillance of the colonial state. This also is a story of families in perpetual transit. The women were Chinese, they migrated to Southeast Asia, and they obtained employment in multiple localities. British officials complained that they could never keep tabs on sojourners from China. Southeast Asia, filled with wealthy Chinese, offered work opportunities for women as amahs, maids, and prostitutes. Like their laboring brothers, these women circulated throughout the Nanyang, pursuing opportunities that were available to anyone willing to uproot herself. They also relied on their sister travelers to care for children they collectively sustained.

A look at the unconventional translocal family enables us to see the conventional family more clearly. Indeed, the conventional was imbricated in the unconventional. Men sailed away to find better employment in Southeast Asia, and their villages back home became numerically dominated by females. Chinese men populated distant colonies, and the brothel became a site of female sojourning, fictive kinship, and biological parenthood. An accelerating rate of migration exacerbated the selling of children, rendering girls born into nice families more susceptible to the predations of translocal networks of female traffickers. One family setback—the death of a father—might transform a beloved daughter into the plaything of a plantation owner three thousand kilometers away.

Chaozhouese peasants witnessed the fateful realities of families who suffered setbacks. Anxieties about financial security compelled people to sojourn abroad, hopeful of supporting families through remittances they sent home. Those remittances resolved many of the economic challenges the Chaozhou region confronted in the twentieth century. The tidal flow of cash encouraged even more people to leave home, thus accelerating the very emigration that exacerbated the challenges of living a conventional family life and transformed those families into a large-scale collectivity.

9

Maritime Chaozhou at Full Moon, 1891–1929

All the shops [in Bangkok] were owned by Chaozhouese. Eventually, those overseas Chinese no longer wanted to speak Chaozhou dialect; they spoke Thai. But back when I went, everyone spoke Chaozhou dialect. Because if you were an Overseas Chinese and couldn't speak Chaozhouese, you couldn't operate a business. . . . The character of Siam was very Chaozhouese.

—CHEN JINHUA

AFTER THE TUMULT of the mid-nineteenth century, Chaozhou experienced an expansion of trade. Merchants maintained control of commerce and continued to benefit from opportunities overseas. Sojourners of all classes remitted significant sums from Southeast Asia and Shanghai. The expanding population of agricultural and skilled laborers found employment on plantation estates and in the operations of translocal enterprise. Their territorial strategy of migrating to overseas colonies and kingdoms accorded them access to land and natural resources.

As the twentieth century dawned, new challenges emerged at home. The sugar trade declined in the face of competition with Southeast Asia. Indian opium was forced underground as the drug once again was outlawed and native opium increasingly satisfied the tastes of recreational users. These challenges were daunting, for the sugar-beancake-opium trade had been a mainstay of the economy since the seventeenth century, but they were not insurmountable. Local farmers turned to the production of other crops, especially opium and fruit, and merchants involved in maritime commerce continued to thrive in Shanghai, Hong Kong, Singapore, Saigon, and Bangkok. Laborers who specialized in sugar milling migrated to the very overseas territories that posed such competition back home. Much "Southeast Asian sugar" was in fact "Chinese sugar." Production shifted offshore as laborers emigrated to work in Chinese-owned enterprises. As the population expanded, maritime Chaozhou offered the resources and work opportunities that enabled its translocal economy to thrive in the years before the Great Depression.

The region's more intractable problems were political. Fang Yao died in 1891, and whatever one thought of his militarized rule, he at least maintained order and facilitated development. With his passing, endemic feuding and piracy reappeared. As we have seen, the Qing dynasty was overthrown in 1912 and the politics of the Republican period (1912–1949) were chaotic. Philanthropies like benevolent halls and merchant organizations filled gaps in the fledgling state-building process, but the violence of the 1911 Revolution, the annoyances of warlordism, the catastrophic typhoon of 1922, and the early communist insurgencies hindered the economic development of eastern Guangdong. Aside from investments in land and small-scale enterprises in Chaozhou, sojourning merchants focused their entrepreneurial energies on overseas ventures, where their interests continued to be protected by kings and colonial authorities. Access to overseas economies and territories became ever more important to familial advancement.

Emigration accelerated dramatically during the early decades of the century and further entangled Chaozhou's soicoeconomic life with Southeast Asia. Foreign currency—Mexican dollars, Hong Kong dollars, French Indochinese piasters, Philippine pesos, Straits dollars, and Japanese yen—inundated local markets as emigrants returned after a few years overseas.[1] Remittances offset trade imbalances, thus benefiting the region as a whole, but they exacerbated social divides because families who enjoyed even minute trickles of funding from abroad achieved a financial security unavailable to those who did not. Families with overseas contacts, especially those with commercial ties, were more likely to purchase land, antagonizing their less fortunate relatives and neighbors. Translocal families were targeted in the peasant insurgencies of the 1920s and 1930s.

The story of maritime Chaozhou at its height is complicated, and for this reason I have chosen to tell it primarily through the experiences of one family, the Liu (Low) of Chao'an (formerly Haiyang) district. They were not typical. Like other titans of overseas commercial achievement, their wealth and status distinguished them from their fellow sojourners. Their exploits nonetheless form a useful porthole for viewing the wider social and economic currents coursing through maritime Chaozhou at this time. They exemplified the tale of the small-time peddler who succeeded beyond all comprehension, an entrepreneur whose business ventures helped fuel an industrial revolution across the globe and elevated his clan into the colonial elite. Successive generations diversified their investments into opium, banking, real estate, and the rice trade Chaozhouese dominated across the South China Sea. The translocal nature of family life; the bifurcation of national identities; the commitment to the welfare of the native place; the blessed remittances from abroad that secured the home folks' interests as the political world disintegrated; the accursed remittances that separated those with an overseas connection from those who lacked one: these trends were channeled through the experiences of three generations of Lius. They return us to the themes of the seventeenth century, when the bounties of maritime life proved both boon and bane.

The period from 1891 to 1929 witnessed the flourishing of maritime Chaozhou at its height. As the *Book of Changes* nonetheless foretold, "When the sun stands at midday it begins to set; when the moon is full, it begins to wane."[2] We now look back and see how the very success of these merchants and even of many laborers cast a shadow over the social world of modern Chaozhou. The ensuing animosities and violence presaged the larger revolution to come.

Migration and Its Discontents

As we have seen, in the eighteenth and nineteenth centuries Chinese assimilated into Siamese society largely through intermarriage with Siamese or Sino-Siamese women and conversion to Theravada Buddhism. G. William Skinner has shown that this tendency to assimilate slowed between 1900 and 1947 as Chinese women began to migrate along with men. Philanthropists also established Chinese schools for their children, which inculcated in them a stronger sense of cultural identity. This identity was reinforced by the rise of Chinese nationalism, which diminished tensions among Chinese dialect groups as they found common cause in support of the Republic.[3] Chen Jinhua migrated to Siam at this time and found the commercial world to have been "very Chaozhouese."

Siamese were becoming more nationalistic themselves, their views predicated on an ethnic vilification of Chinese, who seemed to dominate their economic lives. Such resentments were stoked by King Wachirawat, who, like other Westernizing elites, was influenced by Euro-American anti-Semitism and dogmas about a "yellow peril." In 1914 he authored an anti-Sinitic screed titled *The Jews of the East* in which he railed against what he depicted as a Chinese reverence for money that ostensibly contrasted with the values of his people, who appreciated more noble things in life. He also bemoaned the fact that their sheer numbers were "enough to inundate any country in the world."[4]

Unedifying as the king's meditations were (the biggest beneficiaries of Chinese investments were the Siamese monarchy and aristocracy, after all), they point to one feature of Chinese immigration in the twentieth century: its increasing volume. We have seen the accelerating rate of migration out of Chaozhou, most of which was occasioned by political tumult and environmental disasters. This intensified migration was matched by other Chinese native place groups and collectively transformed Chinese relations with indigenes, not only in Siam but elsewhere in Southeast Asia. In the Chaozhouese case, the nineteenth century was marked by cooperation with local leaders; indeed, they arrived and prospered at the invitation of indigenous elites in Siam, Borneo, and Malaya. Leaders in Johor, a major site of Chaozhouese settlement in Malaya, were actively involved and invested in Chinese enterprise and maintained political authority over Chinese leaders. As the size of the Chinese population expanded in the latter nineteenth century, however, Chinese became ever more tightly organized around their brotherhood societies, and the system in which the Malay sultans exercised authority over the "proliferating numbers of Chinese headmen" began to decline. Across the peninsula, Chinese increasingly bypassed Malay authority and, from the Malay point of view, "tightened their grasp of economic resources."[5] The sheer volume of Chinese migration made it more difficult for indigenous leaders to retain ultimate control over them. This is one way quantitative increases in migration led to qualitative changes in the relations between the Chinese and local people.

This transformation coincided with changes in the political economy of colonialism in Southeast Asia after the 1890s. The global economy was evolving from commercial to industrial capitalism, and colonial authorities in the Straits Settlements and elsewhere shifted from free trade policies toward more state-managed approaches to production. In Skinner's words, "colonial rule became more intensive, more bureaucratic, and more efficient." Colonialists became less tolerant of informal power-sharing arrangements with the Chinese, not only in opium revenue-farming but also with Chinese self-rule in a wider context. In the Straits in particular we see an intensified, direct British authority exercised over their colonial subjects with a mind to eliminate the longstanding *imperium in imperio* wherein Chinese governed themselves through the power of their "secret societies."[6] In the twentieth century the independent political power of Chinese became more circumscribed and their economic ascendancy challenged (but not eliminated) by a determined British effort to participate more directly in commodity production. By then, however, Chaozhouese had accumulated a significant amount of capital and, as in Shanghai, were diversifying their investments into other sectors of the modern economy. Their commercial networks held them in good stead as the world around them changed.

The Heights of Low Ah Jit

Liu Xiri (Low Ah Jit) departed for Singapore on a "red-bowed" junk sometime in the 1840s.[7] He hailed from Liulong village in Haiyang district (renamed Chao'an in 1914). The village was adjacent to Anbu, the traditional port and customs station, and thus a commercial area offering many employment opportunities. At the time, villagers in the vicinity served as porters who loaded and unloaded goods between ships on flat-bottomed lighters. Locally the hamlets were referred to as "villages of the sea" because of their connection to coastal and international shipping.[8]

Although Liu's family was considered "poor and virtuous," it is unlikely that they were as impoverished as his biographies imply. He had the resources to sail to a distant colonial outpost and, upon arrival, was not obliged to toil on a plantation or in a mine. He initially made a living operating a sampan—Chaozhouese dominated the small-trade business on sampans there—and engaged in the classic middleman role of purchasing goods from indigenes and selling them in town. He obviously had sufficient financial backing (perhaps from kin already in Singapore) to acquire a vessel and launch his own firm. Moreover, Xiri's fellow villager, Liu Jianfa (Lau Kiat Huat), is similarly depicted as having been born in poverty. Jianfa departed for the British colony of Sarawak at the same time and founded a pepper and gambier plantation before branching into international trade and opium farming. Jianfa almost singlehandedly galvanized an enormous migration of Chaozhouese to Sarawak and by the 1860s had emerged as the wealthiest and most influential Chinese there.[9] The remarkable biographical trajectory of both men suggests that they had unidentified financial support at the outset of their adventures.

Liu Xiri's story departs from that of earlier generations of Chaozhouese in Singapore who made their initial fortunes in gambier and pepper. In fact, his life's work reflects the transition in Chaozhouese enterprise in southern Malaya from those agricultural goods to rubber and other businesses, for the gambier industry began to decline in the late nineteenth century.[10] In the course of his waterborne peddling, he began to specialize in gutta-percha, a latex rubber naturally produced by the Palaquium (taban) tree that was native to Southeast Asia. The industrial potential of gutta-percha became known circa 1843, and demand for the rubber as an electrical insulator increased steadily. Gutta-percha is well suited to permanent immersion in soil and water—it notably retains its stability and flexibility over time in salt water—and therefore was spectacularly useful as insulation for transoceanic telegraph cables. Because it takes the Palaquium tree twenty-five to thirty years to come into production and has a lower yield than Para rubber, British merchants were not keen to invest in it. They instead imported Para trees from their native habitat in Latin America, and the process of domesticating that transplant delayed serious British rubber production in the Straits until 1895.[11] This left the gutta-percha business to Chinese like Liu Xiri. Recognizing the increasing demand for gutta as submarine cables were installed across the oceans, Liu started a production and wholesaling business known in English as Low Ah Jit (Mandarin: Liu Yari) around 1850. He thus enjoyed an early start in the Malayan rubber business, and the firm emerged as the leading wholesalers of gutta-percha rubber across peninsular Malaya. This commercial interest transformed Liu Xiri into one of the wealthiest men in the Straits. Other kin invested in gutta-percha as well, but Low Ah Jit and Sons (known in Chinese under the style Rongfeng and four associated companies) emerged as the leading enterprise.[12]

Great Britain dominated the manufacture and installation of cable in these years, and there was a voracious demand for gutta-percha there. Liu forged a mutually beneficial relationship with the British firm Paterson, Simons, and Co. This enterprise, founded in Singapore in 1828, was the first to export gutta-percha to Europe and evolved into a major shipping company. Their main client for gutta-percha was the Telegraph Construction and Maintenance Company (Telcon or TC&M), the paramount British firm in the production and installment of cables. By 1900 TC&M had manufactured and placed two-thirds of the world's cables—over 160,000 miles of conductivity across the Atlantic, Indian, and Pacific Oceans, linking London to Bombay and New York and Hong Kong to San Francisco, to name just a few of the multiple nodes of telecommunications on land and sea around the globe.[13]

Liu Xiri was an important part of that story: a small-time sampan peddler from Liulong village who emerged as the major wholesale supplier to a British firm that itself evolved into the main source of insulation to the world's preeminent telecommunications company. Liu was the right man in the right place at the right time, for he founded his company just as submarine cables were being laid, first across the English Channel and Irish Sea in the 1850s and then across the wider oceans from the 1860s to the 1920s.[14] The Lius' role in the gutta-percha trade placed the family at the intersection of colonial resource extraction and the European technological revolution. Their business also was integral to the process that telegraphically linked London to its colonies and naval bases at the height of British imperial expansion. This is surely one of the more remarkable success stories in overseas Chinese history.

The Lius' business relationship with their British exporter in part explains their close identification with the British Empire. We have seen how Liu Xiri's sons Liu Changyi and Liu Mingyi registered as British subjects at the consulate back in Swatow in 1879. Xiri himself had become a naturalized British subject (as Low Ah Jit) in May 1857.[15] They were cosmopolitan subjects of both the British and Chinese Empires, and although there was a cynical logic to their translocal stratagems, they genuinely identified with their native place and the colony in which they acquired fame and fortune. It nevertheless is intriguing that Liu Xiri adopted British citizenship in the middle of the Second Opium War. He may simply have been apolitical, but he probably was not very pro-Qing. In 1865 he was called as a character witness in the criminal trial of four members of the Ghee Hok Society. This "secret society" was heavily involved in female trafficking, prostitution, and feuding in Singapore. The founding brothers were Chaozhouese who had revolted against the Qing and then fled to the Straits in 1853 and 1854. In this case, the accused were convicted of kidnapping several Chinese women who had arrived with their husbands on a junk.[16] It was not unusual for laborers in the Straits to turn to prominent men in their dialect communities when they got into trouble, and Liu Xiri, now a wealthy man, presumably had little to do with the unsavory shenanigans of the underworld. As a former boatman, however, he probably was a member of this sodality formed by refugees in the anti-Qing struggle. Even if he did not believe in its tenets, it is likely he had taken an oath that called for the overthrow of the dynasty. His ties to Chaozhou itself nonetheless remained strong, and he retired to and later died there in 1884.

By then, his third son Liu Changyi (Low Cheang Yee, 1848–1915) and fifth son Liu Kunyi (Low Koon Yee, 1862–1926) had taken over the businesses. The brothers represented different strands of the translocal familial experience. Changyi was the more Anglicized of the two. He was born in Singapore and studied at Raffles Institution, an elite, Anglophone school. When the pro-British Straits Chinese British Association was established in 1900, he was elected an officer. Both brothers were stalwarts of the Sino-British community in Singapore and back in Chaozhou. Together with several kin, for example, they attended a gathering of British subjects at Swatow to celebrate the service of the departing British consul, E. G. Jamieson, when he transferred to another post in 1913. Low Ah Jit also was one of nine Chinese firms in Singapore that contributed to a "Coronation Celebration Subscription" in 1902, the year Edward VII came to throne, a public nod of loyalty to the new king.[17]

Kunyi, on the other hand, was born in Chaozhou, probably of a different mother. He became an officer of the Singapore Chinese Chamber of Commerce, an organization that was founded in 1906 by merchants who were more oriented toward China and Chinese culture. Kunyi had no problem celebrating multiple sovereigns in his peripatetic life, but as someone who was born in China, he felt the cultural tug of the homeland more strongly than his older brother.[18]

By the twentieth century the sons transformed their father's prosperous company into a multinational giant. In addition to Low Ah Jit (or Rongfeng), they fostered the further development of three other "associate companies" (lianhao) under the umbrella of Low Ah Jit and Sons, two focusing on gutta-percha and the general import-export trade between China and the Straits (Rongli and Rongye) and one devoted to gambier production (Rongmao). Rongli evolved into a midlevel player among the North-South network of firms based in Hong Kong that came to dominate the rice trade between Southeast Asia and Guangdong province. Liu Xiri's other son, Liu Xiaoqin, initially managed that firm.[19]

Gutta-percha nonetheless remained their entrepreneurial focus for obvious reasons. At the peak of its value, the rubber sold for seven hundred to eight hundred silver dollars per ton.[20] Singapore was the center of the import and reexport of the entire Southeast Asian gutta-percha trade. The settlement imported gutta from Malaya, Borneo, Sumatra, Riau, and elsewhere and then re-exported it to Europe and the United States. From 1885 through 1896, total exports and reexports of gutta-percha came to 619,377 cwt (69,370,224 imperial pounds) with a total value of £4,855,794 (approximately £555,000,000 in 2019). Combined exports of Singaporean and Malayan–produced gutta-percha alone for those years came to 111,628 cwt (12,502,336 imperial pounds) for a total value of £1,588,441 (roughly £185,200,000 in 2019).[21] Liu Xiaoqin, Xiri's son, informed American colonial authorities in the Philippines that in the half-century between 1850 and 1900, Singapore exported approximately

300,000,000 pounds (American) and that in 1901 the best grades were sold at $260 (American) per picul.[22] It is impossible to know precisely how much of that business belonged to Low Ah Jit, but their firms dominated the wholesaling of gutta-percha across Malaya, including Singapore and British North Borneo, and they surely earned multiple millions during these years. They were known as shrewd traders whose numerous storehouses allowed them to hold onto large stocks until prices peaked before selling. The profitability of the business nonetheless led to an unsustainable "trail of depletion" of the widely dispersed stands of the Palaquium tree in the region.[23]

By the early twentieth century Liu Changyi was the twelfth wealthiest Chinese and fifth wealthiest Chaozhouese in Singapore in terms of property assets.[24] He had enhanced the family fortune by joining a wealthy syndicate that controlled the Singapore Opium Farm from 1898 to 1900. It was not the family's first foray into managing opium monopolies. Low How Kim had served as the chief assistant to the opium farm circa 1877 and controlled the opium farm in the Kota Setia region of Perak from 1883 to 1885.[25] The family fortune did not depend on opium, however. From their headquarters along Boat Quay in Singapore, Low Ah Jit and Sons traded in a range of products, including rice, gambier, pepper, cotton, rattan, opium, and general goods, but their fortune was made in rubber.[26]

Changyi and Kunyi together had thirteen sons and several daughters born in both Chaozhou and Singapore, and most of the men were active in business. The most pioneering of the third generation was Liu Bingyan, better known as Low Peng Yam, the third son of Changyi. Bingyan, as we know, married the daughter of Commander Fang Yao (we are never told her name). The younger Liu was born in Singapore in 1876, and the marriage presumably was arranged by older relations back in China, for Fang interacted with the family in the 1870s. One of their firms, Rongli, had been among the contributors to the native place association he established in Canton, the Chaozhou Native Place Association of the Eight Districts, and at least one family member served with him among its inaugural directors in 1876.[27] The relationship may have been cultivated in Chaozhou. Both Changyi and his brother Mingyi returned for an extended visit in 1877, when Fang was raising funds to rebuild the Longxi Academy, which was near their village. The local gazetteer notably referred to the fact that both Fang and the "gentry and wealthy" (shenfu) collected funds for schools and river dredging throughout the 1870s, and the Lius probably contributed.[28] By the time the Lius emerged as a commercial force, the notion of "local elite" had long been in transformation, and, as a family that thrived in the Straits while maintaining contact with the home folks, they certainly were among "the wealthy" of this area. The nuptials between the Singaporean-born Bingyan and Fang Yao's daughter reflected translocal networking strategies that connected "local" elites with overseas sojourners. The local "gentry and wealthy" as a group were in fact translocal.

Liu Bingyan was best known as a director and shareholder of the most important modern bank serving the needs of overseas Chaozhouese, the Sze Hai Tong Bank. It was also known by its name in translation, the Four Seas Bank, and, reflecting its role in financing Chaozhou rice networks during the twentieth century, had branches in Bangkok and Hong Kong.[29] It was founded in Singapore in 1906 by influential members of the business elite, including Liao Zhengxing (Leow Chia Heng)—who had made his fortune in pepper and gambier and was the bank's longstanding managing director; Chen Ruiqi (Tan Swi Khi)—the son of the gambier planter Chen Mianjie and a son-in-law of the pioneering tycoon, Seah Eu Chin; and Lan Jinsheng (Nga Kim Seng)—who had made his fortune in Siam and Singapore trading in rice and other foodstuffs.[30] The Lius were not members of the original board, but by 1913 both Bingyan and Kunyi had taken on this responsibility. They were joined in 1914 by Seah Peck Seah, the son of Seah Eu Chin and the father-in-law of Liu Bingxian, the oldest son of Liu Kunyi.[31]

Opium had been integral to the economy of the gambier plantations in the nineteenth century. The sale of opium in these settlements was largely in the hands of the "kangchus" (*jiangzhu*), "river chieftains" who managed the gambier and pepper estates for Chaozhouese like the Seahs and Chens.[32] Needless to add, all these families profited from their participation in syndicates that controlled the opium farms of the colony, especially in Singapore.

Thus we again encounter a process in which capital generated in opium was channeled into the banking industry catering to Chaozhouese. Unlike the Chaoyang syndicate in Shanghai, however, many of these overseas Chinese were not exclusively dependent on their opium businesses to raise banking capital. The Lius owed most of their wealth to their fortuitous command of the nineteenth-century gutta-percha trade, and Seah Peck Seah himself invested in the oil industry.[33] The gambier business in the nineteenth century nonetheless had been intimately connected to the political economy of opium at the level of both the plantation settlement and the colonial monopoly, and the heirs to many of those fortunes were now branching into banking.

The bank was run by and for Chaozhouese, and this elicited derision from other Chinese, mostly Fujianese, who equated Chaozhou culture in Singapore with "clannishness" and "traditional Chinese ways."[34] The bank indeed was oriented toward the overseas Chaozhouese community from its founding in 1906 until 1998, when it was absorbed by the larger (Fujianese-founded) Oversea Chinese Banking Corp. The institution advanced the interests of Chaozhouese rice networks across Southeast Asia as well as smaller businesses and depositors who, as newcomers to colonial worlds, were probably more comfortable banking in their own dialect. Aside from the elite, most Chinese did not use European banks, which did not normally accept small deposits and tended to have an "air" about them that some Chinese found to be off-putting. Native place–oriented banks like Sze Hai Tong also mediated between Chinese firms and European banks when those firms needed to access larger capital resources or to trade when foreign exchange was involved. The bank profitably evolved with the expansion of Chaozhou trade networks, financing the commerce in rice, forest and marine products, seafood, and other commodities.[35] It was an institution vital to the modern development of the translocal economy.

Bingyan was celebrated for his fidelity to Sze Hai Tong during a period of instability when World War I broke out in 1914. There had been alarming bank runs as panicky depositors withdrew their money. Unlike other banks its size, the bank weathered the storm, for it had always maintained large reserves. More important, Bingyan loaned the bank $500,000 at the height of the crisis, an act that guaranteed its solvency.[36] Bank collapses deleteriously affect depositors and small businesses alike, so he not only buttressed the bank's reserves but also protected its clients.

Low Ah Jit and Sons survived into the post–World War II era, but in February 1920 the partnership between Liu Kunyi and the sons of his late brother Changyi—Liu Bingyan, Liu Bingfeng, and Liu Bingjia—was dissolved.[37] The reasons for the dissolution were not publicly declared, but one suspects the younger Lius preferred to strike out on their own. Changyi's sons continued to invest in gutta but moved forcefully into their other businesses, especially banking, real estate, and rice. Kunyi's sons, especially Liu Bingsi (Low Peng Cer) and Liu Bingxian (Low Peng Soy), continued to run Low Ah Jit after their father's death in 1926, and they too branched into other businesses, founding the firms Liu Runfeng, which specialized in the import-export business in Siam, and Rongzhang, which engaged in gum production in Siam. The third generation pursued their own agendas after their respective fathers passed from the scene, and they expanded more energetically into the Siamese economy.[38]

Rice Kings: Territorialism without Colonialism

It is not surprising that rubber magnates would keep their oar in the rice trade. Rice had always been a staple of commerce, and this trend accelerated in the 1890s. Rice production in Chaozhou decreased further as local farmers shifted from the cultivation of that grain and sugar to the production of opium, which now offered better returns. The heavy taxation of imported Indian opium and simultaneous improvement of the domestic product inclined Chinese consumers to purchase home-grown varieties. Local farmers also increased production of fruits and ground-nuts (which are used in cooking oil). Rice imports consequently almost tripled in the final decades of the nineteenth century, increasing from 6,631,998 piculs in the decade 1882–1891 to 17,605,517 piculs from 1892 to 1901.[39]

Sugar remained an important export item, but locals faced competition from cheaper Southeast Asian varieties. According to customs officials, sugar was produced in Chaozhou through "small-holding" agriculture, and farmers relied on cash advances by merchants engaged in the export business. They were unwilling to switch to the Southeast Asian mode of production on "large farms worked on an organized system and on modern economic principles."[40] In other words, they did not proletarianize themselves by working on plantation-style estates like those in Siam or the Dutch East Indies. Instead, they suffered the competition while turning to the production of other crops. Fang Yao's district of Puning reflected this transformation. In the 1860s Puning had been a major site of sugar cultivation, but by the 1930s travelers to the region observed with disdain the widespread cultivation of opium poppy.[41] During these years, sugar was the only major Chaozhou export that experienced a notable decline: from 14,941,075 piculs in the decade 1882–1891 to 13,158,944 piculs from 1892 to 1901.[42]

By this time Chaozhouese had incorporated parts of the previously under-populated, resource-rich territories of Southeast Asia into their translocal economy. Overseas entrepreneurs continued their long tradition of producing sugar in Siam on vast estates. They also offshored a good deal of industrial sugar refining to that kingdom, and it was not uncommon to find that all the laborers in Siamese sugar refineries were Chaozhouese.[43] Moreover, in spite of the fact that Chaozhou sugar producers competed with plantations on Java, the majority of sugar-refining labor on that island were also natives of Chaozhou.[44] In fact, Chinese producers in China were largely competing with Chinese magnates in Siam and the Dutch East Indies. Across maritime

Chaozhou, families at home retained access to small plots of farmland while adapting to industrial-scale agriculture overseas either as proletarianized farm or mill labor or as estate and mill owners. Modern class formation was, in part, translocal.

These changes coincided with the increased specialization of Chaozhouese merchants in the rice trade of the South China Sea. Indeed, the history of the modern Southeast Asian rice trade is the story of the rise of maritime Chaozhou. By the late nineteenth century Chaozhou mercantile networks had emerged as dominant players in the business, occupying nodes of longstanding commercial power in Bangkok, Saigon, Hong Kong, and Swatow. Rice constituted more than half the total exports of Siam and French Indochina. In Indochina, that export trade was principally in the hands of such Chaozhouese as Guo Yan (Qúach Đàm, 1863–1927) and his nephew Guo Sigao, whose Tonghe (Thong Hiep) firm was a major processer and exporter out of Saigon.[45] By 1909 Chaozhouese operated 108 firms in Saigon's rice-trading center of Cholon. Laborers from Chaozhou constituted the majority of river boatmen in southern Vietnam as well as the majority of longshoremen who loaded and unloaded cargo in Saigon. More significant, Chaozhouese constituted the majority of farmers who cultivated rice in the regions of Cantho, Soctrang, Travinh, Rachgia, and Baclieu, which were located in the Mekong delta region south of Saigon. The French colony was providing Chaozhou sojourners with investment opportunities, employment for urban and rural laborers, and access to farmland. French colonial officials were not worried about this development. As Jean-André LaFargue noted in his discussion of these farmers, he hoped that the Chinese would "multiply the population of the deserted territories of our Colony" and contribute to its success.[46]

Meanwhile, in Siam, rice milling constituted another example of Chaozhou merchants successfully marginalizing their British competitors. British investors had sought to gain a foothold in the kingdom's rice economy but were thwarted by the sheer domination of Chaozhouese rice networks operating out of Bangkok and Singapore.[47]

In Singapore, the Fujianese traditionally prevailed in the industrial processing of and commerce in rice.[48] This also began to change in the 1890s. Chaozhouese rice networks in the port began to compete more effectively, as investors like Lan Jinsheng, She Yingzhong, Li Weinan, Guo Yan, Chen Cihong, and the Lius began to focus more energetically on Singapore's transnational rice business. They naturally relied on their connections with Chaozhou-dialect speakers in Siam and elsewhere, but one institutional vehicle driving the group's ascendance after 1906 was the Sze Hai Tong Bank.[49] The rice trade required large outlays of capital and posed special challenges with regard to storage and shipping. The bank, with its headquarters in Singapore and branches in Bangkok and Hong Kong, provided financing for the intensified participation of Chaozhouese in the expanding rice trade of the South China Sea. Sze Hai Tong enabled Chaozhouese in Singapore to participate more energetically in the milling and marketing of rice just as the gambier, gutta-percha, and opium-farming businesses were declining and the British were moving more decisively into plantation agricultural production (especially of para rubber). The bank facilitated Chaozhouese commercial interests at a critical moment of transition, serving a translocal clientele in Singapore, Bangkok, and Hong Kong. It facilitated the export of rice from Siam and Saigon to both Singapore—a center of the grain's distribution to the rest of Southeast Asia—and Hong Kong—the center of distribution in the colony as well as southern China.[50] The branch in Hong Kong served as a bank depository as well as a Singaporean and Siamese currency exchange and soon emerged as the bank's East Asian "vital point" for Chaozhouese commerce with Southeast Asia.[51] When Liu Bingyan saved the bank in 1914, he bolstered the ongoing success of the Chaozhou rice network.

His family's involvement in the rice trade is difficult to trace in detail. They had always engaged in the import-export trade in rice and textiles between China and Southeast Asia. Their associate company, Rongli, had been one of seventy enterprises affiliated with Hong Kong's "North-South firms" (*Nanbei hang*), the most important Chaozhouese businesses involved in the trade between China and Southeast Asia.[52] When his father, Liu Changyi, and uncle, Liu Mingyi, registered as British subjects in Swatow in 1879, they identified themselves as merchants engaged in the rice business. They listed the family firm as Rongfeng, which was the principal organization through which their father had pioneered the gutta-percha business in the Straits. That firm, however, simultaneously traded in other commodities, most notably rice. Mingyi also reported that the firm did business with a Swatow rice concern called Chenyuansheng (Tan Gwan Seng), which happened to be owned by his wife's father. That business was an influential member of the Wannianfeng Guild of the port. His father-in-law, Chen Yuting, was also an early investor in the Shanghai Cotton Cloth Mill, one of Li Hongzhang's major Self-Strengthening projects in the 1880s.[53]

This once again reflects the ways the Lius' translocal marital strategies served their far-flung financial interests. The marriage of Liu Bingyan to Fang Yao's daughter cemented their connection to the local strongman, who also hailed from a landowning and commercial lineage. The marriage of Bingyan's uncle to the daughter of the proprietor of Chenyuansheng reinforced their ties to the network of rice-selling wholesalers in the Haiyang district of Chaozhou. Those in-laws also enjoyed links to the Shanghai industrial world. The Lius were building their gutta-percha business back in Singapore, but, significantly, they represented themselves as rice merchants at the Swatow consulate, for their commerce in rice was probably more relevant to the local economy of Chaozhou than were their rubber enterprises. The Lius were middling participants in the rice trade of the South China Sea, but that commerce reinforced their connection to networks of translocal Chaozhou business families in Bangkok, Singapore, Hong Kong, Saigon, Canton, Shanghai, and Chaozhou itself.

Hong Kong and Singapore—rather than Swatow, Canton, or Amoy—emerged as the nexus of the Southeast Asian rice trade with China. Both were "free ports"—they did not tax trade—and they evolved into preeminent Asian entrepots. Moreover, because of its proximity to south China, Hong Kong emerged as the headquarters of the predominantly Chaozhou-dialect-speaking North-South firms. This commercial association of commodity-traders began to coalesce around 1850 (initially "north" and "south" referred to the Chinese ports north and south of the Yangzi River; eventually the meaning of "south" was broadened to incorporate Southeast Asia).[54] The association was led by two leading Chaozhouese firms in Hong Kong, Yuanfa (Yuen Fat Hong), which was founded by Gao Manhua, and Qiantailong (Kin Tye Lung), founded by Chen Huanrong. As Choi Chi-cheung has shown, the similarities between these two commercial standouts were notable. And yet Yuanfa collapsed in 1934 while Qiantailong has endured to the present day as the oldest Chinese import-export firm in Hong Kong. Qiantailong was sustained by an unusually strong network of associated family firms: Wanglee in Bangkok, Tan Guan Lee in Singapore, Tan Wan Lee in Swatow, and Kien Guan Lee in Saigon. In fact, the parent firm was eventually superseded as a global powerhouse by one of its subordinate "associated" firms, the Bangkok-based Wanglee (Hongli) company, which has buttressed the family's network of enterprises since 1871. It was founded by Chen Huanrong's son, Chen Cihong (1841–1920), who along with his own sons and grandsons built Wanglee into one of the largest rice importers and millers in Bangkok and later expanded into shipping, insurance, and banking. Even today the family network is counted among the "Big Five" capitalist groups in Thailand. Choi ascribes the enduring success of the Chens to their family business dynamic. Company control passed to brothers and cousins first before proceeding to the next generation. This kept multiple branches of the Chen lineage financially involved in the firm. In contrast, the Gaos operated "unigeneratively": control was always passed directly from father to son. As a consequence, branches of Gaos believed the company had been "taken over" by Gao Manhua's direct line and were rarely inclined to help inject more cash into it. Gao family networking was inadequate to the task of maintaining far-flung business operations, and the company and its eighteen associated firms collapsed during the Depression.[55] "Kinship" alone did not enable a network of businesses to succeed wondrously over the generations. Multiple branches needed to have a sense of control to ensure that these complicated enterprises endured over the long term.

Although Low Ah Jit and its associated firms survived the Depression and World War II, they were weakened by these events and for reasons similar to the challenges the Gaos faced. Liu Xiri passed his firms down "unigeneratively"; his sons alone inherited his interests, and nephews and cousins did not run them in any significant way after the 1860s. After Xiri's sons died, their own sons—cousins—broke up and redistributed the family firms among themselves. They clearly were committed to "unigenerative" management practices. Brothers ran family businesses together long-term; cousins did not.

The "unigenerative" approach to translocal business worked well in boom times, but it debilitated firms struggling to survive the Depression. As we saw in the previous chapter, Kunyi's sons sold off a large amount of prime Singaporean real estate in 1931, probably because of cash needs. Changyi's son Liu Bingyan experienced worse difficulties. In October 1931 he was sued in the Supreme Court of the Straits Settlements for failure to repay two mortgages totaling $6,000 contracted in 1928 and 1929. He neglected to appear in court and as of 1932 was deemed "no longer residing within the jurisdiction of the courts here." The case remained unresolved through 1934, when he disappeared from the historical record.[56] This was quite a fall for a man who single-handedly salvaged the leading Chaozhouese bank in Southeast Asia with a half-million-dollar loan in 1914. The unigenerative approach to family business did not offer refuge from a truly cataclysmic contraction in global trade.

Waves of Benevolence

The third generation nonetheless continued the family's tradition of translocal philanthropy. Straits-born Liu Bingyan contributed to several British charities during World War I, including the "Our Day Fund"—which remitted money to the British Red Cross to help the war wounded—and the "Malaya Aircraft

Squadron"—which paid for the development of a colonial air force.[57] Significantly, funding for the Our Day Fund, which supported the British back in Europe, was forthcoming only after the colonial secretary requested leading Chinese to make a donation and thus "set an example" for others. In contrast, the subscription campaigns for the Malayan air squadron were spearheaded by Chinese themselves, indicating that these Sino-British subjects were less interested in the British homeland than they were in the colony that had nurtured their success.

Like most sojourning Chinese, they also directed their philanthropy toward their native place, as we see in the wake of the devastating "Swatow Typhoon" of 1922, a catastrophe that compelled the entire translocal world of Chaozhou to focus on their homeland. This tropical cyclone was the worst natural calamity in Chaozhou's modern history. The storm itself was unfathomably violent, accompanied by blinding rain and hurricane force gales that pummeled homes and shops. But the tempest also generated an enormous tidal wave that churned unimpeded across the coastal plain at 11:30 p.m. on August 2, when few could see, much less prepare for the monster wall of inundation. The death toll was incalculable because so many bodies were washed to sea, but at least 34,500 people perished, and some local elites claimed that a total of 70,000 souls may have been lost. Almost 27,000 victims died in Chenghai district alone. Waisha village, once the proud home of opium-smuggling corsairs and defiers of the Chinese state, was totally washed away by the tsunami. Out of approximately 10,000 farmers and fisher folk living there, over 7,000 either drowned instantly or were bludgeoned to death by the heavy debris that the wave propelled along its destructive path. A sixteen-mile swath of agricultural land around Swatow port remained flooded for weeks thereafter, and over 60 percent of the crops were destroyed. The harvests of 1923 were also deleteriously affected by the salt-saturated soil. The Paotai area of Jieyang district experienced less damage from the storm but, in an eerie reenactment of the turmoil of the coastal evacuation of the 1660s, once again became the site of widespread looting as mobs of starving refugees stormed the police, salt, and lijin offices and robbed the premises of anything of value. Compounding the devastation was the near total cessation of fishing, shipping, and commerce in a region heavily dependent on those industries. Customs bureaus and warehouses were washed away, while harbors remained clogged with damaged ships and buildings and the mangled corpses of humans and domestic animals. Witnesses marveled at the sight of an enormous sugar junk stranded on dry land over a mile from any waterway.[58]

Officialdom was unable to provide emergency relief, much less long-term reconstruction assistance. Like many places in China after 1915, the province suffered the throes of warlord conflict. In a hollow gesture of sympathy, the regional strongman, Chen Jiongming, permitted locals to "deduct" 60,000 yuan in disaster relief from a 300,000-yuan "loan" he recently had demanded.[59] Civil officials were no more effective. After the Revolution of 1911 there was little governmental presence beyond Swatow. In the devastated port of Zhanglin, the closest thing to a government office was the police station, which was staffed by people who were overwhelmed by the disaster (the police chief was the only member of his extended family to survive). The old subdistrict magistrate's office had been replaced by the Security Militia (Baowei tuan), an officially sanctioned elite project organized along the lines of a local self-government club. When understaffed officials in Swatow called for the creation of Disaster Relief Bureaus (Qiuzai fensuo), the militias simply reconstituted themselves under the new name.[60] Without effective political institutions, local notables were forced to assume the burden of disaster relief.

Elites did what they could to alleviate the suffering. The Disaster Relief Bureau in Zhanglin raised 9,000 yuan to meet immediate emergency needs and begin rebuilding dikes. Local efforts were supplemented by remittances sent from overseas sojourners in Siam and Singapore to their own kinfolk there.[61] The Southern Merchants Association and the Bangkok Traders' Guild, two influential mercantile organizations in Swatow, successfully petitioned the Native Customs for a temporary cessation of duties and tariffs and for other concessions relating to lost or damaged cargo. Contemporary observers were struck by the alacrity with which local charities buried thousands of unidentified corpses scattered along the coast, for the threat of epidemics loomed.[62]

The devastation was too overwhelming for locals to face alone, however, and networks of overseas Chaozhou natives sprang into action. The Lius joined other merchants in Singapore in responding to requests for assistance. Liu Bingsi was the most prominent son of Liu Kunyi. Like his father and grandfather, he was born and educated in Chaozhou and strongly identified with his native place. Perhaps for this reason he was the most active among his family in raising funds for disaster relief, organizing meetings and opera performances at his club, and personally remitting over $10,000 (Straits) to Swatow.[63]

He was one among a multitude of merchants who wired assistance. Responding to urgent requests from the Swatow Chamber of Commerce, the Hong Kong Chaozhou Native Place Association of the Eight Districts, the Hong Kong Chaozhou Chamber of Commerce of the Eight Districts, the Chaozhou Chamber of Commerce of Saigon, and the Chaozhou Native Place Association of Saigon organized a disaster relief bureau in Hong Kong that collected 600,000 yuan in financial support as well as rice, clothing, and medicine dispatched to their sister organizations in Swatow.[64]

The Chaozhou Native Place Association of Shanghai remitted money on an evolving basis to finance the hospitalization of the wounded, support children left orphaned by the crisis, and fund local charities. At one point they raised fifty-one thousand yuan to rebuild fifteen embankments in Chao'an, Chenghai, Raoping, and Jieyang. The association was dominated by natives of Chaoyang; indeed, many of the meetings concerning disaster relief were personally chaired by Guo Zibin, the former opium tycoon who had branched into manufacturing and banking. He rarely bothered to attend routine meetings, so the presence of this captain of industry attests to the seriousness with which these merchants addressed the crisis (as well as the large sums they were remitting).[65] Like the Lius of Singapore, they sent money where it was needed and not merely to their own villages. Clearly their distant travels had inculcated in them a sense of being "Chaozhouese" and not simply people from a lineage or village. They also responded in the manner of a translocal gentry, pooling their funds, building embankments, and providing charity.

Shantang or "benevolent halls" were charitable organizations located throughout maritime Chaozhou and played a vital role in alleviating catastrophes like the 1922 typhoon. A modern version of the age-old Chinese voluntary or benevolent association, these redemptive societies evolved during the nineteenth and early twentieth centuries to perform altruistic deeds and thereby entitle their practitioners to religious salvation. They provided welfare to the poor and, in particular, dedicated themselves to the performance of funeral rituals, including the recovery and interment of unclaimed corpses.[66] The Cunxin Shantang, founded in 1899 in Swatow, emerged as the most prominent hall in the port by the 1920s. Founded as the city rapidly expanded, it engaged in charitable outreach ranging from the care of indigents to the founding of a hospital and the burial of the victims of epidemics and feuds. The hall evolved into a major institution in the public sphere of Swatow and even established the region's first fire brigade.[67] Given its proximity to the port and its renown among Chaozhouese sojourners, the Cunxin benevolent hall was a major beneficiary of translocal philanthropy in the wake of the typhoon of 1922. When the Chaozhou Native Place Association of Shanghai wired sixty thousand yuan in early September of that year, they earmarked thirty thousand for the devastated district of Chenghai, ten thousand each to the districts of Chaoyang and Raoping, and ten thousand to the Cunxin hall, which is to say they entrusted the organization with as much funding as they sent to entire districts, including their own homeland of Chaoyang. The Chaozhou Chamber of Commerce in Hong Kong also worked in cooperation with the hall.[68] The devoted work of the Cunxin volunteers explains how thousands of corpses were so expeditiously interred as the tsunami waters receded.

The shantang as an institution was transmitted across Southeast Asia by Chaozhouese sojourners and constituted an important vehicle for the dissemination of a religious and philanthropic practice. As Li Zhixian has shown, benevolent halls in Singapore had strong associations with particular Chaozhou lineages and villages.[69] Indeed, shantang and gongsi were the earliest form of village native place associations in the settlement. Sojourners turned to these organizations for assistance, especially in old age. Charitable halls usually retained the name of the hall in their home village, a phenomenon we see among those who sojourned to the Straits from the Liu family village of Liulong. Their village shantang was known as the Hall of Generational Respect (Shiqin tang), and migrants relied on it for charitable assistance until 1960, when a more secular association (the Liulong tongxianghui) was established. Significantly, founders of the tongxianghui explained at the time that the change was occasioned by the emergence of Singapore as "an autonomous and self-governing entity. Our people thus became citizens of Singapore and no longer Overseas Chinese sojourners."[70] This reflected an institutional recognition that new political realities in both China and Singapore ruptured the organic, translocal unity of village and multiethnic colony; Singapore was now its own nation-state.

During the colonial era, however, the shantang was part of the translocal life of the sojourner. Li Zhixian emphasizes the role of shantang in "maintaining the order of the family and the clan." He observes that "a natural feeling of kinship" was reinforced through the charitable and religious programs of the halls. Funeral rites in particular reminded sojourners that they were members of a group, had obligations to it, and could expect benefaction in return. This contributed to their moral edification by reinforcing the bond of kinship while simultaneously encouraging them to act in the public interest. The shantang also encouraged a sense of "ethnic fellowship" among sojourners, interconnecting rites, charity, and group identification at the familial and native place level.[71] The fact that the Lius reestablished their hall in Singapore attests to a desire to foster these virtues overseas.

Among the third generation of Lius in Singapore, Liu Bingsi manifested the strongest commitment to philanthropy, especially philanthropy that strengthened native place ties to Chaozhou. Like his father, Kunyi, he was born in Chaozhou and served in the sinophilic Chinese Chamber of Commerce in Singapore. Educated at modern schools in his village and in Swatow, he did not leave China until age fourteen, when his father summoned him to the colony to learn English and join the family business in 1911.[72] He was bilingual, cosmopolitan, and culturally oriented toward Chaozhou.

He played a role in the establishment of the Native Place Association of the Eight Districts of Chaozhou in Singapore (Singapore Chaozhou bayi huiguan) in 1929. There already existed an organization catering to the Chaozhou population in Singapore, the Ngee Ann Kongsi (Yian Gongsi), which had been founded by Seah Eu Chin in 1845 in coordination with twelve other mercantile families. The gongsi offered assistance to migrants and facilitated the dissemination of Chaozhou religious beliefs and ritual practices relating to the worship of Mazu (the goddess of seafarers) and the popular deity Xian Tian Huangdi. Every Chaozhouese of means was expected to contribute silver, and over the years it acquired an impressive amount of collectively owned, income-generating property. The Seahs and their allies from the Chenghai district of Chaozhou completely controlled the gongsi, which, however, had never issued the usual regulations governing such associations. Merchants from other districts, including the Lius of Haiyang (Chao'an), resented the indomitable hold of the Seahs on all levers of decision-making authority. These tensions came to a boil in 1929, when the anti-Seah faction founded the native place association as an institutional challenge to the gongsi. They also sued Seah's grandson, Seah Eng Tong, in a legal rumble over control of the gongsi's real estate and other assets. In the end, the gongsi was reorganized according to a formal set of regulations. Control of its properties was transferred to a new oversight committee, and management of the collective assets of the Chaozhou community was exercised by a more diverse group of individuals, who now administered both organizations. Bingsi, inaugural treasurer of the native place association, helped make this institutional regularization possible.[73]

The anti-Seah faction strongly identified with the Chinese homeland, a sentiment that informed Liu Bingsi's philanthropic life. He energetically devoted himself to the improvement of the Tuan Mong (Duanmeng) School, largely understood to have been the first institutional challenge to the Seah faction by its detractors among the Chaozhou business community. Founded in 1906 as the pioneering school in Singapore devoted to public education in the Chaozhouese dialect, the school did not list a single Seah among its original twenty-eight founders, which was unusual, for the Seahs never before had been excluded from any significant Chaozhou-related charity. Most of the founders of the school also founded of the Sze Hai Tong Bank, including Liao Zhengxing and Lan Jinsheng. The school formed the original "power base" of the anti-Seah faction and served as an instrument through which the group began to wrest control over philanthropy from the Ngee Ann Gongsi in the years before 1929. Bingsi was too young to have been involved in the school's founding, but his father, Kunyi, had been a major contributor to the endowment, and Bingsi eventually emerged as its patron, serving for many years on its board of trustees.[74]

The school had a "modern" curriculum but, significantly, was dedicated to educating youth in the Chaozhou dialect. This represented a shift, not only from the Anglophone thrust of elite Singaporean education prior to the twentieth century but also from the more "nationalistic" approach in China in which Mandarin became the "standard" dialect of instruction to unify the Chinese people linguistically. Bingsi's devotion to a specifically Chaozhouese culture was reflected in his lifelong sponsorship of the school as well as in the performing arts; he was a major patron of (and occasional performer in) Chaozhouese vernacular plays.[75] He exemplified the Chinese orientation of those who challenged the Seah faction, but in his case these challenges were made in a framework of native place affiliation.

Liu Bingsi maintained the family tradition of friendly relations with the British. When World War II broke out in Europe in 1939, he supported the Malaya Patriotic Fund, serving on the Teochew [Chaozhou] Committee of that organization. This was part of a larger effort across the British Empire to raise funds from the colonies to support the war effort back home. He also raised an enormous amount of money to support the war effort in China itself, chairing the Chaozhou group in the Singapore Chinese Relief Committee and contributing a large, unspecified sum from his personal fortune.[76] In spite of his binational philanthropy, he never bothered to naturalize as a British subject until 1951, after the communists seized power in China and his homeland became less welcoming to capitalist success stories.[77] His connection to Chaozhou remained strong, until it became untenable.

Remittances

Remittances were crucial to the twentieth-century Chaozhou economy. As Chun-hsi Wu defined them, "Remittance is a phrase used to describe [financial] remittance from overseas Chinese to support their families and dependents, to purchase land or houses for the remitter or his family, or to invest in industrial or commercial enterprises."[78] Officials reporting on the "wealthy and populous" regions of Chaozhou usually attributed their bounty to the flow of money from Siam, Singapore, and Indochina in particular.[79] It is impossible to ascertain the exact amount remitted over the years—there were too many ways to send money and too few systematic studies in the pre-1949 period. The amount in the aggregate was enormous, however. Estimates for 1912 and 1913 amounted to approximately twenty-five million Chinese yuan each year, whereas the annual amounts remitted in the 1920s ranged from twenty-seven to thirty million.[80] Locally tabulated estimates from 1926 to 1932 (table 9.1) convey the largesse pouring in from Southeast Asia. The figures are probably too low but reflect relative amounts sent from various lands and change over time.

Not surprisingly, the largest sums were sent from Siam, where 1.5 million Chaozhouese constituted 60 percent of the Chinese population. The estimates for Singapore nonetheless are significant, for the Chaozhouese population in that settlement was 20 percent of the size of that in Siam, and yet they remitted 70 to 79 percent of the amount sent by the Siamese-based group during the pre-Depression years. In one year, 1926, Singaporean remittances to Swatow actually exceeded those from Siam. Even as the Chaozhouese-Singaporean community began to shrink, residents of that thriving colony continued to send large sums home. The Singaporean figures also reflect the fact that Singapore was a center of banking and financial exchange, and Chinese residing in other colonies tended to remit funds via that settlement.[81]

Remittances were a boon because they offset the trade deficits that plagued the region (indeed most of China) in the first half of the twentieth century. Scholars have estimated that remittances during the 1910s ranged from twenty to thirty million yuan annually, and these sums came close to matching the imbalance between imports and exports. Statistics from 1912 (table 9.2) illustrate this phenomenon.

These remittances were derived from overseas commercial and industrial investments as well as wage labor abroad that originally had required little capital out-payment from Chaozhou itself. The return on these activities redounded to the benefit of the home region, constituting a phenomenal repatriation of wealth. Contemporary analysts demonstrated that the funds sustained families and offset deficits.[82]

Japanese wartime authorities in 1943 assessed the reasons for the trade imbalances, noting that Chaozhou had not experienced significant industrial

TABLE 9.1. Remittances to Swatow (selected), 1926–1932 (Chinese yuan)

Origin	1926	1927	1928	1929	1930	1931	1932
Singapore	9,156,000	7,298,000	7,408,000	7,250,000	3,577,000	7,120,000	4,654,000
Siam	9,011,000	9,200,000	9,330,000	12,930,000	13,820,000	8,234,000	6,120,000
Indochina	2,120,000	2,503,000	2,311,000	2,507,000	2,310,000	2,005,000	1,510,000
Sumatra	229,000	192,000	231,000	205,000	262,000	153,000	102,000
Hong Kong	1,210,000	250,000	1,280,000	1,150,000	1,233,000	828,000	750,000
Penang	510,000	455,000	516,000	494,000	638,000	420,000	348,000
Total	**22,236,000**	**19,898,000**	**21,076,000**	**24,536,000**	**21,840,000**	**18,760,000**	**13,484,000**

Source: Shantou zhinan 1933: 134.

Note: It is unclear how the data were compiled. The editors of CSDQ claim that they reflect the personal investigations of Xie Xueying, the editor. The figures roughly accord with the gross estimates of economic historians and appear to have been derived from local knowledge. Some totals were added incorrectly in the original; corrected figures are entered here.

TABLE 9.2. Trade at Swatow, 1912 (yuan)

	Imports	Exports	Deficit
Foreign trade	24,096,300	9,284,958	−14,811,342
Domestic trade	29,682,440	12,290,768	−17,391,672
Total	**53,778,740**	**21,575,726**	**−32,203,014**

Source: Hicks 1993, book 1, 100. For deficits in general, Cheong, Lee, and Lee 2013: 75.

development during the preceding decades and continued to export the man-ufactures they always had sent overseas: porcelain, embroidered goods, fruit and processed foods, and other, primarily nonindustrial products. Many items of daily necessity, including rice but also medicine and manufactured goods, were imported, and the region consumed more than it produced for export.[83] Remittances rendered such consumption possible.

Once again we see that the Chaozhou economy cannot be understood out-side of its translocal dimension.[84] Overseas Chinese industrial and other in-vestments (in mining, plantation agriculture, factory production, real estate, banking, etc.) were integral to the local economy of the native place, reflecting a dynamic in which distant colonial and monarchical bureaucracies protected expensive investments in modern businesses while investments back home sustained traditional enterprises like landowning and commerce. Officials in the region believed that, unlike Cantonese who had emigrated to the United States, Chaozhouese emigrants were not inclined to invest heavily in modern enterprise in their native place after 1911. The reason was the greater insecurity of eastern Guangdong. "Why should [Chaozhou emigrants] send home large amounts to invest? Why should they build more roads [or] set up factories . . . ? Their homes, for the most part, are in one of the 'areas of [anti-communist] pacification' where large numbers of soldiers are stationed to ward off bandits and communists. . . . On a visit home . . . they dare not show their wealth."[85] Village Chaozhou was emerging as a highly insecure "suburb" to the industrial metropole of colonial Southeast Asia, a homestead in which mothers and children dwelled while fathers sailed off to work building the modern global economy. Most industrial investments were made outside of the political bor-ders of Chaozhou, as sectors of Siam, Malaya, Indochina, and Shanghai were incorporated into the Chaozhou translocal economy.[86]

The pathways for sending funds were diffuse, but the most common route in the twentieth century was the *piguan* or private remittance agency. These were cooperatives in both China and Southeast Asia that primarily facilitated remittance orders and money exchanges but also, in China at least, conducted other business like purchasing and selling agricultural produce and foreign goods. The money was remitted from Southeast Asia via telegram order to agencies in Chaozhou that worked on commission. Of the approximately sixty agencies in the area during the 1910s, thirty had working relationships with exchanges in Siam, twenty with those in Singapore, and ten with groups in French Indochina and Penang. Their offices were located in Swatow, while a few of the larger agencies established branches in cities in the interior. Agency staff delivered remittances in Chinese currency as well as any accompanying letters to recipients in town; couriers were hired to make deliveries to remote areas.[87]

Foreign banks located in Hong Kong and Southeast Asia constituted another formal institution for remitting funds, though they tended to transfer larger amounts and were used by wealthier families. Some agencies in Swatow did not have the funds to remit all the orders they received, so they purchased remittance notes from foreign banks. These banks thus played an important, though indirect, role in transmitting remittances.[88] The banks involved in this service included the familiar firms of the colonial era: the Hong Kong and Shanghai Bank (British); Banque de l'Indochine (French); Bank of Taiwan (Japanese); and so on. Sze Hai Tong—the bank that served overseas Chaozhouese interests and on whose board the Lius served—was the Chinese-operated financial institution most identified with the remittance trade during the first two decades of the twentieth century. Significantly, however, it did not have a branch in Chaozhou itself. It operated through an agent, the Guangyiyu firm. This was a traditional Chinese bank that specialized in distributing funds sent from Singapore and Indochina. Guangyiyu had branches in Chenghai, Chaoyang, and Jieyang districts and held a middling amount of assets of roughly 100,000 Chinese dollars circa 1913.[89] Judging from statistics available for the Depression year 1934, Guangyiyu was the most active remitter of overseas funds in Swatow, transmitting 358,725 yuan that had been sent in 23,915 letters and telegrams. No other agency or bank came close to matching this amount.[90] The 1934 figures nonetheless represent a diminution of the sums distributed in the boom years of the late 1910s, as can be seen in table 9.3.

Guangyiyu was the largest remitter of funds from Singapore and Indochina, for no other firm came close to remitting millions of yuan from those two places during the years 1917 to 1919. The 1934 figure, in contrast, reflected the catastrophic affect the global Depression had on colonial economies.

TABLE 9.3. Remittances Distributed by Guangyiyu Agency, Swatow, 1917–1919 (yuan)

Location	1917	1918	1919
Singapore	1,850,000	1,790,000	1,860,000
Indochina	1,560,000	1,680,000	1,740,000

Source: Ma Yuhang 1921: 18–19.

Sze Hai Tong Bank served Chaozhouese sojourners, so why did it not open a branch in their native place? In fact, the Japanese-owned Bank of Taiwan was the only modern, foreign bank to operate a branch in Swatow during the pre–World War II era.[91] After the chaos of the Revolution of 1911, directors of the Chaozhouese bank must have been reluctant to risk significant amounts of capital beyond what was needed to facilitate remittances and the import-export trade. The early months of that struggle witnessed serious factional fighting among military bands purporting to represent the new Republic. Local militarists and revolutionaries resisted control from Canton and split along ethnic lines between Hakka and Hoklo (Chaozhouese speakers). The Guangyi native bank was forced to close its doors temporarily in April 1912 because the leader of one faction, Lin Jizhen, the regional commander of Huizhou, claimed that the bank's manager had spread malicious rumors against him among the powerful merchants of Singapore, so he tried to extort money from him. Lin's troops also pillaged the premises of the Swatow Chamber of Commerce, and widespread looting revealed the fragile security of the port. The Bank of Taiwan temporarily stepped in to serve the banking needs of the Maritime Customs simply because a contingent of Japanese troops was on hand to guard the facilities.[92]

The threats extended beyond the port. Forces aligned with another Hakka faction attacked a temple dedicated to the August Lord of the Dark Heaven just north of Anbu. Generations of worshippers had applied layers of gold leaf to the Daoist god's image, and these troops proceeded to scrape off every speck. Rumor had it that they amassed one hundred pounds of gold, "much to the rage of the 100 villages in the vicinity."[93] Liulong would have been one of those villages, and the Lius were surely aware of the insecurity of specie in a volatile region. After the revolutionary chaos subsided, new problems arose: warlord campaigns; the typhoon of 1922; the eruptions of the Hai-Lu-feng Soviet in Huizhou in 1927; the ongoing communist insurgencies, and finally the Japanese invasion of 1937. It did not make sense to establish a branch of Sze Hai Tong. Their agents managed local remittances, and the Hong Kong branch, protected by the British, was a short steam ride or telegraph message

TABLE 9.4. Sources of Monthly Income, 100 Emigrant Families,
October 1934–September 1935

Monthly income per family (yuan)	Number and social class of families	Average monthly remittance from Southeast Asia		Average monthly income, local sources		Average total monthly income per family (yuan)
		Yuan	% of income	Yuan	% of income	
Below 20	17 "poor"	11.40	75.5	3.70	24.5	15.10
20–49	49 "lower"	25.70	80.6	6.20	19.4	31.90
50–124	21 "middle"	68.10	78.6	18.50	21.4	86.60
125–250	13 "upper"	192.60	84.1	36.30	15.9	228.90
Average/total	**100 families**	**53.90**	**81.4**	**12.30**	**18.6**	**66.20**

Source: Chen Ta 1940: 82 (class designations, 86). Chen identified class by income.

away if one needed the services of a financial institution with international reach. As one local observer noted, "A Hong Kong bank is often chosen [to park money] instead of a bank near the emigrant's home community for [reasons of] greater security."[94] This underscores how the ongoing political problems of eastern Guangdong were inimical to modern development.

Remittances nevertheless were indispensable to families left behind in Chaozhou. From 1934 to 1935 a Chinese sociologist, Chen Ta, led a team of field researchers in southeast coastal sites that included the rural area of Chenghai from which Seah Eu Chin had emigrated to Singapore in 1823.[95] They found that the sums remitted varied widely among the families surveyed but discovered that the local food supply was sufficient to meet consumption needs for only four months of the year; these families relied entirely on cash remittances for the other eight months. These were Depression years, of course, but remittances obviously were crucial to survival. Figures derived from intensive interviews with one hundred families (table 9.4) in this area reinforce this.

Regardless of class, remittances accounted for 75 to 84 percent of the total monthly income of emigrant families in Chenghai. These families prioritized expenditures on basic necessities like food, clothing, and shelter, and only after those needs were met were funds devoted to other concerns like paying for weddings or building a better house. Remittances blessed emigrant families with the necessities of life while simultaneously enhancing the class status of a lucky few. As one member of the Swatow Chamber of Commerce noted, "If remittances should for any reason decline, the livelihood of a large number of families would be seriously endangered."[96] Left unmentioned was the fate of those families that did not enjoy the lifeline of remittances at all.

Things Fall Apart, Again

Remittances did decline, precipitously. Table 9.1 indicates that the global depression had a significant impact on the flow of financial support to Chaozhou. The figures for 1931 and 1932 were catastrophically lower than those of the preceding decade. The Singaporean figures mark the earliest and most dramatic decline, reflecting the fact that a good deal of that colonial economy was oriented toward supplying the resource needs of the industrial West, whose economies crashed in 1929. The rubber and tin industries were particularly hard hit, and the Straits experienced severe unemployment. The rice markets of Bangkok, Singapore, and Saigon were also adversely affected as prices plummeted amid a global oversupply of all grain products. Across Southeast Asia, the contraction in commodity exports was exacerbated by the closing of the Southeast Asian rural frontier as once-ample land grew scarce.[97]

Remittance figures for Chaozhou from 1929 to 1932 reflected the crisis in global commerce and finance. These declines must be considered in tandem with severe restrictions on Chinese emigration that Southeast Asian authorities began to impose to mitigate unemployment. In the Straits, quotas reduced the number of Chinese immigrants from 242,000 in 1930 to 28,000 in 1933. In French Indochina, 1,400 migrants were sent back to China during the first six months of 1931 alone. The Siamese simply increased the fee for Chinese residency permits—from ten baht in 1928 to thirty baht in 1931 to one hundred baht in 1932. This discouraged immigration.[98] Legions of unemployed men began to arrive on ships from Siam, Indochina, and Singapore, many forced to rely on the charity of the Cunxin benevolent hall upon disembarking.[99] As a result, a rare reversal of the migration trend out of Swatow occurred as more Chinese returned to the port than departed (table 9.5).

The figures reflect a dramatic reduction in emigration, but they also demonstrate that more people returned to the local economy than departed for overseas opportunities. Although the situation was slightly alleviated after 1934, these returnees—primarily working-age men—would be added to the unemployed ranks in Chaozhou. The fact that they were working class is significant, for they would have had little to fall back on during the crisis. Moreover, if they had been sending remittances, this source of sustenance for impecunious families was lost.

TABLE 9.5. Passenger Trade Into and Out of Swatow, 1928–1933

Year	Departures	Arrivals
1928	211,977	141,861
1929	no data	no data
1930	123,724	94,726
1931	80,202	81,962
1932	36,824	70,864
1933	44,858	59,722

Source: CSDQZ, 8.

In spite of these reversals, remittances helped the region withstand the downturn in the global economy. The flow of funds contracted, but it did not disappear prior to the war, and contributions began to increase again by the mid-1930s. Some of the ebb and flow of remittances reflected fluctuations in currency exchange rates, of course. When the Nationalist government abandoned the silver standard in 1935, for example, a dramatic devaluation of the Chinese dollar in relation to foreign currencies ensued. That is to say, it is unclear how much of the "recovery" reflected the fact that one Singapore dollar or Siamese baht was now exchanged for many more Chinese dollars. Most scholars nevertheless believe that remittances helped many in China ride out the Depression prior to 1937.[100]

Remittances did nothing for the farming classes who lacked overseas support. In his field studies of the southeast coast, Chen Ta determined that families with an emigrant tradition tended to have commercial ties. His team intensively interviewed the elders of 100 families comprising 626 individuals in Chenghai. Among those individuals, 150 were living overseas in Southeast Asia. Of those 150 emigrants, 81 were engaged in commercial work of some sort (shopkeepers, peddlers, managers, etc.) and 56 were laborers. Thirteen were "unemployed" upon their departure. As we have seen, the remittances these travelers sent home constituted 75 to 84 percent of the income of the home folk.[101]

Chen's team also studied a region of Chenghai district that did not have an emigrant tradition. They found that farming constituted the primary source of income for all but one of the one hundred families interviewed (the exception was a laborer). It was unusual for these farmers to have only one occupation, but their sideline jobs were also connected to agriculture in some way. The nonemigrant families were significantly poorer compared to the predominantly commercial, emigrant communities (table 9.6).

TABLE 9.6. Average Monthly Incomes, Emigrant and Nonemigrant Families, Chenghai, 1934–1935

Class	Emigrant families (yuan)	Nonemigrant families (yuan)	Discrepancy, actual (yuan)	Nonemigrant income as % of emigrant income
Poor	15.10	10.90	4.20	72.18
Lower	31.90	18.14	13.76	56.86
Middle	86.60	28.06	58.54	32.6
Upper	228.90	54.68	174.22	23.88

Source: Compiled from information in Chen Ta 1940: 83, 87.
Note: Chen identified nonemigrant families by "class" and income, but the income totals did not coincide with those that defined class status among emigrant families. He apparently applied a different income standard to identify class.

Emigrant families whose commercially oriented kin remitted funds enjoyed higher incomes than those of farm families who lacked the overseas tie. The differences ran across class lines but grew more decisive at the middle- and upper-class levels. The poorest of the poor were rural, nonemigrant households. The wealthiest by far were upper-class families with overseas connections. Significantly, a "middle-class" nonemigrant peasant family earned less than even a "lower-class" family with a home-remitter abroad. Chen's findings are reinforced by Daniel Kulp's anthropological field work in a different region of Chaozhou, Chao'an (Haiyang), circa 1923. His investigations determined that "extremes of wealth and poverty exist because of the importation of wealth from the areas of emigration."[102] By the 1920s wealth and diaspora were entirely interconnected in regions with emigrant communities.

The translocal nature of the economy structured class differences in Chaozhou and the remittance system exacerbated social antagonisms. Commercial families had long been subject to attack. In 1867, for example, the village of Xinliao (in Jieyang) had entered into a rural league to extort money from merchants exporting sugar along the Rong River. That same year they kidnapped and held for ransom a businessman who had worked for many years in Singapore and acquired British citizenship but had retired to Jieyang. He had been wise to register with the consulate. The local magistrate was reluctant to confront the well-armed village. The British, obliged to send in a gunboat, succeeded in rescuing him. After four months captivity, he was emaciated and had to be carried aboard the ship. British consuls were convinced that "well-to-do" sojourners were always under threat of attack when they returned home.[103] With the success of his pacification campaign of 1869 to 1873, Fang Yao claimed to make life easier for families with overseas connections.

He died in 1891, however, and, as we saw in chapter 5, Chaozhou once again plunged into feuding and piracy. None of his successors—be they warlords or Nationalists—maintained the sort of militarized order he and his allies had inflicted from 1869 to 1891.

The family experiences of Wang Changrui reflected the tense relations between the commercial and rural classes. Changrui was born in the village of Xianxi in 1920. The village was near Anbu port and about a mile from the Liu family homestead. Four branches of the Wang lineage lived in the area. Changrui's own family, the fifth branch, was heavily engaged in trade and had been sojourning abroad for generations; they were quite affluent in the 1920s and even had relatives serving in the local Swatow government. Some of his family sojourned to Singapore because they had prosperous relatives in nearby Johor, but others sailed to Siam, Shanghai, and Hong Kong. The third branch of the Wangs, on the other hand, were almost all farmers, and few of them had ever gone abroad prior to World War II. Changrui explained the different occupational paths in terms of generational inheritance. Because his ancestor "had gone overseas to engage in business, so too most of his descendants engaged in business. If people till the soil in China, then most of their descendants also till the soil."[104]

The relations between Changrui's commercial branch and the farmers of branch three were hostile, and they had long feuded. Members of the third branch frequently slathered "night soil" onto their doorway or flung rocks in their direction, but he also remembered at least one large, violent conflict and one lawsuit over property in the 1920s. The animosity stemmed from class tensions. Changrui's family had actually moved from nearby Lingzi village to Xianxi before he was born (they already possessed property in Xianxi, however). They proceeded to purchase land and houses there, and the poorer, third branch of peasants deeply resented this. In one dispute, he recalled, "The third branch told us that they were poor and we were rich. . . . They thought we were using our money to inveigle them into surrendering [their house]. If we [conditionally] purchased it from them, then they would never regain their capacity to recover their land and then we would compel them to sell it to us outright."[105] He probably was referring to a "conditional sale." After the fifteenth century, land was rarely alienated absolutely on the southeast coast. Property "sales" were usually for a temporary period of time and occasioned by a need for immediate cash by the seller. Once the period of contract had expired, the conditional seller was permitted to redeem the property. Conditional sellers were perennially unable to redeem, however, and this led to disputes that erupted into lawsuits and feuding. Such discord had been common in Chaozhou for generations, and it is not surprising that Changrui's resentful kin feared that they would lose control of their property. Changrui, recalling the altercations decades later in his adopted home in Singapore, understood its underlying causes: "It had to do with the relations between rich and poor. The third branch had a lot of peasants, and my fifth branch had money."[106]

Class antagonism was expressed in other ways. Anbu formed the commercial heart of overseas Chinese in Chao'an (formerly Haiyang) district. There were many wealthy families living there, but they rarely hired local peasants or poor people to work for them as laborers or servants. Changrui's branch was no different. "When members of our family back in the village wanted to hire people to help us out, we would hire people from other places—perhaps from Puning or the prefectural city. People from those places were fairly poor. A lot of their women would come to Anbu to find work." The problem was not simply a refusal to hire local people for menial jobs; locals were reluctant to work for wealthy people in their midst, especially if they were related to them. The farmers in his family refused to work for them: "They were very particular about the issue of face. They knew they were poor. . . . So even if you wanted to hire them, they wouldn't want to work for you."[107]

The rural class dynamic made quite an impression on him. The financial resources of his family enabled them to live in comfort, but his farming kinfolk had their own power: numbers. When his interviewer asked him, "What were you just saying now about 'strong' and 'weak'? Why are some households strong and others fairly weak?," he replied, "Strong means we have a lot of men, we have strength. And if we have a brawl in the village, we will defeat you. That's strength. Weak means you have no power and you have no money." He understood that his family's wealth constituted a form of power, and he occasionally contradicted himself in discussing the relative power of wealth versus numbers, but in the physical dynamic of feuding, he believed his antagonists held the upper hand. "In every village, whichever family has the most men also has the most power." The power of numbers enabled the third branch of Wangs to hold sway in collective meetings among lineage elders. "In the final decision, because [our] people were relatively few in number, [we] definitely did not have their level of satisfaction."[108] Like many financially secure households, his family moved to Swatow during the "unstable situation" of the Hai-Lu-feng Soviet in 1927, and this terminated their participation in the family feud.

The Lius in nearby Liulong village experienced far worse travails than the Wangs for both similar and slightly different reasons. They too were a

commercially successful emigrant community in a port region filled with peasants who lacked the overseas lifeline. They nonetheless were wealthier and had
more problematic political connections than the Wangs. Liu Changyi, as we
have seen, registered title deeds to 406 *mu* of land he had purchased as rental
property for 1,050 silver taels back in 1879, and this was land at some distance
from their already sizable village. He expected the British Consulate to protect
it. Considering that the average homestead in eastern Guangdong in the early
1930s was 9.43 *mu*, this single acquisition alone catapulted the family into the
landowning stratosphere.[109] Located three miles from Swatow, it was suitable
for fish-farming and likely part of the Ox-Field Sea development promoted by
Fang Yao in Chaoyang. The project reclaimed much-needed land and enhanced the hydraulic infrastructure of the region, but it was built with the
forced labor of local farmers whose descendants fume over it to this day. The
Lius' prosperity overseas was the result of hard work and fortuitous investments, but their property back home seemed to have been safeguarded by the
local strongman and the consulate of British imperialists. They could never
camouflage their translocal and transtemporal entanglement with the notorious Fangs. They had married into the family. Through kinship and common
interests, they were implicated in a campaign that had driven thousands of
others overseas. They were among those families who dwelled in Fang's "undisturbed security" after 1869 while so many others seethed with resentment.

The marital and political strategies they adopted to secure their far-flung
interests over the course of three generations had served them well, but they
were inadequate to withstand the rise of an organized peasant movement that
began to target rural elites in the Anbu area in the 1920s. They suffered assaults
during the brief Hai-Lu-feng Soviet period of 1927 and early 1928. Even more
serious was an onslaught by communists in 1934. Cai Hu, a native of Longtian
village in Chenghai, had been induced by his older brother to join the revolutionary movement in 1932. His guerilla band operated for a time around Anbu.
With twenty small boats at their disposal, they pillaged commercial shipping
along the Han River and raided nearby villages for two years. By January 1934
they had reorganized themselves into the Red Third Regiment (Hong san lian)
and were regularly attacking "rich families" on the riverine stretch between
Chao'an and Chenghai. The Lius were among those families. "On the night of
February 2 [1934], we gathered for an attack on Liulong village in the Anbu
area," Cai later recalled. "This was the largest battle in the lower plains. The
Anbu guerilla squadron along with several hundred irregulars went into action and the fighting went well. We killed the head of the [Liulong] militia

guard and captured two rifles, thirty spears, and a telephone. We also captured six or seven despotic gentry landlords." The regiment then proceeded to other areas.[110]

Considering the prosperity of some of their overseas kinfolk, this was a surprisingly meager haul. The Lius did not appear to have been as well-armed as Fang's descendants in Puning. The true targets of the attack clearly were the six or seven "gentry landlords" who presumably had been seized for ransom, for kidnapping was a routine tactic in the repertoire of revolutionary survival in these years. This insurgent group eventually merged with Red Army regulars who had escaped southward—rather than northward on the Long March— after Chiang Kai-shek's Nationalists routed the Jiangxi Soviet in 1934. They launched what has been called the "Three-Year War" (1934–1937) in South China. To survive the lean years of Nationalist counterinsurgency, these southern revolutionaries kidnaped for ransom. They captured women, children, and gentry leaders; designated them as "local bullies"; imprisoned them in "tuhao huts" in the mountains; and released them upon payment.[111]

These practices were reminiscent of the feuding and piratical tactics of earlier years, only now a revolutionary ideology sanctioned them in the name of "the people." Although the wealthier Lius had secured most of their assets overseas, the communists back home devised a way to capture some of their fortune through ransom demands. The family had contributed large sums to support impoverished locals, especially after the earthquake of 1918 and typhoon of 1922, and one could argue that they had done more for "the people" at home and abroad than a succession of local governments. They could not escape their own history, however. The communists were forging new social realities, and in the records they began to compile, the Lius were cosigned to the revolutionary category of translocal "bullies," entangled in a past that now began to tighten around them.

Conclusion

Every ten years the Maritime Customs issued a "decennial report" on the conditions of trade in each treaty port in China. The Swatow report for the years 1912 to 1921 did not attribute the declining prospects of the region to economic challenges. Indeed, even the "moribund sugar trade" seemed on the rebound by then. Instead, officials asserted, the problem stemmed from political and social disorder, looting by disbanded soldiers, and "forced loans demanded by military authorities." The report for 1922 to 1931 was similarly bullish on the commercial prospects of the region were it not for these ongoing problems, which were exacerbated by the catastrophic typhoon of 1922; the rise of communist insurgencies; and the high tariffs Chiang Kai-shek's government imposed after achieving tariff autonomy, which fostered the age-old problem of smuggling.[112]

Chaozhou nonetheless had overcome these sorts of impediments to commercial vitality for generations. Indeed, the translocal economy was poised once again to transcend its limitations and overcome the challenges of the Great Depression before the war broke out in China in 1937 and across Southeast Asia in 1941. Whatever the region's destiny in the 1930s, the explosion of total war followed by civil war and revolution traumatically terminated the rise of maritime Chaozhou.

War ruptured the historic connection between Chaozhou and the lands of the South China Sea. The number of remittance letters plunged in 1941, and the system never fully recovered after 1945.[113] Trade was disrupted, with dire consequences everywhere. Recalling the wartime deprivations of Singapore, Wang Changrui recalled that the warehouses in a neighborhood filled with Chaozhouese-owned shops were completely empty. Businesses that specialized in imports from China were particularly hard hit.[114] Back in Chaozhou, the collapse of the rice trade led to a disastrous famine. One magazine reported that "coffins were lined up at a certain place by a charitable Buddhist organization, and the people staggered there to lie down in the coffins to await death. In that way, they were sure of some sort of burial."[115]

Our story of maritime Chaozhou thus ends much the way it began, with mass starvation caused by severe rice shortages. Famines like the one so vividly depicted by Lan Dingyuan from 1725 to 1727 alerted provincial authorities to the necessity of reopening local markets to direct trade with Southeast Asia. Across the generations, the population expanded, harvests failed, and scarcities ensued, but the junks and steamers of Chaozhouese rice traders always averted catastrophe.

Local communists understood that the promise of land redistribution might not solve the demographic challenges of the modern era. As Li Lisan reported in 1927, the party decided to expropriate the property of landlords with over 200 *mu* of land. Upon hearing this, their comrades in eastern Guangdong were "very skeptical," he wrote. "En route, we found the Guangdong peasants among the troops discussing it, and one peasant very bitterly said, 'If we confiscate the land of the big landlords having 200 or more mu, then the tiller won't get his land,' because in Guangdong ... there are very few big landlords with over 200 mu. This sort of talk made a lot of the comrades nervous."[116] There simply was not enough "big landlord" land in eastern Guangdong to redistribute to the multitudes of poor farmers and fisher folk. Until the 1930s, however, there was ample territory in Southeast Asia. Mass migration alleviated many of the problems the region confronted after the seventeenth century. The overseas connection did not simply enrich investors or provide employment to laborers, it ensured the very survival of the people of Chaozhou. After 1929 new solutions would have to be found.

CONCLUSION

Territorialism and the State

Europeans have a saying: "The Europeans here [in Singapore] raise all the
cattle, but the Chinese get all the milk."

—MUTUAL AID SOCIETY OF SHANTOU OVERSEAS
CHINESE IN THE NANYANG, 1934

THE HEYDAY OF MARITIME Chaozhou arced from the triumphant rise of the
Chaozhou-Siamese king of Siam, Taksin, in 1767 to the catastrophic collapse of
the global economy after 1929. Chaozhou merchants joined the ranks of the
Fujianese and Cantonese as commanding players in the commerce and commodity production of Southeast Asia, while legions of laborers sustained their
families by sojourning abroad to work. From 1869 to 1948 almost six million
Chinese (5,855,557) departed the port of Swatow and 3,960,320 returned, an
excess of 1,836,824 departures.[1] Employed primarily by Chaozhouese-owned
businesses, they produced gambier, pepper, rice, sugar, rubber, and fruit on
overseas plantations, or they toiled in mines or served as boatmen and sailors.
Capital derived from overseas investments primarily was reinvested abroad
while the home folk grew dependent on remittances. The culture and economy
of Chaozhou grew entangled with those of Shanghai, Bangkok, Malaya, Borneo,
and Hong Kong. That is to say, the period from 1767 to 1929 witnessed a great
convergence of southeastern China with territorial outposts across the South
China Sea. Southeast coastal Chinese were not trapped in an "ecological cul-
de-sac." Like the colonizing nations of Europe, they gained access to overseas
land, resources, and work opportunities after the mid-eighteenth century.

Was the history of maritime Chaozhou a colonial history? Early twentieth-
century Chinese scholars tended to depict their overseas compatriots as hav-

ing manifested a spirit of colonial conquest and entrepreneurial dynamism. The reformist intellectual Liang Qichao (1873–1929) referred to the founders of early modern overseas communities as "colonialists," pointedly adopting that term, *zhimin*, rather than the more common nomenclature of sojourners (*kemin*) or migrants (*yumin*)—not to mention the early Qing epithet, "traitors." He designated eight individuals in particular as the "grandees of Chinese colonialism" (*Zhongguo zhimin ba da weiren*). Tellingly, two of these "grandees" were Chaozhouese and three were from the Hakka regions of Jiaying-zhou that once had been in the administrative territory of Chaozhou prefecture.[2] Liang depicted men like Taksin and Luo Fangbo as militarily and economically talented overlords who defended Chinese interests against Western interlopers. He depicted the half-Chaozhouese Taksin in particular as the sort of political leader China needed in his own day to extirpate the humiliations of military defeat and semicolonialism. "Ayutthaya [Siam] fell," he wrote, "then it rose under the leadership of Taksin, who like King Goujian of Yue, united his people and returned them to glory. During the Qianlong reign . . . they rose up in righteousness and made war with Burma three times and three times did they smite them. They recaptured all of their territory and the Siamese people supported him as their King."[3] The reference to King Goujian (r. 496–465 BCE) of the ancient Chinese state of Yue was a classical allusion to the erasure of humiliation through perseverance and military triumph, and Liang enthusiastically represented Taksin in this tradition of resourceful men who redeemed their beleaguered states. Liang neglected to acknowledge that Taksin usurped the Siamese throne and that many Siamese and the Qing themselves did not recognize his status as king (the court in Beijing referred to him as a "headman").[4]

Liang's celebration of overseas Chinese pioneers bordered on an espousal of Chinese colonialism. He famously declared that the majority of the people of Southeast Asia descended from the Chinese Yellow Emperor and therefore "whether from the standpoint of geoscience (*dishi*) or of history, it really is only natural that these [lands] serve as the colonial territories of our race (*shi tianran wo zu zhi zhimin di ye*)."[5] His Southeast Asia was an arena in which Chinese had unshackled themselves from an enervating political culture back home and manifested the dynamic, audacious traits needed to revitalize the nation. It was scientifically and historically obvious to him that Chinese should rule over the indigenous people of these lands. Siew-min Sai has depicted this sort of thinking in early-twentieth-century Chinese intellectual circles as a "Sinocentric" form of colonialism in which Chinese expansion into the region was natural, predicated as it was on the largely peaceful infiltration of culturally similar Chinese.[6]

Scholars like Prasenjit Duara have considered the transnational dimensions of early twentieth-century Chinese nationalism. Nationalists sought to reincorporate sojourners into the politics of the homeland while simultaneously justifying Chinese control over foreign lands. Patriotic intellectuals, he wrote, "deployed their narratives to nationalize transnationals ... to establish a bond ... and to turn the loyalties of these forgetful 'sojourners' back to the [Chinese] geobody." This was part of a larger agenda to "domesticate transnationality" whether by utilizing Pan-Asianism to incorporate borderland peoples into the Chinese nation or by inculcating Han Chinese "racial" identity and "Confucian culturalism" in overseas Chinese.[7] Shelly Chan similarly refers to a "diaspora moment of Chinese national formation," when scholars affiliated with Jinan University in Shanghai sought to link Chinese national identity to Chinese emigrants. These specialists in "Nanyang" or South Seas studies portrayed Overseas Chinese as "incomplete colonists without China's protection ... [and] geopolitical incorporation." In this understanding, true colonialism could be achieved only after overseas settlements were absorbed by the Chinese state.[8]

Some Republican-era Chaozhouese participated in this "domestication" of their translocal traditions. The publishers of a report on behalf of the Mutual Aid Society of Shantou [Swatow] Overseas Chinese in the Nanyang depicted Chaozhouese migrants as having operated in the national interest:

> The rule of the imperialists is certainly very cruel, but the forbearance of the Overseas Chinese in the face of adversity is of a highly unusual quality. They live under the oppression of the government. They don't consider it wonderful. They just relentlessly endure their suffering. In the spirit of chopping down the wilderness and filling in the seas, they go off to consolidate their economic position. ... On behalf of Han Chinese nationality [minzu] they gloriously advance toward the twentieth century.[9]

This was an anachronistic interpretation of the history of these sojourners in an age of Chinese nationalism. It also disregards the suffering of their own forebears who defied the violent sea bans of the Ming and Qing to "gloriously advance" the coastal frontier for the sake of their families and villages rather than a culturally abstract neologism like minzu. Some Chaozhouese nevertheless interpreted their overseas history as a natural extension of the history of their southeast coastal homeland. In a commemorative volume celebrating the illustrious figures of "Chaozhou history" in Malaya, for example, no distinction was made between those who made their mark back in China and those who had succeeded in Malaya.[10] This tendency reflected the translocal geographical framework in which Chaozhouese collectively lived, of course, but it also must be seen in the context of nationalistic claims to overseas territory.

These emerging discourses of frontier expansion had the potential to evolve into an ideology undergirding formal colonial expansion. Li Changfu wrote the most influential history of "Chinese colonialism" in the first half of the twentieth century (indeed, it continues to be cited to the present day). Published in 1937, *A History of Chinese Colonialism* (*Zhongguo zhimin shi*) was a sweeping panorama of Chinese migration to Southeast Asia and elsewhere from the earliest times. He distinguished Chinese "colonialism" from the European (and increasingly Japanese) variety, which was predicated on military power and economic exploitation. Instead, he asserted, the Chinese version was characterized by mass migration to and settlement in Southeast Asia and was a natural, geographical extension of the two provinces that were home to roughly 95 percent of the Chinese who moved there: Fujian and Guangdong. With long, winding coastlines along the southeastern frontier, their inhabitants enjoyed a longstanding relationship with the sea and familiarity with the territories beyond China's borders. Li also resorted to northern Chinese stereotypes of the people of these regions (he was a native of Jiangsu). Not only were southeast coastal residents depicted as "late bloomers" in the adoption of such "Confucian" civilizational norms as staying rooted in family burial grounds, but also "their character tended toward violence, piracy, and perversity."[11] In accounting for their unusual overseas triumphs, Li conflated the natural environment with what he construed as the inherent cultural proclivities of southeast coastal frontiersmen.

In his view, the natural expansion of southeastern China over six centuries was thwarted only by the rise of Western colonialism in Southeast Asia. The nineteenth and twentieth centuries constituted the "Age of Western Power," a period of Chinese subordination to European and American domination that coincided with the rise of capitalism and the greater formalization of European colonial control. The triumphant trajectory of Chinese expansion was distorted in the nineteenth century, not so much by the arrival of Europeans per se but by the advantages afforded Westerners by the coterminous evolution of industrial capitalism and, most important, the strong backing of the modern nation-state. This was the key variable for him: the overseas Chinese were on their own and were neither protected nor supported by the military power of the Ming and Qing.[12]

Mainland Chinese scholars have continued to complain about dynastic negligence to the present day. Historians in the People's Republic of China no longer make the politically incorrect claim that overseas Chinese were "colonialists." Instead they argue that late imperial Chinese "opened up new land for human settlement" or claim that the "style" of Chinese migration and investment in Southeast Asia was morally distinct from that of the Western powers and Japan.[13] In his study of Chinese migration to Taiwan and the Philippines, Zeng Shaocong emphasized that the Chinese "did not take the colonialist path, which is to say China did not establish overseas colonies. This is the special feature of Chinese maritime migration." Instead, "China's overseas migration was a popularly spontaneous activity, the road they took was one of peaceful coexistence and mutual development in concert with native peoples.... The [peaceful] overseas migration to Taiwan and the Philippines profoundly reflects China's historical maritime character."[14] Having established—with justifiable pride—the nonbelligerent nature of Chinese migration, Zeng somewhat incongruously laments that the overseas Chinese suffered in their rivalry with Europeans because the latter "received governmental and military support." He cited the example of our great sixteenth-century Chaozhouese pirate, Lin Feng, who came close to wresting control of Luzon from its Spanish overlords. Not only did the Ming not support him, they subjected him to their maritime proscriptions and opposed him in every way. Zeng views this as "a great tragedy," for it reflected the ways Chinese were forced to fend for themselves in foreign lands. Even more problematic, in his view, was the absence of any dynastic response to the slaughter of thousands of Chinese over the course of several anti-Chinese massacres in early modern Java and Luzon. "The Chinese government did nothing to protect them," he complained. "The Ming and Qing courts did not care that overseas Chinese were being massacred.... Without government support, overseas Chinese lacked sufficient power to overthrow the heartless and exploitive rule of the colonialists."[15]

This, of course, was the point and in turn underscores one reason why the experiences of overseas Chinese merchants and laborers cannot be construed as an alternative form of European colonialism. The Ming and Qing did not permit the "colonial" tail to wag the metropolitan dog in Southeast Asia. They were never dragged into colonial-style wars in an effort to make the South China Sea safe for Chinese merchant adventurers. Indeed, the Chinese state had little to do with the success of nontributary, Chinese capitalist enterprise or, aside from expelling people in pacification campaigns, overseas migration.

Textbook interpretations of European imperialism describe it as a "process by which an expanding state dominates the territory, population, and resources of less powerful states or regions." The multiplication of European colonial states was a complicated, multifaceted process that changed over time, but the ability to wrest territorial control over the long term depended on the extension of the European state form, usually through the use (or threat) of military power.[16] Even under "informal colonialism," a system of economic domination that does not involve direct colonial governance, the backing of the state is essential. When Jürgen Osterhammel teased out the difference between "informal colonialism" and mere hegemony, he pointed to the institutional element. Informal colonialism is characterized by a "system of business firms and political-military agencies (the pro-consul-type of diplomat, a naval squadron, troops or police forces under foreign command, and so on) capable of translating potential superiority into effective influence and control."[17] This informal, nonstate-driven, business-oriented colonialism is predicated on the institutional presence of state actors. The reason the British even gained access to Shanghai, the semicolonial treaty port par excellence, was that they waged war against the Qing. The unequal treaty system, imposed on China to facilitate Western and Japanese enterprise, was largely a product of war and diplomatic pressure and endured under the shadow of the gunboat.

The process of lashing the state to capitalist enterprise was not always premeditated, and occasionally the escapades of European merchants forced their governments to resort to armed force. The First Opium War (1839–1842) is the classic case in point. During the course of their anti-opium campaign, Qing officials confiscated the opium stocks of British merchant-smugglers. The "China Lobby" back in London demanded a punitive response, and the prime minister (Melbourne) dispatched a naval force to the China coast, where British gunboats inflicted a decisive defeat on the Chinese. As a consequence, the British acquired Hong Kong, one of the most enduring colonies in the British Empire. This was not the result of a grand, premeditated scheme initiated by London but a response to overseas British complaints that the Chinese threatened their persons and property. In this way, the British Empire began to expand more formally into East Asia.

The contrast with the Ming and Qing response to the massacres of Chinese in the Philippines, Dutch East Indies, and Siam could not be more explicit. Overseas Chinese were very much on their own, but the absence of Chinese state power in fact enabled those Chinese to engage in territorial access, resource extraction, and commercial domination in a manner that was more enduring and perhaps even more successful than that of the Europeans prior to the twentieth century. As P. J. Cain and A. G. Hopkins have noted, imperialism "involves an incursion, or an attempted incursion, into the sovereignty of another state."[18] And the marvel of Chinese demographic and economic expansion into Southeast Asia prior to 1929 was its nonstatist, informal character. Indigenous people may have railed against Chinese economic power or subjected Chinese to an odious anti-Sinicism, but there was no formal Chinese colonial structure to resist and overthrow.[19]

Chinese settlement overseas had long served the interests of southeast coastal families and villages. Nationalist discourses sought to hitch that tradition to the rising star of the centralizing nation-state. This effort to channel popular and diffuse patterns of migration toward a larger national purpose reflected the weakness of the Chinese state in the international arena. What the government could not achieve militarily or diplomatically—foreign recognition of its political relevance to Southeast Asia—it might achieve discursively and culturally. This tendency was not unique to China. Narratives about diaspora and emigration played an important role in the making, or at least the imagining, of the Italian nation-state after 1871. Policy makers characterized the mass out-migration of Italians as a manifestation of their country's international power and depicted Italian emigrants as part of a "Greater Italy," who required the tutelage of Rome to ensure they remained culturally and politically "Italian." The Italian experience was largely comparable to that of the Chinese: as in Ming and Qing China, the Italian state initially characterized emigrants as "criminals" or "irresponsible adventurers" and only belatedly came to appreciate them as a dynamic, modernizing force. The level of migration from both countries was astronomical and resulted in enormous overseas settlements. Remittances constituted a phenomenal repatriation of capital to impoverished homelands. Italian and Chinese nationalists alike regretted that their imperial glory days all seemed to be in the distant past and hoped that incorporating their sojourning compatriots into an organic whole might lead to national rejuvenation. Both made a virtue of international weakness, asserting that their own traditions of maritime expansion—the late medieval polities of Venice and Genoa in the Italian case and the self-governing gongsi partnerships of Chinese merchants—were predicated on peaceful commercial intercourse. These traditions served as a model of wealth and power that was superior to that of Great Britain.[20] Such transnational identifications constituted a tool of modern state-building, but they also consoled ambitious nationalists who were frustrated that their countries did not play a more important role in international affairs.

The transnational imaginary of Chinese nationalism arose at a historically significant moment in the early twentieth century. It constituted an incipient, potentially aggressive type of Chinese Pan-Sinicism that arose simultaneously with the Japanese Pan-Asian variety to challenge the domination of Euro-American colonialism. The Japanese "southward advance" into the Pacific was initially commercial in nature, but by the 1930s it had become infused with an "ultranationalism" that celebrated the mystical destiny of the Japanese "race" to impose the "Greater East Asia Co-Prosperity Sphere" across East and Southeast Asia. Avowedly "anticolonial," it was conceptualized as a new form of internationalism, led by Japan, that would sweep aside the decadent tyranny of European territorial conquest and inaugurate "co-prosperous economic blocs" controlled by "Asians" themselves. As Japan's wartime expansion ground on, of course, the concept came to serve as the ideological underpinning of Japan's own territorial domination of its neighbors.[21]

As Shelly Chan has noted, Chinese scholars affiliated with Jinan University developed their ideas about Southeast Asia with Japan very much in mind (indeed, many had studied there). The Chinese shared some international assumptions with the Japanese: a sense that the wrong civilization had usurped their nation's "natural colonies"; the conviction that the state must play the organizing role in colonization; a belief that their own "race" was culturally superior to that of the indigenous people with whom they settled. Aside from these shared convictions, the Chinese invented new ones, most notably that "migration was colonization."[22]

It is hypothetical to speculate whether the Chinese might have acted on these ideas had their domestic history in the 1930s been different. They continued to lack the governmental power and military capacity to put it their ideas into effect prior to the outbreak of war in 1937. These Chinese discourses only succeeded in antagonizing Southeast Asian nationalists, who themselves were beginning to fight for their independence from Europeans and resented the efforts of the Nationalist government in Nanjing to "renationalize overseas Chinese" by adopting policies like issuing Chinese passports to them.[23] Eventually the discourses were swept aside by the sheer violence of World War II, and it is the Japanese, like the Europeans, who now suffer the historical infamy of colonial conquest.

Twentieth-century nationalists adopted the logic of European statism in which sovereignty is claimed over territory and ultimately preserved by military force. The territorialism explored in this study is a phenomenon that encompasses the entire range of human geospatial behavior to "control resources"; it is "a geographical expression of social power."[24] Humans engage in a variety of efforts to maximize benefits derived from access to land. We have seen the strategies employed by Chaozhouese across their maritime sphere. Sometimes they advanced their interests through violence: for example, the militarized feuding among lineages in the postevacuation era and the contests among Chinese dialect groups along the Gulf of Siam. Usually, however, Chaozhouese left sovereign control to others as they attended to their personal and group agendas. They also relied on European colonial offices and diplomatic services to secure their economic interests.

The informal, nonstatist approach to economic aggrandizement was an effective means of resource extraction. Indeed, the lack of administrative control enhanced the Chaozhouese advantage across a much wider, translocal world than political sovereignty would have made possible in any specific locale. By the late eighteenth century Chaozhouese on West Borneo were as focused on Singapore and Bangkok as loci of their import-export trade as they were on Kalimantan.[25] A "rice king" like Guo Yan became wealthy in the grain-milling business of Saigon even as he emerged as a major property owner in Singapore. The Lius made a fortune in rubber, opium, and banking in Singapore; the rice trade connecting Swatow, Hong Kong, Saigon, Singapore, and Bangkok; and the gum industry in Siam. They were among the biggest landowners in Singapore; they were also among the biggest landowners in Chaozhou. What does this say about their territorial strategies? Their marital, migratory, and commercial endeavors gained them access to the ample resources of foreign lands. They—along with other Chinese—abjured the juridico-political administration of territory and instead controlled commodities and sectors of the labor market, which enabled them to dominate much of the commerce of the port cities of the South China Sea. Their industrializing metropoles included Bangkok, Singapore, Saigon, and Hong Kong. Republican-era nationalists who lamented the Chinese "failure" to wrest control of these colonial outposts from the West did not fully appreciate that it indeed was better to "get all the milk" while the Europeans took responsibility for safeguarding the pastureland. They controlled economic resources without territorial sovereignty. One is tempted to compare the Chinese habitation on overseas colonial, monarchical, and sultanic territory to "two masters of the field" (*yitian liangzhu*), the land tenure system of southeast coastal China in which landlords technically owned the subsoil and expected rental payments from tenants while the tenants "owned" the surface rights and whatever the land produced.

Today the leaders of the People's Republic of China are building on the colonial imaginary of their predecessors, the Nationalists, to assert territorial authority over the vast water world connecting China to Southeast Asia. Both governments contrived a "Nine-Dash Line," a boundary drawn to stake hard, sovereign control over the disputed islands of the South China Sea. The line brushes against the littoral of every one of their southeastern neighbors in contravention of the UN Convention on the Law of the Sea, to which the PRC is a signatory. Beijing itself has remained silent on the specifics of this claim, relying instead on government-affiliated experts in international law to lay the foundation for incorporating these islands and the sea around them into their nation-state. These jurists justify their arguments on the basis of "historic title," title predicated on a tradition of Chinese sea travel, commerce, and map-making "since time immemorial." They dismiss, for example, the Vietnamese claim to some of the Paracel (Xisha) islands, a claim based on Vietnamese occupation of these islands in 1816. This claim is invalid, Chinese jurists assert, because "Vietnam remained a tributary to China until 1884." In reimagining the old tributary system as a modern political phenomenon in which their neighbors submitted to the sovereignty of the Chinese state, they appear to embrace a European model of colonial state-making. Indeed, these scholars refer to the "dominion of the Chinese state over the sea routes from East Asia to the Mediterranean."[26] These are not the sort of assertions that our Chaozhouese sojourners made, or needed to make, as they sailed away to make their fortunes along those very sea lanes.

"The strong do what they have the power to do and the weak accept what they have to accept." Thus Thucydides ruminated on the moral complexities of power and empire as he explained why the Athenians so unjustly slaughtered the men of Melos before establishing a colony of five hundred settlers there in 416 BCE.[27] This familiar quotation is often cited by the "realist" school in political science to explain the power dynamics and moral logic of international relations (to wit, "might makes right").[28] In the nineteenth and twentieth centuries Europeans, Americans, and Japanese wielded military power to compel others to accede to their territorial conquests across the South China Sea. Chinese sojourners did not have the naval power to wage war with the Europeans after the eighteenth century, but they did not need to. They achieved all the benefits of colonialism—land, resources, work and investment opportunities—without any of the cost, bother, and infamy of territorial administration. They left that to the colonial states that served as their nominal overlords. Among the "weaker" parties in Southeast Asia, these Chinese made do with the humble task of territorial access, resource extraction, and capital accumulation. This is a lesson the government of today's People's Republic of China—so intent on staking hard territorial sovereignty across the South China Sea—would do well to learn. Statist, militarily aggressive approaches to territorial aggrandizement are not always the best way to assure access to natural resources, especially when one's neighbors also have long memories of colonialism and celebrate their history of resisting it.

ACKNOWLEDGMENTS

"IT IS EASY to see the beginnings of things, and harder to see the ends" wrote Joan Didion as she reminisced about the early days of her great adventure as a journalist. Her remark might equally apply to the history of this book. The challenge I confronted upon embarking on a long journey across three centuries and several national histories was to live up to the impossible vision I had of the project at its inception and to sense when it was time to just let go. There are many ways to tell a local history in its global context. I managed to find my own way thanks to many institutions and individuals who sustained my efforts over the years.

This book was made possible through the financial support of institutions that were not only generous but also flexible about funding the research of someone with a severe case of scholarly wanderlust. Most of the research was funded by the American Council of Learned Societies' National Program for Advanced Study and Research in China; a Fulbright-Hays Faculty Research Abroad Fellowship; and an International and Area Studies Fellowship from the American Council of Learned Societies, the Social Science Research Council, and the National Endowment for the Humanities. The writing was supported by fellowships from the National Endowment for the Humanities, the Starr Foundation East Asian Studies Endowment Fund of the Institute for Advanced Study, the Kaplan Institute for the Humanities, and funding in support of the Gerald F. and Marjorie G. Fitzgerald Chair in Economic History.

I am grateful to Hou Dejian for permitting me to quote the powerful lyrics to "Chaozhou Man," translated by Linda Jaivin in *The Monkey and the Dragon* (Melbourne: Text Pub. Co., 2001), p. 65. Portions of Chapters 4 and 5 were previously published in Melissa Macauley, "Entangled States: The Translocal Repercussions of Rural Pacification in China, 1869–1873. *American Historical Review* 121.3 (June 2016): 755–79 and appear by permission of Oxford University Press. I am grateful to include brief excerpts from my article on smuggling, "Small Time Crooks," Copyright © 2009 Johns Hopkins University

Press and the Society for Qing Studies. This article was first published in *Late Imperial China* 30.1 (2009): 1–47 and is reprinted with permission by Johns Hopkins University Press. The excerpts from the Oral History Centre of the National Archives of Singapore (NAS/OHC) cited in the introduction and Chapters 3, 5, and 9, original audio recordings and transcripts in Chinese, can be accessed on the Archives Online portal of the National Archives of Singapore (http://www.nas.gov.sg/archivesonline).

I owe debts to too many individuals to list here, but I must acknowledge the intellectual, professional, and personal support over the years of Joseph Esherick, Madeleine Zelin, Peter Perdue, Nicola Di Cosmo, Tobie Meyer-Fong, and the late Frederic Wakeman. At this point they must dread seeing my incoming emails. Others who have helped in immeasurable ways include Chen Chunsheng, Chen Jingxi, John Wong, Kaoru Sugihara, Chen Hua, Prasenjit Duara, Ross Yelsey, Joseph Lee, Martin Barrow, Blaine Gaustad, Janet Theiss, Maram Epstein, Susan Naquin, Seng Guo-Quan, Andrea Goldman, Li Chen, Anne Reinhardt, Tong Lam, and the late Thomas Buckley, S.J. Many friends and colleagues, too numerous to mention, have helped me puzzle my way through this project at presentations and conferences at two dozen institutions. Scholars who read sections of the manuscript and offered much-needed feedback include Helen Siu (who drilled into me the importance of the Dan), Michael Szonyi (who drilled out of me my obsession with "cultures of violence"), Lucille Chia, Adam McKeown, Amy Stanley, Daniel Immerwahr, and Laura Hein. Haydon Cherry, Peter Carroll, Sunil Amrith, and Eunike Setiadarma generously read the entire manuscript and offered excellent advice. Two anonymous readers for the press were extraordinarily conscientious and insightful in trying to help me turn the manuscript into a better book. That I could not follow all their advice is owing to my own failures, though I must point out that the final revisions were made under a Chicago-land lockdown occasioned by the worst pandemic in a century.

It has been a pleasure to work with Princeton University Press. Thalia Leaf, my insightful editor, patiently steered me from a bloated manuscript through a "baggy" one (one reader's term) to a manuscript that is not quite buff but is at least a readable length. I am grateful to Jeremy Adelman, Sunil Amrith, and Emma Rothschild for including my book in their series "Histories of Economic Life." Anita O'Brien did a superb job of copyediting, while David Cox expertly charted the maps. Jenny Wolkowicki efficiently managed all production matters.

Friends and family have carried me through the usual challenges that always send a book to the back burner. Mark, Jim, Blaine, Meg, Toni, Bronwyn, Ken, Jim, Jon, Ann, Jane, Len, Tim, Debbie, Erin, and Mitchell contributed less to the book than to the life lived outside of it. I cannot thank Bill and Tom enough for the wine lessons, loving support, and many adventures. This book is dedicated to the memory of my mother, whose short life was fatefully entangled in the history of the South China Sea.

APPENDIX

Total Value of Trade (Imports and Exports), Ten Leading Treaty Ports, 1875–1879 (Haiguan taels)

Treaty port (population, 1891)	1875	1876	1877	1878
Guangzhou/Canton (1,600,424)	24,788,043	25,739,690	23,888,177	25,115,980
Tianjin/Tientsin (950,852)	17,058,711	18,741,493	22,942,468	20,773,479
Hankou/Hankow (800,370)	32,955,514	33,580,934	29,396,672	29,488,544
Fuzhou/Foochow (636,351)	18,098,568	15,871,907	15,554,429	17,059,328
Shanghai (404,956)	44,866,937	59,182,062	49,565,966	47,383,945
Ningbo/Ningpo (250,209)	12,846,315	12,404,421	12,451,653	12,650,602
Zhenjiang/Chinkiang (135,220)	12,403,137	10,992,235	11,198,936	14,857,312
Xiamen/Amoy (96,370)	9,032,686	9,065,201	10,138,097	9,074,116
Jiujiang/Kiukiang (53,101)	12,829,172	12,950,558	11,828,054	12,087,847
Shantou/Swatow (40,216)	16,612,747	18,241,968	18,608,019	19,237,846
Total (including 9 additional ports)	175,977,748	190,922,821	180,336,000	187,151,963
Opium imports as percentage of total value of imports	**37.39%**	**39.87%**	**41.32%**	**45.57%**

Source: IMC, *Reports on Trade at Treaty Ports, 1878*, xvi–xx; population figures, DR 1882–1891, xxix–xxxi. Haiguan tael = £1 in 1874.

ABBREVIATIONS

AJMR	*Asiatic Journal and Monthly Register for British India and Its Dependencies*
ARLCSS	*Annual Reports, Legislative Council of the Straits Settlements*
CBYWSM	*Chouban yiwu shimo (Xianfeng chao)*
CHD	*Chaozhou haiguan dang'an*
CHYB	*Chaozhou huiguan yi'an beicha*
CMGJ	*Chaoyang minjian gushi jingxuan*
CO	[British] Colonial Office
CSDQZ	*Chao Shan diqu qiaopiye ziliao*
CZZ	*Chaozhou zhi*
DR	*Decennial Reports*
DYCGNGM	*Diyici guonei geming zhanzheng shiqi de nongmin yundong*
FO	[British] Foreign Office
GDTC	*Gia-dinh-thung-chi: Histoire et description de la Basse Cochinchine*
GPA	Guangdong Provincial Archives, Guangzhou, China
GPA/FO 931	Guangdong Provincial Archives, stored in National Archives of Great Britain
GXCZPZZ	*Guangxuchao zhupi zouzhe*
JMA/SWATOW/LHL	Jardine Matheson Archives/In-Correspondence/ Unbound Letters/Swatow/Local House Letters
KYQSCRFDZ	*Kang Yong Qian shiqi chengxiang renmin fankang douzheng ziliao*

LDYLCWJ	*Lan Dingyuan lun Chao wenji*
LGCSSZJT	*Lü Gang Chaozhou shanghui sanshi zhounian jinian tekan*
MCT	*Malaiya Chaoqiao tongjian*
MQSLCZSJ	*Ming Qing shilu Chaozhou shiji*
NAS/OHC/HFQ	National Archives of Singapore/Oral History Centre/Huaren fangyan qun
NAS/OHC/XXR	National Archives of Singapore/Oral History Centre/Xinjiapo xianqu renwu
NCH	*North China Herald*
PLCSS	*Proceedings of the Legislative Council of the Straits Settlements*
QDBX	*Qingdai dizu boxiao xingtai*
QTCBMMSHA	*Qingting chaban mimi shehui an*
SB	Shenbao: *Guangdong ziliao xuanji*
SBZX	*Shanghai beike ziliao xuanji*
SDQ	*Shalongshi difeng qinglu*
SKJKQHSZ	*Shantou kaibu ji kaibu qian hou sheqing ziliao*
SNHHSB	*Shantou Nanyang huaqiao huzhu shewu baogao*
SPER	*Shanghai: Political and Economic Reports*
ST	*Straits Times*
XCBHJJ	*Xinjiapo Chaozhou bayi huiguan jinxi jiniankan*
XKTBWA	*Xingke tiben, weijin, anjian*
YZDS	*Yapian zhanzheng dang'an shiliao*
ZGDS	*Zhaoxuan gong du shiyi*
ZJZ	*Zhongguo jindushi ziliao*
ZZFL	*Zhupi zouzhe falü lüli*

NOTES

Introduction

1. NAS/OHC/HFQ/Chen Jinhua (Tan Kim Wah)/ reel 1. On farm size in Guangdong, Alfred Lin 1997: 36.

2. NAS/OHC/HFQ/Chen Jinhua/ reels 1–10.

3. Ng 1990: 312.

4. Oakes and Schein 2006: xii–xiii, 1–35. On translocalism in the Asian context, Raphael 1995; Cartier 2001; essays in Oakes and Schein 2006. See also Appadurai 1996; Brickell and Datta 2011.

5. On post–Cold War translocalism, Oakes and Schein 2006: 5; Appadurai 1996: 3–9; Smith 2011: 181–98. On the transformative effects of steamships and the telegraph across the South China Sea, Baker 1981: 330–31; Latham and Neal 1983: 274.

6. Werner and Zimmerman 2006. References to China and Malaya are mine. For a consideration of entangled history in the Atlantic world that focuses on the importance of peripheries in colonial encounters, Gould 2007.

7. Brickell and Datta 2011: 8–10; also "AHR Conversation: How Size Matters."

8. Kuhn 2008: 111–12; Wu Fengbin 1993: 260–67; Yen 1986: 1–3; Li Changfu 1966: 19; Wei 1967, 1: 423.

9. Pomeranz 2000.

10. On the availability of land in Siam, Skinner 1957b: 30; on Borneo, Heidhues 2003: 33; in Johor, Turnbull 1959: 44; in Cochinchina, LaFargue 1909: 282. They also became the major shopkeeping class in Cambodia (Delvert 1961: 27, 511–23). There was much migration within Qing China itself. On this, most recently, see Miles 2017.

11. Begbie 1967: 303–12; Doty and Pohlman 1839: 305; Phipps 1836: 204; Crawfurd 1830, 2: 121; Fernando and Bulbeck 1992: 183; Blussé 1981: 160. Fujianese were the dominant Chinese group in Java.

12. Hobson 1938: 71–93. Critics of the economic interpretation include Schumpeter 1951, who argued that capitalism diminished the ancient and atavistic joy of conquest, and Langer 1935 and 1968, who noted that the United States and Russia were debtor nations when they embarked on imperialist adventures and that France exported more capital to Russia and the Ottoman Empire than they ever did to their colonies. The "Neo-Marxist" interpretation (Langer's term) of imperialism, most famously expressed by Lenin (1939), spawned a minor cottage industry in the Anglo-American academy that critiqued economic arguments and emphasized cultural explanations. More recently, Cain and Hopkins (2016) have shown that that

the capital accumulation of the British Empire depended more on the service sector (especially banking, shipping, and insurance) than on manufacturing.

13. Swettenham 1975: 232. On the Chinese role in Southeast Asian economies, see essays in Tagliacozzo and Chang 2011.

14. SNHHSB 1934: preface. The economic situation in the Straits was complicated. For a study of the ways British rubber planters began to supplant Chinese in the twentieth century, Jackson 1968. The Chinese nonetheless maintained a commanding presence in the economy.

15. Jackson 1968: xv–xvi. Gould (2007) claims that colonial peripheries—where interactions and adaptations were part of daily experience—offer richer opportunities for exploring entangled transformations than is possible with a focus on metropoles. McCoy (2009: 8–40) has called on historians to "recenter the periphery" in analyzing U.S. colonialism in the Philippines, for the encounter was "mutually transformative" for colonizer and colonized.

16. Cherry 2011; Li Tana 2004: 261–69. On Chaozhou domination of the rice trade, see chap. 9 of this book.

17. CO 275/28 (27–32), PLCSS, 28 February 1883. Also CO 275/29 (187–93), "Report of Chinese Protectorate," 6 May 1884.

18. NAS, PLCSS, Microfilm NL 1101 (1872): 2. By the 1880s revenues were adequate to pay for most expenses. See CO 275/32 (266).

19. CO 275/25 (268), PLCSS, 29 December 1881. There were seventy-one females among the British forces.

20. CO 275/25 (177–78), PLCSS, 11 October 1881.

21. W. A. Pickering, inaugural protector of the Chinese, offered extensive services to them. NAS/ NL 1103, PLCSS, 20 May 1880; and Doc. 6, tables B and C. He was bludgeoned with an axe in 1887 by a Chaozhouese who opposed his efforts to regulate "secret societies."

22. Elden 2013: 322–29; Raustiala 2009: 5–10.

23. Sack 1986: 1–2.

24. Vaccaro, Dawson, and Zanotti 2014: 3.

25. Po 2018: 17–23, 73–77.

26. Turner 1920: 3–52; also Klein 1997: 7–16.

27. Tiedge translated in Mangan 1859: 227.

28. Osterhammel 2014: 322–24.

29. Building on Sahlins 1985; Sewell 2005.

30. Rogaski 2004; Carroll 2005; Goodman and Goodman 2012. Osterhammel (1986) offers an incisive structural framework for studying imperialism in China, but his ideas about "asymmetrical power" and "business systems" illustrate the semicolonial dynamics of Shanghai and Tianjin rather than those of treaty ports with powerful commercial networks across Southeast Asia. On the brutality of the wars of imperialism, Hevia 2003.

Chapter 1

1. Skinner 1977: 211–49. Chapter epigraph quoted in Hsieh 1932: 569.

2. Cooke and Li 2004: xii.

3. Huang Ting and Chen Zhanshan 2001: 18–19.

4. On harbors, Liu Sen 1996: 124; on the problems of "fluvial hydrosystems, Campbell 2012: 4–11, 110–15, and Cuthbert William Johnson 1842: 78–82; on alluviation and litigation in Chaozhou, Huang Ting 2007: 150–51.

5. LGCSSZJT (Essay on "Xianggang chaoren shangye diaocha gaikuang"), 1; Du 1997: 12–13; MCT, 28.

6. Jiang Risheng 1986: 432.

7. Viraphol 1977 1–31; also Wills 2011; Mancall 1968; Schottenhammer 2007; Huang Ting 1996; Daphon Ho 2011: 63–65.

8. On Chaozhou's economy from Song to Ming, Huang Ting 1996: 5–8. On shipbuilding, Huang Ting 1996; Jiang and Fang 1993: 246.

9. Antony 2003; Daphon Ho 2011; Ptak 1998; Huang Ting 1996.

10. Dai 1982: 30.

11. David Kilcullen, quoted in Packer 2006: 63.

12. Huang Ting 1996: 9; Dai 1982: 26–27, 56–57. On the patrol route, CBYWSM, 1: 102.

13. Qu 1985, 2: 428–32.

14. MQSLCZSJ, 13.

15. MQSLCZSJ, 15.

16. So 1975: 44–58, 122–40; also Brook 1998.

17. So 1975: 69; Antony 2003: 22.

18. Andaya and Andaya (2001: 134–35) describe a similar phenomenon in precolonial Malaya.

19. On Lin Daoqian, Dai 1982: 26, 56–64; Li Changfu 1966: 142–43; MCT, 26; Chaozhou fuzhi 1893, 38: 939; Chaoyang xianzhi 1884: 172. Daoqian ultimately settled in Pattani where by 1616 there were more Chinese than Malays. See Anderson 1890: 80.

20. On Lin Guoxian, CZZ 2005: 2621–2622 and 2630; and Chaozhou fuzhi (1893), 38: 936. On the personal dynamics of the gang, Dai 1982: 26–27. On the birth year of Lin Feng, Calanca 2001: 120.

21. MQSLCZSJ, 56, 59–61; Dai 1982: 55–56.

22. Quoted in Dai 1982: 64.

23. MQSLCZSJ, 60.

24. Chen Chunsheng 2000: 78.

25. Chen Jinghe 1963: 27, 34–35.

26. Zeng Shaocong 1998: 105.

27. González de Mendoza 1854, 2: 6–10.

28. Kamen 2003: 139; Kelsey 1998: passim.

29. González de Mendoza 1586, 2: 10–11. I have relied on the 1854 version of this text, but the language of that translation is idiosyncratic. The quotes are my own, based on the 1586 text. On Shōkō, see Li Changfu 1966: 144.

30. Chen Jinghe 1963: 37–38; Li Changfu 1966: 143–45; González de Mendoza 1854, 2: 15–18.

31. González de Mendoza 1854, 2: 18. Chen Jinghe (1963: 39) believes that these women and children were Chinese, but it is possible that some were Japanese or Filipina.

32. González de Mendoza 1854, 2: 21–25; Chen Jinghe 1963: 38–43.

33. Zeng Shaocong 1998: 221–22.

34. Dai 1982: 56, 60–63.

35. Patton (2008: xvii). On Drake, Kelsey 1998: 86, 392. Drake grew up in Devon, where piracy was morally criticized but widely practiced (Kelsey, 12), a situation similar to that of Chaozhou.

36. Dai 1982: 59–60; Wade 2005: WL 8.8.25. Lin and Yang, however, had managed to reside in Cambodia for years.

37. Dai 1982: 56.

38. Ptak 1998: 187. Calanca (2010: 86) notes that restrictions were again imposed in 1572, 1592, 1626, 1628, and 1639 and is less sanguine about the recovery of foreign trade for the duration of the Ming.

39. Lamley 1990; Zheng Zhenman 2001.

40. Chen Chunsheng 2000: 88–89.

41. Chen Chunsheng 2000: 90–96; Chen Zehong 2001: 366–67.

42. Mao Cheng 1879, 1: 2.

43. Chen Chunsheng 2000: 79–88, relating story of Xu Chaoguang.

44. Ng 1983: 53. The ban fostered the emergence of the Amoy trade network. On the Ming-Qing transition and the Zhengs, Wakeman 1985; Struve 1984; Dahpon Ho 2011; Hang 2015. On Guangdong, Jiang and Fang 1993: 329–32.

45. Jiang and Fang 1993: 330–31. The policy was not uniformly implemented across Guangdong. Faure (2007: 174) notes that the Canton region was not "entirely emptied of people," though it did experience a "human disaster."

46. MQSLCZSJ, 102.

47. Huang Ting 2007: 142; Lin Dehou's calculations in CZZ 1949, Hukou zhi (1), 4–5.

48. CZZ 1949, "Yan'ge zhi," 20, 35, 69; Jiang and Fang 1993: 330.

49. CZZ 1949, "Yan'ge zhi," 20, 69.

50. Rao 1996: 310–11.

51. CZZ 1949, "Dashi zhi," 14b.

52. CZZ 1949, "Dashi zhi," 43, 69; Huilai xianzhi 1731: 89.

53. On the Su empire, Marks 1984: 29.

54. MQSLCZSJ, 84–85.

55. On the mutiny, Huilai xianzhi 1731, 2: 396–97; MQSLCZSJ, 89; Lin Tian and Cai Qionghong 2002: 151; Jiang and Fang 1993: 332.

56. Huilai xianzhi 1731, 1: 171.

57. Marks 1984: 29

58. Huang Ting 2007: 145–46.

59. Rao 1996: 310.

60. Huang Ting 2007: 142.

61. On Xu's life, Chenghai xianzhi 1815, 19: 14; Chenghai xianzhi 1992: 840.

62. Huang Ting 2007: 140; also Chen Chunsheng 2001: 101–2.

63. Chaoyang xianzhi 1884, 4: 13; Lan Dingyuan 1985: 239.

64. Huang Ting 2007: 142, quoting from Ji genealogy.

65. Chaoyang xianzhi 1884, 13: 16.

66. Huang Ting 2007: 142.

67. On Qiu's Dan followers, Jiang Risheng 1986: 230. On Dan in general, Ye Xian'en 1995: 83–88; Ouyang Zongshu 1998: 97–119.

68. *Chaoyang xianzhi* 1884, 13: 17; *Chaoyang xianzhi* 1997: 26–28; CZZ 1949, "Yan'ge zhi," 14. On genealogical records, Huang Ting 2007: 147.

69. MQSLCZSJ, 104.

70. CZZ 1949, "Da shi zhi" (2), 22. On popular accounts, Jiang Risheng 1986: 412; Foccardi 1986: 120.

71. MQSLCZSJ, 90–104; *Qingshi gao* 1928, 172: 5803.

72. CBYWSM, 1: 102.

73. Loubère 1969: 112.

74. Hang 2016. On the Fujianese "Amoy Network," Ng 1983; 1990.

75. Chen Chunsheng 2000: 103–4.

Chapter 2

1. *Ka'i hentai*, 2: 931–39, 952, 979, 1023–24.

2. Ta Chen 1940: 50–51; Skinner 1957b: 16–17; Viraphol 1977: 56–57, 86; Ishii 1998: 243.

3. LaFargue 1909: 282.

4. Viraphol 1977: 82–103.

5. CZZ 2005: 2704–5. The Fu-Chao yanghang was established in 1760 and evolved out of the South Seas Guild.

6. Fan 1992: 247.

7. Ng 1983: 130, 146; Viraphol 1977: 100.

8. Lan, LDYLCWJ, 186. On feuding in Chaozhou, ZZFL, JQ 10.6.6.

9. Lan 1985: 1–7; CZZ 2005: 2700.

10. SDQ, 12, 42, 70, 216–19.

11. XKTBWA, DG 4.5.21; Macauley 2009: 1–3, 22.

12. *Chaoyang xianzhi* 1884: 318.

13. CZZ 2005: 2704; MQSLCZSJ, 144–45; KYQSCRFDZ, 2: 653–54. On Qing food riots, R. Bin Wong 1982.

14. Du 1997: 37. On official demands to limit overseas trade to stem opium imports, ZJZ, 4.

15. *Shantou haiguan zhi*, 15. Importers of 10,000 *shi* of rice saw duty reduced by 50 percent; those who carried over 5,000 *shi* received a 30 percent reduction. As Skinner notes (1957b: 17), Siamese merchants sold rice in China under Qing auspices after 1722.

16. *Haiyang xianzhi* 1900, juan 7: 230; *Chenghai xianzhi* 1764, juan 19: 899–900.

17. *Chaozhou fuzhi* 1893, juan 34: 836; Ye Xian'en 1989, 1: 188, 224.

18. Chen Chingho 1977, 2: 1538, 1543–44. Taksin is known in Chinese as Zheng Zhao, the name he used in his correspondence with the Qing.

19. Chen Chingho 1977, 2: 1543–44; Launay 2000, 2: 276.

20. Turpin 1908: 156–87. Also Wyatt 2003: 122–28; Leng 1999: 190–228; Chen Chingho 1977: 1535–75. The Qing considered him a usurper and referred to him as "headman." See MQSLCZSJ, 181.

21. Cushman 1993: 50.

22. MCT: 29; Wyatt 2003: 122–28; Leng 1999: 190–228.

23. Chen Chingho 1977, 2: 1549–53; Sakurai and Kitagawa 1999: 189.

24. Chen Chingho 1977, 2: 1534–35; also Sakurai and Kitagawa 1999: 151–54; Ouyang Enliang and Chao Longqi 2002, 4: 468–70.

25. GDTC, 29–30; Chen Chingho 1977, 2: 1537–38, 1552; Sakurai and Kitagawa 1999: 154–59, 177–78; Sellers 1983: 15; Skinner 1957b: 12.

26. Sakarai and Kitagawa 1999: 151. For a discussion of the term "port polity," Rungswasdisab 1994: 85. Following convention, I refer to the Macs as "Cantonese," but they actually were from Leizhou. The Leizhou dialect, like Chaozhouese, is a variant of the southern Min dialect.

27. GDTC, 177; *Da Nan shilu*, 11, 21.

28. Chen Chingho 1977: 1553–55; Sakarai 2004: 45.

29. For details of these struggles, GDTC, 1969; *Da Nan shilu*, 11–12, 87; Chen Chingho 1977; Sakarai 2004; Rungswasdisab 1995. Tran Lien is called Hau Tran Lien in Vietnamese and Phraya Phiphit in Siamese.

30. Reid 2004: 23.

31. Turpin 1908: 178; Crawfurd 1830, 2: 154; Viraphol 1977: 104–9.

32. Dhiravat na Pomberja 2004: 346–48; Viraphol 1977. Taksin grew paranoid and/or religiously fanatical and was overthrown (Wyatt 2003: 127). Fr. M. Descourvières claimed in 1782 that he began to vex his subjects by "forcing them to abandon [commerce] almost completely" (journal excerpt, Launay 2000, 2: 309). His dismayed Chinese supporters quietly abandoned him at the time of the coup.

33. Crawfurd 1830, 2: 174.

34. Viraphol 1977: 104. Chaozhouese continued to purchase rice in the Lower Yangzi, but by the mid-nineteenth century Chaozhou's supplemental rice needs were largely met by imports from Siam and Saigon (via Hong Kong). See JM/IC/UL/reel 552/Swatow/LHL 1232.

35. Viraphol 1977: 171–73.

36. For Siamese figures, Crawfurd 1830, 2: 221–22. Based on Skinner's critique of his methodology (1957: 70), I rely on Crawfurd's figures before he manipulated them. For Chaozhou's population, CZZ 2005: 2106, 2133.

37. Turpin 1908: 185–87; Wang Yuanlin and Liu Qiang 2005: 83.

38. *Trade Report for Swatow, 1879*, 207–8. The site described in 1879 had been in operation since 1829.

39. *Siam Repository* 4 (1872): 483–84.

40. AJMR 18 (1824): 326.

41. Crawfurd 1830, 1: 76; 2: 159; Phipps 1836: 205; Viraphol 1977: 181; Leng 1999: 74–75.

42. Ruschenberger 1838: 313. This included junks that sailed from elsewhere in China. His source was missionaries who catered to the medical needs of Chinese sailors. Also Gutzlaff 1840: 84–85; Bowring 1857, 1: 247.

43. Crawfurd 1830, 2: 160–61. The pilot and accountant alone were salaried and entitled to 50 piculs of tonnage. On crew as "shareholders," Bowring 1857, 1: 249.

44. Shen Binghong 2001: 22–23; Zhang Yingqiu 1991: 242. On the company, Choi 1998.

45. Nidhi Eoseewong 2005: 75.

46. AJMR 27 (1829): 435; 28 (1829): 489; Turpin 1908: 202–8.

47. Crawfurd 1830, 2: 161–62.

48. Crawfurd 1830, 2: 177–78.

49. Pallegoix 1854, 1: 80, 101–2.

50. Crawfurd 1830, 2: 177–78.

51. Pallegoix 1854, 1: 310. Statistics for 1840s.

52. Crawfurd 1830, 2: 178 and 181.

53. Nidhi Eoseewong 2005: 75–114.

54. Ye Xian'en 1989, 1: 224–25.

55. Viraphol 1977: 104. Merchants with other surnames also were honored. One, Yang Licai, imported 2,700 piculs from Vietnam. See Wang Yuanlin and Liu Qiang 2005: 83.

56. Ye Xian'en 1989: 224–25; *Chaozhou fuzhi* 1762: 3270 (electronic).

57. Ye Xian'en 1989: 225–26, quoting a Daoguang-era stele.

58. Crawfurd 1830, 2: 328.

59. The East India Company administered the territory after Thomas Raffles "raised the flag" over Singapore in 1819. A separate colony was established in 1867.

60. Xie Qinggao 1962: 37–38; AJMR 8 (1819): 305; Poh Ping Lee 1978: 27–30. My focus on Chaozhouese is not to dismiss the commercial significance of Fujianese in Singapore. The agricultural economy nonetheless was dominated by Chaozhouese.

61. Siah U Chin [Seah Eu Chin] 1848: 290. Seah was a leading gambier producer.

62. Phipps 1836: 324–25; Crawfurd 1830, 2: 352–53.

63. AJMR 18 (1824): 256. On Sarawak Chaozhouese, *Anbu zhi* 1990: 353; on plantations, Reid 2004.

64. MCT, 29, 78–80; Song Ong Siang: 19–20.

65. Trocki 1979: 142–43; Yen 1986: 232; MCT, 136. Seng Poh was born at Ipoh and technically was "Straits Chinese." The family hailed from Haiyang.

66. *Anbu zhi* 1990: 353; CO 275/19, App. 2 ("Emig. Report," 1876); STR, 1870; Siah 1848: 290; Chin 1981: 74.

67. MCT, 42–43, 285.

68. Trocki 1979: 113–14; Trocki 1990: 119, 139. Historians (Trocki; Yen 1986: 264) conventionally render *kangzhu* as *gangzhu*, "port chiefs," but Yap Pheng Geck (1982: 1), whose father was a jiangchu in Johor, explained that *kangzhu* approximated the Chaozhou pronunciation of *jiangzhu*, "river chief."

69. Carstens 2005: 10.

70. Xie Qinggao 1962: 14–15. Chapter epigraph from Xie Qinggao 1962: 49–50.

71. Crawfurd 1830, 2: 385.

72. Siah 1848: 288–89; on Guangdong wages, Mazumdar (1998: 283), citing monthly wage of 500–700 cash.

73. Wei Yuan 1847, 2: 487–88. Pontianak was known in Chinese as Kundian.

74. Liang 1905: 53; Heidhues 2003: 60 (quoting de Groot); Yuan 2000.

75. Heidhues 2003: 40, 54–55; Wang Tai Peng 1994: 78–79; Blussé and Merens 1993. Yuan Bingling (2000) emphasizes religious features.

76. Heidhues 2003: 50–55; Wang Tai Peng 1994: 60.

77. Liang 1957; 53; Luo Xianglin 1961: 1.

78. CZZ 2005: 2702.

79. Luo Xianglin 1961: 137–46 and passim; Yuan 2000: 48–55; Heidhues 2003: 64–65.

80. Yuan 2000: 16, 31; Heidhues 2003: 31, 36. Leo (2015: 179–80) asserts that half-mountain Hakka were culturally Hakka.

81. Yuan 2000: 31, 47–48.

82. Yuan 2000: 40; Heidhues 2003.

83. Wu Fengbin 1993: 433.

84. Quotes from Cator 1936: 150; also Heidhues 1993: 76–79; Yuan 2003: 43, 52, 247.

85. Heidhues 2003: 48–50.

86. Cator 1936: 149–50. Cator suspects that Raffles's estimates were excessive because the latter assumed that every adult Chinese male living there was a miner.

87. Fu 1966: 517–19; Zheng Yangwen 2005: 15–18; *Ming huidian*, 106:576.

88. Qu Dajun 1985, 2: 428–32.

89. ZJZ, 4, memorial dated YZ 6.11.6.

90. *Chenghai xianzhi* 1815, 6: 3.

91. Siah 1848: 284–85.

92. MQSLCZSJ, 232–33.

93. Zhao 1995: 155–56; Farooqui 1998: 13–14.

94. JMA/Namoa/reel 585/ PL 1, 2, 4; Zhao 1995: 154–58. On Christianity in Chaozhou, Joseph Tse-hei Lee 2003.

95. JMA/Namoa/reel 585/ PL 38, 82; 84 (all 1838).

96. JMA/Namoa/reel 585/ PL 34, 35, and 67.

97. Crawfurd 1830, 2: 362; JM/Local Namoa/reel 544, LHL 4; JM/Swatow/reel 550/LHL 177, 272.

98. Phipps 1836: 201; YZDS, 1: 427.

99. ZJZ, 14–15 (1815 case memorial).

100. Begbie 1967: 304–8; Trocki 1979: 32–33. Begbie refers to them as the "Canton campong," but Europeans used the term "Canton" to denote "Guangdong"; these almost certainly were natives of Chaozhou.

101. Trocki 1990: 151–54. Fujianese also dominated the farms.

102. QTCBMMSHA, 38:11479–80, 11485.

103. XKTBWA, DG 4.5.21.

Chapter 3

1. Murray 1994; Wu Fengbin 1994: 425–27; Ownby 2001; Faure 2004. I employ TDH as generic shorthand for a variety of organizations that evolved out of its traditions.

2. Packer 2006: 60; Kilcullen 2006: 117.

3. Feierman 1990: 18–24.

4. Qin 1988: 118–19.

5. CZZ 2005: 2106 (Lin's estimate); Wei Yuan 1847, 1: 423; SKJKQHSZ, 304.

6. Logan 1847: 36; Hong 2006: 24.

7. Qin 1988: 119.

8. On lineage reconstruction, Bao Wei 2005. On feuds emanating from the evacuation, Huang Ting 2007; Chen Chunsheng 2000.

9. Muir 1993: 245.

10. Lan 1985: 239; Macauley 1998. On property disputes, QDBX, 2: 497–646.

11. Qin 1988; Murray 1994; Ownby 1996: vii; Ownby 1993: 3–11; ter Haar 1993: 153–76; 1998.

12. QTCBMMSHA, 20: 4918–4925.

13. CO 275/19 (1876).

14. Turnbull 1959: 45.

15. NAS/OHC/ HFQ/Chen Jinhua/ reel 3.

16. Taiguo Chaozhou huiguan chengli wushi zhounian jinian tekan 1988: 13.

17. Ownby 1996: 96–97. For other instances of resistance to Qing forces, CZZ 2005: 2702; MQSLCZSJ, 169–72; Jieyang xianzhi 1993: 18; Chen Zehong 2001: 363.

18. QTCBMMSHA, 31: 8796–8801.

19. QTCBMMSHA, 31: 8801. This is the source of this chapter's epigraph.

20. Ter Haar 1993: 168. He believes these sorts of slogans reflected a messianic rather than a political message.

21. CO 275/8, App. 17, 107–22.

22. Macauley 2009. Statistics culled from XKTBWA, 1790–1860.

23. I rely on QTCBMMSHA, a forty-volume compendium of cases held in the First Historical Archives; that archive's XKTBWA collection; YZDS; and ZJZ.

24. QTCBMMSHA, 7: 567–71; 7: 845–46; 18: 4351–54; and 29: 8193.

25. QTCBMMSHA, 30: 8679–82.

26. Murray 1994: 62.

27. QTCBMMSHA, 30: 8676–78.

28. Wu Fengbin 1993: 433–34.

29. Examples of cases involving Hoklos, QTCBMMSHA, 20: 4915–83 (in this 1787 dragnet against the TDH, officials usually offered exculpatory evidence for Hoklos. In contrast, even innocent Hakka were punished, for example 20: 4979–83). For exemplary cases in Hakka regions, 20: 4921; 29: 8193; 30: 8676–78; 31: 8781–47.

30. QTCBMMSHA, 3: 1114–15; 30: 8521–25; 30: 8691–95; 30: 8742–46; 31: 8796–8901; 31: 8781 (these include individuals who were from these places but arrested elsewhere).

31. FO 228/439 (123–24).

32. FO 228/439 (123–24, 160–61). On the animosity between Hoklos and Hakkas at Swatow, CHD, 1330: 5963.

33. XKTBWA, 1790–1860; Macauley 2009: 28–35.

34. Ter Haar 1998: 70, 78, 335–36.

35. For biographical accounts, *Chaoyang xianzhi* 1884: 13:19–20; *Chaoyang xianzhi* 1997: 1080–81. Details of rebellion in CZZ 1949, "dashi zhi," 33b–34; *Chaoyang xianzhi* 1884, 13: 19–20; *Jieyang xianxuzhi* 1890: 440–44; *Neige daku dang'an*, #194387–001; *Chaoyang xianzhi* 1997: 33–34; Ouyang Enliang and Chao Longqi 2002, 4: 413–14.

36. SKJKQHSZ, 307; CZZ 1949, "Dashi zhi," 34.

37. Yuan Bingling 2000: 43–45.

38. For Huang's punishment, *Chaoyang xianzhi* 1884, 13: 20; for the others', MQSLCZSJ, 253; CZZ 1949, "dashi zhi," 34; SKJKQHSZ, 307; Hu Zhusheng 1996: 203. On the shrine, Tanaka 1993: 50–57; Chng 1999: 69.

39. Lin 1997: 98–102.

40. He Zhiqing and Wu Zhaoqing 1996: 271–72.

41. Lan 1985: 239 (18th c.); CMGJ, 291 (19th c.); IMC, "The Fisheries of Swatow," 1883: 1. On women, *Chaozhou fuzhi* 1893: 130.

42. JMA/Swatow LHL 1880; 2033; 2034.

43. ZJZ, 103 (*Lufu zouzhe*, DG 18.11.16).

44. Wakeman 1966; Wagner 1982; Shih 1967; Platt 2012; Meyer-Fong 2014.

45. CZZ 1949, "Dashi zhi," 34b; MQSLCZSJ, 261.

46. On financial pressures, J. Y. Wong 1976: 95–119.

47. CCZ 2005: 2717–23; Chen Zehong 2001: 363–64. The Zhengs of Meihua had longstanding grievances against local officials. See CMGJ, 291.

48. Zeng Guoquan 1969, 614: 1964–66.

49. Michael 1966: 118

50. Zhao Huifeng 1998: 174–84.

51. *Chaoyang xianzhi* 1997: 34, 539–44, 564; CCZ 2005: 2727–28; Jiang Zuyan and Fang Zhiqin 1993: 467–69.

52. Wu's report in GPA/FO/931/1394. Yamen functionaries were unreliable because many were themselves longstanding members of brotherhoods. See QTCBMMSHA, 31: 8802–06.

53. JMA/Swatow/reel 550/LHL 440. An additional 65,000 was raised in September. FO 17/278 (303–310).

54. MQSLCZSJ, 272–73; FO 228/354 (92–93).

55. FO 228/480 (22–28); Chinese version of guild notice, FO 228/924 (162).

56. JMA/Swatow/reel 552/LHL 1058, reel 552. Back in 1854, a Jardine representative reported (LHL 93) that the "bulk of the people are against the Insurgents."

57. QTCBMMSHA, 38: 10331–33; 38: 10329–30; 38: 10335–37. For a colonial complaint, CO275/19.

58. There was a cluster of cases in Chaozhou in 1786, including QTCBMMSHA, 20: 4918–28; 20: 4941–44; 20: 4979–83. For Borneo, Yuan Bingling 2000: 40, 42–44.

Chapter 4

1. JMA/Swatow/LHL, 123 (quote), 776.

2. GPA/FO 931/1654.

3. ZJZ, 106–7; YZDS, 1: 444–45, 448.

4. On rebel songs and ideology, Wu Kuixin 1997; on the rebellion, CZZ 2005: 2719–23; *Haiyang xianzhi* 1900: 256.

5. Bruinsma and Bernasco 2004: 79, 87.

6. Kilcullen 2006: 117; see also Packer 2006: 60.

7. GPA/FO 931/1654 (deposition).

8. JMA/Swatow/LHL, 131; Scarth 1860: 54–55.

9. Jiang Risheng 1986: 412.

10. JMA/Swatow/LHL 336, reel 550.

11. GPA/FO 931/1654.

12. *Chenghai xianzhi* 1815, 8: 7.

13. QTCBMMSHA, 4: 1404; 36: 10814–21.

14. Ter Haar 1998: 351–60; Linda Cooke Johnson 1995: 283.

15. CO 275/19.

16. QTCBMMSHA, 38: 10341; Ter Haar 1998: 359.

17. QTCBMMSHA, 38: 10329–30, 10335–37.

18. Observations inspired by older work on the French Revolution, especially Hunt, 1984: 12–16.

19. MQSLCZSJ, 288. Also SB 1: 80–82; *Peking Gazette*, 14 November 1873.

20. On Fang's genealogical descent and ancestral hall, *Chaozhou Fangshi zupu*, 8–10, 28, 31. On their prominence in gazetteers, *Puning xianzhi* (1747), 6: 285–97. On their Guangdong ties, *Peking Gazette*, May 2, 1891; *Qingdai Yueren zhuan*, 2: 575–79.

21. *Chaoyang xianzhi* 1884, 21: 91–92.

22. Zeng Guoquan 1969 (1882 memorial), 614: 1966.

23. On militia, GPA/FO/931/1120; biography in *Qingdai Yueren zhuan*, 2: 563–79; *Puning xianzhi* 1995: 676–77.

24. On Ruilin, *Qingshi gao*, 388: 11710.

25. MQSLCZSJ, 288.

26. SB, 1: 81 (memorial by Ruilin and Gov. Zhang Zhaodong in 1873); *Chaoyang xianzhi* 1884, 21: 91–92. This was not unusual in post-Taiping Guangdong, as seen in the annual assessments of high-ranking military officers: GXCZPZZ, 36: 321, 743; 37: 24–25, 831.

27. SB, 1: 80–82 (Ruilin's comment); 3: 404–5 (Zeng's). On Huizhou, GXCZPZZ, 42: 205; ZGDS, juan 3, n.p.

28. On military mode, Gregory 2015; on Fang's declaration of mode, MQSLCZSJ: 288; on its application in a Puning bandit eradication campaign in 1836, GPA/FO 931/88; MQSLCSJ; 243.

29. ZGDS, juan 4, n.p. Most official accounts repeat these statistics, so clearly Fang was the source of government information about the campaign.

30. SB, 1: 80–82.

31. SB, 1: 80–82; ZGDS, juan 4, n.p.; GXCZPZZ, 42: 205.

32. Lan Dingyuan 1985: 2. On violence, *Neige daku dang'an* 197020–001, JQ 10.2 (report of 1805); *Chaoyang xianzhi* 1884: 176–77; ZGDS, juan 4, n.p. For popular, local accounts, CMGJ: 291–96.

33. SDQ: 42; 70.

34. *Chaoyang xianzhi* 1884, 4: 13 (p. 46); for quote: CMGJ, 356.

35. ZGDS, juan 4, n.p.

36. CMGJ, 356–57.

37. CMGJ, 355–60.

38. Lida Ashmore 1920: 152; ZGDS, juan 4, n.p.

39. JMA/Swatow/reel 551/LHL 597, 646.

40. FO 228/479 (240–47).

41. Alabaster reporting gossip of Chinese informants, FO 228/479 (268–69).

42. GXCZPZZ, 38: 371.

43. FO 228/493 (268–76).

44. SB, 1: 80–82. On Fang's award, MQSLCZSJ, 291.

45. SB, 3: 404. Fang was heavily involved in judicial matters after 1873. See *Jieyang xian xuzhi* 1890, 1: 89–90; FO 228/855 (20–42); FO 228/867 (16–24).

46. SB, 3: 405.

47. Zeng Guoquan 1969 (1882 memorial), 614: 1963–64; *Chaoyang xianzhi* 1884: 216; ZGDS, juan 4, n.p.

48. SB, 3: 405.

49. SB 3: 405. Routine cases proceeded through normal channels. For example, *Xingbu dang'an/Guangdong si/* case 20081, GX 8; or case 20520, GX 14.4.9.

50. SB, 3: 405.

51. FO 228/891 (249).

52. MQSLCZSJ, 272.

53. MQSLCZSJ, 296–97.

54. Zeng Guoquan 1969, 614: 1964–66. Communist organizers in 1927 insisted that Fang's family had killed and expelled the villagers of Horse Yard Bridge village. See DYCGNGM, 158–59; *Shantou shizhi* 1999, 4:779. On other aspects of De'anli, Lin Kailong 2004: 142–45; *Chao Shan mingren yu guju* 2006: 155–56.

55. Zeng Guoquan 1969, 614: 1963–64; SB, 1: 80–82.

56. GXCZPZZ, 38: 371; 39: 543, 704–5, 776, 863–64; *Qingdai Yueren zhuan*, 2: 575; Chen Zehong 2001: 326–29; *Qingshi gao*, 244: 12677; FO 228/835 (281–90).

57. GXCZPZZ, 38: 818; Liu's comments, 36: 743; 37: 224–25.

58. GXCZPZZ, 41: 403–5. For qingxiang elsewhere in Guangdong, GXCZPZZ, 109: 614–16; 109: 726–27; *Qingdai Yueren zhuan*, 2: 575; *Peking Gazette*, 5 October 1889; 26 November 1889; 14 March 1892; 24 May 1892.

59. GXCZPZZ, 37: 831.

60. R. Bin Wong (2000: 203) describes a "political economy of opium" in general.

61. JM/Swatow/reel 551/LHL 587; LHL 637.

62. *Shantou haiguan zhi*, 17; JMA/Swatow/reel 551/LHL 753; reel 553/LHL 1699.

63. MQSLCZSJ, 272–73; FO 228/354 (92–93).

64. FO 17/505 (237–38); FO 228/458 (257–58); FO 228/493 (312–34, 336–42, 277–96).

65. FO 228/479 (194–239). On *lijin* generated in 1869, Luo Yudong 2010: 628.

66. FO 228/439 (158–68) includes letter from superintendent to Ruilin.

67. FO 228/480 (1–11), quoting from proclamation of circuit intendant of Chao-Hui-Jia.

68. FO 228/479 (194–239).

69. FO 228/439 (141–57); JMA/Swatow/LHL 796; LHL 799; LHL 812; LHL 919. Xie Xiquan (2001: 38) notes that many Shalong Zhengs got their start in the opium business here.

70. FO 228/557 (167–85, 173–74); FO 228/595 (65, 205–6); FO 228/855 (20–42); JM/Swatow/reel553/LHL 1872. On 1878 figures, "Reports on the Treaty Ports, 1878," xvi–xx.

71. On communist fulmination, DYCGNGM, 158–70. On post-Mao accounts, *Chaoyang xianzhi* 1997: 34–35.

72. *Chaoyang xianzhi* 1997: 34–35; CZZ 2005: 2731; on the labor tax, Huang Haohan 2012; CMGJ, 417.

73. *Haiyang xianzhi* 1900, 21: 198; 22: 208; 25: 259; CZZ 2005: 2731; *Chaoyang xianzhi* 1997: 34–35; *Peking Gazette*, May 31, 1888.

74. *Haiyang xianzhi* 1900, 25: 258; 40: 408; Huang Ting 2004: 68. On the Straits, *Anbu zhi* 1990: 361–62, 401.

75. *Jieyang xian xuzhi* (1890), 1: 39; *Haiyang xianzhi* 1900, 25: 260; *Shantou shizhi* 1999, 4: 779; Huang Haohan 2012. On gentry management in general, Kuhn 1970: 211–14.

76. On the projects, *Haiyang xianzhi* 1900, 21: 198; 21: 200; 22: 208; 25: 259. On Haiyang's large granaries, GPA/FO/254.

77. Zeng Guoquan 1969, 614: 1960–61.

78. *Peking Gazette*, 17 September 1874. On a scandal in which Fang coerced a Fujianese into contributing 8,000 taels, "Notes and Queries," JCBRAS 40.4 (2 January 1886): 181–82.

79. Huang Xianzhang 2010: n.p.; Halwart and Gupta 2004: 10–36; also Luo and Han 1990: 299–322; FO 228/867 (92–111).

80. On Fang operations in Ox-Field Sea, *Chaoyang xianzhi* 1997: 35; Huang Xianzhang 2010; FO 228/855 (20–42).

81. CMGJ, 417.

82. "Xianggang Chaoren shangye diaocha gaikuang" in LGCSSZJT, 1–4.

83. The directors of the huiguan included Ding Richang, Chaozhouese governor of Fujian and ally of Fang.

84. *Chaoyang xianzhi* 1884, 6: 97–99; 1997: 35; *Haiyang xianzhi* 1900, 19: 47, 176; 20: 192.

85. Fang's response to undated supervisory report by Zhang Xiangshua, recorded in ZGDS, n.d., n.p.

86. ZGDS, n.d., n.p.

87. *Chaoyang xianzhi* 1884, 21: 91–92.

88. *Chaoyang xianzhi* 1884, 21: 91–92.

89. *Analects* 1979, 5: 16; 14: 9; *Han Feizi* 2001: 342.

Chapter 5

1. FO 228/536 (188), relating comments by Fang.

2. Armitage 2012; Guldi and Armitage 2014: 15, 125.

3. In a Thai refugee camp, the Chinese rocker, Hou Dejian, met a man whose family had emigrated to Vietnam. "Capitalist" peddlers of soymilk, they fled postwar Vietnam for Cambodia, only to flee the Khmer Rouge in the late 1970s. For the historical context of Hou's rock song and the English translation of the lyrics, Jaivin 2001: 65.

4. For example, the suppression of both Huang Wukong's uprising in 1844 and multiple uprisings in 1854. See Tanaka 1993: 52–57.

5. FO 228/503 (245) and (174). Most were campaign targets, but some were landowners who planned to return when the fighting subsided. FO 228/493 (256).

6. Gardner 1897: 622.

7. IMC, Swatow Trade Report, 1870: 132; FO 228/503 (245).

8. SDQ, 64; Zheng Baitao 1993: 36.

9. CZZ, 2005: 2733–40.

10. *Chaoyang xianzhi* 1997: 36.

11. CZZ, 2005: 2165.

12. Fielde 1887: 141. On substitution in village feuds, Macauley 1998: 266–71.

13. Fielde 1887: 142.

14. FO 228/503 (202–20); Chinese-language placards in FO 228/946 (178–83).

15. MQSLCZSJ, 245–46, a *xiedou* in Puning, 1832.

16. CZZ, 2005: 2208–10.

17. Cui Bingyan 1908, n.p., "Chaoyang fengsu," item 16.

18. On problems relating to emigration, CO 275/19 (ccxl–cclxxxii). For a case in which 880 Chaozhouese coolies were incarcerated by "secret societies," ccxlii. Travel by credit ticket had been outlawed at Amoy, transforming Swatow into the port of embarkation for the southeastern poor.

19. JMA/Swatow/LHL 1563 (1871 price); LHL 1903 (1874); LHL 2027 (1875).

20. Phipps 1836: 324–25; Siah 1848: 290.

21. FO 228/503 (248).

22. CO 275/13 (248–49).

23. CO 275/12 (20); CO 275/13 (24).

24. CO 275/13 (8–9). Italics in original.

25. FO 228/493 (256).

26. CO 275/13 (xci–xciv). On the evolution of policing in general, Turnbull 1972: 86–100.

27. Comber 1959: 138.

28. PLCSS, 16 June 1873, appendix 27: cxii.

29. PLCSS, 16 June 1873, appendix 27: cix–cx. On the antagonism between brotherhood societies, Blythe 1969; Yen 1986.

30. FO 228/354 (165).

31. CO 275/16, "Report . . . Riots of October, 1872," 48. Business leaders helped resolve the hawkers' complaints.

32. CO 275/16, 3, 5. On the fame of Chaozhou's fighters, Wakeman 1966: 22–23.

33. CO 275/16, 3.

34. CO 275/32, ARLCSS, 4 March 1887: 155–75.

35. PLCSS, 29 October 1875, "Report of the Inspector-General of Police . . . 1874," cccxxxiv–cccxl; also ARLCSS, 1874 (Singapore, 1875): 109–11.

36. Purcell 1948: 103–14; Andaya and Andaya 2001: 158–60; Leo 2015: 288.

37. GXCZPZZ 42: 125–26; DYCGNGM, 162.

38. DR, 1892–1901, 150; *Chaoyang xianzhi* 1997: 36; Ashmore 1897. On piracy, *New York Times*, 29 September 1891; 15 October 1891.

39. *Shantou haiguan zhi*, 24.

40. Rhoads 1975: 101.

41. Review based on Yen 1976; Rhoads 1975. Further specifics of the Chaozhou experience derived from MCT, 233–40; QTCBMMSHA, 4: 1707–9.

42. Ding Shenzun et al. 2004, 1: 68.

43. MCT, 237; CZZ, 2749–50.

44. Summary based on Rhoads 1975: 110–13; Ding Shenzun et al. 2004, 1: 68–70; additional material from QTCBMMSHA, 4: 1707–9; 39: 12020–23; CZZ, 2005: 2749–50; MCT, 233.

45. MCT, 234.

46. Cui Binyan 1908, n.p.

47. CHD, 464: 1186–87, 8 August 1923.

48. SB, 3: 405.

49. Galbiati 1985.

50. DYCGNGM, 161–62.

51. DYCGNGM, 161–62.

52. DYCGNGM, 161–63. The organizer of the Puning Communist Party in 1927, Chen Kuiya, was a native of Haifeng, not Puning. See Hai-Lu-feng geming genju dishi, 218.

53. Galbiati 1985: 205–7; Marks 1977: 92–94.

54. Other landlords and merchants usually remained unnamed. See DYCGNGM, 165; *Hai-Lu-feng geming genju dishi*, 218. On the marauding Tuyang Fangs, MQSLCZSJ, 241; GPA/FO 931/88 (the Tuyang and Hongyang Fangs had migrated to Puning from Putian, Fujian but had different founding ancestors).

55. Zhang Guotao 1964: 33. On the early communist movement in eastern Guangdong, Galbiati 1985; Hofheinz 1977; Marks 1984.

56. DYCGNGM, 159.

57. *Fang Fang yanjiu*, 2: 2.

58. *Puning xianzhi* 1995: 698–99.

59. On this war in South China, Benton 1992.

60. *Shantou zhinan* 1933: 354–55. Haiyang was renamed Chao'an in 1914.

61. NAS/OHC/HFQ/Wang Changrui (Heng Chiang Swee)/ reel 2.

62. CZZ, 2005: 2765–72.

63. *Hai-Lu-feng geming genju dishi*, 218 (Puning); Marks 1984: 268 (Haifeng).

64. *Hai-Lu-feng geming genju dishi*, 222.

65. NAS/OHC/XXR/Fang Yanshan/ reel 1.

66. NAS/OHC/XXR/Fang Yanshan/ reel 1.

67. NAS/OHC/XXR/Fang Yanshan/ reel 1.

68. NAS/OHC/XXR/Fang Yanshan/ reel 1.

69. NAS/OHC/HFQ/Chen Jinhua/ reel 1.

70. NAS/OHC/HFQ/Chen Jinhua/ reel 1.

71. NAS/OHC/HFQ/Chen Jinhua/ reel 1.

72. ARLCSS, 1928: 41, 55–58; *China Weekly Review*, 28 April 1928.

73. Willmott 1967: 15–18.

74. Willmott 1967: 17–18; Chandler 1992: 160; Delvert 1961: 27.

75. Delvert 1961: 511; Willmott 1967: 59.

76. Delvert 1961: 511–12, 523.

77. *Zhongguo jingji wang*, 16 December 2011, "Fang Qiaosheng: Cong nanmin dao yinhongjia." On Fang Qiaosheng's *guxiang* as Hongyang, http://www.jyql.org/pic_detail.asp?id=109.

78. Fawthrop and Jarvis 2005: 83.

79. *Associated Press News Archive*, June 17, 2001.

80. Kiernan 1996: 295–98, 458–63. Hinton (2005: 15) notes that genocide was complemented by an "autogenocide" of 1,327,000 Khmers.

81. Qiaosheng went into banking. His aunt and uncle eventually recognized Hun Sen's government and helped negotiate an end to the civil war. They encouraged Chaozhouese, like their nephew, to return to Cambodia to rebuild the economy.

Chapter 6

1. Sibing He 2012; Stelle 1940. Trocki (1999) argues that opium buttressed the rise of capitalism and colonialism.

2. Zheng Yingshi 1965: 13–14.

3. XKTBWA, DG 22.12.5; JQ 25.3.15; DG 25.12.10; DG 19.4.25; Macauley 2009.

4. Zheng Yingshi 1965: 1.

5. JMA/Namoa/reel 585/PL 3 (1834).

6. Ye Xian'en 1989, 1: 189. On beancake trade, JMA/Swatow/reel 552/LHL 1113.

7. JMA/Namoa/reel 585/PL 35.

8. JMA/Namoa/reel 585/PL 38.

9. JMA/Namoa/reel 585, PL 2-PL5; PL 30; PL 35; PL 42 (for 1837–1838).

10. JMA/Namoa/reel 585/PL 87; Zhao 1995: 154–58.

11. JMA/Namoa/reel 585/PL 5; PL 8; PL 34; PL 40.

12. JMA/Namoa/reel 585/PL 44; also PL 40.

13. ZJZ, 103 (LFZZ dated DG 18.11.16).

14. AJMR 27 (1829): 435.

15. Ye Xian'en 1989, 1: 189–90; Mazumdar 1998: 311.

16. On these associations in China, Goodman 1995.

17. Ye Xian'en 1989, 1: 190 (Shanghai); MCT, 71–214 (Straits); Viraphol 1977: 104 (Siam).

18. Wang Tao 1960 (orig. 1853), 1: 6a, 21.

19. Ye Xian'en 1989, 1: 190, quoting SBZX, 325, which does not record the amount.

20. Goodman 1995: 58, 131–32.

21. ZJZ, 14–15 (LFZZ, JQ 20.2.21).

22. SBZX, 326.

23. SBZX, 325–30; on dates, Xu Ke 1984, 5: 2318; on control of Desheng, FO 228/804 (366–419).

24. *Chaoyang xianzhi* 1997: 1090; Zhang Guanlan 1987; *Chao Shan baike quanshu* 1994: 202–3. For his banking investments, Shanghai qianzhuang shiliao 1960: 107–9, 756–62. Goodman (1995: 71) notes he learned English working as a cook for foreigners.

25. SBZX, 327.

26. Zheng Yingshi 1965: 1–2; Ping Jinya 1999: 313; Fang Xiaolan and Zhou Xiao 2001: 39; *Chao Shan baike quanshu*: 729.

27. Goodman 1995: 70; Zheng Yingshi 1965: 7.

28. SPER, 8: 221–23; on Zheng Jiechen as defendant, *Shenbao*, 1879.09.03.

29. Zheng Yingshi 1965: 7; Xie Xiquan 2001: 38.

30. ZGDS, juan 3, n.p.; CMGJ, 357–60.

31. Zheng Ruiting 2001: 81–82; SDQ, 73, 226–32. Other descendants of Zheng Xiangde, notably Zheng Wulou (b. 1913), grew wealthy in Siam. See SDQ, 80; *Tai Hua mingren huizhi* 1963: 9.

32. On Yaochen, SDQ, 228; Zheng Ruiting 2001: 83. On Hardoon, Betta 2002; Zheng Yingshi 1965: 2. Hardoon married a woman of Euro-Chinese descent and traveled in Chinese social circles.

33. On Yaochen, SDQ, 228; Zheng Ruiting 2001: 83–84. On his domination of Zhenjiang, Zheng Yingshi 1965: 8; on his role in the huiguan, CHYB, 118/9/8 (12 and 18 March 1917).

34. Zheng Ruiting 2001: 81–87; Zheng Yingshi, 1965.

35. Zheng Ruiting 2001: 82–84.

36. Zheng Ruiting 2001: 86–87; *Chaoyang dashiji*, 59–60.

37. Zheng Ruiting 2001: 86.

38. MQSLCSSJ, 296–97; Zeng Guoquan 1969, 614: 1966; *Peking Gazette*, September 20, 1882. According to Zheng oral tradition, Fang and the military *jinshi*, Zheng Zhicai, hated each other, and Zheng and his brother were victims of a false accusation by Fang. They were saved only by Zhicai's status and connections. SDQ, 72; 209–11.

39. *Shenbao*, GX 11.1.11 (February 25, 1885); FO 228/804 (155–56); 228/855 (20–40). On Li Yuheng (aka Li Sheng), FO 228/634 (136); Cai Rongfang 2001: 28; www.lingkee.com/1900.

40. Wang Tao (1960), 1: 6a, 21.

41. Zheng Yingshi 1965: 7–9.

42. NCH, 10 October 1879: 360; 17 October 1879: 386.

43. SPER, 8: 142, 219.

44. SPER, 8: 142, 219.

45. Murphy 1977: 183–84; Hamilton 1977; Goodman 1995: 130–33; Motono 2000: 92–116. Swatow was the treaty port in Chaozhou and served as shorthand in English for the region.

46. SPER, 8: 220; NCH, 17 October 17: 386; Goodman 1995: 131.

47. JMA/IC/UL/Shanghai/reel 556/LHL 2897.

48. SPER, 8: 220.

49. Hamilton 1977: 54; SPER, 8: 384–91; NCH, 17 October 1879: 384. Historical accounts do not identify the Chaoyang defendants but focus on the Cantonese comprador for Jardine Matheson, Tang Mouzhi, who helped manage the monopoly. Shenbao (1879.09.03) identifies three Chaoyang defendants as Zheng Jiechen, Zheng Shize, and Li Guanzhi. For other disputes involving the Chaoyang bang, Zheng Yingshi 1965: 3–4.

50. FO 228/804 (244–305).

51. On defense arguments, NCH, 17 October 1879, 384–91; SPER, 8: 222–24; Hamilton 1977: 55–59.

52. Zheng Yingshi 1965: 8.

53. SPER, 8: 142, 219.

54. *British Parliamentary Papers*, vol. 31, "Opium War and Opium Trade:" 424–31; Trocki 1990.

55. LeFevour 1968: 16–17; JMA/Swatow/reel 550/LHL 277.

56. JMA/IC/UL/Shanghai/LHL 10764 to 10769 (quote from LHL 10767). Motono (2000: 95) erroneously claims that the foreigners were opposed to the deal out of a commitment to "free trade."

57. Wright and Cartwright 1908: 516; Chen Tong 2005.

58. FO 233/96 (282–93), for example. Zheng Yingshi (1965: 9–10) asserts that Japanese courts invariably sided with Japanese disputants.

59. FO 228/805 (271–72).

60. Numbers computed from table in Luo Yudong 2010: 493.

61. Johnson 2000, 1: 272. Some Chaozhouese sailors remained in Shanghai to work in the opium industry. See QTCBMMSHA, 35: 10479.

62. FO 228/805 (255, 282).

63. FO 228/805 (252).

64. FO 228/805 (281).

65. FO 228/805 (265–66, 281).

66. FO 228/479 (12–49, 156–66, 248–54).

67. FO 228/479 (241).

68. The British could have resolved their lijin problem by ratifying the Chefoo Convention of 1876, in which the Maritime Customs was to collect both the import tariff and lijin, but concern for the interests of British India delayed the agreement to 1887. Owen 1934: 251–78.

69. *Shanghai qianzhuang shiliao* 1960: 107–9, 757–58.

70. Zheng Yifang 1981: 37.

71. *Shanghai qianzhuang shiliao* 1960, 109. View of a bank manager who had married into a Chaoyang opium-dealing family.

72. *Shanghai qianzhuang shiliao*1960: 107–8 (statistics compiled from data on 107–8 and 757). The sources for this collection were former bankers "interviewed" by unnamed compilers.

73. *Shanghai qianzhuang shiliao* 1960: 769–70. Mann Jones (1974) shows that the Ningbo bang controlled native banking in nineteenth-century Shanghai.

74. Murphy 1977: 181–82; Linsun Cheng 2003: 15–16, 138–39, Mann Jones 1972: 47, 71–72.

75. Zheng Ruiting 2001: 84; Zheng Yifang 1981: 36; Song Zuanyou 2007: 45. Young (1931: 682) estimated that the Shanghai tael was worth 32 cents in 1931 U.S. currency. Jianming's investment was worth about $1,044,000 in 2018 U.S. dollars.

76. *Shenbao*, 1895.08.21; 1895.08.23; 1895.08.30; 1895.10.12; 1896.03.19.

77. Zheng Yingshi 1965: 14–15. Yingshi, Zijia's son (p. 20), did not know the amount of the bribe because it was paid by the Yangyao gongsuo.

78. Wakeman 1995: 35–36; Martin 1996: 46.

79. Zheng Yingshi 1965: 15–16.

80. Zheng Yingshi 1965: 10–11.

81. Zheng Yingshi 1965: 13–14.

82. For Chiang's opium policies, Zheng Yingshi 1965: 16–30; Wakeman 1995; Martin 1996.

83. Zheng Yingshi 1995: 16–18. Others unsuccessfully branched into morphine (18–20).

84. Zheng Yingshi 1965: 22–25.

85. Keswick (1982) edited a family business history that refers to the role of opium in their rise even as it celebrated 150 years of commercial success, a level of historical honesty rarely matched in China and the United States.

86. Précis of his life in Ingham 1983: 824–26, which does not mention the opium trade.

87. XKTBWA, DG 21.2.9; YPZZ, 1: 361–62; ZJZ, 5.

88. FO 17/278 (85–100).

89. Michie 1900, 1: 369. On lobbyist influence, FO 17/279 (102–4).

90. NCH, 13 October 1879: 470.

91. NCH, 17 October 1879: 384.

92. CO 273/534/24; FO 228/613.

93. Hou 1965: 17, 51.

Chapter 7

1. Spence 1999: 181–82; Rowe 2009: 192–93; Hevia 2003: 39.

2. Zhao 1995: 163–67; MQSLCZSJ, 268.

3. Zhao 1995: 162; CZZ 1949, "Yan'ge zhi": 16, 50; FO 228/595 (66).

4. Scarth 1860: 55–56.

5. FO 228/557 (168–69). On multinationalism of British crews, FO 656/25 (2).

6. Chen Zehong 2001: 132–33; Zhao 1995: 158; Dennys and Mayers 1867: 232. For depositions of forty-one coolies rescued from kidnappers off the Guangdong coast, FO 17/320 (153–99). Locals resented the firm Bradley and Co. Charles Bradley was the Swatow agent in the 1850s for

Tait and Co., a major shipper of coolie labor. Indeed, James Tait had been designated "vice-consul for Spain" at Amoy, and Bradley circulated the "royal decrees" of the Spanish court in an effort to recruit migrants to Cuba and Puerto Rico (JMA/Swatow/reel 550/LHL 206).

7. On abuses related to the trade between Chaozhou and the Straits, CO 275/19, "Report of Committee Appointed to Consider . . . Condition of Chinese Labour in the Colony," 1876.

8. CZZ 2005: 2725. FO 228/293 (2–3).

9. FO 228/315 (3: 1–6); FO 228/333 (2: 4–7).

10. FO 17/435 (405).

11. FO 228/315 (2: 19–24); JMA/Swatow/reel 551/LHL 763.

12. *Shantou haiguan zhi*, 17; FO 228/293 (1: 43–60).

13. FO 228/293 (1: 54–55); Chinese version FO 228/296 (28–30). Quotation combines both versions.

14. Cohen 2003: 151

15. Wakeman 1966: 56.

16. Zeng Guoquan 1969, 614: 1957–1969.

17. Zeng Guoquan 1969, 614: 1957–1969; *Haiyang xianzhi* 1900, 15: 31–34; 28: 1098; 40: 1576–77; FO 228/315 (3: 33–70).

18. FO 228/293; 228/315; 228/333; 228/354. On spying, FO 228/293 (59) and FO 17/435 (411); on ship attacks, FO 228/315 (2: 49) and FO 228/296 (48). Also Dennys 1867: 233.

19. FO 228/396 (104–12); FO 17/435 (417). On Christianity, Joseph Lee 2003.

20. FO 228/458 (254–67); FO 228/536 (130). Richardson was the British partner in Bradley and Co.

21. MQSLCZSJ, 281–86; GXCZPZZ, 42: 205.

22. FO 228/458 (82–100).

23. JMA/Chin Chew[Quanzhou]/reel 525/LHL 15; JMA/Namoa/reel 544/LHL 10 and LHL 1 to 27 (1844–1860).

24. JMA/Swatow/reel 551/LHL 506.

25. JMA/Swatow/reel 550/LHL 441 and reel 551/LHL 591.

26. Munn 2000: 107.

27. JMA/Swatow/reel 550/LHL 294; LHL 425. Shanghai also experienced silver shortages. See JMA/Shanghai reel 373/LHL 14. On SE Asia as a source of silver, JMA/Swatow/reel 550/LHL 94; LHL 32; JMA/Swatow/reel 551/LHL 535.

28. JMA/Swatow/reel 551/LHL 563; LHL 564.

29. FO 228/354 (169–77); JM/Swatow/reel 551/LHL 591. The "government bank" was the Haiguan bank, which was a branch of a Cantonese bank solely responsible for remitting government revenue to Canton. DR 1892–1901: 163.

30. JMA/Swatow/reel 550/LHL 12; LHL 35; LHL 245; LHL 269.

31. JMA/Swatow/reel 550/LHL 35; LHL 86.

32. Hamashita (2008: 138–39) has shown that British traders resorted to barter in Shanghai. In Swatow we see both Chinese (JM/Swatow/reel 550/LHL 172) and British (LHL 456) bartering opium for other goods. But in Swatow, Chinese tea and sugar sellers preferred cash, not opium, from British customers because they feared they might be attacked by other Chinese protecting their opium markets. See JM/Swatow/reel 550/LHL 463.

33. Chang 1964: 38–39.

34. DR 1892–1901: 163–64.

35. FO 17/457 (69–70).

36. JMA/Swatow/reel 552/LHL 1154 and LHL 1780; FO 228/634 (136–40).

37. FO 228/458 (n.p.).

38. Eighteenth-century revenues, *Shantou haiguan zhi*, 15; for 1870s, *Reports on the Trade at the Treaty Ports, 1878*, lxxv; for 1891 figures, DR 1882–1891: xxix–xxxi.

39. *Report on Trade at the Treaty Ports in China, 1875*, 28.

40. *Swatow Trade Report, 1875*, 272; 1886: 330; 1895: 407. For sugar, FO 17/411 (24); FO 228/880 (Annex B). In 1874 the haiguan tael was worth £1.

41. FO 228/880 (180).

42. JMA/Swatow/reel 552/LHL 1190.

43. FO 228/835 (259–62, 285–309).

44. Reports on Trade at Treaty Ports, 1880 (1881): 9; 1881 (1882): 244–45.

45. Mazumdar 1998: 383–85.

46. Republic of China, *Sugar Trade in China, 1928*, 1069–78.

47. FO 228/595 (205–6).

48. *Reports on Trade at Treaty Ports, 1880*, 243. Peasants purchased fertilizer on long credit, so the expanded use of beancake represented greater confidence in assuming debt. Ye Xian'en 1989, 1: 190.

49. Cui Bingyan 1908, n.p.

50. CSDQZ, 7.

51. Jiang Zuyuan and Fang Zhiqin 1993: 372–73.

52. FO 228/458 (82–100).

53. FO 228/480 (35–43).

54. FO 228/835 (259–62; 285–309); *Trade Report for Swatow, 1889*, 378.

55. FO 228/613 (23).

56. Dennys and Mayers 1867: 235.

57. On the company, Zhu 2012: 4, 172.

58. Chen Haizhong 2011: 83–85; DR 1882–91: 537. It evolved out of the old Zhangzhou-Chaozhou guild.

59. FO 228/536 (246).

60. FO 228/536 (242–43); Chinese-language version, FO 228/946 (145).

61. FO 228/536 (242–43); FO 228/946 (145).

62. FO 228/536 (246).

63. FO 228/536 (247).

64. JM/Swatow/reel 555/LHL 2664; LHL 2670.

65. JM/Swatow/reel 555/LHL 2664; LHL 2670; FO 228/855 (11–14, 43–61).

66. FO 228/293 (3: 17–19); Chinese version, FO 228/296 (9–10); FO 228/294 (105); Thomson 1875: 287.

67. NAS/OHC/HFQ/Wang Changrui/ reel 3.

68. CHD 463: 607 (8.15/1922); 464: 928 (1/22/1923).

69. JMA/Swatow/reel 554/LHL 1880.

70. Wright and Cartwright 1908, 1: 216, 836.

71. Zhao 1995: 159; JM/Swatow/reel 550/LHL 460; FO 17/536 (141–42); FO 228/536 (181).

72. *Swatow Trade Report, 1879*, 206–8.

73. *Swatow Trade Report, 1879,* 207–08.

74. China, *Native Customs, 1902–1906, Swatow Report,* 90.

75. FO 228/557 (168–69).

76. On this Supreme Court, see memoirs of its first chief justice, Edward Hornby 1928: 191–330.

77. FO 17/397 (236–41); FO 17/414 (1–6).

78. FO 17/435 (352–57).

79. Statistics culled from semiannual reports, FO 656 (25–63).

80. Alcock observed in 1869 that this phenomenon was not unknown in China. FO 881/1861 (5–7), but there is no record of it at Swatow.

81. FO 656/25 (2–3); FO 228/595 (138–41).

82. King 1924: 33.

83. FO 656/25 to 656/63. The sodomy case (FO 228/333 [1: 8–9]) was deemed a false accusation in spite of the fact that it included nine witnesses for the accuser, a Chinese servant. In the case of the insulted wife, a drunken sailor verbally abused her on deck, declaring that a scrape on her nose had been caused by her own excessive drinking. FO 656/25 (11).

84. FO 228/557 (70).

85. FO 228, years 1860 through 1890. Some debt cases might have been resolved without the consulate reporting the fact. See FO 228/880 (182–206). The cases of murder and attempted murder were never solved, but the Chinese officials did their best to find the culprits. I did not include an unresolved case involving a robbery of the consulate, for Caine himself was the likely perpetrator of the crime.

86. Huang 1993.

87. DR 1882–1891: 538–39.

88. FO 881/1861, No. 68. ("China Report: Swatow").

89. FO 228/634 (23–24); FO 228/480 (14–21).

90. CO 275/13, 13 November 1871.

91. FO 228/480 (38).

92. FO 228/373 (177–236); FO 228/354 (147–64); FO 228/396 (122). Compromise reached—in Singapore—after two years.

93. FO 656/63 (2); FO 228/354 (238).

94. Hertslet 1896, 2: 558; Norton-Kyshe 1898: 99; Great Britain, *Report of the Royal Commissions for Inquiries into the Laws of Naturalization and Allegiance* 1869: 64. The Singaporean-born leader of the Small Sword Society claimed extraterritorial immunity. He was executed anyway, as we have seen (QTCBMMSHA, 35: 10335–37).

95. Brooks 2000; Man-houng Lin 2001; Thilly 2018.

96. Norton-Kyshe 1898: 164; FO 656/25 (6); FO 228/419 (306–8).

97. FO 228/634 (5–10); CSDQZ: 7; FO 228/419 (306–8).

98. FO 228/634 (5–10). In 1881 six women also registered, but their names were not recorded. FO 228/688 (18–19).

99. MCT, 199–200.

100. MCT, 199. Changyi first registered with consulate in 1867, FO 656/25 (5).

101. FO 228/634 (246–47). Other diaspora Chinese registered land at Swatow, FO 656/25 (5); FO 656/25 (6).

102. Song Ong Siang 1984: 142.

103. FO 656/63 (1). On Yap's naturalization, FO 228/634 (5–10); on Jury List, FO 656/25 (8).

104. CO 275/19 (134–36); CO 275/12 (24). On the great commercial clans of Penang, including the Khoos, Yee Tuan Wong (2007). For a biography of Teang Poh, Yee Tuan Wong (2011). The Khoos had moved to Malaya in 1527.

105. Thean Tek was sentenced to death, but Yee Tuan Wong (2011: 148) and Blythe (1969: 138–48) note that the British feared that Penang Fujianese would riot if their leader were executed.

106. Colonial authorities were aware of the abuses of the coolie trade among Swatow, the Straits, and Sumatra. See CO 275/19, "Report of Committee Appointed to Consider . . . Condition of Chinese Labourers in the Colony."

107. FO 228/574 (43–68, 133–55). On guild rejection of emigration firms, FO 228/536 (234–48); FO 228/557 (188–200).

108. Carroll 2005.

109. CO 882/5/17 (7–10, 28–32). The Qing similarly failed to force Chaozhouese to abandon the Mexican dollar in the 1830s. See MQSLCZSJ, 242, 244.

Chapter 8

1. PLCSS, 24 July 1879, "Annual Report . . . Protector . . . 1879," xlv–liii.

2. *Chaozhou fuzhi* 1893, juan 12: 130; Cui Bingyan 1908: 5b, 11a.

3. Cui Bingyan 1908: 11a (quote); *Chaozhou fuzhi* 1893, juan 12: 130. Both sources appear to address obliquely the less constrained lives of Hakka and half-mountain Hakka women, who tended to live in mountainous areas.

4. JMA/Swatow/reel 554/LHL 2325.

5. MCT, 396. Data include forty-nine foreigners.

6. Ma 1921: 1–37; DR 1912–1921: 178; population figures (for 1923), CZZ 2005: 2142. Cui Bingyan (1908: 11b) noted that lineage girls' schools were established in rural areas.

7. CSDQ, 7–8.

8. Ping-ti Ho 1959: 58–62; Rowe 2007: 18; Lee and Feng 1999: 47–65; Lillian Li 2007: 315. Lee and Campbell (1997: 65–70, 95–96) demonstrate that one-fifth to one-quarter of all girls born between 1774 and 1873 in the region they studied were infanticide victims.

9. SDQ, 64–65.

10. *Nanyō ni okeru kakyō* 1914: 46. Most *kezhan* patrons were from Jiayingzhou, Dabu, and Fengshun, for Chaoyang and Chenghai villagers traveled directly to port from home.

11. PLCSS, 24 July 1879, "Annual Report, Protector, 1878," xlv–liii.

12. CO 275/25: 306.

13. Skinner (1996: 63) describes the bilateral kinship practices of the Straits-born.

14. CO 275/25: 322–42.

15. Skinner 1957b: 61, 126. On the twentieth century, GPA, G2013-*Huaqiao shiliao*-0044.

16. *Straits Settlements, Report for 1921* (1922): 42.

17. Smedley 1956: 207.

18. Smedley 1956: 207.

19. Kulp 1925: 332–33.

20. Sang 2003.

21. Kulp 1925: 278–81. Bao (2005: 36) writes perceptively about these women in post-1930s China. For a post-1930s account of Fujianese "left-behind wives," Huifen Shen 2012.

22. Smedley 1956: 207.

23. Kulp 1925: 185. This probably had always been the case but was represented as a new and "increasing" development.

24. Lee and Feng (1999: 70–72), who added that 10 to 20 percent of males went unmarried and that the percentage of bachelor males in South China was lower than in North China.

25. Chen Ta 1940: 137.

26. NAS/OHC/HFQ/Chen Jinhua/ reel 1.

27. NAS/OHC/HFQ/Chen Jinhua/ reel 4.

28. NAS/OHC/HFQ/Wang Chunquan/ reel 1. Wang's great-grandfather was from Hainan, but successive generations married Chaozhouese, and the younger generation were Chaozhou speakers. They also were shareholders in Sze Hai Tong Bank.

29. NAS/OHC/HFQ/Chen Jinhua/ reel 4.

30. NAS/OHC/HFQ/Wang Changrui/ reel 3.

31. Remer 1933: 178.

32. On *liangtou jia* in post-1930s Siam and China, Bai 2005: 48.

33. NAS/OHC/HFQ/Wang Chunquan/ reel 1.

34. NAS/OHC/HFQ/Chen Jinhua/ reels 1, 3, and 4.

35. MCT, 181.

36. NAS/OHC/HFQ/Wang Changrui/ reel 4.

37. Jung-fang Tsai 1993: 73.

38. MCT, 199–200.

39. On the complicated case details, see ST, 26 June 1929: 17; 7 July 1932: 12; 29 July 1932: 12; 19 April 1933: 6; 21 April 1933: 6; 6 July 1933: 4.

40. Bernhardt 1999: 101–3, 141.

41. NAS, PLCSS, 2 April 1877, "Report of Committee Appointed to Enquire into . . . Contagious Disease Ordinance," xliii.

42. Lin Dachuan 1857, 2: 12–15. Lin flourished from the late eighteenth to nineteenth century.

43. Ju Han 1989: 192–94, 200 (quotes Yuan and Zhao at length). On Dan prostitutes, Yu 1994, 743; Ju Han 1989: 200; Hansson 1996: 130.

44. Gutzlaff 1968: 88–89.

45. Lin Juncong 1987; Hai 1989.

46. Shen Fu 2011 [orig. 1811?]: 105–7; Shen Fu (Chinese version) 2008, juan 4, n.p.; Hansson (1996: 129) notes that many prostitutes were not Dan, but Cantonese disdained them anyway.

47. Xu Ke 1869–1928, 10: 4914. On prostitution in Shanghai in general, Hershatter 1997.

48. *Chaozhou fuzhi* 1893, juan 12:6, 131.

49. *Shantou zhinan* 1933: 108–9.

50. CO 275/19, appendix 2.

51. Lim 1958.

52. NAS, PLCSS, 2 April 1877, "Report . . . Contagious Disease," xliii, xlviii. Macaoese spoke Cantonese.

53. NAS, PLCSS, 2 April 1877: xliii–xlvii, lxi–lxii. Warren (1993) claimed that most prostitutes were "Cantonese," but he relied on English-language sources and may not have been aware of the British tendency to use "Canton" to identify both the city (Guangzhou) and the province of which it was the capital, Guangdong.

54. Details from NAS, PLCSS, 2 April 1877, xliii–lix. For a history of prostitution that focuses on the difficulties, Warren 1993.

55. NAS, PLCSS, 2 April 1877, appendix B and K. On boys: lxiii–lxiv. Turnbull (1977: 87) claimed that most male prostitutes were Hainanese.

56. NAS, PLCSS, 2 April 1877, lx. On children calling them "mother," CO 275/32, "Annual Report, Civil Hospitals, 1886," 48–50; and CO 275/34, PLCSS, 12 December 1888: 109–22.

57. Sommer 2000.

58. Sommer 2015.

59. NAS, PLCSS, 2 April 1877, lxix; NLS, Kyshe's Reports, Microfilm 3499: 385–86, case of mother selling underage daughter to brothel in 1888.

60. CO 275/30, PLCSS, 24 March 1885, "Report, Chinese Protectorate, 1884."

61. Wolf 1972: 208. For a similar Japanese dynamic, Stanley 2012; Warren 1993: 194.

62. NAS, PLCSS, 2 April 1877, xliv.

63. CO 275/30, PLCSS, 24 March 1885, "Report, Chinese Protectorate, 1884."

64. Warren 1993: 320–23.

65. NLS, Kyshe's Reports, Microfilm 3499: 685–88.

Chapter 9

1. DR 1902–1911: 119.

2. *I Ching*, 670.

3. Skinner 1957a; Skinner 1957b: 244–48.

4. Skinner 1957a: 243; Skinner 1957b: 244–48; Kuhn 2008: 298.

5. Andaya and Andaya 2001: 139–47; Huen 2003. Amrith (2011: 11) assesses the scholarship describing the tendency of all Asian groups to gather into ethnic "enclaves."

6. Skinner 1996: 85–86, building on Trocki 1990: 233–39.

7. Biography in MCT, 199.

8. Ye Xian'en 1989, 1: 224–25. Village dated to the seventeenth century. *Chaozhou fuzhi* 1676, juan 1: 1676.

9. On Jianfa's early life, *Anbu zhi* 1990: 353; on Sarawak, Chin 1981: 43–56, 73–74; Lockard 1971: 197–200. On the Chaozhou sampan monopoly in Singapore, *Nanyō ni okeru kakyō* 1914: 58.

10. MCT, 285.

11. Drabble 1973: 1–24.

12. MCT, 199–200. Liu Sen, Liu Hanxi, and Liu Xiaoqin (Low How Kim) were also in the business. On the leading role of the Lius in the business, Kathirithamby-Wells 2005: 102.

13. On Low Ah Jit and Paterson, Simons, MCT, 199. On Paterson, Simons, Macmillan 1907: 290. On TC&M, Headrick 1988: 102; http://Atlantic-cable.com/CableCos/BritishMfrs/.

14. On cable installation, Headrick 1988: 98–108.

15. NAS, *Governor's Diary*, Microfilm NL 159: 71.

16. On case, ST, 21 January 1865: 1; on brotherhood, Blythe 1969: 79–80, 114, 161.

17. NCH, 27 December 1913; ST, 28 May 1902: 4.

18. On Kunyi's election to the chamber, MCT, 200; on the chamber, Yen 1986: 190.

19. On associate firms, MCT, 199; on Rongli, LGCSSZJT, 4. On Xiaoqin's management of Rongli, Song 1984: 191. Choi (2015: 74) describes *lianhao* as "companies whose shares are cross-owned by close relatives but are financially and administratively independent."

20. MTC, 199. They do not specify a year.

21. Clouth 1903: 213–15; noting that "the Chinese have nearly the whole of the trade."

22. Wood, Taft, et al. 1902: 39.

23. Kathirithamby-Wells 2005: 102; on their Borneo interests, ST, 17 July 1893: 2 and 19 July 1893: 2. Kathirithamby-Wells (2005: 45–47, 69–70) notes that the Orang Asli, the aboriginal people of the Malay Peninsula, were the "best collectors" of gutta because they were familiar with the forest terrain and were skilled at felling and tapping the trees. Chinese and Malays supervised the work and marketed the product. Its rising price led to "indiscriminate" felling of trees as all parties sought to benefit from the forests' bounty. The ruler of Johor also established a monopoly over its production at one point.

24. *Nanyō ni okeru kakyō* 1914: 74–76.

25. On the syndicate, Trocki 1990: 197. On How Kim's farm, Wynne 2000: 344.

26. MCT, 199–200; *Nanyō ni okeru kakyō* 1914: 75; *Kaikyō shokuminchi gairan* 1918: 188.

27. "Xianggang chaoren shangye diaocha gaikuang," in LGCSSZJT, 3–4.

28. *Haiyang xianzhi* 1900, 19:45, 175; and 25: 28, 259.

29. Tan Ee Leong 1961: 456–57.

30. On Liao, MCT, 181–82. On Lan, MCT, 211.

31. For original board, MCT, 16; for 1913 board, ST, 30 December 1913: 14; for Seah's ascension to board, ST, 13 April 1914: 14.

32. On kangchus and opium, Yen 1986: 264. Trocki (1979; 1990) has written extensively of the connection between the gambier economy and opium.

33. Song 1984: 21.

34. NAS/OHC/*Economic Development of Singapore*/David Beng Hwee Chew, reel 5.

35. Yap 1982: 36; Yuen 2013: 353.

36. ST, 9 February 1915: 9 (annual report for 1914). The report for 1915 stated that the bank repaid the loan, indicating that it was otherwise in good financial condition. ST, 31 January 1916: 8.

37. ST, 13 September 1920: 5; MCT, 200.

38. MCT, 200. Kunyi's sons assumed Low Ah Jit's liabilities, which is why their aunt Low Soon Wah sued them but not Changyi's sons. In 1950 the firm was run by Liu Fanmao, Kunyi's grandson.

39. DR 1892–1901, 2:153–54. Rice was imported from Southeast Asia and the Lower Yangzi.

40. DR 1892–1901, 2: 155.

41. *Shantou zhinan* 1933: 354–55; on the 1860s, FO 228/458 (map, n.p.).

42. DR 1892–1901, 2: 154.

43. NAS/OHC/HFQ/Chen Jinhua, reel 3. Tenant harvesters were Thai.

44. DR 1891–1902, 2: 155. Rush (1990: 102) notes that half the sugar plantations on Java were Chinese-owned, but the native place of most of those owners was Fujian.

45. On Chaozhouese dominance in general, Latham and Neal 1983: 274; Godley 1981: 47; Choi 2015: 53. On the Guos, MCT, 169; *Anbu zhi* 1990: 355, 361–62, 405.

46. LaFargue 1909: 282. He estimated that 20,000 Chaozhouese resided there in 1909.

47. Wright, Cartwright, and Breakspear 1908: 146.

48. On the Singapore-Saigon rice trade prior to 1850, Li Tana 2004.

49. Brown 1994: 129. Chen Cihong was not part of the Sze Hai Tong network.

50. Yuen 2013: 353. On capital needs of the rice trade, Li Tana 2004: 267.

51. "Xianggang chaoren shangye diaocha gaikuang," LGCSSZJT, 14.

52. LGCSSZJT, 1–5.

53. FO 228/634 (5–10), which records one Chinese character for Tan Gwan Seng incorrectly. On the firm's role in the Guild, FO 228/978 (257). On the cloth mill, *Zhongguo jindai gongyeshi ziliao*, 2: 1048–49, quoting *Shenbao*, 17 November 1880. It is possible that the father-in-law was one of Yuting's brothers, Chen Quande or Chen Yanchu. Yuting, however, was considered the primary founder of the firm. On the Chens, https://read01.com/nMNE2e.html. On the Chens as a prominent Anbu family with overseas connections, *Shantou shizhi* 1999, 4: 575.

54. "Xianggang chaoren shangye diaocha gaikuang," LGCSSZJT, 1–2.

55. Choi 1995, 1998, and 2015; also Tsai 1993: 72–75; Suehiro 1989: 118; Wright, Cartwright, and Breakspear 1908: 169.

56. NLS, Supreme Court Suit #1320 of year 1931 (NSL online), http://mms.elibraryhub.com/SHC/Koh%20Seow%20Chuan%20Collection/Writ%20Of%20Summons/040000519.pdf . Also *Le Bao*, 13 November 1931: 7.

57. ST, 14 October. 1916: 9; 26 September 1918: 20; 18 March 1916: 8.

58. Details in CHD, 463: 619–39, 23 August 1922; 464: 1095–98. Also CZZ 2005: 2767; LGCSSZJT (essay on "Huishi jiyao"), 4–8. CZZ estimates that 34,500 people died, and the Customs reported 70,000 perished. Typhoon referred to in Chinese sources as the Ba'er fengzai (the hurricane of 2 August). *Shantou zhinan* 1933: 105. See also *Le Bao*, 7 August 1922: 3; 8 August 1922: 3.

59. Report of the General Committee of the Hongkong General Chamber of Commerce, 1922: 395.

60. Chen Chunsheng 1997: 374–75, 388.

61. Chen Chunsheng 1997: 377, 382.

62. CHD 463: 705–7; CZZ 2005: 2767; *Shantou haiguan zhi* 1988: 24.

63. MCT, 200.

64. *Shantou zhinan* 1933: 105–6; Chen Chunsheng 1997: 382–83. The Wannianfeng Guild evolved into the Chamber of Commerce in 1901.

65. *Shanghai Chaozhou huiguan yi'an beicha* 118: 13 (21 November 1922); meeting concerning embankments, chaired by Guo (11 August and 27 September 1922). See also 22 August, 4 September, and 10 September 1922.

66. On the ritual practices and social organization of *shantang*, Shiga 2008; Chee-Beng Tan 2012; Li Zhixian 2004; 2006. By the Republican period there were 170 shantang throughout Chaozhou, most dedicated to the spiritual messages of Master Song Dafeng (Song Dafeng zushi), a popular local deity.

67. Shiga 2008: 44; Chee-Beng Tan 2012: 82.

68. *Chaozhou huiguan yi'an beicha* 118: 13 (4 September 1922); LGCSSZJT (essay on "Huishi jiyao"), 5. Shalong Zhengs sent relief to their own benevolent hall, the Xiude Benevolent Hall of Shalong. See SDFQL, 232.

69. Li Zhixian 2004: 242; on Siam, Tamaki 2007.

70. On the Shiqin tang and the Liulong tongxianghui, see *Xinjiapo Chaozhou bayi huiguan jinxi ji'nian kan* 1980: 165; Shijie Chaoshang, http://ww.wchbp.com.

71. Li Zhixian 2006: 63–74.

72. MCT, 200.

73. On these struggles, Yen 1986: 188–91; MCT, 331–33. On the Lius' role, *Xinjiapo Chaozhou bayi huiguan jinxi jiniankan*, 154. On obligation to pay silver, NAS/OHC/*Pioneers of Singapore*/ Lien Ying Chao/ reel 13.

74. On the anti-Seah faction, Yen 1986: 190. On Lius, MCT, 16, 200; *Xinjiapo Duanmeng xuexiao sanshi zhounian jiniance* 1936: 11 and chap. 3, n.p.

75. MCT, 200.

76. ST, 16 September 1939; MCT, 200.

77. ST, 14 July 1951: 2.

78. Chun-hsi Wu 1967: 15.

79. Cui Bingyan 1908: 4b.

80. Pre–World War I figures Hicks 1993, book 1: 65; 1920s figures, Remer 1933: 182–83 (his estimates were based on research into Hong Kong and American banks and tend to be higher than those compiled locally).

81. Hicks 1993, book 1: 78; population figures book 2: 124.

82. Remer 1933: 179; DR 1922–1931, 2: 155; Chun-hsi Wu 1967: 15.

83. Hicks 1993, book 2: 153.

84. On this also see Chen Liyuan 2007.

85. Quoted in Chen Ta 1940: 75; also Yow 2013: 31.

86. There was modern development in Chaozhou. Overseas Chinese and the Japanese invested in a railroad connecting Swatow to Chaozhou city. Modern factories were also established. But this cannot be compared to the economic development fostered by Chaozhouese in Southeast Asia or Shanghai. The Mutual Aid Society of Shantou Overseas Chinese in the Nanyang encouraged overseas Chinese to foster industrialization. Significantly, however, the funds they raised from 1931 to 1934 mostly went to sustaining the organization itself (salaries, stationery, food, etc.). SNHHSB 1934, sections on "Organization," 1–2 and "Finances," 1–4.

87. Hicks 1993, book 1: 65–70, 96.

88. Hicks 1993, book 1: 74.

89. On Guangyiyu, Hicks 1993, book 1: 78, 96–98; Cai Peirong 2002: 128; Chen Liyuan 2007: 52–53.

90. CSDQZ, 98.

91. Hicks 1993, book 1: 97.

92. CHD, 1330: 5982–84, 24 April 1912 (on Guangyi bank); 1330: 5963–66 (on Lin); 1330: 5971–76, 21 March 1912 (on Chamber of Commerce). Lin, a Hakka, was rumored to have embarked on a ship with two thousand soldiers to "take forcible possession of whatever funds he could find."

93. CHD, 1330: 5936–38, 25 December 25 1911. The faction was led by Zhang Licun.

94. Chen Ta 1940: 78.

95. Chen Ta 1940: 6–7. The region studied, "Z," was located in the vicinity of Yuepu village.

96. Chen Ta 1940: 82–84.

97. On Siamese rice markets, Sompop Manarungsan 2000: 189–90; on those of Saigon and Cambodia, Norlund 2000: 206–9. Siamese rice exports rose in these years, but the price plunged. Boomgaard and Brown (2000a) caution that it is difficult to generalize about the Depression in Southeast Asia. The crisis had disparate impacts.

98. Turnbull 2005: 146; Khanh 1986: 144; Skinner 1957b: 177.

99. GPA, G2013: *Huaqiao shiliao* 0055; also 0057, 0058, 0059.

100. Hicks 1993, book 2: 153; Cheong, Lee, and Lee 2013: 75 and 91.

101. Chen Ta 1940: 86.

102. Kulp 1925: xxiii, 104–5.

103. FO 228/439 (94–112); FO 228/419 (306–8).

104. NAS/OHC/HFQ/Wang Changrui/ reel 1. On sojourning destinations of branch five, reel 2.

105. NAS/OHC/HFQ/Wang Changrui/ reel 1. On night soil incidents, reel 3.

106. NAS/OHC/HFQ/Wang Changrui/ reel 1. On conditional sales and feuds in the eighteenth century, Macauley 1998: 229–78.

107. NAS/OHC/HFQ/Wang Changrui/ reel 3.

108. NAS/OHC/HFQ/Wang Changrui/ reels 1 and 3.

109. FO 228/634 (246–47). On average farm size, Alfred H. Y. Lin 1997: 36.

110. On the 1934 attack, *Min Yue bianqu sannian youji zhanzheng shiliao huibian* 1985, 2: 64–67. In 1927 a ninety-person delegation from the village traveled to Swatow to seek refuge and government assistance. See *Anbu zhi* 1990: 421–22.

111. On communist kidnapping tactics, Benton 1992: 78, 92, 147, 308.

112. DR 1912–1921: 169; 1922–1931: 155, 165.

113. Chen Liyuan 2007: 234; Cheong, Lee, and Lee 2013: 92–93.

114. NAS/OHC/HFQ/Wang Changrui/ reel 1.

115. NAS/OHC/HFQ/Wang Changrui/ reel 1; on coffins, *Time Magazine*, 4 February 1946: 34; on famine, Hong Kong PRO, HKMS2021–10: 67–68.

116. Li Li-san 1964: 16–17.

Conclusion

1. CSDQZ, 7–8. Numbers do not include those who departed from smaller ports.

2. Liang 1957: 51–55. On nomenclature, Sai 2013: 60; Wang Gungwu 1981b. Liang identifies Ye Lai (Yap Ah Loy) as having hailed from Jiayingzhou but Carstens (2005: 13) identifies him as a Huizhou Hakka.

3. Liang 1957: 52–53. On Goujian as a cultural hero, Cohen 2009.

4. MQSLCZSJ, 181. Headman (*toumu*) is the term used in the Ming dynastic history to refer to the "pirate" chieftain of Old Port Palembang, Chen Zuyi, who was defeated by Zheng He in 1407. See *Mingshi*, 324: 8408.

5. Liang 1957: 55.

6. Sai 2013, building on Wang Gungwu 1981b.

7. Duara 1997: 1049. Others who have considered the transnationalism of nationalist discourses include Kuhn 2008; Jing 2006: 247 (who refers to a "diasporic frontier" that was "reincorporated into the national imagination"); Carstens 2005.

8. Chan 2018: 64. She refers to this as "a great convergence."

9. SNHHSB 1934: preface.

10. MCT, 354–64.

11. Li Changfu 1966: 4–6.

12. Li Changfu 1966: 14–20. He charted four periods of Chinese colonialism starting in the thirteenth century.

13. On "settlement," *Chenghai xianzhi* 1992: 838–39; on "style," Zeng Shaocong 1998: 199.

14. Zeng Shaocong 1998: 199, 227–28. He repeats the phrase "peaceful coexistence and mutual development" three times in two pages. He is aware that the Qing incorporated Taiwan into their empire, but in this part of his analysis he does not consider that to have been comparable to colonial conquest. Li Changfu (1966: 3–4) advances similar interpretations with regard to the Qing conquest of Central Asia.

15. Zeng Shaocong 1998: 222, 225–26. Liang Qichao (1957) advanced similar arguments.

16. For quote, Conklin and Fletcher 1999: 1. On the scholarly consensus that colonial conquest depended on states relying on superior military power, Barua 2003: 1. On the role of culture and "knowledge production" in colonial control, Cohn 1996.

17. Osterhammel 1986: 298.

18. Cain and Hopkins 2016: 59.

19. On anti-Sinicism in Siam, see chapter 9; also Kuhn 2008: 226–29, 287–318. For comparisons between European anti-Semitism and Southeast Asian anti-Sinicism, Chirot and Reid 1997. For a rumination on the European conflation of anti-Semitism and anti-Sinicism, Geller 2011: 50–87.

20. On Italian emigration and state-building, Choate 2008: 1–58. Comparison to China mine.

21. Peattie 1984: 123–25.

22. Chan 2018: 55–65.

23. Purcell 1965: 153.

24. Sack 1986: 1–2.

25. Heidhues 2003: 78–79.

26. Gao and Jia 2013; claims rebutted in U.S. Department of State 2014.

27. Thucydides 1972: 402–8, 614–16. Athenians advanced this argument to convince the people of Melos to surrender and pay tribute to Athens even though the Melians sought to remain neutral in the Peloponnesian War. When the Melians refused, the Athenians slaughtered the men and made slaves of the women and children. They then established a "colony" to complete the conquest of the island.

28. Zakaria 1999: 19, among others.

BIBLIOGRAPHY

Archival and Unpublished Sources

FIRST HISTORICAL ARCHIVES OF CHINA, BEIJING

Xingbu dang'an/anjuan/Guangdong si/ touqiang, hunjia, tuzhai, qita [Archives of the Board of Punishments/cases/Guangdong division/robbery, marriage, land and debts, and miscellaneous categories].

Xingke tiben, weijin anjian [Routine memorials of the Board of Punishments, contraband cases].

Zhupi zouzhe, falü, lüli [Imperially rescripted palace memorials, legal category, statutes and substatutes].

Zhupi zouzhe, falü, qita [Imperially rescripted palace memorials, legal category, miscellaneous].

GUANGDONG PROVINCIAL ARCHIVES, GUANGZHOU

Chaozhou haiguan dang'an [Maritime customs archives of Chaozhou].

G2013—*Huaqiao shiliao* [Historical materials on overseas Chinese].

GUANGDONG PROVINCIAL LIBRARY, GUANGZHOU

Mao Cheng. 1879. *Chao du ou cun* [Chaoyang documents accidentally preserved]. N.p. (preface 1877).

Shantou Nanyang huaqiao huzhu shewu baogao [Report on the Social Services of the Mutual Aid Society of Shantou Overseas Chinese in the Nanyang]. Shantou, n.p. Manuscript.

HONG KONG, PUBLIC RECORD OFFICE, HKMS202-1-10, WAR OFFICE

Kwangtung: Reports on Conditions, 1940–1946

INSTITUTE OF HISTORY AND PHILOLOGY, TAIWAN

Neige daku dang'an [Grand Secretariat Archives] (digital).

JARDINE MATHESON ARCHIVES, UNIVERSITY OF
CAMBRIDGE LIBRARY, CAMBRIDGE, UK

In-Correspondence/Unbound Letters/Private/Namoa, 1834–1839.
In-Correspondence/Unbound Letters/Local House Letters, Namoa, 1844–1860.
In-Correspondence/Unbound Letters/Local House Letters, Shanghai, 1844–1891.
In-Correspondence/Unbound Letters/Local House Letters, Swatow, 1853–1894.

NATIONAL ARCHIVES OF GREAT BRITAIN

Colonial Office

CO 273/Straits Settlements, Original Correspondence, 1838–1946.
CO 275/Straits Settlements, Sessional Papers, 1855–1940.
CO 882/5/17: Hong Kong-Straits Settlements: Coinage of a British Dollar for Circulation in Hong
Kong and the Straits Settlements. Minutes of Evidence Taken before a Departmental Committee
and Correspondence. 1894.

Foreign Office

FO 17/Political and Other Departments/General Correspondence before 1906.
FO 228/ Foreign Office, Consulates and Legation, China, Swatow, General Correspondence,
Series 1.
FO 233/96, Northern Department and Foreign Office, Consulates and Legation, China, Miscellaneous
Papers and Reports, 1727–1951, Shanghai: Mixed Court and Miscellaneous.
FO 656, Supreme Court, Shanghai, China, General Correspondence, Swatow, 1866–1898.
FO 881, Confidential Print (Numerical Series), 1827–1914.
FO 931, Guangdong Provincial Archives [Qingdai Guangdongsheng dang'an].

NATIONAL ARCHIVES OF SINGAPORE

Governor's Diary. 1852–1866.
Oral History Centre. Economic Development of Singapore (Xinjiapo jingji fazhanshi).
Oral History Centre. Huaren fangyan qun [Chinese Dialect Group Project]. Recorded in
Chaozhouese, transcribed in Chinese.
Oral History Centre. Xinjiapo xianqu renwu [Pioneers of Singapore Project]. Chaozhou/
Chinese transcript.

NATIONAL LIBRARY OF SINGAPORE

Cases Heard and Determined in Her Majesty's Supreme Court of the Straits Settlements. Vol. 4,
1885–1890. Edited by James William Norton Kyshe. Singapore: Singapore and Straits Printing Office, 1890.
Koh Seow Chuan Collection. Supreme Court of the Straits Settlements, Cases, 1910 [part 4], Suits
85–100. Manuscript [10 folders], 1910.

SHANGHAI MUNICIPAL ARCHIVES

Chaozhou huiguan yi'an beicha [Minutes of the meetings of the Chaozhou huiguan of Shanghai], 1914–1936.

SHANTOU MUNICIPAL LIBRARY

Cui Binyan. 1908. *Chaoyang xian minqing* [Conditions of the people of Chaoyang district]. Unpublished manuscript.

Zhaoxuan gong du shiyi [Collected writings of Mr. Zhaoxuan (Fang Yao)]. Vols. 3–4. Unpublished Manuscript..

Published Sources

"AHR Conversation: How Size Matters." 2013. *American Historical Review* 118.5 (December): 1430–72.

Amrith, Sunil. 2011. *Migration and Diaspora in Modern Asia*. New York: Cambridge University Press.

Analects. 1979. Translated by D. C. Lau. New York: Penguin.

Anbu zhi [Gazetteer of Anbu]. 1990. Gen. ed. Lin Rensheng. N.p.: Xinhua chubanshe.

Andaya, Barbara, and Leonard Andaya. 2001. *A History of Malaysia*. 2nd ed. Honolulu: University of Hawaii Press.

Anderson, John. 1890. *English Intercourse with Siam in the Seventeenth Century*. London: Kegan Paul.

Antony, Robert. 2003. *Like Froth Floating on the Sea*. Berkeley: Institute of East Asian Studies.

Appadurai, Arjun. 1996. *Modernity at Large*. Minneapolis: University of Minnesota Press.

Armitage, David. 2012. "What's the Big Idea?" *History of European Ideas* 38.4 (June): 493–507.

Ashmore, Lida Scott. 1920. *The South China Mission of the American Baptist Foreign Mission Society*. Shanghai: American Baptist Foreign Mission Society.

Ashmore, William. 1897. "A Clan Feud Near Swatow." *Chinese Recorder* 28.5: 214–23.

Asiatic Journal and Monthly Register for British India and Its Dependencies. 1816–1829.

Augustine of Hippo. 1998. *The City of God against the Pagans*. Cambridge: Cambridge University Press.

Baker, Christopher. 1981. "Economic Reorganization and the Slump in South and Southeast Asia." *Comparative Studies in Society and History* 23.3: 325–49.

Balzac, Honoré de. 1962. *Père Goriot*. New York: Signet Classics.

Bao, Jiemin. 2005. *Marital Acts: Gender, Sexuality, and Identity among the Chinese Thai Diaspora*. Honolulu: University of Hawai'i Press.

Bao Wei. 2005. "Fu jie hou de zongzu zhongjian: Chenghai Lin shi zongzu de ge'an yanjiu" [The reestablishment of lineages after the return from the evacuation border: An examination into the case of the Lins of Chenghai]. *Chaoxue yanjiu* 12: 186–96.

Barua, Pradeep. 2003. *Gentlemen of the Raj*. Westport, CT: Praeger.

Begbie, P. J. 1967 [1834]. *The Malayan Peninsula*. London: Oxford University Press.

Benton, Gregor. 1992. *Mountain Fires: The Red Army's Three-Year War in South China, 1934–1938*. Berkeley: University of California Press.

Bernhardt, Kathryn. 1999. *Women and Property in China, 960–1949.* Stanford, CA: Stanford University Press.

Betta, Chiara. 2002. "Silas Aaron Hardoon." *The Scribe: Journal of Babylonian Jewry* 75 (Autumn). Electronic.

———. 2003. "From Orientals to Imagined Britons: Baghdadi Jews in Shanghai." *Modern Asian Studies* 37.4 (October): 999–1023.

Blussé, Leonard. 1981. "Batavia, 1619–1740: The Rise and Fall of a Chinese Colonial Town." *Journal of Southeast Asian Studies* 12.1 (March): 159–78.

Blussé, Leonard, and Ank Merens. 1993. "Nuggets from the Gold Mines: Three Tales of the Ta-Kong Kongsi of West Kalimantan." In *Conflict and Accommodation in Early Modern East Asia,* edited by Leonard Blussé and Harriet Zurndorfer, 284–321. Leiden: Brill.

Blythe, Wilfred. 1969. *The Impact of the Chinese Secret Societies in Malaya.* London: Oxford University Press.

Boomgaard, Peter, and Ian Brown. 2000a. "The Economies of Southeast Asia in the 1930s Depression." In *Weathering the Storm,* edited by Peter Boomgaard and Ian Brown, 1–19. Singapore: Institute of Southeast Asian Studies.

———. eds. 2000b. *Weathering the Storm: The Economies of Southeast Asia in the 1930s Depression.* Singapore: Institute of Southeast Asian Studies.

Bowring, John. 1857. *The Kingdom and People of Siam.* 2 vols. London: Parker and Son.

Brickell, Katherine, and Ayona Datta, eds. 2011. *Translocal Geographies: Spaces, Places, Connections.* Surrey, UK: Ashgate.

Brook, Timothy. 1998. *The Confusions of Pleasure: Commerce and Culture in Ming China.* Berkeley: University of California Press.

Brooks, Barbara. 2000. "Japanese Colonial Citizenship in Treaty-Port China." In *New Frontiers,* edited by Robert Bickers and Christian Henriot. Manchester, UK: Manchester University Press.

Brown, Rajeswary Ampalavanar. 1994. *Capital and Entrepreneurship in South-East Asia.* New York: St. Martin's Press.

Bruinsma, Gerben, and Wim Bernasco. 2004. "Criminal Groups and Transnational Illegal Markets." *Crime, Law, and Social Change* 41: 79–94.

Cai Peirong. 2002. *Qingji zhu Xinjiapo lingshi zhi tantao, 1877–1911* [A study of the late-Qing consulate in Singapore, 1877–1911]. Singapore: Xinjiapo guoli daxue zhongwenxi.

Cain, P. J., and A. G. Hopkins. 2016. *British Imperialism.* 3rd ed. New York: Routledge.

Calanca, Paola. 2001. "Aspects spécifiques de la piraterie à Hainan." In *Hainan: de la Chine à l'Asie du Sud-Est,* edited by Claudine Salmon and Roderich Ptak, 111–38. Wiesbaden: Harrassowitz.

———. 2010. "Piracy and Coastal Security in Southeastern China, 1600–1780." In *Elusive Pirates, Pervasive Smugglers,* edited by Robert Antony, 85–98. Hong Kong: Hong Kong University Press.

Campbell, Brian. 2012. *Rivers and the Power of Ancient Rome.* Chapel Hill: University of North Carolina Press.

Carroll, John. 2005. *Edge of Empires: Chinese Elites and British Colonials in Hong Kong.* Cambridge, MA: Harvard University Press.

Carstens, Sharon. 2005. *Histories, Cultures, Identities: Studies in Malaysian Chinese Worlds.* Singapore: Singapore University Press.

Cartier, Carolyn. 2001. *Globalizing South China*. Oxford: Oxford University Press.

Cator, Writser Jans. 1936. *The Economic Position of the Chinese in the Netherlands Indies*. Chicago: University of Chicago Press.

Census of British Malaya, 1921 (The Straits Settlements, Federated Malay States, and Protected States of Johore, Kedah, Perlis, Kelantan, Trengganu, and Brunei). 1922. Compiled by J. E. Nathan. London: Waterlow and Sons.

Chan, Shelly. 2018. *Diaspora's Homeland: Modern China in the Age of Global Migration*. Durham, NC: Duke University Press.

Chang, Hsin-pao. 1964. *Commissioner Lin and the Opium War*. New York: Norton.

Chao Shan baike quanshu [Encyclopedia of Chaozhou and Shantou]. 1994. Beijing: Zhongguo da baike quanshu chubanshe.

Chao Shan diqu qiaopiye ziliao [Historical sources for the overseas remittance industry in the Chaozhou-Shantou region]. 2004. Edited by Yang Qunxi. Shantou: Chao Shan lishi wenhua yanjiu zhongxin.

Chaoyang dashiji [Historical chronicle of Chaoyang]. 2005. Shantou: Shantou daxue chubanshe.

Chaoyang minjian gushi jingxuan [Selection of popular lore in Chaoyang]. 2005. Edited by Weng Mushun. Shantou: Gongyuan chuban youxian gongsi.

Chaoyang xianzhi [Chaoyang gazetteer]. 1884, 1997.

Chaozhou Fangshi zupu [Genealogical records of the Fangs of Chaozhou]. 1963. Edited by Fang Shaowei. N.p.

Chaozhou fuzhi [Chaozhou prefectural gazetteer]. 1679 (electronic), 1762 (electronic), 1893.

Chaozhou zhi [Chaozhou gazetteer]. 1949. Edited by Rao Zongyi. Shantou.

Chaozhou zhi. 2005 (Reprint of 1949 ed.). Edited by Rao Zongyi. Hong Kong.

Chen Chingho [see also Chen Jinghe]. 1977. "Mac Thien Tu and Phraya Taksin: A Survey of Their Political Stand, Conflicts, and Background." *Proceedings of the Seventh IAHA Conference*, 1535–75. Bangkok: n.p.

Chen Chunsheng. 1997. "Baer fengzai suo jian zhi minguo chunian Chao Shan qiaoxiang: yi Zhanglin wei li" [The August 2nd typhoon as seen in the emigrant villages of early Republican-era Chao Shan: the example of Zhanglin]. *Chaoxue yanjiu* 6: 369–95.

———. 2000. "Cong 'wolun' dao 'qianhai': Mingmo Qingchu Chaozhou difang dongluan yu xiangcun shehui biancheng" [From the wokou chaos to the coastal evacuation: local disorder in Chaozhou and rural change in the late Ming and early Qing] *Ming Qing longcun* 2.2: 73–106.

Chen Haizhong. 2011. *Jindai shanghui yu difang jinrong: yi Shantou wei zhongxin de yanjiu* [Modern chambers of commerce and local finance: research centered on Shantou]. Guangzhou: Guangdong renmin chubanshe.

Chen Jinghe [see also Chen Chingho]. 1963. *Shiliu shiji zhi feilübin Huaqiao* [The overseas Chinese in the Philippines in the sixteenth century]. Hong Kong: New Asia Research Institute.

Chen Kun. 1870. "Zhi Chao chuyan" [My humble opinions on governing Chaozhou]. Reproduced in Xie Shi, "Chen Kun 'Ru bu ji zhai congshu' yu Qingdai Xian-Tong nianjian Chaozhou shehui [Chen Kun's "Ru bu ji zhai congshu" and Chaozhou society during the Xianfeng and Tongzhi eras]. *Chaoxue yanjiu* 14 (2008): 111–54.

Chen Liyuan. 2007. "Hua'nan yu Dongnanya huaren shehui de hudong guanxi: yi Chaoren qiaopi wangluo wei zhongxin (1911–1949)" [The Interactions between South China and the

Chinese communities of Southeast Asia: with a focus on the Chaozhou remittance networks, 1911–1949]. Ph.D. dissertation, National University of Singapore.

Chen Ta. 1940. *Emigrant Communities in South China*. New York: Institute of Pacific Relations.

Chen Tong. 2005. "Luelun jindai Shanghai waiji lüshi de falü huodong ji yingxiang [The legal activities of foreign lawyers in modern Shanghai and their influence]. *Shilin* 3: 20–38.

Chen Zehong. 2001. *Chao Shan wenhua gaishuo* [An overview of Chaoshan culture]. Guangzhou: Guangdong renmin chubanshe.

Chenghai xianzhi. 1764, 1815, 1992.

Cheong, Kee Cheok, Lee Am Hing, and Lee Poh Ping. 2013. "Chinese Overseas Remittances to China: The Perspective from Southeast Asia." *Journal of Contemporary Asia* 43.1 (February): 75–101.

Cherry, Haydon. 2011. "Down and Out in Saigon." Ph.D. dissertation, Yale University.

Chin, John. 1981. *The Sarawak Chinese*. Oxford: Oxford University Press.

China, Imperial Maritime Customs. 1882–1891; 1892–1901; 1902–1911; 1912–1921; 1922–1931. *Decennial Reports*.

———. 1883. "The Fisheries of Swatow." Shanghai: Statistical Department of the Inspectorate General.

———. 1866–1912. *Reports on the Trade at the Treaty Ports in China*.

———. 1871–1896. *Swatow Trade Reports, 1870–1895*. Shanghai: Inspectorate General of Customs.

———. 1888. *Opium, Crude and Prepared*. Shanghai: Inspectorate General of Customs.

China, Republic of. 1928. "Sugar Trade in China." *Chinese Economic Journal* 36 (December): 1069–78.

Chirot, Daniel, and Anthony Reid, eds. 1997. *Essential Outsiders*. Seattle: University of Washington Press.

Chng, David. 1999. *Heroic Images of Ming Loyalists: A Study of the Spirit Tablets of Ghee Hin Kongsi Leaders in Singapore*. Singapore: Singapore Society of Asian Studies.

Choate, Mark. 2008. *Emigrant Nation: The Making of Italy Abroad*. Cambridge, MA: Harvard University Press.

Choi, Chi-cheung. 1995. "Competition among Brothers." In *Chinese Business Enterprise in Asia*, edited by Rajeswary Ampalavanar Brown, 96–114. London: Routledge.

———. 1998. "Kinship and Business." *Business History* 40.1 (January): 26–49.

———. 2015. "Rice, Treaty Ports, and the Chaozhou Chinese *Lianhao* Associate Companies." In *Merchant Communities in Asia, 1600–1980*, edited by Lin Yu-ju and Madeleine Zelin, 53–77. London: Pickering and Chatto.

Chouban yiwu shimo (Xianfeng reign) [Complete account of the management of alien affairs]. 1979. 8 vols. Beijing: Zhonghua shuju; orig. 1930.

Clouth, Franz. 1903. *Rubber, Gutta-Percha and Balata*. London: MacLaren and Sons; orig. (German) 1899.

Coates, P. D. 1988. *The China Consuls*. Hong Kong: Oxford University Press.

Cohen, Paul. 2003. "Remembering and Forgetting National Humiliation in Twentieth-Century China." In *China Unbound*, edited by Paul Cohen, 148–84. New York: Routledge.

———. 2009. *Speaking to History: The Story of Goujian in Twentieth-Century China*. Berkeley: University of California Press.

Cohn, Bernard. 1996. *Colonialism and Its Forms of Knowledge*. Princeton, NJ: Princeton University Press.

Comber, L. F. 1959. *Chinese Secret Societies in Malaya*. Locust Valley, NY: Augustin.

Conklin, Alice L., and Ian Fletcher. 1999. *European Imperialism, 1830–1930*. Boston: Houghton Mifflin.

Cooke, Nola, and Li Tana, eds. 2004. *Water Frontier: Commerce and the Chinese in the Lower Mekong Region, 1750–1880*. Lanham, MD: Rowman and Littlefield.

Crawfurd, John. 1820. *History of the Indian Archipelago*. 3 vols. Edinburgh: Archibald Constable.

———. 1830. *Journal of an Embassy from the Governor-General of India to the Courts of Siam and Cochin China*. 2 vols. 2nd ed. London: Colburn and Bentley.

Cushman, Jennifer. 1993. *Fields from the Sea: Chinese Junk Trade with Siam during the Late Eighteenth and Early Nineteenth Centuries*. Ithaca, NY: Cornell Southeast Asia Program.

Da Nan shilu: Qing-Yue guanxi shiliao huibian [The Veritable Records of Vietnam (Dai Nam thuc luc): a compendium of sources on Qing-Vietnamese relations]. 2000. Edited by Xu Wentang and Xie Qiyi. Taipei: Academia Sinica; orig. 1811–1909.

Dai Yixuan. 1982. *Mingdai Jia Long jian de wokou haidao yu Zhongguo ziben zhuyi de mengya* [The wokou pirates of the Ming Jiajing and Longqing eras and the sprouts of Chinese capitalism]. Beijing: Zhongguo shehui kexue chubanshe.

Delvert, Jean. 1961. *Le paysan cambodgien*. Paris: Mouton.

Dennys, N. B., and W. F. Mayers. 1867. *Treaty Ports of China and Japan*. London: Trubner and Sons.

Dhiravat na Pombejra. 2004. "Administrative and Military Roles of the Chinese in Siam during an Age of Turmoil." In *Maritime China in Transition*, edited by Wang Gungwu and Ng Chin-keong, 335–53. Wiesbaden: Harrassowitz.

Ding Shenzun et al. 2004. *Guangdong Minguo shi* [A history of Guangdong in the Republican era]. 2 vols. Guangzhou: Guangdong renmin chubanshe.

Diyici guonei geming zhanzheng shiqi de nongmin yundong [The peasant movement during the first revolutionary civil war]. 1953. Beijing: Renmin chubanshe.

Doty, E., and W. J. Pohlman. 1839. "Tour in Borneo." *Chinese Repository* 8 (October): 283–310.

Drabble, J. H. 1973. *Rubber in Malaya*. Kuala Lumpur: Oxford University Press.

Du Guifang. 1997. *Chaoshan haiwai yimin* [Overseas migrants from Chaozhou and Shantou]. Shantou: Shantou daxue chubanshe.

Duara, Prasenjit. 1997. "Transnationalism and the Predicament of Sovereignty: China, 1900–1945." *American Historical Review* 102.4.

Dusinberre, Martin. 2012. *Hard Times in the Hometown: A History of Community Survival in Modern Japan*. Honolulu: University of Hawai'i Press.

Elden, Stuart. 2013. *The Birth of Territory*. Chicago: University of Chicago Press.

Fan, I-chun. 1992. "Long-Distance Trade and Market Integration in the Ming-Ch'ing Period." Ph.D. dissertation, Stanford University.

Fang Fang yanjiu [Studying Fang Fang]. 1996. Edited by Zhonggong Guangdong Shengwei, Dangshi Yanjiu Shi. Guangzhou: Guangdong renmin chubanshe.

Fang Xiaolan and Zhou Xiao. 2001. *Chaoren xianbei zai Shanghai* [The forebears of Chaozhouese in Shanghai]. Hong Kong: Yiyuan chubanshe.

Farooqui, Amar. 1998. *Smuggling as Subversion*. New Delhi: New Age International.

Faure, David. 2004. "The Heaven and Earth Society in the Nineteenth Century." In *Heterodoxy in Late Imperial China*, edited by Kwang-ching Liu and Richard Shek, 365–92. Honolulu: University of Hawai'i Press.

———. 2007. *Emperor and Ancestor: State and Lineage in South China*. Stanford, CA: Stanford University Press.

Fawthrop, Tom, and Helen Jarvis. 2005. *Getting Away with Genocide?* Sydney: UNSW Press.

Feierman, Steven. 1990. *Peasant Intellectuals*. Madison: University of Wisconsin Press.

Fernando, M. R., and David Bulbeck, eds. 1992. *Chinese Economic Activity in Netherlands India*. Singapore: ISEAS.

Fielde, Adele. 1887. *Pagoda Shadows*. London: T. Ogilvie Smith.

Foccardi, Gabriele. 1986. *The Last Warrior*. Wiesbaden: Harrassowitz.

Fu, Lo-shu, ed. 1966. *A Documentary Chronicle of Sino-Western Relations*. Tucson: University of Arizona Press.

Galbiati, Fernando. 1985. *P'eng P'ai and the Hai-Lu-feng Soviet*. Stanford, CA: Stanford University Press.

Gao, Zhiguo, and Bingbing Jia. 2013. "The Nine-Dash Line in the South China Sea: History, Status, and Implications." *American Journal of International Law* 107.1 (January): 98–124.

Gardner, Christopher. 1897. "Amoy Emigration to the Straits." *China Review* 22.4: 621–26.

Geller, Jay. 2011. *The Other Jewish Question*. New York: Fordham University Press.

Gia-dinh-thung-chi: Histoire et description de la Basse Cochinchine [Gazetteer of Gia-dinh]. 1863. Translated by Gabriel Aubaret. Paris: Imprimerie imperial.

Godley, Michael. 1981. *The Mandarin Capitalists from Nanyang*. Cambridge: Cambridge University Press.

Gongzhongdang Yongzhengchao zouzhe [Imperially-inscripted memorials of the Yongzheng reign]. 1977–1980. Taibei: Guoli gugong bowuyuan, [1723–1736].

González de Mendoza, Juan. 1586. *Historia de las cosas mas notables, ritos y costumbres del gran reyno de la China*. Madrid: Casa de Pedro Madrigal.

———. 1854. *The History of the Great and Mighty Kingdom of China, and the Situation Thereof*. 2 vols. Translated by Robert Parke. London: Hakluyt Society.

Goodman, Bryna. 1995. *Native Place, City, and Nation*. Stanford, CA: Stanford University Press.

Goodman, Bryna, and David Goodman, eds. 2012. *Twentieth-Century Colonialism and China*. New York: Routledge.

Gould, Eliga. 2007. "Entangled Histories, Entangled Worlds: The English-Speaking Atlantic as a Spanish Periphery." *American Historical Review* 112.3 (June): 764–86.

Great Britain. 1869. *Report of the Royal Commissioners for Inquiries into the Laws of Naturalization and Allegiance*. London: Her Majesty's Stationery Office.

———. 1971. *British Parliamentary Papers, China: 31, Correspondence . . . Respecting the Opium War and Opium Trade in China, 1840–85*. Shannon: Irish University Press.

Gregory, John. 2015. "Militarized Adjudication and the Frontier." Paper delivered at Association for Asian Studies conference.

"Guangdong Shantou Niutianyang de lishibianqian" [The historical evolution of Ox-Field Sea in Shantou, Guangdong]. *Zhongguo shuichan yangzhi wang* [China Aquaculture Network]. Website.

Guangxuchao zhupi zouzhe [Imperially-inscripted palace memorials of the Guangxu reign]. 1995–1996. 120 vols. Edited by First Historical Archives. Beijing: Zhonghua shuju.

Guldi, Jo, and David Armitage. 2014. *The History Manifesto*. Cambridge: Cambridge University Press.

Gutzlaff, Charles. 1968. *Journal of Three Voyages Along the Coast of China in 1831, 1832, and 1833*. Taipei: Ch'engwen Publishing; orig. 1834.

Hai-Lu-Feng geming genju dishi [The Hai-Lu-Feng revolution as told in local accounts]. 2000. Edited by Ye Zuoneng. Beijing: Zhonggong zhongyang dangxiao chubanshe.

Hai Ying. 1989. "Nan'ao jiguan zatan" [Miscellaneous discussions about the brothels of Nan'ao]. *Shantou wenshi* 6: 209–10.

Haiyang xianzhi [Gazetteer of Haiyang district]. 1900. Electronic.

Halsey, Stephen. 2015. *Quest for Power: European Imperialism and the Making of Chinese Statecraft*. Cambridge, MA: Harvard University Press.

Halwart, Matthias, and Modadugu V. Gupta. 2004. *Cultures of Fish in Rice Fields*. Penang: World Fish Center.

Hamashita, Takeshi. 2008. *China, East Asia and the Global Economy*. Edited by Linda Grove and Mark Selden. New York: Routledge.

Hamilton, Gary. 1977. "Nineteenth-Century Chinese Merchant Associations." *Ch'ing-shih wen-t'i* 3.8 (December): 50–71.

Han Feizi. 2001. "On the Prominent Schools of Thought." In *Readings in Classical Chinese Philosophy*, edited by Philip J. Ivanhoe and Bryan W. Van Norden, 335–42. New York: Seven Bridges.

Hang, Xing. 2015. *Conflict and Commerce in Maritime East Asia*. New York: Cambridge University Press.

Hansson, Anders. 1996. *Chinese Outcasts: Discrimination and Emancipation in Late Imperial China*. Leiden: Brill.

Hao, Yen-ping. 1970. *The Comprador in Nineteenth-Century China*. Cambridge, MA: Harvard University Press.

Hayes, James. 1979. "The Nam Pak Hong Commercial Association of Hong Kong." *Journal of the Hong Kong Branch of the Royal Asiatic Society* 19:216–26.

He, Sibing. 2012. "Russell and Company and the Imperialism of Anglo-American Free Trade." In *Narratives of Free Trade*, edited by Kendall Johnson, 84–98. Hong Kong: Hong Kong University Press.

He Zhiqing and Wu Zhaoqing. 1996. *Zhongguo banghui shi* [History of Chinese Brotherhoods]. Taipei: Wenjin chubanshe.

Headrick, Daniel. 1988. *The Tentacles of Progress*. New York: Oxford University Press.

Heidhues, Mary Somers. 1993. "Chinese Organizations in West Borneo and Bangka: Kongsis and Hui." In *"Secret Societies" Reconsidered*, edited by David Ownby and Mary Somers Heidhues, 68–85. Armonk, NY: M. E. Sharpe.

———. 2003. *Goldiggers, Farmers, and Traders in the 'Chinese Districts' of West Kalimantan, Indonesia*. Ithaca, NY: Cornell Southeast Asia Program.

Hertslet, Edward. 1896. *Treaties between Great Britain and China*. London: Harrison and Sons.

Hevia, James. 2003. *English Lessons*. Durham, NC: Duke University Press.

Hicks, George. 1993. *Overseas Chinese Remittances from Southeast Asia*. Singapore: Select Books.

Hinton, Alexander. 2005. *Why Did They Kill? Cambodia in the Shadow of Genocide*. Berkeley: University of California Press.

Ho, Dahpon. 2011. "Sealords Live in Vain." Ph.D. dissertation, University of California, San Diego.

Ho, Ping-ti. 1959. *Studies on the Population of China*. Cambridge, MA: Harvard University Press.

———. 1964. *The Ladder of Success in Imperial China*. New York: Columbia University Press.

Hobson, J. A. 1938. *Imperialism: A Study*. 3rd ed. London: George Allen and Unwin; orig. 1902.

Hofheinz, Roy. 1977. *The Broken Wave*. Berkeley: University of California Press.

Hong Kong General Chamber of Commerce. 1923. *Report of the General Committee of the Hong Kong Chamber of Commerce, 1922*. Hong Kong: South China Morning Post.

Hong Lin. 2006. "Taiguo qiaopi yu yinxingju chuyi" [Discussion of the remittances and silver letters of Thailand]. In *Taiguo qiaopi wenhua* [The Thai culture of remittances], edited by Hong Lin and Li Daogang. Bangkok: Tai Zhong xuehui congshu.

Hornby, Sir Edmund. 1928. *An Autobiography*. Boston: Houghton Mifflin.

Hou, Chi-ming. 1965. *Foreign Investment in China, 1840–1937*. Cambridge, MA: Harvard University Press.

Hsieh, Kuo Ching. 1932. "Removal of Coastal Population in Early Tsing Period." *Chinese Social and Political Science Review* 15: 559–96.

Hsu, Madeline. 2000. *Dreaming of Gold, Dreaming of Home*. Stanford, CA: Stanford University Press.

Hu Zhusheng. *Qingdai Hongmen shi* [History of the Hong League]. Shenyang: Liaoning renmin chubanshe, 1996.

Huang Haohan. 2012. "Niutianyang de lishi bianqian." [Historical evolution of the Ox-Field Sea]. *Shantou daxue tushuguan: Chao Shan tezang wang* [Website of the Special Collections division of the Shantou University Library].

Huang, Philip. 1993. "Between Informal Mediation and Formal Adjudication: The Third Realm of Qing Civil Justice." *Modern China* 17.3: 25–198.

Huang Ting. 1996. "Mingdai haijin zhengce dui Mingdai Chaozhou shehui de yingxiang" [The influence of the Ming maritime proscriptions on Chaozhou society]. *Hanshan shifan xueyuan bao* [Journal of the Hanshan Teachers College] 1996.1 (March): 5–16.

———. 2004. "Difang wenxian yu quyu lishi yanjiu: yi wan Qing Haiyang Wu Zhongshu shijian wei li" [Local source materials and the study of regional history: the example of the Wu Zhongshu incident in Haiyang in the late Qing]. *Chaoxue yanjiu* 11: 45–74.

———. 2007. "Qingchu qianhai shijianzhong de Chaozhou zongzu" [Chaozhou lineages during the coastal evacuation of the early Qing]. *Shehui kexue* 2007.3: 139–51.

Huang Ting and Chen Zhanshan. 2001. *Chaoshan shi* [History of Chaoshan]. Vol. 1. Shantou: Guangdong renmin chubanshe.

Huang Xianzhang. 2010. "Fangcuo ju he Daren tian" [The Fang family bureau and the Big Man's land]. Blog entry. http://www.chaozhinan.com/blog/hxz/article/15747.html.

Huen, P. Lim Pui. 2003. "Continuity and Connectedness." In *New Terrains in Southeast Asian History*, edited by Abu Talib Ahmad and Tan Liok Ee, 301–27. Athens: Ohio University Press.

Huilai xianzhi [Gazetteer of Huilai district]. 1731.

Huizhou fuzhi [Gazetteer of Huizhou prefecture]. 1966; orig. 1881.

I Ching. 1967. Translated by Richard Wilhelm and Cary Baynes. Princeton, NJ: Princeton University Press.

Ingham, John. 1983. *Biographical Dictionary of American Business Leaders*. Westport, CT: Greenwood.

Ishii Yoneo. 1998. *The Junk Trade from Southeast Asia: Translations from the Tosen Fusetsu-gaki, 1674–1723*. Singapore: ISEAS.

Jackson, James C. 1968. *Planters and Speculators: Chinese and European Agricultural Enterprise in Malaya, 1786–1921*. Kuala Lumpur: University of Malaya Press.

Jaivin, Linda. 2001. *The Monkey and the Dragon*. Melbourne: Text Pub.

Jiang Risheng. 1986. *Taiwan waizhi* [Unofficial history of Taiwan]. Shanghai: Shanghai guji chubanshe; orig. 1704.

Jiang Zuyuan and Fang Zhiqin. 1993. *Jianming Guangdong shi* [Concise history of Guangdong]. Guangzhou: Guangdong renmin chubanshe.

Jieyang xianxuzhi [Gazetteer of Jieyang district]. 1890.

Jing Tsu. 2006. "Extinction and Adventures on the Chinese Diasporic Frontier." *Journal of Chinese Overseas* 2.2: 247–68.

Johnson, Cuthbert William. 1842. *The Farmer's Encyclopaedia and Dictionary of Rural Affairs*. London: Longman, Brown, Green, and Longmans.

Johnson, Linda Cooke. 1995. *Shanghai: From Market Town to Treaty Port, 1074–1858*. Stanford, CA: Stanford University Press.

———. 2000. "Dock Labour at Shanghai." In *Dock Workers: International Explorations in Comparative Labour History*, edited by Sam Davies et al., vol. 1, 269–89. London: Routledge.

Ju Han. 1989. "Chaozhou liu peng chuan shulue" [An account of the canopied boats of Chaozhou]. *Shantou wenshi* 6: 192–200.

Ka'i hentai [Chinese metamorphosed into foreigners]. 1958–1959. Compiled by Hayashi Shunsai and Hayashi Hōkō; edited by Ura Ren'ichi. 3 vols. Tokyo: Toyo Bunko; orig. circa 1732.

Kaikyō shokuminchi gairan [An overview of the Straits Settlements]. 1918. Edited by Ministry of Foreign Affairs, Bureau of Commerce. Tokyo: Gaimushō Tsūshōkyoku.

Kamen, Henry. 2003. *Empire: How Spain Became a World Power*. New York: Harper Collins.

Kang Yong Qian shiqi chengxiang renmin fankang douzheng ziliao [Historical sources on popular resistance struggles in urban and rural areas during the Kangxi, Yongzheng, and Qianlong eras]. 1979. 2 vols. Beijing: Zhonghua shuju.

Kathirithamby-Wells, Jeyamalar. 2005. *Nature and Nation: Forests and Development in Peninsular Malaysia*. Honolulu: University of Hawaii Press.

Kelsey, Harry. 1998. *Sir Francis Drake: The Queen's Pirate*. New Haven, CT: Yale University Press.

Keswick, Maggie, ed. 1982. *The Thistle and the Jade*. London: Octopus Books.

Khanh, Huynh Kim. 1986. *Vietnamese Communism*. Ithaca, NY: Cornell University Press.

Kiernan, Ben. 1996. *The Pol Pot Regime*. New Haven, CT: Yale University Press.

Kilcullen, David. 2006. "Counter-Insurgency Redux." *Survival* 48.4 (Winter): 111–31.

King, Paul. 1924. *In the Chinese Customs Service*. London: T. Fisher Unwin.

Klein, Kerwin. 1997. *Frontiers of Historical Imagination*. Berkeley: University of California Press.

Kuhn, Philip. 1970. *Rebellion and Its Enemies in Late Imperial China*. Cambridge, MA: Harvard University Press.

Kuhn, Philip. 2008. *Chinese Among Others: Emigration in Modern Times*. Lanham, MD: Rowman and Littlefield.

Kulp, Daniel. 1925. *Country Life in South China*. 2 vols. New York: Columbia Teachers College.

LaFargue, Jean-André. 1909. *L'immigration chinois en Indochine: sa réglementation, ses conséquences économiques et politiques*. Paris: Henri Jouve.

Lamley, Harry. 1990. "Lineage Feuding in Southern Fujian and Eastern Guangdong under Qing Rule." In *Violence in China*, edited by Jonathan Lipman and Steven Harrell, 27–64. Albany: SUNY Press.

Lan Dingyuan. 1726. "Chaozhou haifang tushuo" [Chaozhou's coastal defenses illustrated]. In *Lan Dingyuan lun Chao wenji*, 53–57.

———. 1985. *Luzhou gong'an* [The cases of Luzhou]. Guizhou: Qunzhong chubanshe; orig. 1729.

———. 1993. *Lan Dingyuan lun Chao wenji* [Lan Dingyuan's collected essays on Chaozhou culture]. Shenzhen: Hai tian chubanshe.

Langer, William. 1935. "A Critique of Imperialism." *Foreign Affairs* 14.2: 102–19.

———. 1968. *The Diplomacy of Imperialism*. 2nd ed. New York: Knopf; orig. 1935.

Latham, A.J.H., and Larry Neal. 1983. "The International Market in Rice and Wheat, 1868–1914." *Economic History Review* 36.2: 260–80.

Launay, Adrien. 2000. *Histoire de la mission de Siam, 1662–1811*. 3 vols. Paris: Missions Étrangères; orig. 1920.

Le Bao [Lat Pau, Singapore Reporter]. 1922–1931.

Lee, James Z., and Cameron Campbell. 1997. *Fate and Fortune in Rural China*. New York: Cambridge University Press.

Lee, James Z., and Wang Feng. 1999. *One Quarter of Humanity*. Cambridge, MA: Harvard University Press.

Lee, Poh Ping. 1978. *Chinese Society in Nineteenth-Century Singapore*. Kuala Lumpur: Oxford University Press.

Lee, Joseph Tse-hei. 2003. *The Bible and the Gun: Christianity in South China*. London: Routledge.

LeFevour, Edward. 1968. *Western Enterprise in Late Ch'ing China*. Cambridge, MA: Harvard East Asia Monographs.

Leng Dong. 1999. *Dongnanya haiwai Chaoren yanjiu* [A study of overseas Chaozhouese in Southeast Asia]. Beijing: Zhonghua huaqiao banshe.

Lenin, V. I. 1939. *Imperialism: The Highest Stage of Capitalism*. New York: International Publishers; orig. 1917.

Leo, Jessica. 2015. *Global Hakka*. Leiden: Brill.

Li Changfu. 1966. *Zhongguo zhimin shi* [History of Chinese colonialism]. Taibei: Commercial Press; orig. 1937.

Li Li-san. 1964. "Li Li-san's Report: The Experience and Lessons of the August 1st Revolution." In "The Ashes of Defeat," translated and edited by C. Martin Wilbur, 9-24. In *China Quarterly* 18 (April–June): 3–54; orig. 1927.

Li, Lillian. 2007. *Fighting Famine in North China*. Stanford, CA: Stanford University Press.

Li, Tana. 1998. *Nguyen Cochinchina*. Ithaca, NY: Cornell Southeast Asia Program.

————. 2004. "Rice from Saigon: The Singapore Chinese and the Saigon Trade of the 19th Century." In *Maritime China in Transition*, edited by Wang Gungwu and Ng Chin-keong, 261–69. Wiesbaden: Harrassowitz.

Li Zhixian [Lee Chee Hiang]. 2004. "Xinjiapo Chaoren shantang suyuan: jian lun qi zai zaoqi yimin shehui de jiangou jichu" [The origins of the Chaozhou shantang in Singapore with a discussion of their structural foundation in early immigrant society]. *Chaoxue yanjiu* 11: 240–70.

————. 2006. "A Study of the Religious Culture of Teochew 'Shantang' (Hall of Charity): Benefaction and Spirit-Writing Rites." *Asian Culture* 30 (June): 57–77.

Liang Qichao. 1957. "Zhongguo zhimin ba da weiren zhuan" [Biographies of eight grandees of Chinese colonialism]. In *Zhongguo weiren zhuan wuzhong*, 51–55. Taibei: Taiwan Zhonghua shuju; orig. 1905.

Lim, Janet Chiu Mei. 1958. *Sold for Silver*. Cleveland, OH: World Publishing.

Lin, Alfred H. Y. 1997. *The Rural Economy of Guangdong*. New York: St. Martin's.

Lin Dachuan. 1990. *Han jiang ji* [Records of the Han River]. Hong Kong: n.p.; orig. 1857.

Lin Juncong. 1987. "Nan'ao haidao tuanhuo 'Sanhe gongsi' shimo" [The entire story of the Nan'ao piratical gang's "Sanhe gongsi"]. *Shantou wenshi* 4: 160–69.

Lin, Man-houng. 2001. "Overseas Chinese Merchants and Multiple Nationality." *Modern Asian Studies* 35.4: 985–1009.

Lin Tian and Cai Qionghong, eds. 2002. *Song, Yuan, Ming, Qing Chaozhou minbian ziliao* [Sources on Chaozhouese popular change under the Song, Yuan, Ming, and Qing]. Puning: Chao Shan lishi wenhua yanjiu zhongxin.

Liu Sen. 1996. *Ming Qing yanhai dangdi kaifa yanjiu* [A study of the opening of coastal marshlands during the Ming and Qing]. Jieyang: Shantou University Press.

Lockard, Craig. 1971. "Leadership and Power within the Chinese Community at Sarawak: A Historical Survey." *Journal of Southeast Asian Studies* 2.2: 195–217.

Logan, James Richardson. 1847. "Annual Remittances by Chinese Immigrants in Singapore to Their Families in China." *Journal of the Indian Archipelago and Eastern Asia* 1: 34–37.

Lombard, Denys. 1998. "Une autre 'Méditerranée' dans le Sud-Est asiatique." *Hérodote* 88: 184–93.

Loubère, Simon de la. 1969. *The Kingdom of Siam*. Translated by A. P. Gen. London: Oxford University Press; orig. 1691.

Lü Gang Chaozhou shanghui sanshi zhounian jinian tekan [Thirtieth anniversary special issue of the Chaozhou Chamber of Commerce of Hong Kong]. 1951. Hong Kong: Lü Gang Chaozhou shanghui.

Luo Xianglin. 1961. *Xi Poluozhou Luo Fangbo deng suo jian gongheguo kao* [A study of the establishment of a republic in West Borneo by Luo Fangbo]. Hong Kong: Zhongguo xueshi.

Luo Yudong. 2010. *Zhongguo lijinshi* [History of Chinese lijin]. Beijing: Shangwu yinshuguan; orig. 1936.

Ma Yuhang. 1921. *Shantou jinkuang yiban* [Shantou's current situation in a nutshell]. Shantou: n.p.

Macauley, Melissa. 1998. *Social Power and Legal Culture*. Stanford, CA: Stanford University Press.

Macauley, Melissa. 2009. "Small Time Crooks: Crime, Migration, and the War on Drugs in China, 1819–1860." *Late Imperial China* 30.1 (June): 1–47.

———. 2016. "Entangled States." *American Historical Review* 121.3 (June): 755–79.

Macmillan, Allister. 1907. *Seaports of the Far East*. London: Allister Macmillan.

Malaiya Chaoqiao tongjian [Chronicle of Chaozhouese in Malaya]. 1950. Edited by Pan Xing-nong. Singapore: Nandao chubanshe.

Manarungsan, Sompop. 2000. "The Rice Economy of Thailand in the 1930s Depression." In *Weathering the Storm*, edited by Peter Boomgaard and Ian Brown, 189–97. Singapore: ISEAS.

Mancall, Mark. 1968. "The Ch'ing Tribute System." In *The Chinese World Order*, edited by John Fairbank, 63–89. Cambridge, MA: Harvard University Press.

Mangan, James Clarence. 1859. *Poems*. New York: Haverty.

Mann Jones, Susan. 1972. "Finance in Ningbo." In *Economic Organization in Chinese Society*, edited by W. E. Wilmot, 47–77. Stanford, CA: Stanford University Press.

———. 1974. "The Ningpo Pang and Financial Power at Shanghai." In *The Chinese City between Two Worlds*, edited by Mark Elvin and William Skinner, 73–96. Stanford, CA: Stanford University Press.

Marks, Robert. 1977. "The World Can Change! Guangdong Peasants in Revolution." *Modern China* 3.1 (January): 65–100.

———. 1984. *Rural Revolution in South China*. Madison: University of Wisconsin Press.

Martin, Brian. 1996. *The Shanghai Green Gang*. Berkeley: University of California Press.

Mayer, William F., and N. B. Dennys. 1867. *The Treaty Ports of China and Japan*. London: Trubner.

Mazumdar, Sucheta. 1998. *Sugar and Society in China*. Cambridge, MA: Harvard East Asia Center.

McCoy, Alfred. 2009. *Policing America's Empire*. Madison: University of Wisconsin Press.

McKeown, Adam. 2001. *Chinese Migrant Networks and Cultural Change*. Chicago: University of Chicago Press.

Meyer-Fong, Tobie. 2013. *What Remains: Coming to Terms with Civil War in Nineteenth-Century China*. Stanford, CA: Stanford University Press.

Michael, Franz. 1966. *The Taiping Rebellion*. Seattle: University of Washington.

Michie, Alexander. 1900. *The Englishman in China During the Victorian Era*. 2 vols. Edinburgh: William Blackwood and Sons.

Miles, Steven B. 2017. *Upriver Journeys: Diaspora and Empire in Southern China*. Cambridge, MA: Harvard University Asia Center.

Min Yue bianqu sannian youji zhanzheng shiliao huibian [A compendium of historical sources on the three-year guerilla war in the Fujian-Guangdong border region]. 1985. 2 vols. Edited by Zhonggong Fujiansheng Longxi diwei dangshi ban'gongshi and Zhonggong Guangdong-sheng Shantou shiwei dangshi ban'gongshi. Hua'an, n.p. [neibu].

Ming huidian (Wanli ed.). 1989. Beijing: Zhonghua shuju; orig. 1587.

Ming Qing shilu Chaozhou shiji [Compilation of matters relating to Chaozhou in the *Veritable Records* of the Ming and Qing]. 1998. Hong Kong: Yiyuan chubanshe.

Mingshi [Dynastic history of the Ming]. 1739. Beijing. Electronic.

Molina, Antonio. 1984. *Historia de Filipinas*. 2 vols. Madrid: Ediciones Cultura Hispánica del Instituto de Cooperación Iberoamericana.

Motono, Eiichi. 2000. *Conflict and Cooperation in Sino-British Business*. New York: St. Martin's.

Muir, Edward W. 1993. *Mad Blood Stirring*. Baltimore: Johns Hopkins University Press.

Munn, Christopher. 2000. "The Hong Kong Opium Revenue." In *Opium Regimes*, edited by Timothy Brook and Bob Tadashi Wakabayashi, 105–26. Berkeley: University of California Press.

Murphy, Rhoads. 1977. *The Outsiders*. Ann Arbor: University of Michigan Center for Chinese Studies.

Murray, Dian, with Qin Baoqi. 1994. *The Origins of the Tiandihui*. Stanford, CA: Stanford University Press.

Nanyō ni okeru kakyō (Shina ijūmin) [The overseas Chinese of the Nanyang (Chinese migrants)]. 1914. Edited by Taiwan Ginkō [Bank of Taiwan]. Taihoku-shi: Taiwan Ginkō.

Ng, Chin-keong. 1983. *Trade and Society*. Singapore: Singapore University Press.

———. 1990. "The South Fukienese Junk Trade at Amoy from the Seventeenth to Early Nineteen Centuries." In *Development and Decline of Fukien Province in the 17th and 18th Centuries*, edited by E. B. Vermeer, 297–316. Leiden: Brill.

Nidhi Eoseewong. 2005. *Pen and Sail: Literature and History in Early Bangkok*. Chiang Mai: Silkworm.

Norlund, Irene. 2000. "Rice and the Colonial Lobby: The Economic Crisis in French Indo-China in the 1920s and the 1930s." In *Weathering the Storm*, edited by Peter Boomgaard and Ian Brown, 198-226. Singapore: Institute of Southeast Asian Studies.

Norton-Kyshe, James William. 1898. *History of the Laws and Courts of Hong Kong*. London: Unwin.

Oakes, Tim, and Louisa Schein. 2006. "Preface" and "Introduction." In *Translocal China*, edited by Tim Oakes and Louisa Schein, xii–xiii and 1–35. New York: Routledge.

Ong, Aihwa, and Donald Nonini, eds. 1997. *Ungrounded Empires: The Cultural Politics of Modern Chinese Nationalism*. New York: Routledge.

Osterhammel, Jürgen. 1986. "Semi-Colonialism and Informal Empire in Twentieth-Century China." In *Imperialism and After*, edited by Wolfgang Mommsen and Jürgen Osterhammel, 290–314. London: Allen and Unwin.

———. 2014. *The Transformation of the World*. Princeton, NJ: Princeton University Press.

Ouyang Enliang and Chao Longqi. 2002. *Zhongguo mimi shehui* [Chinese secret societies]. Vol. 4: *Qingdai huidang* [Qing groups]. Fuzhou: Fujian renmin chubanshe.

Ouyang Zongshu. 1998. *Haishang renjia: Haiyang yuye jingji yu yumin shehui* [Families of the seashore: Maritime fishing economies and fishing communities]. Nanchang: Jiangxi gaoxiao chubanshe.

Owen, David. 1934. *British Opium Policy in China and India*. New Haven, CT: Yale University Press.

Ownby, David. 1993. "Introduction." In *"Secret Societies" Reconsidered*, edited by David Ownby and Mary Somers Heidhues, 3–33. Armonk, NY: M. E. Sharpe.

———. 1996. *Brotherhoods and Secret Societies in Early and Mid-Qing China*. Stanford, CA: Stanford University Press.

———. 2001. "Recent Chinese Scholarship on the History of Chinese Secret Societies." *Late Imperial China* 22.1 (June): 139–58.

Ownby, David, and Mary Somers Heidhues, eds. 1993. *"Secret Societies" Reconsidered*. Armonk, NY: M. E. Sharpe.

Packer, George. 2006. "Knowing the Enemy." *New Yorker* (December 18): 60–69.

Pallegoix, Jean-Baptiste. 1854. *Déscription du royaume Thai ou Siam*. 2 vols. Paris: n.p.

Patton, Robert H. 2008. *Patriot Pirates*. New York: Vintage.

Peattie, Mark. 1984. "Japanese Attitudes toward Colonialism." In *The Japanese Colonial Empire, 1895–1945*, edited by Ramon Myers and Mark Peattie, 80–127. Princeton, NJ: Princeton University Press.

Peking Gazette. 1872–1886. Shanghai: North China Herald and Supreme Court and Consular Gazette.

Perdue, Peter. 2005. *China Marches West*. Cambridge, MA: Harvard University Press.

Phipps, John. 1836. *A Practical Treatise on the China and Eastern Trade*. London: W. H. Allen.

Ping Jinya. 1999. "Jiu Shanghai de yandu" [The opiate poison of old Shanghai]. In *Ershi shiji Shanghai wenshi ziliao wenku* [Library of historical materials of Shanghai in the twentieth century], vol. 10: 313–20. Shanghai: Shanghai Shudian chubanshe.

Po, Ronald. 2018. *The Blue Frontier*. Cambridge: Cambridge University Press.

Pomeranz, Kenneth. 2000. *The Great Divergence: China, Europe, and the Making of the Modern World Economy*. Princeton, NJ: Princeton University Press.

Ptak, Roderich. 1998. "Ming Maritime Trade to Southeast Asia." In *From the Mediterranean to the China Sea*, edited by Claude Guillot, Denys Lombard, and Roderich Ptak, 157–91. Wiesbaden: Harrassowitz.

Puning xianzhi [Gazetteer of Puning district]. 1747, 1995.

Purcell, Victor. 1948. *The Chinese in Malaya*. London: Oxford University Press.

———. 1965. *South and East Asia since 1800*. Cambridge: Cambridge University Press.

Qin Baoqi. 1988. *Qingdai qianqi Tiandihui yanjiu* [A study of the Tiandihui of the early Qing]. Beijing: Zhongguo Renmin Daxue chubanshe.

———. 2004. *Zhongguo dixia shehui* [The underworld society of China]. Beijing: Xueyuan chubanshe.

Qingdai dizu boxiao xingtai [Forms of rent exploitation during the Qing]. 1982. 2 vols. Beijing: Zhonghua shuju.

Qingdai Yueren zhuan [Biographies of Guangdong people of the Qing]. 2001. 3 vols. Beijing: Zhonghua quanguo tushuguan wenxiansuo wei fu zhi zhongxin.

Qingshi gao [Draft history of the Qing]. 1928. Electronic.

Qingting chaban mimi shehui an [Secret society cases as investigated by the Qing]. 2006. Edited by Liu Ziyang. 40 vols. Beijing: Xianzhuang shuju.

Qu Dajun. 1985. *Guangdong xinyu* [New words from Guangdong]. 2 vols. Beijing: Zhonghua shuju chubanshe; orig. 1690s.

Raphael, Vicente L. 1995. *Discrepant Histories: Translocal Essays on Filipino Cultures*. Philadelphia: Temple University Press.

Rao Zongyi. 1995. "Nan'ao: Taihai yu dalu jian de tiaoban [Nan'ao: gangplank between maritime Taiwan and the Chinese mainland]. *Chaoxue yanjiu* 3: 1–5.

———. 1996. "Qingchu Chaozhou qianjie kao" [A study of the coastal evacuation of Chaozhou in the early Qing]. In *Rao Zongyi Chao Shan difang shi lunji* [The collected writings on Chao Shan local history of Rao Zongyi], edited by Huang Ting, 306–13. Shantou: Shantou daxue chubanshe; orig. 1947.

Raustiala, Kai. 2009. *Does the Constitution Follow the Flag? The Evolution of Territoriality in American Law*. New York: Oxford University Press.

Reid, Anthony. 2004. "Chinese Trade and Southeast Asian Economic Expansion in the Later Eighteenth and Early Nineteenth Centuries." In *Water Frontier*, edited by Nola Cooke and Li Tana, 21–34. Lanham, MD: Rowman and Littlefield.

Remer, C. F. 1933. *Foreign Investments in China*. New York: Macmillan.

Rhoads. Edward. 1975. *China's Republican Revolution: The Case of Kwangtung, 1895-1913*. Cambridge, MA: Harvard University Press.

Rogaski, Ruth. 2004. *Hygienic Modernity*. Berkeley: University of California Press.

Rowe, William. 2007. *Crimson Rain: Seven Centuries of Violence in a Chinese County*. Stanford, CA: Stanford University Press.

———. 2009. *China's Last Empire*. Cambridge, MA: Harvard University Press.

Rungswasdisab, Puangthong. 1994. "Monopolize Cambodian Trade: Siamese Invasion of Hatien in the Eighteenth and early Nineteenth Centuries." In *Thailand and Her Neighbors (II): Laos, Vietnam, and Cambodia*, edited by Thanet Aphornsuvan, 83–121. Bangkok: Thammasat University Press.

———. 1995. "War and Trade: Siamese Intervention in Cambodia, 1767–1851." Ph.D. dissertation, University of Wollongong.

Ruschenberger, W.S.W. 1838. *A Voyage Round the World, Including an Embassy to Muscat and Siam in 1835, 1836, and 1837*. Philadelphia: Carey, Lea, and Blanchard.

Rush, James R. 1990. *Opium to Java: Revenue Farming and Chinese Enterprise in Colonial Indonesia, 1860–1910*. Ithaca, NY: Cornell University Press.

Sack, Robert David. 1986. *Human Territoriality: Its Theory and History*. New York: Cambridge University Press.

Sahlins, Marshall. 1985. *Islands of History*. Chicago: University of Chicago Press.

Sai, Siew-min. 2013. "The Nanyang Diasporic Imaginary." In *Chinese Indonesians Reassessed*, edited by Siew-min Sai and Chang-Yau Hoon, 45–64. New York: Routledge.

Sakarai, Yumio. 2004. "Eighteenth-Century Chinese Pioneers on the Water Frontier of Indochina." In *Water Frontier*, edited by Nola Cooke and Li Tana, 35–52. Lanham, MD: Rowman and Littlefield.

Sakarai, Yumio, and Takako Kitagawa. 1999. "Ha Tien or Banteay Meas in the Time of the Fall of Ayutthaya." In *From Japan to Arabia*, edited by Kennon Breazeale, 150–220. Bangkok: Foundation for the Promotion of Social Sciences and Humanities Textbooks Project.

Salmon, Claudine, and Roderich Ptak, eds. *Hainan: de la Chine à l'Asie du Sud-Est*. Wiesbaden: Harrassowitz, 2001.

Sang, Tze-Lan D. 2003. *The Emerging Lesbian: Female Same-Sex Desire in Modern China*. Chicago: University of Chicago Press.

Scarth, John. 1860. *Twelve Years in China*. Edinburgh: Thomas Constable.

Schottenhammer, Angela. 2007. "Introduction." In *The East Asian Maritime World, 1400–1800*, edited by Angela Schottenhammer, 1–86. Wiesbaden: Harrassowitz.

Schumpeter, Joseph. 1951. "The Sociology of Imperialisms." In *Two Essays by Joseph Schumpeter*, 1–98. New York: New American Library; orig. 1918.

Scott, James. 2009. *The Art of Not Being Governed*. New Haven, CT: Yale University Press.

Sellers, Nicholas. 1983. *The Princes of Ha-Tien (1682–1867)*. Brussels: Thanh-Long.

Sewell, William H. 2005. *Logics of History*. Chicago: University of Chicago Press.

Shalong shi difeng qinglu [A historical record of Shalong's local customs]. 2001. Edited by Zheng Ruiting. Chaoyang: Chaoyang shi Shalong wenhuazhan yinhong.

Shanghai beike ziliao xuanji [Selections from historical materials on inscriptions in Shanghai]. 1980. Shanghai: Shanghai renmin chubanshe.

Shanghai qianzhuang shiliao [Historical sources on Shanghai native banking]. 1960. Shanghai: Shanghai renmin chubanshe.

Shanghai: Political and Economic Reports, 1842–1943. 2008. 10 vols. Edited by Robert L. Jarman. Slough, UK: Archive Editions, 2008.

Shantou haiguan zhi [Gazetteer of the Shantou Customs Bureau]. 1988. Shantou: Shantou haiguan bianzhi bangongshi.

Shantou shizhi [Shantou municipal gazetteer]. 1999. 4 vols. Beijing: Xinhua chubanshe.

Shantou zhinan [Shantou guidebook]. 1933. Edited by Xie Xueying. Shantou: Shantou shishi tongxunshe.

Shen Binghong. 2001. *Lingnan diyi qiaozhai* [The leading overseas Chinese residence of Lingnan]. Shantou: Shantou daxue chubanshe.

Shen Fu. 2008. *Fu sheng liu ji* [Six records of a floating life]. Gutenberg Ebook.

———. 2011. *Six Records of a Life Adrift*. Translated by Graham Sanders. Indianapolis: Hackett.

Shen, Huifen. 2012. *China's Left-Behind Wives*. Honolulu: University of Hawai'i Press.

Shenbao. 1872–1949. Electronic.

Shenbao: Guangdong ziliao xuanji (1872–1949) [Selected materials relating to Guangdong in "Shenbao," 1872–1949]. 1995–1996. 17 vols. Guangzhou: Guangdong Provincial Archives.

Shiga Ichiko. 2008. "Chūgoku Kantonshō Chō-San chiiki no zendō [The benevolent halls in the Chao Shan region of Guangdong, China]. *Ibaraki kirisutokyō daigaku kyō* 42: 197–216.

Shih, Vincent. 1967. *The Taiping Ideology*. Seattle: University of Washington Press.

Siah U Chin. 1848. "The Chinese in Singapore." *Journal of the Indian Archipelago and Eastern Asia* 2: 283–90.

Siam Repository. 1872.

Siu, Helen, ed. 2010. *Merchants' Daughters*. Hong Kong: Hong Kong University Press.

Skinner, G. William. 1957a. "Chinese Assimilation and Thai Politics." *Journal of Asian Studies* 16.2 (February): 237–50.

———. 1957b. *Chinese Society in Thailand*. Ithaca, NY: Cornell University Press.

———. 1996. "Creolized Chinese Societies in Southeast Asia." In *Sojourners and Settlers*, edited by Anthony Reid, 51–93. Honolulu: University of Hawaii Press.

———. 1977a. "Introduction." In *The City in Late Imperial China*, edited by G. William Skinner, 3–31. Stanford, CA: Stanford University Press.

———. 1977b. "Regional Urbanization in Nineteenth-Century China." In *The City in Late Imperial China*, edited by G. William Skinner, 211–49. Stanford, CA: Stanford University Press.

Smedley, Agnes. 1956. *The Great Road*. New York: Monthly Review Press.

Smith, Michael Peter. 2001. "Translocality: A Critical Reflection." In *Translocal Geographies*, edited by Katherine Brickell and Ayona Datta, 181–98. Surrey, UK: Ashgate.

So, Kwan-wai. 1975. *Japanese Piracy in Ming China during the 16th Century*. East Lansing: Michigan State University Press.

Sommer, Matthew. 2000. *Sex, Law, and Society in Late Imperial China.* Stanford, Calif.: Stanford University Press.

———. 2015. *Polyandry and Wife-Selling in China.* Berkeley: University of California Press.

Song Ong Siang. 1984. *One Hundred Years History of the Chinese in Singapore.* Singapore: Oxford University Press; orig. 1902.

Song Zuanyou. 2007. *Guangdongren zai Shanghai, 1843–1949.* Shanghai: Renmin chubanshe.

Spence, Jonathan. 1996. *God's Chinese Son.* New York: Norton.

———. 1999. *The Search for Modern China.* 2nd ed. New York: Norton.

Stanley, Amy. 2012. *Selling Women.* Berkeley: University of California Press.

Stelle, Charles. 1940. "American Trade in Opium Prior to 1820." *Pacific Historical Review* 9.4 (December): 425–44.

Straits Settlements. 1922. *Report for 1921.* London: His Majesty's Stationery Office.

———. 1940. *Report for 1938.* London: His Majesty's Stationery Office.

Straits Times. 1845–1980.

Struve, Lynn. 1984. *The Southern Ming, 1644–1662.* New Haven, CT: Yale University Press.

Suehiro, Akira. 1989. *Capital Accumulation in Thailand, 1855–1985.* Tokyo: Centre for East Asian Cultural Studies.

Swettenham, Frank. 1975. *British Malaya.* New York: AMS Press; orig. 1948.

Tagliacozzo, Eric, and Wen-Chin Chang, eds. 2011. *Chinese Circulations.* Durham, NC: Duke University Press.

Taiguo Chaozhou huiguan chengli wushi zhounian tekan [Special commemoration of the fiftieth anniversary of the founding of the Chaozhou huiguan of Thailand]. 1988. Bangkok: Taiguo Chaozhou huiguan.

Tai Hua mingren huizhi [Collectanea of famous Chinese in Thailand]. Edited by Huang Ziyi. Bangkok: Nanhai congshu chubanshe, 1963.

Tamaki, Mitsuko. 2007. "The Prevalence of the Worship of Goddess Lin Guniang by the Ethnic Chinese in Southern Thailand." G-Sec Working Paper 22 (online).

Tan, Chee-Beng. 2012. "Shantang: Charitable Temples in China, Singapore, and Malaysia." *Asian Ethnology* 71.1: 76–107.

Tan Ee Leong. 1961. "The Chinese Banks Incorporated in Singapore & the Federation of Malaya." In *Readings in Malayan Economics,* edited by T. H. Silcock, 454–79. Singapore: Eastern Universities Press.

Tanaka Issei. 1993. "Xinjiapo Wuhuci yishi kao: Chaozhou Tiandihui huidang yu Xinjiapo Yixing gongsi de guanxi" [A study of the patriotic guardsmen of Singapore's Five Tiger Shrine: on the relationship between the Tiandihui of Chaozhou and Singapore's Yixing gongsi]. In *Qingzhu Rao Zongyi jiaoshou qishiwu sui lunwenji* [A festschrift in honor of Professor Rao Zongyi on the occasion of his seventy-fifth birthday], 43–58. Hong Kong: Hong Kong zhongwen daxue.

Tarling, Nicholas. 1992. *The Cambridge History of Southeast Asia from Early Times to 1800.* Cambridge: Cambridge University Press.

Ter Haar, Barend. 1993. "Messianism and the Heaven and Earth Society." In *"Secret Societies" Reconsidered,* edited by David Ownby and Mary Somers Heidhues, 153–76. Armonk, NY: M. E. Sharpe.

———. 1998. *Ritual and Mythology of the Chinese Triads.* Leiden: Brill.

Thilly, Peter. 2018. "The Fujitsuru Mystery." *Cross-Currents* 7.1 (May): 93–117.

Thomson, John. 1875. *The Straits of Malacca, Indo-China, and China*. London: Sampson Low, Marston, Low, and Searle.

Thucydides. 1972. *The Peloponnesian War*. New York: Penguin.

Tiandihui [The Heaven and Earth Society]. 1981–1989. 7 vols. Beijing: Renmin daxue chubanshe.

Tilly, Charles. 1990. *Coercion, Capital and European States*. Cambridge, MA: Harvard University Press.

Trocki, Carl. 1979. *Prince of Pirates*. Singapore: Singapore University Press.

———. 1990. *Opium and Empire*. Ithaca, NY: Cornell University Press.

———. 1999. *Opium, Empire, and the Global Political Economy*. London: Routledge.

Tsai, Jung-fang. 1993. *Hong Kong in Chinese History*. New York: Columbia University Press.

Turnbull, C. M. 1959. "The Johore Gambier and Pepper Trade in the Mid-19th Century." *Nanyang xuebao* 15.1 (June): 43–55.

———. 1972. *The Straits Settlements, 1826–67*. London: Athlone Press.

———. 2005. *A History of Modern Singapore*. Singapore: NUS Press.

Turner, Frederic Jackson. 1920. *The Frontier in American History*. New York: Holt.

Turpin, F. H. 1908. *History of the Kingdom of Siam*. Translated by B. O. Cartwright. Bangkok: American Presbyterian Missionary Press; orig. 1771.

U.S. Department of State. 2014. "Limits in the Seas, No. 143, China: Maritime Claims in the South China Sea."

Vaccaro, Ismael, Allan Charles Dawson, and Laura Zanotti. 2014. "Negotiating Territoriality: Spatial Dialogues between State and Tradition." In *Negotiating Territoriality*, edited by Ismael Vaccaro, Allan Charles Dawson, and Laura Zanotti, 1–19. New York: Routledge.

Viraphol, Sarasin. 1977. *Tribute and Profit: Sino-Siamese Trade, 1652–1853*. Cambridge, MA: Harvard East Asia Monographs.

Wade, Geoff, ed. 2005. *Southeast Asia in the Ming Shilu*. Digital.

Wakeman, Frederic. 1966. *Strangers at the Gate*. Berkeley: University of California Press.

———. 1985. *The Great Enterprise*. 2 vols. Berkeley: University of California Press.

———. 1995. *Policing Shanghai*. Berkeley: University of California Press.

Wang Gungwu. 1981a. *Community and Nation*. Singapore: Heinemann Educational.

———. 1981b. "Southeast Asian *Hua-Ch'iao* in Chinese History-Writing." *Journal of Southeast Asian Studies* 12.1 (March): 1–14.

Wang Gungwu and Chin-keong Ng, eds. 2004. *Maritime China in Transition*. Wiesbaden: Harrassowitz.

Wang, Tai Peng. 1994. *The Origins of Chinese Kongsi*. Selangor Darul Ehsan: Pelanduk Pub.

Wang Tao. 1960. *Ying ruan zazhi* [Miscellany of the seaside]. Taipei: Guangwen shuju; orig. 1853.

Wang Yuanlin and Liu Qiang. 2005. "Qing qianzhongqi Chaozhou dui wai maoyi yanjiu" [The foreign trade of Chaozhou during the early Qing]. *Shantou daxue xuebao* 21.2: 81–92.

Wanguo jixin bianlan [International Chinese Business Directory of the World (bilingual)]. 1913. San Francisco: n.p.

Warren, James. 1993. *Ah Ku and Karayuki-san*. Oxford: Oxford University Press.

Wei Yuan. 1967. *Haiguo tuzhi* [Treatise on the sea kingdoms]. 7 vols. Taibei: Chengwen chubanshe; orig. 1847.

Werner, Michael, and Bénédicte Zimmermann. 2006. "Beyond Comparison." *History and Theory* 45.1 (February): 30–50.

Wilbur, C. Martin. 1964. "The Ashes of Defeat." *China Quarterly* 18 (April–June): 3–54.

Willmott, W. E. 1967. *The Chinese in Cambodia*. Vancouver: UBC Press.

Wills, John E. 2011. "Introduction." In *China and Maritime Europe*, edited by John Wills, 1–23. New York: Cambridge University Press.

Wolf, Margery. 1972. *Women and the Family in Rural Taiwan*. Stanford, CA: Stanford University Press.

Wong, J. Y. 1976. *Yeh Ming-ch'en*. Cambridge: Cambridge University Press.

———. 1998. *Deadly Dreams: Opium and the Arrow War (1856–1860) in China*. Cambridge: Cambridge University Press.

Wong, R. Bin. 1982. "Food Riots in the Qing Dynasty." *Journal of Asian Studies* 41.4 (August): 767–88.

———. 1997. *China Transformed: Historical Change and the Limits of European Experience*. Ithaca, NY: Cornell University Press.

———. 2000. "Opium and Modern Chinese State-Making." In *Opium Regimes*, edited by Timothy Brook and Bob Tadashi Wakabayashi, 189–211. Berkeley: University of California Press.

Wong, Yee Tuan. 2007. "The Big Five Families in Penang, 1830s-1890s." *Chinese Southern Diaspora Studies* 1: 106–15.

———. 2011. "Uncovering the Myths of Two 19th-Century Hokkien Business Personalities in the Straits Settlements." *Chinese Southern Diaspora Studies* 5: 146–56.

Wood, Leonard, William H. Taft, et al. 1902. *Opportunities in the Colonies and Cuba*. New York: Lewis, Scribner.

Wright, Arnold, and H. A. Cartwright, eds. 1908. *Twentieth-Century Impressions of Hongkong, Shanghai, and Other Treaty Ports of China*. London: Lloyd's Greater Britain.

Wright, Arnold, H. A. Cartwright, and Oliver T. Breakspear. 1908. *Twentieth-Century Impressions of Siam*. London: Lloyds.

Wu, Chun-hsi. 1967. *Dollars, Dependents, and Dogma: Overseas Remittances to Communist China*. Stanford, CA: Hoover Institution Press.

Wu Fengbin. 1993. *Dongnanya huaqiao tongshi* [History of Overseas Chinese in Southeast Asia]. Fuzhou: Fujian renmin chubanshe.

Wu Kuixin. 1997. "Chaozhou gece 'Wu Zhongshu' de renminxing yu lishi yiyi" [The popular character and historical significance of the Chaozhou songbook, "Wu Zhongshu"]. *Chaoxue yanjiu* 6: 195–207.

Wyatt, David K. 2003. *Thailand: A Short History*. 2nd ed. New Haven, CT: Yale University Press.

Wynne, Mervyn. 2000. *Triad and Tabut*. New York: Routledge; orig. 1941.

Xie Qinggao. 1962. *Hailu zhu* [*Record of the Seas, Annotated*]. Taibei: Taiwan Shangwu yinshuguan; orig. 1820.

Xie Shi. 2008. "Chen Kun 'Ru bu ji zhai congshu' yu Qingdai Xian-Tong nianjian Chaozhou shehui [Chen Kun's "Ru bu ji zhai congshu" and Chaozhou society during the Xianfeng and Tongzhi eras]. *Chaoxue yanjiu* 14: 111–54.

Xie Xiquan. 2001. "Zheng Yingshi de yishu daolu [The artistic path of Zheng Yingshi]. *Chaoyang wenshi* 18: 38–43.

Xie Xueying, ed. 1933. *Shantou zhinan* [Shantou guidebook]. Shantou: Shantou shishi tongxunshe.

Xinjiapo Chaozhou bayi huiguan jinxi jiniankan [The golden jubilee souvenir magazine of the Chaozhou Eight-District huiguan]. 1980. Edited by Pan Xingnong. Singapore: Chaozhou bayi huiguan.

Xinjiapo Duanmeng xuexiao sanshi zhounian jiniance [The Thirtieth Anniversary Album of the Tuan Mong School of Singapore]. 1936. Singapore: Shanghai Zhonghua shuju.

Xu Ke. 1984. *Qing bai lei chao* [Classified collection of Qing anecdotes]. Beijing: Zhonghua shuju; orig. 1917.

Yap Pheng Geck. 1982. *Scholar, Banker, Gentleman Soldier*. Singapore: Times Books.

Yapian zhanzheng dang'an shiliao [Archival sources for the history of the Opium War]. 1992. 7 vols. Tianjin: Tianjin guji chubanshe.

Ye Xian'en. 1989. *Guangdong hangyun shi* [History of Guangdong shipping]. 2 vols. Beijing: Renmin jiaotong chubanshe.

———. 1995. "Notes on the Territorial Connections of the Dan." Translated by David Faure. In *Down to Earth: The Territorial Bond in South China*, edited by David Faure and Helen F. Siu, 83–88. Stanford, CA: Stanford University Press.

Yen, Ching-hwang. 1976. *The Overseas Chinese and the 1911 Revolution*. Kuala Lumpur: Oxford University Press.

———. 1986. *Social History of the Chinese in Singapore and Malaya*. New York: Oxford University Press.

Young, John Parke. 1931. "The Shanghai Tael." *American Economic Review* 21.4 (December): 682–84.

Yow, Cheun Hoe. 2013. *Guangdong and Chinese Disapora: The Changing Landscape of Qiaoxiang*. New York: Routledge.

Yu Jiao. 1994. *Chao Jia fengyue ji* [A record of feminine seduction in Chaozhou and Jiayingzhou]. In *Congshu jicheng xubian*, 96: 743–60. Shanghai: Shanghai Shudian.

Yuan, Bingling. 2000. *Chinese Democracies: A Study of the Kongsis of West Borneo, 1776–1884*. Leiden: Research School of Asian, African, and Amerindian Studies.

Yuen, William Tai. 2013. *Chinese Capitalism in Colonial Malaya, 1900–1941*. Bangi: Penerbit Universiti Kebangsaan Malaysia.

Zakaria, Fareed. 1999. *From Wealth to Power*. Princeton, NJ: Princeton University Press.

Zeng Guoquan. 1969. *Zeng Zhongxiang gong quanji* [Complete writings of Zeng Zhongxiang]. Taipei: Chengwen chubanshe; orig. 1903.

Zeng Shaocong. 1998. *Dongyang hanglu yimin: Ming Qing haiyang yimin Taiwan yu Feilübin de bijiao yanjiu* [Migrants on the sea routes of the Eastern Sea: A comparative study of maritime sojourners to Taiwan and the Philippines during the Ming and Qing]. Nanchang: Jiangxi gaoxiao chubanshe.

Zhang Guanlan. 1987. "Rexin gongyi shiye de shiyejia Guo Zibin" [The public spirited industrialist Guo Zibin]. *Chaoyang wenshi* 2: 19–22.

Zhang Guotao. 1964. "Chang Kuo-t'ao's Report." In "The Ashes of Defeat," translated and edited by C. Martin Wilbur, 31–34. In *China Quarterly* 18 (April-June): 3–54; orig. 1927.

Zhao Chunchen. 1995. "Shantou kai bu shi shikao" [A historical investigation into the opening of Shantou]. *Chaoxue yanjiu* 3: 154–70.

Zheng Baitao. 1993. "Chaoyang ren quguo suotan" [Fragmentary conversations about Chaoyang people emigrating abroad]. *Chaoyang wenshi* 10: 36–41.

Zheng Ruiting. 2001. "Qingmo Minguo shiqi Shalong de Shanghai ke [Shanghai sojourners from Shalong in the late Qing and Republican period]." *Chaoyang wenshi* 18: 81–87.

Zheng, Yangwen. 2005. *The Social Life of Opium in China*. Cambridge: Cambridge University Press.

Zheng Yifang. 1981. *Shanghai qianzhuang, 1843–1937* [Chinese native banks, 1843–1937]. Taibei: Zhongyang yanjiuyuan.

Zheng Yingshi. 1965. "Chaoji yapianyanshang zai Shanghai de huodong ji qi yu Jiang Jieshi zhengquan de guanxi" [The activities of the Chaozhou opium merchants in Shanghai and their connection to the political power of Chiang Kai-shek]. *Guangdong wenshi ziliao* 21: 1–30.

Zheng Zhenman. 2001. *Family Lineage Organization and Social Change in Ming and Qing Fujian*. Translated by Michael Szonyi. Honolulu: University of Hawaii Press.

Zhongguo jindai gongyeshi ziliao [Sources on China's modern industrial history]. 1957. Shanghai: Kexue chubanshe.

Zhongguo jindushi ziliao, 1729–1949 [Documents on the history of Chinese narcotics proscriptions, 1729–1949]. 1998. Tianjin: Tianjin renmin chubanshe.

Zhou Jiarong. 2012. *Xianggang Chaozhou shanghui jiushinian fazhanshi* [Ninety years historical development of Chaozhou Chambers of Commerce in Hong Kong]. Hong Kong: Zhonghua shuju.

Zhu, Marlon. 2012. "Typhoons, Meteorological Intelligence and the Inter-Port Mercantile Community in 19th-Century China." Ph.D. dissertation, Binghamton University.

INDEX

Alabaster, Chaloner, 110, 118, 174–76, 192, 199, 210–11

alluviation, 23, 56, 120, 149

Americans, 7, 157–58, 178, 182, 186, 207, 252–53, 269, 291

Anbu (Ampoh), 50–51, 61–62, 92, 120–21, 162, 188, 204–5, 271; and overseas Chinese, 120, 143, 237, 249, 276–79, 326n53

Annam. *See* Vietnam

anti-Sinicism, 32, 60, 153–55, 247–48, 286–88

Army of the Green Standard, 98–99, 104–6, 120–21, 143–45, 155–56, 161; and legal procedure, 111–17. *See also* Fang Yao

assimilation, 59–60, 166, 223, 247

Bangkok, 4, 14, 43, 51, 54–57, 123, 152, 213, 245–46, 254–55, 257–60, 273. *See also* Siam; Taksin

banking, 176–78, 194–96, 260, 267, 270; Sze Hai Tong Bank and, 232–33, 254–55, 258, 266, 270–72

beancake, 160, 193–94, 197, 199

boatmen, 38, 61, 63, 82–83, 257, 282; sampans and, 249–51

borderlands, 22, 23, 26, 35, 43, 48, 73, 83–87, 102–3; in Southeast Asia, 52–54

Borneo, 4, 7, 64–69, 86, 88, 252–53

British, 132, 172–74, 250–51, 266; at Chaozhou, 69, 71–72, 110, 139, 186–216, 252, 275, 278; as colonizers for others, 7–11, 187, 198, 211–16, 223–25, 234, 246, 269, 271, 290; East India Company, 61–62, 71; at Hong Kong, 102; in Shanghai, 157–

85. *See also* British Straits Settlements; colonialism; Hong Kong; Sarawak; shipping industry; translocalism

British Straits Settlements (British Malaya), 15–16, 61–64, 105, 129–30, 136–43, 151, 210–16, 235–36, 238–44, 260–61, 273; brotherhoods in, 79, 89, 103 214, 235, 248–49; communist movement and, 152–53; demographics of, 221–26; opium farms in, 73, 172; shift from commercial to industrial capitalism in, 248–49. *See also* Malay Peninsula; Singapore

brotherhoods (mutual aid societies), 11, 65–69, 74–96, 104, 139, 143–45, 249; and coolie trade, 79, 136, 214–15; and criminal underworld, 73–74, 83–87, 100, 212, 214, 238, 251; as Double Sword Society, 68, 86–90; and militias, 93–94; and network theory, 84–85, 100–101, 232–33; and opium trade, 46, 67, 73–74, 86–87; and overseas plantation power, 63–64; in settled agricultural communities, 68, 77, 88–89; as Small Sword Society, 102–3; and translocalism, 46, 60, 67–68, 79, 82–88, 95, 103, 144–45

Burma, 51–52, 130

business networks, 11, 43, 163–85, 193–96, 200–203, 212, 249, 254–60; and Siam, 51–55, 65, 159, 209–10, 262–63; women and, 2, 232–33, 258–59

Cambodia, 4, 7, 33, 52–54, 152–55, 226. *See also* French Indochina

Depression, Great, 18, 234, 238, 260, 270, 272–75, 280, 282
dialects, 66–67, 71, 139, 214, 237, 245, 247, 254–55, 257, 265–66, 306n26.
Drummond, W.V., 171, 173–74
Dutch East Indies, 7, 52, 62, 64–69, 71, 88, 136, 142, 189, 214, 243–44, 256–57

emigrant communities, 4, 217–34, 272–75; commercial ties of, 274–79
entangled history, 46, 56–59, 74, 77, 129–30, 137–43, 244–47, 278–79, 282; defined, 4–6; and opium, 87

famine, 18, 48, 50, 280
Fang Bingzhen (Pung Peng Cheng), 154–55
Fang Fang (Fang Siqiong), 148, 150
Fang Qiaosheng (Pung Kheav Se), 154–55
Fang Yao, 150–51, 155, 165–67, 192, 214–15, 246, 278–79; biography of, 104–6; death of, 143–46; and lineage power, 111–17, 121–22, 143, 146–47, 150, 315n54; as military idealist, 123–25; pacification campaign of, 97–125, 198–99, 220–21, 275; as state-builder, 119–25; as tax enforcer, 118–19, 196; translocal power of, 105, 122–23, 134, 213, 253–54
Fang Yanshan, 150–51, 154
Fengshun, 38, 67
Fielde, Adele, 134–35
fishing industry: domestic 37, 41, 43, 49, 83, 121–22, 132, 213, 261, 278; overseas, 2, 8
food panics, 135
France, 155, 180; colonialism of, 7, 153; Sino-French wars and, 113, 116, 186
French Indochina, 6, 116, 151–55, 179, 226, 257, 267, 270–71, 273
fruit industry, 57, 151, 256; overseas, 2, 7, 226
Fujian, 3, 5, 7, 57, 76, 83–86, 104, 119, 162, 200–201, 285; Amoy network of, 36, 44, 47–48, 56, 114, 282, 297; and piracy 26–28, 102–3; and smuggling, 70, 72–73, 160; and southeast coastal macroregion, 21–22, 139; and Straits Settlements, 61, 139, 214–16, 223–26, 229, 254–55, 257

gambier, 7, 59, 61–64, 137, 249–50, 252, 254; and pepper, 7, 59, 61–64, 226, 249
gambling, 51, 53, 100, 113, 237
Gao Manhua, 233, 259–60
gongsi partnerships, 11, 64–69, 264–66, 288
González de Mendoza, Juan, 30–32
Goodman, Bryna, 163
Guangdong province, 16, 117–19, 285. See also Canton; state-building
Guangxi, 49, 91
guilds. See native place
Gulf of Siam, 4, 52–55, 60; and coastal evacuation, 43, 52–55
Guo Tingji, 120–21
Guo Yan, 61, 257, 290
Guo Zibin, 163–64, 167, 177, 182, 185, 263
Gutzlaff, Charles, 71, 237

Ha Tien, 53–54
Haimen, 42, 49, 119, 161
hair, 101–2, 238, 243–44
Haiyang (Chao'an), 34, 38, 42, 100, 120–21, 123, 143–45, 148, 162–63, 191, 211, 213, 221–22, 227, 232, 235, 246–47, 259, 263, 265–66, 275–77; communists in, 146, 278–79; and junk trade, 51, 61, 249
Hakka, 65–69, 82, 86–87, 91–96, 132, 142, 226–27, 271, 322n3; and opium trade, 73, 86–87, 182. See also Taipings
Hardoon, Silas, 166
Heidhues, Mary Somers, 65
Hong Kong, 4, 14, 101–2, 116, 135, 238–39, 287; and Chinese business, 58, 122–23, 193–94, 198–200, 254–55, 210, 215–16, 258–59, 262–63
Huang Ting, 37
Huang Zunxian, 93
Huanggang, 144, 188
Huilai, 38–39, 67–69, 85–86, 108, 110, 146, 163
Huizhou prefecture, 22, 28, 38–39, 66–69, 116, 144, 229, 271; communists in, 146–49, 220; and opium smuggling, 86–87, 182; qingxiang campaign in, 106, 192

A NOTE ON THE TYPE

This book has been composed in Arno, an Old-style serif typeface in the
classic Venetian tradition, designed by Robert Slimbach at Adobe.